Achieving Open Justice through Citizen Participation and Transparency

Carlos E. Jiménez-Gómez
Department of Justice of the Autonomous Government of Catalonia, Spain

Mila Gascó-Hernández
Institute of Public Governance and Management, ESADE Business and Law School, Spain

A volume in the Advances in Public Policy and Administration (APPA) Book Series

IGI Global
DISSEMINATOR OF KNOWLEDGE

www.igi-global.com

Published in the United States of America by
IGI Global
Information Science Reference (an imprint of IGI Global)
701 E. Chocolate Avenue
Hershey PA, USA 17033
Tel: 717-533-8845
Fax: 717-533-8661
E-mail: cust@igi-global.com
Web site: http://www.igi-global.com

Library of Congress Cataloging-in-Publication Data

Names: Jiménez-Gómez, Carlos E., 1968- editor. | Gásco-Hernández, Mila, editor.
Title: Achieving open justice through citizen participation and transparency / Carlos E. Jiménez-Gómez and Mila Gásco-Hernández, editors.
Description: Hershey PA : Information Science Reference, 2017. | Series: Advances in public policy and administration | Includes bibliographical references and index.
Identifiers: LCCN 2016024300| ISBN 9781522507178 (hardcover) | ISBN 9781522507185 (ebook)
Subjects: LCSH: Justice, Administration of--Citizen participation. | Justice, Administration of--Information technology. | Transparency in government. | Electronic government information. | Due process of law. | Freedom of information.
Classification: LCC K2100 .A927 2017 | DDC 353.4/23802854678--dc23
LC record available at https://lccn.loc.gov/2016024300

This book is published in the IGI Global book series Advances in Public Policy and Administration (APPA) (ISSN: Pending; eISSN: Pending)

British Cataloguing in Publication Data
A Cataloguing in Publication record for this book is available from the British Library.

All work contributed to this book is new, previously-unpublished material. The views expressed in this book are those of the authors, but not necessarily of the publisher.

For electronic access to this publication, please contact: eresources@igi-global.com.

Advances in Public Policy and Administration (APPA) Book Series

ISSN: Pending
EISSN: Pending

Mission

Proper management of the public sphere is necessary in order to maintain order in modern society. Research developments in the field of public policy and administration can assist in uncovering the latest tools, practices, and methodologies for governing societies around the world.

The **Advances in Public Policy and Administration (APPA) Book Series** aims to publish scholarly publications focused on topics pertaining to the governance of the public domain. APPA's focus on timely topics relating to government, public funding, politics, public safety, policy, and law enforcement is particularly relevant to academicians, government officials, and upper-level students seeking the most up-to-date research in their field.

Coverage

- Government
- Law enforcement
- Political Economy
- Politics
- Public Administration
- Public Funding
- Public Policy
- Resource allocation
- Urban Planning

IGI Global is currently accepting manuscripts for publication within this series. To submit a proposal for a volume in this series, please contact our Acquisition Editors at Acquisitions@igi-global.com or visit: http://www.igi-global.com/publish/.

The Advances in Public Policy and Administration (APPA) Book Series (ISSN Pending) is published by IGI Global, 701 E. Chocolate Avenue, Hershey, PA 17033-1240, USA, www.igi-global.com. This series is composed of titles available for purchase individually; each title is edited to be contextually exclusive from any other title within the series. For pricing and ordering information please visit http://www.igi-global.com/book-series/advances-public-policy-administration/97862. Postmaster: Send all address changes to above address.

Titles in this Series

For a list of additional titles in this series, please visit: www.igi-global.com

Comparative Studies and Regionally-Focused Cases Examining Local Governments
Ugur Sadioglu (Hacettepe University, Turkey) and Kadir Dede (Hacettepe University, Turkey)
Information Science Reference • copyright 2016 • 502pp • H/C (ISBN: 9781522503200) • US $205.00 (our price)

Theoretical Foundations and Discussions on the Reformation Process in Local Governments
Ugur Sadioglu (Hacettepe University, Turkey) and Kadir Dede (Hacettepe University, Turkey)
Information Science Reference • copyright 2016 • 555pp • H/C (ISBN: 9781522503170) • US $195.00 (our price)

Handbook of Research on Public Finance in Europe and the MENA Region
M. Mustafa Erdoğdu (Marmara University, Turkey) and Bryan Christiansen (PryMarke, LLC, USA)
Business Science Reference • copyright 2016 • 618pp • H/C (ISBN: 9781522500537) • US $300.00 (our price)

(R)evolutionizing Political Communication through Social Media
Tomaž Deželan (University of Ljubljana, Slovenia) and Igor Vobič (University of Ljubljana, Slovenia)
Information Science Reference • copyright 2016 • 333pp • H/C (ISBN: 9781466698796) • US $170.00 (our price)

Social, Economic, and Political Perspectives on Public Health Policy-Making
Rahmatollah Gholipour (University of Tehran, Iran) and Khadijeh Rouzbehani (University of Tehran, Iran)
Medical Information Science Reference • copyright 2016 • 329pp • H/C (ISBN: 9781466699441) • US $195.00 (our price)

Ethical Issues and Citizen Rights in the Era of Digital Government Surveillance
Robert A. Cropf (Saint Louis University, USA) and Timothy C. Bagwell (American Public University System, USA)
Information Science Reference • copyright 2016 • 303pp • H/C (ISBN: 9781466699052) • US $180.00 (our price)

Handbook of Research on Transitional Justice and Peace Building in Turbulent Regions
Fredy Cante (Universidad del Rosario, Colombia) and Hartmut Quehl (Felsberg Institute, Germany)
Information Science Reference • copyright 2016 • 559pp • H/C (ISBN: 9781466696754) • US $295.00 (our price)

Managing Big Data Integration in the Public Sector
Anil Aggarwal (University of Baltimore, USA)
Information Science Reference • copyright 2016 • 337pp • H/C (ISBN: 9781466696495) • US $205.00 (our price)

Management and Participation in the Public Sphere
Mika Markus Merviö (Kibi International University, Japan)
Information Science Reference • copyright 2015 • 399pp • H/C (ISBN: 9781466685536) • US $200.00 (our price)

IGI GLOBAL
DISSEMINATOR OF KNOWLEDGE
www.igi-global.com

701 E. Chocolate Ave., Hershey, PA 17033
Order online at www.igi-global.com or call 717-533-8845 x100
To place a standing order for titles released in this series, contact: cust@igi-global.com
Mon-Fri 8:00 am - 5:00 pm (est) or fax 24 hours a day 717-533-8661

Editorial Advisory Board

Table of Contents

Detailed Table of Contents

Despite its origins, openness in the judiciary has expanded beyond transparency and, therefore, beyond the common law open justice principle. Several initiatives worldwide are echoing this trend and a new term, open judiciary, is arising as a way to address openness in the justice field. This chapter gives an overview of open judiciary initiatives worldwide, focusing on some of the most successful, in order to identify drivers of adoption, critical success factors, and preliminary results. The research is embedded in a broader exploratory study on the state of the art of open judiciary. The chapter is addressed to answer two of the research questions: What are some learning practices that can be identified worldwide in relation to openness in the judiciary? What are some of the most important lessons that can be learnt from these practices?

Open access to accurate and reliable records is essential to participation in the judicial process and government transparency. As the judiciary and other branches of government increasingly rely on records which are created and maintained in digital form, a new set of challenges faces policy makers to ensure ongoing access and authenticity. One of the keys to this effort is the development of a set of principles and related performance standards which provide a framework and a system for measuring success. Using the recently adopted records management standards published by the U.S. Conference of State Court Administrators as a basis, this chapter discusses their application to digital record-keeping and how existing court performance standards addressing records management already developed by judicial organizations and the records management industry can be brought together to create a new set of performance measures to ensure that court records remain open, accessible, and trustworthy in the digital age.

With this work, it is hoped to offer an insight into open judiciary applied to the specific context of constitutional courts in the Civil Law system from both a legal and technological point of view. The advances in IT are now becoming the drivers of social change and new ways for citizens and public administrations to interrelate. Information technology has enabled a different way for citizens to access public services under an e-Government umbrella to a greater or lesser degree of success. In the area of e-Justice it would appear that advances are perceived in different ways, particularly in the higher courts. This chapter will set out how constitutional justice is integrated into the world of electronic justice as an example of a genuine challenge that is full of paradoxes.

This chapter examines the open government initiative and the application of open government principles to the court system in China in order to illustrate what "open judiciary"—and, ultimately, an "open state"—looks like in a relatively closed society. The authors present a comprehensive background of China's open government initiative and related court reform efforts, along with critical analysis of trends in "Guiding Cases" ("GCs"), de facto binding precedents released by the Supreme People's Court (SPC) of China, and subsequent cases ("SCs") that cite GCs. Drawing on these theoretical and empirical studies, the authors discuss the prospects of leveraging China's open government and open judiciary efforts to develop an open state in the country and identify key factors for promoting open judiciary in other closed societies around the world.

This paper presents analyses of impacts of lay adjudicators' participation in criminal matters in Japan due to the introduction of the new lay adjudication system – the Citizen Judge System [Saiban-in Seido] – in 2009. Since the late twentieth century, the introduction of the lay adjudication system seems to have been in international movement democratising the criminal justice system. This paper is devoted

In the last one or two years, the growing demand for an open state has sped up the adoption of ICT aimed at improving access to justice, making the judiciary more transparent, increasing cooperation between legal authorities, and strengthening the justice system itself. Of particular importance are interoperability initiatives since they guarantee collaboration as well as the harmonic and cohesive functioning of different existing systems, processes, and applications that, in the justice field, are many as a result of the big variety of actors that are involved: judicial institutions but, also, different public administrations, such as those responsible of police forces, and law professionals. The chapter describes and analyzes GRP (Gestió de Requeriments Policials), a project that allows for the exchange of information between the Department of Justice and the Department of the Interior in the framework of the Autonomous Government of Catalonia (Spain).

Legal texts represent a fundamental building block in all democratic states. As such, legal information must be accessible to all members of society to the widest possible extent, to aid inclusiveness and to enable participation in public decision-making. In recognition of this, the EU and its Member States work to make laws, court decisions, etc. publicly available online. The sheer mass of legal norms, instruments, and interpretations in court decisions, commentaries and other sources, makes it increasingly difficult for citizens, civil society, businesses, and all involved stakeholders in legal practices to locate the relevant law. The challenge is to interlink local legal information and to have structures in place to enrich this information through aggregation and mass customization. The technological possibilities to achieve this goal do exist. The European project openlaws.eu aims for initiating a platform and to develop a vision for Big Open Legal Data (BOLD): an open framework for legislation, case law, and legal literature from across Europe.

This paper examines consumer access to justice in the EU by analysing how Alternative Dispute Resolution (ADR) and Online Dispute Resolution (ODR) can improve this access, especially in the case of low-value cross-border disputes, which constitute the majority of consumer contract complaints. The discussion is based on a widened concept of open justice that not only seeks to provide greater transparency, but also greater participation and collaboration as a means to improve consumer access to justice. The approach deals with the subjective and objective obstacles to accessing justice and the role of participatory justice. Finally, the paper examines the decisions taken by the EU in its attempt to foster both ADRs and ODRs for consumer disputes and determines which obstacles have been eliminated in promoting access to justice.

The study focuses on the openness of judicial data in seven countries in Latin America. The judiciary continues to be among the least willing institutions to implement policies on transparency and access to information, generally because of their conservative tradition and lack of accountability practices. The study adopted an exploratory design in order to analyze enabling country and judicial contexts for open data, as well as whether judicial data publication meets open data standards of accessibility, sustainability, re-usability and non-discrimination. Study results show that even though access to judicial information is increasing and that there is also an increase in transparency policies for the judiciary, the publication of judicial data in open formats is still infrequent. This research seeks to build a baseline for an initial measurement that can be compared with future measurements, so as to be able to evaluate progress made in Latin American judiciaries.

The new trend of information technology and communications has been adopted by court systems. A similar path follows other powers in the republics: executive branches with e-government portals and legislative branches with informative and participatory portals. Despite the fact that technology has reached the judiciary branch, we know very little about the changes, advantages or disadvantages of this adoption. The purpose of this chapter is to explore the use of technology, especially in the websites portals in the Latin America region. An assessment model, which has been developed by Sandoval and Gil-García (2015) and that has four components: information, interaction, integration and participation, has been implemented on a sample of 25 countries during the month of July, 2015. Findings reveal a great disparity among the different countries in the region.

Preface

On January 2009, President Obama signed the Memorandum on Transparency and Open Government that declares the new Administration's commitment to creating an unprecedented level of openness in government and establishing a system linking three principles: transparency, public participation and collaboration. Since then, public administrations around the world have embarked on open government initiatives and have worked to redefine their relationship with citizens and with each other. The benefits attributed to open government are many. They include the claims that open government leads to more effective decision making and services, safeguards against corruption, enables public scrutiny, and promotes citizens' trust in government, included better achievements of effectiveness, efficiency or accountability.

Although many open government initiatives have been implemented around the world, most of them have been related to the executive and legislative powers and institutions. However, open government does not seem to apply to the judiciary for, maybe, this has always been a "closed" field. As a result, there is a need to know what openness in justice is, to explore its implementation, and to understand what it can do to improve government, society and democracy.

As in the case of open government, in the judiciary, openness has been originally linked to transparency, that is, the right to know, the right to public scrutiny (Reinhard, 1995). In particular, the starting point has been said to be the open justice principle, a constitutional principle to be found not in a written text but in the common law. The principle states that judicial procedures should be open to the public, including contents and information of judicial records and public hearings. According to Neuberger of Abbotsbury (2013), in this context, openness is a justice fundamental right.

Authors such as Reinhardt (1995), Jiménez-Gómez (2013) and Rodrick (2007) state that the open justice principle enhances the integrity, accountability, and performance of those who are involved in the administration of justice. *For example, it is supposed that openness makes judges more accountable for the manner in which they exercise the judicial power that is vested in them; secret courts are regarded as having a propensity to spawn corruption. Witnesses are thought to be more likely to tell the truth if they have to testify orally in open court. For their part, the public, having observed responsible and truthful behaviour on the part of the judges and witnesses, will have increased confidence in the operation of the courts and a greater understanding of society's laws and legal system. Any perceived shortcomings in the behaviour of particular individuals or in the substance of the law or its application in a particular case can be publicly scrutinised and, perhaps, corrected* (Rodrick, 2007: 172).

Dyson (2013) confirms that the open justice principle allows for a better understanding of the activities that are carried out but, also, for an increasing trust in judicial independence. However, the author goes a little further and also recognizes the important role that technology plays in judicial openness. Specifically, the author refers to televising courts or using social media, tools that support the opening of processes but that are not exempt of challenges (such as sensationalism or the effects of real time diffusion). The potential of ICT is also assessed by Jiménez-Gómez (2013) and Gamero (2012).

Despite its origins, openness in the judiciary has expanded beyond transparency and, therefore, beyond the common law open justice principle (Stefan & Alemanno, 2014). Jiménez-Gómez (2014) has widely referred to the application and adaptation of the open government dimensions to the judiciary: transparency and accountability but collaboration and participation, as well. He calls this new open government-inspired philosophy open judiciary. Jiménez-Gómez (2014) also refers to the significant role innovation and ICT play in open judiciary. Finally, as Williams III (2007) does, he maintains that this shift is aligned with the structural and unprecedented changes in the judiciary that several countries have undertaken and that focus on meeting today's social demands, such as accountability, effectiveness, protection rights, democratic participation, and trust.

OPEN JUDICIARY: VISION AND VOICE

In the academic literature, openness has been approached from two different perspectives: (Meijer et al., 2012): transparency and participation. The literature on transparency revolves around terms such as freedom of information, Internet, active dissemination of information, access to documents and usability of websites (Curtin & Mendes, 2011). The core question tackled by these works is: what is being made visible/transparent? Literature discusses, among other issues, the nature and scope of transparency, the usefulness of information, and the timing of the release of documents. The premise underlying these studies is that transparency yields to accountability. At the same time, a more accountable government is a more legitimate one (Sandóval-Almazán, 2011). At the same time, the literature on participation literature stresses terms such as interactive policy-making, consultations, dialogue and stakeholder involvement. The central question for participation is: whose voice is heard? Empirical and theoretical analyses focus on inequalities in access to participation meetings.

Curtin and Mendes (2011) refer to these components of openness as vision and voice. Citizens need information to see what is going on inside government and participation to voice their opinions about this. We find this distinction extremely useful for an in-depth approach to open judiciary.

Open Judiciary and Transparency (Vision)

As we have already presented, judiciary openness is highly related to transparency and, in its roots, to the common law open justice principle. Transparency means, in this context, openness to public scrutiny and, therefore, it is linked to the right of information, active dissemination of information, and access to documents or web usability (Rodrick, 2007).

Several authors have addressed transparency in the judiciary from different perspectives. For example, Devanesan and Aresty (2013) affirm that transparency is a key element for Online Dispute Resolution (ODR) models while Ruggieri (2010) states that it should be inherent in mediation processes. Meanwhile, Conley et al. (2012) refer to both the right to access hearings and the right to access judicial documentation for inspection and copy. What's more, the authors declare that courts should review the rules that allow for the creation and access to documents, introducing online tools that will actively promote transparency. This statement shows the relevant role ICT play in transparency initiatives, as is the case when talking about open government.

Two additional authors, Stefan and Alemanno (2014), state that transparency in this field is more than just accessing documents or being present at hearings. They actually refer to further goals, such as legitimacy, accountability, and good governance. For them, transparency is just a means to achieve these ultimate objectives. Along the same lines as Conley et al. (2012), Stefan and Alemanno (2014) also recognize the contribution of ICT and media not only in allowing access to the information but, also, in helping undertand it.

However, being transparent is not easy (Bannister & Connolly, 2011). In addition to the challenges of technology (for example, those related to the characteristics of social media such as immediacy, ubiquity and speed), transparency initiatives are also associated to privacy and security issues, distortion of information, and sensationalism (Gorham, 2012; Winn, 2004; McLachlin, 2003; Cameron, 1986). The case of the Court of Justice of the European Union (CJEU), which has been not able to keep a balance between the pervasive rethoric of transparency and the implementation of real transparency initiatives (Stefan & Alemanno, 2014), clearly shows these difficulties. Despite the slow evolution towards greater transparency, the lack of defined transparency and openness standards as well as the absent of a detailed regulatory framework in this regard hinder openness efforts.

Open Judiciary and Participation (Voice)

In terms of open government, Gascó (2014) differentiates between collaboration and participation. The author refers to a collaborative government as one that involves citizens and other external and internal actors in the design, delivery, and evaluation of public services whereas she states that a participative government is one that promotes citizen engagement in political processes and, particularly, in the design of public policies. Although both definitions focus on different elements (public services, on one hand, public policy/political processes, on the other), boh clearly bring up the issue of engagement, involvement, and cooperation. In sum, they both raise the subject of voice, which is easier to apply when addressing open judiciary.

According to Meijer et al. (2012), the link between vision and voice may seem self-evident but is rarely explored in the literature:

Sometimes, in research into government transparency the question is raised whether information is actually used to strengthen participation, but generally this does not feature prominently in the debate. Likewise, some of the research into participation does pay attention to the question whether citizens have been informed properly and can have access to the information they need to participate but, again, this is the exception rather than the rule (p. 11-12).

Interestingly enough, this has also been the case in the justice field although a few authors have addressed the links between transparency and participation and, furthermore, they have connected both dimensions to trust and legitimacy. Abrahamson (2002), for example, reports the lack of trust in judicial institutions. He links information activities (particularly related to achieving a closer relationship between lawyers and judges and citizens, to increasing the communication with the executive and legislative powers, and to getting input from non-legal professionals, such as volunteers) with public participation. Stepniak (2006), as other authors do, declares that the open justice principle is not only about public scrutiny but about true participation. García (1998) adds that citizens' participation in courts helps these citizens understand the role of courts, increasing trust in what they do and the decisions they made. Similarly, the National Association for Court Management (2001) links openness, hearings and collaboration to increasing citizens' trust in justice. Rottman (1998) speaks on the same lines and states that citizen engagement boosts citizens' trust in the judiciary.

Participation has been approached from several points of view. One of the most popular perspectives has to do with the concept of participatory justice (Stephens, 1986), a model according to which the common people become participants in those matters which are of importance to them instead of just onlookers (that is, they become the producers of solutions and not mere consumers). Participatory justice implies the use of alternative dispute resolution mechanisms, such as meditation, conciliation and arbitration, which focus on prevention and cooperation instead of on confrontation. In sum, participatory justice is an approach that engages everyone affected by conflict in finding a satisfactory resolution (Law Commission of Canada, 2003).

Participatory justice has highly benefitted from ICT (Vilalta, 2010) and other more recent ideas such as crowdsourcing. Martic (2014), for example, acknowledges this fact and proposes a conceptual model of Crowdsourced Online Dispute Resolution (CODR) that relies on multiple anonymous participants and that guarantees a higher level of confidentiality, secrecy and privacy preservation along with leveraging the so-called "wisdom of the crowds".

A different set of initiatives has had to do with voluntareeism. Terry III (2000) mention courts in Wisconsin (United States), which take advantage of the participation of citizens in several programs (ADR, prison, legal services, etc.). Similarly, Barendrecht & Nispen (2008) refer to micro-justice services addressed to poor people, some of which are altruistically delivered by volunteers. According to Brown (2007) and the Justice Management Institute (2010), volunteers add value in terms of costs (saving time) but, also, in terms of boosting innovation.

Committees and commissions are another way of participation, particularly related to stakeholders' engagement in judicial initiatives (Lenaola, 2011). For instance, the Committee on State Justice Initiatives of the American Bar Association (ABA) (2003) has, since 1995, supported the role of commissions as collaborative entities that bring together courts, the Bar, civil legal aid providers, and other stakeholders in an effort to remove barriers to civil justice for low-income and disadvantaged people. ABA actually hosts several groups (committees, commissions, centers,...) that rely on collaboration among different stakeholder and that address a wide variety of topics.

Involvement of stakeholders is actually promoted in many countries, such as the United States, the United Kingdom, Canada, and South Africa. This active engagement has given rise to the concept of community court defined as neighbourhood-focused problem-solving court that applies a problem-solving approach to local crime and safety concerns (Wolf, 2007). Community courts can take many forms, but all strive to create new relationships, both within the justice system and with outside stakeholders such as residents, merchants, churches and schools. Community courts emphasize collaboration, crime prevention, and improved outcomes, including lower recidivism and safer communities. Ultimately, community courts attempt to harness the power of the justice system to address local problems. They strive to engage stakeholders in new ways in an effort to bolster public trust in justice (Casey & Rottman, 2005; Berman & Anderson, 1997; Mackenzie, 1994).

An evolution of this collaborative approach is the case of the Center for Court Innovation, described by Goldstein (1997) as a judicial incubator aimend at developing and evaluating new approaches to administering justice. The Center was indeed founded as a public-private partnership between the New York State Unified Court System and the Fund for the City of New York to assist judges in devising strategies and technologies for improving the judicial system.

Despite the success of worldwide initiatives, participation in the judiciary has a long way to go. Rottman et al. (2002) show that collaboration in the justice field will grow more in the future. The authors refer to the specific case of the United States although we believe the situation is replicable to other parts of the world. Rottman et al. (2002) start showing there is high social dissatisfaction with American courts. The gap between courts and citizens seem to grow wider because courts are not meeting the community's needs. The maladjustments of traditional legal procedures embedded in real life circumstances hinder addressing the society's current problems. Only by opening up and involving citizens and communities in their operation, courts will be able to understand and, therefore, really meet citizens' demands. In doing so, trust in justice and its ability to solve current societal challenges will also increase (National Center for State Courts, 1996).

ABOUT THIS BOOK

Aim of the Book

Despite previous developments regarding openness in the judiciary, the lack of specific literature on the topic, combining vision and voice and therefore adopting the philosophy of open government, shows that this is still an unexplored field. What's more, although numerous initiatives aimed at openness have been undertaken, generally speaking, judicial institutions have followed different directions and interpretations when it has come to implement them. As a result, nowadays, it can be said that the development of open judiciary is unequal and heterogeneous. There is confusion about the concept itself (open judiciary versus open justice), about its implementation process, and about its real impact.

In this context, the aim of this book is to shed light on the concept of openness in the judiciary and to identify and analyze worldwide initiatives that focus on opening the judicial organizations by making them more transparent and collaborative/participative. Our ultimate goal is to show that an open government is not enough. There is a need to talk about an open state and, therefore, to make sure, openness is guaranteed in the three state's branches. No other publication has approached open government from the state perspective emphasizing the need to also have an open justice/open judiciary[1].

In particular, the book aims:

- To provide comprehensive knowledge of recent major developments of open juidiciary/open justice around the world.
- To analyze the importance of open judiciary/open justice efforts for the judiciary and the society, as well as for the modernization of the courts and of the justice field generally speaking.
- To provide insightful analysis about those factors that are critical when designing, implementing and evaluating open judiciary/open justice.
- To assess the role of information and communication technologies, and specifically of web 2.0 tools, regarding the acceleration of the opening processes.
- To discuss how contextual factors affect open judiciary/open justice's success or failure.
- To propose strategies to move forward and to address future challenges in an international context.

Organization of the Book

This collective work is structured in four sections and twelve chapters. Section 1 opens the book with general reflections on the concept of open judiciary. Carlos E. Jiménez-Gómez's chapter gives an overwiew of open judiciary initiatives worldwide, focusing on some of the most successful in order to identify drivers of adoption, critical success factors, and preliminary results. The author's research is embedded in a broader study on the state of the art of open judiciary (Chapter 1).

Nial Raaen's text focuses on one of the dimensions of open judiciary: transparency. The author states that open access to accurate and reliable records is essential to participation in the judicial process. He, therefore, links vision and voice and approaches the former as a condition to achieve the latter. In particular, Raaen discusses the application of the recently adopted records management principles published by the U.S. Conference of State Court Administrators to set up a framework and a list of performance measures that ensure that court records remain open, accessible, and trustworthy in the digital age (Chapter 2).

Finally, Jesús Cano, Luis Pomed, Carlos E. Jiménez-Gómez, and Roberto Hernández address the specific contribution of information and communicartion technologies to openness in the judiciary. The authors connect the concept of electronic justice (e-justice) to that of open judiciary/open justice. In doing so, they develop an e-justice tool aimed achieven more open judicial organizations (Chapter 3).

Section 2 is devoted to open judiciary initiatives in Asia. In particular, Mei Gechlik, Di Dai, and Jordan Corrente Beck present the case of China while Yumiko Kita refers to the case of Japan. The former examine the application of open government principles to the reform of the court system in China and identify the key factors to promote judicial openness in a closed society (Chapter 4). The latter describes and analyzes the Japanese citizen judge system, in place since 2001, a judicial model that randomly selects citizens to hear and discuss evidence, to reach a guilty/non-guilty verdict, and to deliver their judgments in cooperation with profesional judges. The author's analytical framework is related to democracy and open justice (Chapter 5).

Section 3 includes five chapters on European initiatives. The first one, by Rui Pedro Lourenço, Paula Fernando, and Conceição Gomes, present the evolution from e-justice to open justice in Portugal. The authors look into open justice initiatives and compared them with succesful development in the fields of e-government and open government (CHAPTER 6). A more specific experience is described in Mortaza S. Bargh, Sunil Choenni, and Ronald F. Meijer's text, who explain the Dutch approach for integrating the data sets of the judiciary systems in The Netherlands and for opening the data integration outcomes to the public and/or to specific groups. The authors identify some challenges in using the term open data and coin the concept of semi-open data as one that encompasses data dissemination solutions aimed at transparency, compliance, collaboration, innovation, and decision-making support, among other, but do not comply with all open data requirements (Chapter 7).

Mila Gascó-Hernández also focuses on a specific initiative, related to collaboration among stakeholders (the Department of the Interior and the Department of Justice of the Autonomous Government of Catalonia, in Spain). In particular, the author introduces the concept of interoperability in the justice field and links it to the collaboration dimension of openness (Chapter 8). Of extreme interest is the case of openlaws.eu, analyzed by Thomas J. Lampoltshammer, Andres Guadamuz, Clemens Wass, and Thomas Heistracher in their chapter. Openlaws.eu is a European project aimed at initiating a platform and at developing a vision for big open legal data: an open framework for legislation, case law, and legal literature from across. According to the authors, the project contributes to better access to legal information and, ultimately, to better governance, both of which build the foundation for open justice in the long run (Chapter 9). Last, Inmaculada Barral-Viñals addresses participation in the judiciary. In her chapter, Barral-Viñals adopts the participatory justice approach and, explicitly, analyzes a specific kind of justice in which participatory access is not necessarily guaranteed: consumer conflicts. The author claims that greater emphasis on collaboration and participation is needed in judicial openness (Chapter 10).

The closing section of the book, section 4, is devoted to experiences in Latin America. The first text, by Rodrigo Sandoval-Almazán, explores the use of technology in open judiciary. In particular, the author assesses the judiciary portals in 25 Latin American countries using a four-component model: information, interaction, integration, and participation. His findings show that the information component is the strongest one, a result which is aligned with the idea that the common law open justice principle is still the prevailing one in the field and that more research is needed to link it with a broader concept of open judiciary that also stresses citizens and stakeholders' collaboration and participation (Chapter 11).

The final chapter, authored by Sandra Elena and François van Schalkwyk, presents a study on the openness of judicial data in seven countries in the region aimed at analyzing enabling country and judicial contexts for open data and at assessing whether judicial data publication meets open data standards of accessibility, sustainability, re-usability, and non-discrimination. Its authors conclude that the seven countries have, to some extent, open judicial data but that this information does not meet the specific requierements of open data (Chapter 12).

In sum, the book presents a collection of chapters that is not comprehensive but that tackles different issues related to open judiciary/open justice that may be of interest for both researchers and practitioners. It shows the state of open judiciary initiatives in some parts of the world and it draws insightful ideas regarding their implementation, but it also presents some interesting conceptual perspectives on transparency and participation, on vision and voice, in achieving greater openness in the judiciary. More could be said about open judiciary/open justice. *Achieving Open Justice through Citizen Participation and Transparency* is only a first approach to the field. We hope that the authors' contributions encourage the reader to keep strengthening the study and practice of open judiciary around the world.

Carlos E. Jiménez-Gómez
Department of Justice of the Autonomous Government of Catalonia, Spain

Mila Gascó-Hernández
Institute of Public Governance and Management, ESADE Business and Law School, Spain

Barcelona (Spain), March 2016

REFERENCES

ABA. Committee on State Justice Initiatives. (2003). Summary of State and Local Justice Improvement Activities. Chicago: American Bar Association, Coalition for Justice.

Abrahamson, S. S. (2002). Involving individual citizens with courts and tribunals: initiatives in the United States and Canada. In *Citizenship and Citizen Participation in the Administration of Justice*. Montreal: Editions Thémis.

Bannister, F., & Connolly, R. (2011). The Trouble with Transparency: A Critical Review of Openness in e-Government. *Policy & Internet*, *3*(1), 1–30.

Barendrecht, M., & Nispen, P. v. (2008, February). Microjustice. TILEC Discussion.

Berman, G., & Anderson, D. (1997). *Engaging the community: a guide for community justice planners*. New York: Center for Court Innovation.

Brown, G. S. (1997). Court Monitoring: A say for citizens in their Justice system. *Judicature*, *80*(5), 219–221.

Cameron, J. (1986). Comment: The Constitutional Domestication of Our Courts-Openness and Publicity in Judicial Proceedings Under the Charter. In P. a. Anisman (Ed.), *The media, the courts and the Charter*.

Casey, P. M., & Rottman, D. B. (2005). Problem-solving courts: Models and trends. *Justice System Journal, 26* (1).

Conley, A., Datta, A., Nissenbaum, H., & Sharma, D. (2012). Sustaining Privacy and Open Justice in the Transition to Online Court Records: A Multidisciplinary Inquiry. *Maryland Law Review (Baltimore, Md.)*, 71.

Curtin, D., & Mendes, J. (2011). Transparences et participation: Des principes democratiques pour l'administration de l'Union Européenne. *Revue Française d'Administration Publique*, *137-138*, 101–121.

Devanesan, R., & Aresty, J. (2013). ODR and Justice. In *M. Abdel Wahab, E. Katsh, & D. Rainey, Online Dispute Resolution Theory and Practice*. The Hague, Netherlands: Eleven International Publishing.

Dyson, J. (2013, 10 18). Advances in open justice in England and Wales. Hong Kong, China: Master of the Rolls.

Gamero, E. (2012). El objeto de la Ley 18/2011 y su posición entre las normas relativas a las tecnologías de la información. In *J. Valero Torrijos, & E. Gamero Casado, Las tecnologías de la información y la comunicación en la Administración de Justicia. Análisis sistemático de la Ley 18/2011, de 5 de julio* (pp. 45–88). Pamplona: Aranzadi.

García, P. (1998). *Community involvement: the key to successful justice reform*. Chicago: American Bar Association, Office of Justice Initiatives.

Gascó, M. (2014). *Guía de Buenas Prácticas en Gobierno Abierto*. Bogotá: Universidad Externado de Colombia. Observatorio de Sociedad, Gobierno y Tecnologías de la Información.

Goldstein, M. (1997). 2 6). Couts, foundation team up to try new strategies. *New York Law Journal*, 1.

Gorham, U. (2012). State courts, e-filing, and diffusion of innovation: a proposed framework of analysis. *13th Annual International Conference on Digital Government Research*. Washington, DC: ACM.

Jiménez-Gómez, C. E. (2013). *Impacto de la Ley Reguladora del Uso de las TIC en la Administración de Justicia*. Barcelona: Centro de Estudios Jurídicos y Formación Especializada.

Jiménez-Gómez, C. E. (2014). *Justicia Abierta: transparencia y proximidad de la justicia en el actual contexto de Open Government.* Barcelona, Barcelona, España: Centro de Estudios Jurídicos y Formación Especializada. Generalidad de Cataluña.

Justice Management Institute. (2000). *Courts as collaborators: opportunities ans issues for courts involved in justice system innovations. Criminal Courts Technical Assistance Project.* Washington, DC: American University.

Law Commission of Canada. (2013). *Transforming relationships through participatory justice.* Ottawa: Law Commission of Canada.

Lenaola, I. (2011). *Public Participation in Judicial Processes* (K. L. Journal, Ed.).

Mackenzie, B. W. (1994). A community-based approach to domestic violence. *The Special Court News, 15* (2).

Martic, D. (2014). Blind Arbitration. *Sintelnet WG5 Workshop on Crowd Intelligence: Foundations, Methods and Practices.* Barcelona.

McLachlin, B. (2003). Courts, Transparency and Public Confidence -To the Better Administration of Justice. *Deakin Law Review* (8).

Meijer, A., Curtin, D., & Hillebrandt, M. (2012). Open government: Connecting vision and voice. *International Review of Administrative Sciences, 78*(1), 10–29.

National Association for Court Management. (2001). *Community, creativity, collaboration: a community dialogue for the courts.* Williamsburg: National Association for Court Management.

National Center for State Courts. (1996). 1995 National Town Hall Meeting on Improving Court and Community Collaboration. *1995 National Town Hall Meeting on Improving Court and Community Collaboration.* Williamsburg: National Center for State Courts.

Neuberger of Abbotsbury, L. (2013, July 2). Openness a 'fundamental principle' of justice, says Britain's most senior judge. *The Telegraph.* (D. Barrett, Interviewer) UK.

Reinhardt, S. (1995). Judicial Speech and the Open Judiciary. *Loyola of Los Angeles Law Review*, 805–813.

Rodrick, S. (2007). Open Justice and Suppressing Evidence of Police Methods: The Positions in Canada and Australia - Part One. *Melbourne University Law Review, 31*, 171–200.

Rottman, D., Efkeman, H., Hansen, R., & Stump, S. (2002). *A Leadership Guide to Statewide Court and Community Collaboration.* National Center for State Courts.

Rottman, D. B. (1998). On public trust and confidence: does experience with the courts promote or diminish it? *Court Review, Winter*, 14-22.

Ruggieri, L. (2010). ADR y ODR y su taxonomía. La identificación de caracteres. *IDP. Revista de Internet, Derecho y Política* (10), 32-41.

Sandóval-Almazán, R. (2011). The two door perspective: An assessment framework for open government. *eJournal of eDemocracy and Open Government, 3*(2), 166-181.

Stefan, O., & Alemanno, A. (2014). Openness at the Court of Justice of the European Union: Toppling a taboo. *Common Market Law Review*, *51*(1), 97–139.

Stephens, G. (1986). Participatory justice: The politics of the future. *Justice Quarterly*, *1*(3), 67–82.

Stepniak, D. (2006). The therapeutic value of Open Justice.*3rd International Conference on Therapeutic Jurisprudence.*Perth.

Terry III, W. (2000, Abril). Opening the courts to the community. *Bureau of Justice Assistance Bulletin* (NCJ 178935), pp. 1-19.

Vilalta, A. E. (2010). Justicia relacional y métodos electrónicos de resolución (ODR): hacia una armonización técnica y legal. *IDP. Revista de Internet, Derecho y Política* (10).

Williams, F. V. III. (2007). Reinventing the Courts: The Frontiers of Judicial Activism in the State Courts. *Campbell Law Review*, 29.

Winn, P. A. (2004). Online Court Records: Balancing Judicial Accountability and Privacy in an Age of Electronic Information. *Washington Law Review (Seattle, Wash.)*, *79*(1).

Wolf, R. (2007). *Principles of problem-solving justice*. New York: Center for Court Innovation.

ENDNOTE

1 We have previously shown that open justice refers to the open justice principle (and, therefore, is mainly related to public scrutiny) while open judiciary combines both transparency and participation. However, this distinction is not always clearly stated in the literature. As a result, we have decided to use both terms indistinctively throughout the book. However, our perspective is broad. We understand open justice/open judiciary as the framework that links vision and voice within the judiciary.

Acknowledgment

The editors would like to acknowledge the help of all involved in the collation and review process of the book, without whose support the project could not have been satisfactorily completed.

Special thanks also go to all the staff at IGI Global, whose contributions throughout the whole process from inception of the initial idea to final publication have been invaluable.

We also want to sincerely thank all those who offered constructive and comprehensive input for the different chapters. And, above all, we wish to thank all the authors for their insights and excellent contributions to this book, and to most of them for making an effort to translate their texts into English. Thank you to all of you for helping us to disseminate your expertise and knowledge about open judiciary/open justice initiatives.

This book is dedicated to Marcos, Carla, and Hawa.

Carlos E. Jiménez-Gómez
Department of Justice of the Autonomous Government of Catalonia, Spain

Mila Gascó-Hernández
Institute of Public Governance and Management, ESADE Business and Law School, Spain

Barcelona (Spain), March 2016

Section 1
Overview

Chapter 1
Open Judiciary Worldwide: Best Practices and Lessons Learnt

Carlos E. Jiménez-Gómez
Department of Justice of the Autonomous Government of Catalonia, Spain

ABSTRACT

Despite its origins, openness in the judiciary has expanded beyond transparency and, therefore, beyond the common law open justice principle. Several initiatives worldwide are echoing this trend and a new term, open judiciary, is arising as a way to address openness in the justice field. This chapter gives an overview of open judiciary initiatives worldwide, focusing on some of the most successful, in order to identify drivers of adoption, critical success factors, and preliminary results. The research is embedded in a broader exploratory study on the state of the art of open judiciary. The chapter is addressed to answer two of the research questions: What are some learning practices that can be identified worldwide in relation to openness in the judiciary? What are some of the most important lessons that can be learnt from these practices?

INTRODUCTION

Although the term of open government was first used back in 1957 (Parks, 1957), it was not until the end of the seventies in the UK when the government gave more importance to initiatives addressed in order to reduce opacity, giving citizens more access to institutional information as well as to governmental activities (Chapman & Hunt, 1987, 2006). With President Obama's Open Government and Transparency Memorandum (Obama, 2009), the concept of open government became even more popular, also gaining a different dimension.

Open government guarantees transparency, accountability and openness of government, while increasing the opportunities of citizen participation (OCDE, 2003). Openness is therefore a key word when associated with access to information within the institutions, in contrast to secrecy, as well as collaboration and cooperation's management, in democratic processes (Peters & Britez, 2008). Although many open government initiatives have been implemented around the world, most of them have been related to the executive and legislative powers and institutions. Albeit, the concept of open government

DOI: 10.4018/978-1-5225-0717-8.ch001

in democratic societies is usually linked to the executive power, special attention must be given to the idea that -even if the judiciary has specific and contextualized characteristics- it is possible to apply the open government philosophy to the judiciary.

The open justice principle of the common law has been originally linked to the right to know and public scrutiny (Reinhardt, 1995). This principle states that judicial procedures should be open to the public, including information of judicial records and public hearings. But openness in the judiciary has currently expanded beyond this view. Jiménez-Gómez (2014) refers to *Open Judiciary* as the application and adaptation of the open government dimensions (transparency and accountability, collaboration and participation) to the judiciary. But despite the importance of this openness-in-justice view, this remains an unexplored area of research.

In this context, the aim of this chapter is to contribute to bridging this gap. In particular, the chapter addresses two main research questions:

1. What are some learning practices that can be identified worldwide in relation to openness in the judiciary?
2. What are some of the most important lessons (in terms of drivers of adoption, critical success factors, and preliminary results) that can be learnt from these practices?

The study presented in this chapter is part of a wider research about the state of the art of open judiciary funded by the Department of Justice of the Autonomous Government of Catalonia (and, in particular, funded by the Centre for Legal Studies and Specialized Training). Such research aimed at exploring open government's processes and principles in the context of judiciary in the civil law, as a basis of a modern view of Administration of Justice. It was conducted between December of 2013 and November 2014.[1]

The remainder of this chapter is organized as follows. In the next section, we present the data and methods used to identify and analyze learning/best practices. Subsequently, we select, describe and assess three of the more meaningful initiatives, highlighting three crucial aspects: drivers of adoption, critical success factors, and preliminary results. Finally, we draw some conclusions, emphasizing the practical implications of our findings and what further steps are to be taken.

METHODOLOGY: IDENTIFYING OPEN JUDICIARY INITIATIVES

Due to the lack of literature, this study (as well as the broader one) was exploratory in nature. Thus, we did not have a specific and clear theoretical framework guiding our research. Instead, we were open to identify initiatives in the justice field aimed at increasing transparency and/or collaboration/participation generally speaking. As stated, our objective was to contribute to the development of the conceptual body of open judiciary by starting to understand what drives adoption, what implementation critical factors are, and what results are being achieved.

Although the broader research, where the results presented in this chapter are embedded in, adopted a multi-method approach, only qualitative methods were used in the collection of information with regard to the identification and analysis of learning/best practices.

Qualitative analysis is a powerful method to identify topics and their interconnections if the phenomena under study are largely unexplored, as was the case here. Thus, first of all, desk research was conducted in order to identify initiatives in the justice field aimed at increasing transparency and/or collaboration/participation. Some initiatives were identified during the literature review we conducted. Many others were the result of using search engines, such as Google. Key words included open justice, open judiciary, transparency and justice, participation and justice, openness and justice, and collaborative justice. We conducted our search in English, Spanish, and Catalan. Thus, results were somewhat limited to these languages.

Initial desk research was complemented with nine in-depth semi-structured interviews with international experts based in Australia, Canada, the United States, and Spain. We were interested in the insights of both academics and practitioners with experience in law and transparency, justice reform, modernization processes, law and technology, open judiciary, and modernization processes of public institutions. Our goal was to look deeply into the opinion of experts to gain better knowledge and understanding of our topic of research as well as to identify initiatives that could be considered as good learning practices.

Well-established methodological guidelines regarding case study research were followed by carefully preparing a structured interview protocol (Yin, 2009). The open-ended questions were used to collect rich, context-specific and qualitative information on three specific topics:

1. Modernization, justice, and the role of ICT,
2. Openness in the judiciary (with specific sections devoted to transparency and participation/collaboration)
3. Innovation in the judiciary.

Interviews lasted between one and two hours. All of them were recorded and later transcribed.

In total, 105 initiatives were identified in order to be analyzed (see Table 1).

In order to initially classify and analyze the initiatives, we combined two main criteria. On one hand, we used categories related to the concept of administration of justice (Gamero, 2012). On the other, we used categories related to the concept of open judiciary. To give more details to the classification of initiatives, we added additional variables such as effectiveness, level of administration, public or private orientation, level of government, etc.

Taking all the information into account (desk research results, information extracted from the interviews, initial analysis of initiatives), we chose three initiatives, our so-called learning practices: Reinventing Justice 2022 in the United States, Open Justice – Making Sense of Justice in the United Kingdom, and the Inter-American Program of Judicial Facilitators (led by the Organization of American States).

An in-depth analysis was then conducted. Several types of documents were reviewed and examined such as legislation, official policy documents, strategic and operational plans, websites, and pieces of news.

ANALYZING LEARNING PRACTICES OF OPEN JUDICIARY

As stated, we selected three initiatives for further analysis, which are different but have some common elements. In particular, we identified two shared trends. On one hand, although all the initiatives can be considered as innovative, not all of them have to do with technology. This is very relevant and feeds the discussion about openness and ICT, which has taken place for a while around the concept of open government. Actually, this trend contributes to the stream that understands that openness does not necessarily have to do with technology but that also states that technology speeds up opening processes.

Table 1. List of initiatives under study

Initiatives Analyzed
1. A2J Author Community
2. America Decoded Laws Network
3. App for access to e-files via mobile (Android, OS X)
4. Australian Collaborative Practice Guidelines for Lawyers
5. Baltimore Decoded
6. California Collaborative Justice Courts Foundation
7. California Court and Community Collaboration
8. CENDOJ CGPJ
9. Center for Court Innovation
10. Chicago Decoded
11. Collaborative Justice
12. Community Justice Exchange
13. Community-focused courts development initiative
14. Community, Creativity, Collaboration: A community dialogue for the courts (guide)
15. Community/Homeless Courts
16. Community/Homeless Courts
17. Concursos Transparentes
18. Contracts Wiki
19. Court Network
20. Court Reminder Project
21. DC Decoded
22. Docracy
23. Domestic Violence Courts
24. Domestic Violence/Dating/Youth Courts
25. Drug Courts
26. DUI Court in Schools
27. DUI Courts
28. e-Court
29. Educaloi
30. Elder Abuse Courts
31. Judicial Facilitators Argentina
32. Judicial Facilitators Costa Rica
33. Judicial Facilitators Guatemala
34. Judicial Facilitators Honduras
35. Judicial Facilitators Nicaragua
36. Judicial Facilitators Panamá
37. Judicial Facilitators Paraguay
38. Free Legal Help Connecticut
39. Georgetown Iron Tech Lawyer Competition
40. Hackcess to Justice
41. Hawai'i State Judiciary - Community Outreach
42. Israel Platform ODR
43. Juvenile Drug Courts
44. Law Without Walls
45. Legal Aid Interagency Roundtable Toolkit
46. 151. Legal Atlas -HILL 2012 Award/WJC 2014 Award-
47. Legal Design Jam
48. Legal Hackers
49. Legal Open Document Hackathon
50. Legal Tech Start-up for Justice
51. LegalHackathon.org MIT Co-creation of Computational Law
52. LIME (Language Independent Markup Editor)
53. MarylandCode.org
54. Mental Health Courts
55. Micro Justice
56. Midtown Community Court. New York
57. Modria.com Resolution Center
58. National Association for Court Management - Court Community Communication
59. New Jersey Youtube Channel (volunteering)
60. ODR Hackathon
61. Open Courts
62. Open Courts Act 2013
63. Open Courts Bench Book
64. Open Gov - Justice
65. Open Justice
66. Open Justice (2)
67. Open Law/ Web of Law
68. Open Laws
69. OregonLaws.org
70. Peer/Youth Courts
71. Plain Site
72. Transparency portal of the CGPJ
73. Program for Legal Tech Design
74. Inter-American Program of Judicial Facilitators -HILL 2011 Innovation Award-
75. Public Access to Court Electronic Records (PACER)
76. Ravel Law
77. Reading List (Library)
78. Red Hook Community Justice Center (RHCJC) US's first multi-jurisdictional community court
79. Reentry Courts
80. Reinvent Law Channel
81. Reinventing Justice 2022 (1992). Massachusetts
82. Rule of Law Project
83. Russian Criminal Justice Atlas
84. San Francisco Decoded
85. Schede trasparenza istituti penitenziari
86. Self-Represented Litigation Network (SRLN)
87. Stanford Computable Contracts Initiative
88. Judicial Auctions online I Blog - Official
89. Sunshine Statutes (Florida)
90. The eKantonrechter: direct digital court access for citizens
91. The Guardianship Navigator Project
92. The Reinvent Law laboratory
93. The State Decoded (AM Legal Decoder)
94. Transparency CGPJ
95. TV Justiça do Brasil
96. Ventura county court - volunteering
97. Veterans Courts
98. Video: How to apply for a divorce: serving divorce papers
99. Virginia Decoded
100. Visual Law Library
101. Visualization for Lawyers
102. Volunteers Service. New Jersey Courts
103. Wisconsin Volunteers
104. You, the Juror (Open Captioned)
105. Youstice

Compiled by author, 2016.

On the other, most of the initiatives have a focus on transparency and access to justice. Again, this is aligned with open government in the executive. In this respect, we could say that these initiatives are linked with the common law open justice principle and, therefore, to the right to know, the right to public scrutiny (Reinhard, 1995). Fewer initiatives refer to participation and collaboration. The former have usually to do with citizen participation although the participation dimension of open government cannot apply here (there are no political processes in the justice field). The latter emphasize cooperation between courts, research institutions, foundations, and non-profit organizations, among other.

Next, we describe and analyze three selected initiatives: Reinventing Justice 2022, Open Justice: Making Sense of Justice, and the Inter-American Program of Judicial Facilitators.

Reinventing Justice and the Strategic Systemic Approach

As Williams III (2007) states, the work of reinventing the state courts in the United States took a giant leap forward in 1990 with the *National Conference on the Future and the Courts*. This conference would be the seed for strategic plans addressed to achieve the preferred future courts by the year 2020. *Reinventing Justice 2022* is one of these first plans, an initiative from the state of Massachusetts. It is one of the most interesting initiatives we have identified. It is a plan with a special focus on the modernization of justice and, therefore, it adopts a strategic approach although it also takes into account operational implementation guidelines. It started back in the early 90s.

In the early 90s, an important alienation and divide between courts and society was identified. There was a considerable degree of citizen dissatisfaction with judicial processes, and distrust in courts. Additionally, an important level of frustration within society was evident, with growing problems whose causes (social ones) were not being properly addressed (solutions were aimed at attacking the symptoms). There was a clear situation of what systems engineering calls "shifting the burden archetype": when solutions are oriented to only solving symptoms, serious negative consequences arise. In these cases, it is wise to adopt a systemic approach (Jiménez-Gómez, 2014).

This is what Massachusetts did by re-connecting courts to citizens through collaboration (Braun, 2002). Thus, in 1990, authorities started a plan addressed to changing the institutional orientation. For two years, the Commission on the Future of the Courts -an expert's committee- worked on a strategic plan, led by the Supreme Judicial Court. This committee included people from the judiciary but, also, from other fields of knowledge and institutions such as the Massachusetts Institute of Technology (MIT) and Harvard University.

The development of the Reinventing Justice 2022's strategic plan would give rise to a new model of justice, addressed to achieving a full transformation of the field (Supreme Judicial Court Commonwealth of Massachusetts, 1992). The plan was prospective and it tried to give an answer to the following question: how should courts be in thirty years? The document analyzed international trends on management and technology and it adopted a true future vision, looking for a new model of justice with a philosophy of true commitment of courts and the community to guarantee continuous openness and effectiveness for everyone in the judicial system. The model aimed at solving problems in its origin and at increasing trust from citizens. It took into account equality and a citizen-centric orientation, multi-optional dispute resolution methods, and new leadership models. Enormous reforms would be required in order to achieve the above-mentioned goals.

In words of (Rottman, Efkeman, & Casey, 1998, p. 2) "Massachusetts is pioneering a systemic approach to court and community collaboration, and California is taking significant strides in that direction". Yes indeed, Reinventing Justice 2022 is a pioneering strategic systemic approach, but it is not the only one. A strategic approach would be also adopted by other states such California in 1993 with the *Justice in the Balance 2020* plan, addressed to create a judicial system radically different by strategies for building public trust and confidence in the courts, where community has a key role. Based on the public trust and confidence in the courts, in the first years of 90's the state of California created the *Collaborative Justice Court* initiative, a similar initiative to the *Mid-Town Community Court* of the state of New York.

The idea behind these initiatives was to enhance collaboration with the community, making relationships stronger and encouraging mutual tolerance and recognition and partnership building (Rottman, Efkeman, & Casey, 1998). In both cases, specialized centers were key actor: the Center for Court Innovation and the National Center for State Courts. In sum, there was a focus on a citizen-centric orientation of the administration of justice. These initiatives throw interesting results. On one hand, they were highly reproducible and quickly extended to different types of courts (such as youth or drugs) and states. On the other, savings were considerable reaching several million dollars (Sviridoff, Rottman, Ostrom & Curtis, 1997; Wolf, 2005; Malone, Cheuk, Rowe, Kriegman, Wong, & Fein, 2010; Waller, Carey, Farley, & Rempel, 2013).

As a result, eventually, the steps done on reinventing the state courts during the 90's headed toward a *National Action Plan* in 2000, as a guide for national organizations in order to relate their strategic plans and programs to state strategies for building public trust and confidence in the courts.

Open Justice: Making Sense of Justice in the UK

United Kingdom is considered to be a reference when it comes to the adoption of ICT in the public sector, to open government. Also related openness in judiciary, an important example is the initiative *Open Justice: Making Sense of Justice* (UK Government, 2015). It is a transversal that particularly benefits from the characteristics of ICT by online tools. Also, it is the result of adopting a public policy perspective aimed at bridging the gap between citizens and the judiciary in the UK.

In December 2010, the UK Government opened the consultation *Breaking the Cycle: Effective Punishment, Rehabilitation and Sentencing of Offenders* in order to get information about the society's opinion with regard to specific changes that had been proposed regarding penalties, judicial decisions, and rehabilitation of offenders. Preventive measures, community participation, and transparency were some of the aspects that were included in the consultation process. In June 2011, the UK Government published the document *Breaking the Cycle: Government Response*, providing replies to citizens' questions and opinions. The document included significant statements such as: *we must open up justice so that victims and the public have a better understanding of how we are performing and more opportunities to get involved.* The document explained why the UK had to open justice, as well as it specified targets and actions to be taken.

In May 2012, the UK issued an Act aimed at decreasing recidivism and at pursuing local involvement. As in the Reinventing Justice 2022 initiative, the goal was to eradicate the problem, at its origin. This was thought to be more important that reshaping penalties. This citizen-oriented initiative puts also special emphasis on the role of volunteers. Neuberger (2009) refers to volunteers in the UK and links volunteerism to participation in the justice field. He says: *it is of course about putting people at its heart, with volunteering being an excellent way of doing this*. In sum, it is about having the capability of regarding volunteers as a bridge in order to connect courts and community and society in criminal justice.

As important elements, this initiative:

1. Aims at explaining to citizens how courts work as well as the difference among different judicial institutions,
2. Includes interactive data and statistics as well as graphic visualization (infographics),
3. Measures length of trials, from the very beginning (report) to the trial,
4. Strengthens links among citizens, inviting them to become volunteers,
5. Uses online tools, such as the game *You Be the Judge*, to educate the youth and to train teachers,
6. Is open to ideas proposed by citizens as well as discuss judges' sentences and, last, but not least,
7. True accountability is being achieved, by measurable and understandable information and continuous statistics about the results of the UK justice system.

The Organization of American States (OAS) Program of Judicial Facilitators

The Inter-American Program of Judicial Facilitators (Organization of American States, 2015) is a multi-country program of the Organization of American States aimed at increasing access to justice, mainly to citizens who live in more outlying rural areas, by a volunteering citizen collaboration mechanism. Mediation is a central element in this program. The service deployed in eight Latin-American countries (Argentina, Costa Rica, El Salvador, Guatemala, Honduras, Nicaragua, Panamá and Paraguay) has national coverage and is administered by the respective Departments of Justice (Republic of Panamá Government, 2015). It is therefore covered by an OAS mandate but also by specific regulations (Organization of American States, 2015). Also, it is technically supported by OAS as well as by other countries such as Italy, Spain, Sweden, and The Netherlands. In 2015, there were more than 9,000 volunteers.

This initiative was awarded in 2011 as an innovative program in the justice field, by The Hague Institute for the Internationalization of Law. The Institute remarked that the initiative brought justice to people who would otherwise be excluded from the system due to practical barriers, helped get the population involved in the justice system, and bridged the gap that so often exists between the formal legal system and true justice for those who need it most.

The initiative is not new at all. It was born in the late 90s to support local judges in isolated communities. The experience threw effective results. The program has expanded over time, particularly since 2007 when OAS offered specific support but, also, as the result of several agreements among countries in the region, such as the 100 Reglas de Brasilia, particularly focused on vulnerable people.

Within the program, facilitators are the ones that bridge the gap between judges and the community. These are volunteers that are usually perceived as leaders in their community or district. Volunteers are first chosen by their community and, later on, they are appointed by the judiciary as collaborating volunteers. They increasingly contribute to getting access to justice, particularly regarding vulnerable citizens. They focus on prevention, providing legal advice to citizens, and use conflict resolution mechanisms. Thus, facilitators are mediators. They also teach them about justice and support them, if necessary, when they have to go to trial.

Regarding impact, OAS has particularly emphasized the increasing number of participants in the program and the lower number of trials. The service has had its main impact on prevention and reduction of conflict and crime rate, it has increased the access to justice. Related to judiciary, it has become more efficient and humanized justice.

Key Factors in Order to Achieve Open Judiciary

The previous initiatives show that there are certain factors (we may call them critical success factors) that are key in order to achieve results that encourage further implementation of the programs. In particular, we want to refer to:

1. Strategic and systemic approach,
2. **Implementation Roadmap:** Test and pilot programs, role of volunteers, education and training,
3. Institutional framework.

The initiatives show how important the strategic approach is. To have a long term vision of what needs to be achieved is key. Open judiciary is not about organizational changes but about a change of culture. Therefore, to have a systemic approach to open judiciary initiatives is very relevant. Other factors are important as well.

Roadmaps help with the implementation process. Of particular significance is the conduction of pilots, which can be considered a first step to identify what works and what does not work. Also, staff needs to be aligned with the new practices. In this respect, education and training programs are key. In sum, organization change strategies need to be considered as well. Finally, in terms of implementation, volunteers, as some of the projects show, are important means to achieve openness in the justice field. The role of volunteers is closely linked to collaboration and participation and, therefore, to the dimensions of an open judiciary.

The institutional framework is very relevant as well. Leadership, laws and regulations and institutional cooperation need to be in place for these projects to be successful.

These insights have also been confirmed by other studies such as those of the Law Commission of Canada (2003) and Wolf (2005).

CONCLUSION AND PRACTICAL IMPLICATIONS

The analysis of the previous experiences show that the philosophy of open government can also be applied to the judiciary. Beyond transparency and access to justice (the common law principle of open justice), collaboration and participation also matter and have actually contributed to improve judicial systems.

If this is so, and we also take into account the works conducted by other authors on open parliaments, we can confirm that, more and more, a new concept prevails: open state (Jiménez-Gómez, 2015). An open state pursues openness in the executive, the legislative and the judiciary, considering the specific legal, organizational, cultural, technological, economic, and social factors that affect each branch. An open state takes advantage of the possibilities offered by the new technologies and by the information and knowledge society (Varella, 2014; Funken, 2013). But achieving openness is not exempt of challenges.

In the next paragraphs, and as a result of our previous analysis, we highlight some of the main issues that have to be taken into account in the particular case of open judiciary.

Openness as an Engine to Access and Modernize Justice

Research not only shows that there is a high degree of connection between closeness and openness in justice, but that open government principles can also be applied to justice. Initiatives analyzed have shown that it is possible to adopt this perspective in justice and, more importantly, experts and professionals agree that more openness in justice is possible, aligned to the open government principles, but true will is necessary in order to apply it.

It also seems right to affirm that adequate ICT use would imply, in general, more open processes in justice; ICT is only a tool and therefore, if modernization is correlated to openness, it seems right to affirm that it would mean an increase, first, in resource optimization, and second, in access to justice. This is a general worry detected in the study. Justice should seriously be adapted to the information society era. There is no justice without judicial independence, but neither without celerity. Access to justice in every dimension is a fundamental need, and from the looks of it, a challenge facing us in the next few years. It is important to closely view citizens as the core of justice services. The low degree of quality that justice has for interviewed and survey respondents is an important symptom. Modernization of justice should be equated to citizen-oriented justice.

Change Management and the Law's Principles

It is well known that changes in justice come up against more barriers than in any other field. Research shows that the biggest barriers for modernization are organizational structural changes. In addition, a main barrier to openness in justice is internal resistance. In order to achieve initiatives with a positive impact, a strategic change that would imply a new way of thinking about justice in a transversal way would be needed.

Only a strategic change and support that would come from figures like a National Treaty could allow this new perspective to gain ground. Collaboration between political parties, authorities and citizens needs clear leadership, and a strategic planning in collaboration among all actors in the state. ICT won't solve problems if there isn't a general improvement of philosophy. Experts highlight the need to see justice as a service and not only as a main power, in other words, a "service mode" in justice with an open-minded view is needed. But this change is really difficult when such an enormous resistance to change exists.

Principles and other elements should be analyzed to determine how they would be affected. For instance, an expert interviewed cites the principle *Iura Novit Curia* versus the *Common-wisdom fallacy* that Petersen (2011) talks about. Related to scientific-based judicial knowledge, innovation's impact could be key in achieving accountability and control mechanisms. ICT could be an opportunity to achieve an important impact from an epistemic perspective, which could closely place the object of the process, and make quality and quantity of information available. It could also help judges acquire greater jurisdictional control.

In general, those interviewed have highlighted the importance of mixing other disciplines with the legal field (ICT, psychology, economy, etc.), which requires an open-minded view that would also be needed in the civil law system. This matter links us to the classical debate between trends in legal methodology. On one hand, the reading and its interpretation of legal text (*bouche de la loi*) and, on the other hand, the sector that sees this view outdated/or as a dead language and states that today's law has to be multidisciplinary and closer to society. Common law legal literature backs up this last point of view, attributing common law judiciary to a more practical attitude than that of civil law. It could determine the degree of openness towards some innovations in the legal field. Usually, civil law practitioners adopt a strong perspective based on the axiomatic principles, which makes inclusion of changes difficult and generates a "blind faith" in effectiveness of other people.

Innovation and Collaboration in Justice

Innovation is key for modernization in justice. This element appears continuously in the initiatives analyzed. It wasn't included in the research as a basic open government principle, but results shows that innovation is really a very important variable. Thus, it seems that we should do an approximation to modernization in justice, by structural modernization as well as by proximity to citizens, simultaneously, with important doses of innovation and a citizen-centric approach. This view of Open Judiciary would allow transparency, collaboration and participation principles, to be a central axis in justice, with more transparency, effectiveness and efficiency, aligned to the old legal principles, but from a present perspective.

Innovative activities are fundamental for developing organizations. As Rogers (1998) states, these activities cannot be produced separately from the organization's core activities, thus innovation should be addressed to find new solutions in solving problems. This view once again is legitimately aligned with the openness concept. Public administrations are transforming public services by being more open, accessible and collaborative. Since reinforcement of justice has to be legitimated by citizens, it is especially interesting to quote here Chesbrough *et al.* (2011, pág. 24) who says that, "the idea of open government can be extended to areas where the government is a monopolist."

We have seen how legal professionals and lawyers have new business models thanks to ICT, which can involve new dynamics to access justice. Some experts say that self-advocacy could be viable with ICT if the justice service could actually be available to citizens. Innovation could be especially useful when accessing justice.

Some authors state that excessive emphasis on judicial independence could be detrimental to judicial accountability. Indeed, it seems that accountability in justice is underdeveloped in comparison to other public services. It would be necessary to find tools that effectively carry out the citizens' needs in the realm of justice. Mechanisms that get the citizen's perspective are needed, which also means openness to innovate in definition and basic organization (rules, processes, ICT, etc.).

Collaboration and participation principles are two elements that -further from the traditional kind (jury, jurisdictional cooperation, etc.)- are not being explored enough in civil law systems from a broader perspective. It seems that these elements have lots of barriers, especially from the legal point of view, if structural changes aren't adopted at a procedural and organizational level. The initiatives analyzed show that they exist and could be positive, but a more open-minded society is needed in order to advance in this direction.

Collaboration from citizens can be also useful, in which volunteering organizations and foundations could give a new perspective; we could even to think in a public-private-people partnership. Collaborative Justice and Community Courts are interesting examples that can show how the court's activities could be addressed in order to solve the origin of problems, and not just the symptoms. But it is also important to remark at this point, that differences between legal systems will be also key in order to adopt these perspectives, as Jiménez-Gómez (2015) explains related to collaboration in justice.

Transparency and Accountability: Open Data and More

As expected, transparency is the most tackled element by literature, especially in the field of access to information. From a practical point of view, the cases analyzed include an important number in this category. The precedent characteristic of common law and the access to cases has a prevalent importance, linked to traditional concepts of the open justice principle.

Taking into account open judiciary as a broader concept, special mention to open data is required. From a statistical and data managerial view, this element would favor accountability in courts, which would allow the possibility to monitor the justice system by the citizens themselves.

In this manner, literature highlights the need of balance between transparency and privacy. Experts consider that it is completely compatible. We also see impartiality as an important element to take into account when publicity restriction is necessary in order to avoid parallel judgments. Some authors say administrative functions from the jurisdictional kind would have to be especially separated in order to clearly define the application of the principles. But literature also points out that sometimes this separation is difficult because administrative aspects could finally have influence on jurisdictional principles.

It seems that transparency and codes of conduct are more advanced in common law countries, where a more conscientious citizen's attention has increased, or at least more than in other political aspects. This transparency is mainly due to open data that could have an impact on elements such as the court's performance, decisions, information about processes, access, language, self-representing, etc. but a true wish to be open, as well as the understanding of society's needs is necessary.

Access, Participation, and Closeness of Justice

Survey results suggest that society's mentality needs to shift towards a broader participation in justice. Transparency is the most cited principle but, even if participation and collaboration are less common, especially in civil law, they exist and are reaching interesting milestones. Access is a previous *condictio sine qua non*. Access is one of the most addressed elements, not only related to information in courts or rights in a more general concept, but also related to the possibility to understand the legal jargon, text and its mechanisms by citizens.

ICT is an accelerator for more open procedures. In this manner, crowdsourcing could help achieve a closer form of justice, a more accessible justice as well as a distinct way of deciding in trials. But again, goodwill is required. If a citizen wants to understand and use legal text, it shouldn't be necessary to be an expert in law.

When considering participation, alternative mechanisms could give ways to increase a more participatory culture in justice. Both mediation or negotiation are good examples of where parties or mediators can play a more active role, proposing solutions where only the judge will validate the final agreements. ICT can strongly help achieve other distinct options that are greater than the older or more outdated models in justice. At this point, ODR and ADR mechanisms could help in this endeavor. Countries like Australia have a large activity in regards to mediation and ODR use, at times, mandatorily before even reaching a confrontation in court. This is the direction in which the 2013 ODR European Directive is shifting towards.

Another important element here is social media. Administration and public institutions should have a stronger presence where citizens are, in order to inform citizens but to also hear their requirements and requests. Communication and participation via these channels can have an important added value to justice from the transparency standpoint, as well as educational. The role of social networks can also be important for participation and collaboration, linking these elements not only to communication in justice, but also related to citizens' collaboration and participation in justice via social media or other tools like interactive TV.

Educational Reform in Order to Regenerate the Model

Education is also an element that will be key. Everyone interviewed has pointed this factor out. We have seen how hearings can be instruments whereas transparency and learning can be placed or found together onsite or online via social media.

An important point here is the redesign of some professional and educational curriculums linked to the legal field, because these changes could imply the Information & Knowledge Society and ICT in justice. Especially interesting in this field, is the case of the USA, where, since more than 20 years ago, this is mandatory in law schools to also having knowledge of other disciplines distinct than law (law & ICT, law & economics, etc.). The idea is that law must be multidisciplinary and, indeed, we find that more and more Schools of Law employers also require a PhD in branches of knowledge distinct to law. This characteristic has an impact on the quality of education and the nature of the doctrine. This is the reason why, for instance, Harvard Law Review publications are from a multidisciplinary point of view. Thus, Common Law is becoming more flexible in including new tools, and law graduates are better prepared in complementary fields of knowledge distinct to law.

For the interviewees, a law professional's education is one of the biggest concerns, because eventually it impacts the knowledge that judges, attorneys and civil servants in the field of justice receive. This is especially monolithic in the case of Spain's norm in the positive use of law, where more and more, disputes seem to require deeper knowledge in other fields different from those concerning law (economy, technology, etc.) that cannot be replaced by an expert opinion.

CONCLUDING WITH SOME ADVICE AS FIRST STEPS

It seems that we are going towards an open state. In the same way that legislative and executive powers are being more and more open, judiciary power needs a more open view too. Open judiciary will be key in the next few years, if Judiciary branches want to achieve a true modernization of the justice and closeness to citizenship. States and institutions should be prepared to move in this direction too. The transversal transformations will require treaties at a national level, where all political forces agree. In addition, centers for innovation in justice will be helpful to assist in building and materializing the steps needed to take towards new and better solutions in justice overall as well as in the XXI century, where information and knowledge society has given institutions the opportunity to better connect with citizens.

We are in a new era, where spirit of openness is advancing also in the judiciary. Very close to this spirit were the words of Stephen Reinhardt, Judge of the Ninth Circuit of the United States Circuit of Appeals when he stated that "judicial openness, I believe, will provide a stronger foundation for our legitimacy. Under a truly democratic system, the public's confidence in our decisions should be based upon its knowledge rather than upon its ignorance, upon openness, not mystery. We are in a position of public trust: there is no justification for hiding from public scrutiny" (Reinhardt, 1995, p. 813).

REFERENCES

Braun, W. (2002). The System Archetypes. *System*, 27.

Chapman, R. A., & Hunt, M. (1987). *Open government. A study of the prospects of open government within the limitations of the British political system*. Londres: Routledge.

Chapman, R. A., & Hunt, M. (2006). *Open Government in a theroretical and practical context*. Surrey: Ashgate.

Chesbrough, H., Vanhaverbeke, W., Bakici, T., & López, H. (2011). *Open innovation and public policy in Europe*. ESADE Business School & the Science I Business Innovation Board AISBL. Science Business.

Gamero, E. (2012). El objeto de la Ley 18/2011 y su posición entre las normas relativas a las tecnologías de la información. In *Las tecnologías de la información y la comunicación en la Administración de Justicia. Análisis sistemático de la Ley 18/2011, de 5 de julio* (pp. 45–88). Pamplona: Aranzadi.

Jiménez-Gómez, C. E. (2014). *Justicia Abierta: transparencia y proximidad de la justicia en el actual contexto de Open Government*. Barcelona, España: Centro de Estudios Jurídicos y Formación Especializada. Generalidad de Cataluña.

Jiménez-Gómez, C. E. (2015). Colaboración Público-Privada y apertura de la justicia.*VI Congreso Internacional en Gobierno, Administración y Políticas Públicas GIGAPP.*Madrid: GIGAPP.

Jiménez-Gómez, C. E. (2015). Principios inspiradores de un Estado Abierto en el contexto del Poder Judicial. Análisis y experiencias. *XX Congreso Internacional del CLAD sobre la Reforma del Estado y la Administración Pública*. Lima: CLAD.

Law Commission of Canada. (2003). *Transforming Relationship Throught Participatory Justice*. Ottawa: Law Commission of Canada.

Malone, P., Cheuk, A., Rowe, S., Kriegman, I., Wong, S., & Fein, D. (2010). *Best Practices in the Use of Technology to Facilitate Access to Justice Initiatives*. Harvard University. Berkman Center for Internet and Society.

Neuberger, J. (2009). Volunteering across the criminal justice system. Academic Press.

Obama, B. (2009, January 26). Transparency and Open Government. (Memorandum for the heads of executive departments and agencies). *Presidential Documents, 74*(15), 4685-4686.

OCDE. (2003). *Open Government: Fostering dialogue with civil society*. Paris: OCDE.

Organization of American States. (2015b). *Inter-American Program of Judicial Facilitators. Regulation.* Retrieved from http://www.oas.org/es/sla/docs/facilitadores_judiciales_reglamento.pdf

Organization of American States. (2015a). *Inter-American Program of Judicial Facilitators*. Retrieved from http://www.oas.org/en/sla/judicial_facilitators.asp

Parks, W. (1957). The open government principle: Applying the right to know under the Constitution. *The George Washington Law Review, 26*(1).

Peters, M. A., & Britez, R. G. (2008). *Open education and education for openness*. Sense Publishers.

Petersen, N. (2011). Avoiding the Common Wisdom Fallacy: The Role of Social Sciences in Constitutional Adjudication. *International Journal of Constitutional Law, No, 2011*(22).

Reinhardt, S. (1995). Judicial Speech and the Open Judiciary. *Loyola of Los Angeles Law Review*, 805–813.

Republic of Panamá Government. (2015). *Órgano Judicial de la República de Panamá*. Retrieved from Programa de Facilitadores Judiciales Comunitarios de Panamá: http://www.organojudicial.gob.pa/wp-content/uploads/2014/04/PROGRAMA-DE-FACILITADORES-JUDICIALES-2009-2010.pdf

Rogers, M. (1998). *5). The definition and measurement of innovation*. Parkville, Australia: Melbourne Institute of Applied Economic and Social Research.

Rottman, D. B., Efkeman, H. S., & Casey, P. (1998). *A guide to court and community collaboration*. National Center for State Courts.

Supreme Judicial Court Commonwealth of Massachusetts. (1992). Reinventing Justice 2022. Boston: Author.

Sviridoff, M., Rottman, D., Ostrom, B., & Curtis, R. (1997). *Dispensing Justice Locally. The Implementation and Effects of the Midtown Community Court*. Amsterdam: Harwood Academic Publishers.

UK Government. (2015). *Open Justice. Making Sense of Justice*. Retrieved from http://open.justice.gov.uk/

Waller, M., Carey, S., Farley, E., & Rempel, M. (2013). *Testing the Cost Savings of Judicial Diversion*. New York: Academic Press.

Williams, F. V. III. (2007). Reinventing the Courts: The Frontiers of Judicial Activism in the State Courts. *Campbell Law Review*, *29*, 591–735.

Wolf, R. (2005). *California's Collaborative Justice Courts*. Judicial Council of California. Administrative Office of the Courts. Judicial Council of California, Administrative Office of the Courts.

KEY TERMS AND DEFINITIONS

Modernization of Justice: The improvement on the Administration of justice, which is addressed to achieving public service quality in justice, similar to most advanced public services, up-to-date, agile, effective, and efficient, guaranteeing access to justice, and achieving citizens' expectations.

Open Judiciary: Extension of open government's philosophy and principles (mainly transparency, participation and collaboration) applied and contextualized in the justice field, where innovation and ICT will be key tools in order to achieve it (Jiménez-Gómez, 2014).

ENDNOTE

1 More information about the broader research at: http://justicia.gencat.cat/ca/ambits/formacio_recerca_documentacio/recerca/cataleg_d_investigacions/per_ordre_cronologic/2015/justicia-oberta-transparencia-i-proximitat-open-government/

Chapter 2
Open and Transparent Judicial Records in the Digital Age:
Applying Principles and Performance Measures

Nial Raaen
National Center for State Courts, USA

ABSTRACT

Open access to accurate and reliable records is essential to participation in the judicial process and government transparency. As the judiciary and other branches of government increasingly rely on records which are created and maintained in digital form, a new set of challenges faces policy makers to ensure ongoing access and authenticity. One of the keys to this effort is the development of a set of principles and related performance standards which provide a framework and a system for measuring success. Using the recently adopted records management standards published by the U.S. Conference of State Court Administrators as a basis, this chapter discusses their application to digital record-keeping and how existing court performance standards addressing records management already developed by judicial organizations and the records management industry can be brought together to create a new set of performance measures to ensure that court records remain open, accessible, and trustworthy in the digital age.

INTRODUCTION

Recordkeeping has always been a core component of the judicial process. While most organizations create and maintain records as part of their business function, the purposes and uses of records in a governmental organization are often directly related to maintaining the democratic process and preserving the rights and obligations of citizens and organizations. This is particularly the case in the judicial branch. An effective records management program in the judiciary supports several critical functions: (Raaen, 2014)

DOI: 10.4018/978-1-5225-0717-8.ch002

- Support for judicial decision-making,
- Documentation of legal status and rights,
- Public access to court proceedings and decisions,
- Enforcement of court orders and judgments,
- Preservation of records for appellate review,
- Preservation of historical information.

Citizen participation in the judicial process is a critical part of open government. Public access helps ensure that court proceedings are conducted fairly and in a way that promotes confidence in judges and the courts as an institution. Public access also allows citizens to monitor the ability of society to address matters relating to crime, punishment and rehabilitation. The ability to access court records in a timely manner, along with the expectation that records will be accurate and complete, are fundamental to open justice and public participation. This chapter focuses on the issues surrounding the creation and maintenance of case records and their importance to transparency and participation by citizens in the judicial process in the digital age, and argues for the adoption of comprehensive performance measures based on fundamental principles to ensure that judicial organizations are able to provide open access to digital court records, while at the same time ensuring their authenticity and preservation over time.

BACKGROUND

The emergence of digital record keeping capabilities is causing a profound shift in the way that government agencies do business and interact with the public. Government agencies have turned to electronic records as a means to increase operational efficiency, improve access and security, and reduce their reliance on paper as the primary record. Although it must be said that in many regards technology has actually created an increase in paper documents since office automation products have made it easier to create, duplicate, and distribute documents and other records. As a result, many government agencies are working in a "hybrid" records environment as they make the transition from paper-based processes and record keeping to greater reliance on digital technology. Across the world, as well as within state and provincial jurisdictions, courts are at varying levels of adoption of electronic record-keeping. Already, however, some judicial agencies have fully adopted electronic record-keeping systems, effectively operating in a "paper-on-demand" environment.

In a 2003 World Bank forum on legal and judicial reform and record keeping, participants from over thirty countries identified a number of emerging issues for consideration in the digital age which have potential impact on the availability and usability of judicial records: (World Bank, 2003)

- The volume of judicial records, and resulting problem of storage, duplication, and obsolescence are major concerns for those responsible for the creation and maintenance of those records.
- The rapid adoption of technology and its continuing evolution have often out-paced the ability of law and policy-makers to ensure that the legal and statutory framework for creation, maintenance, and access to digital records is in harmony with current technological capabilities.

- The accessibility and ease of distribution of judicial data and documents has created a new frontier in public access. Large volumes of information, much of it of a personal or proprietary nature, are now available for distribution. Access and distribution of judicial information must be balanced against privacy concerns and individual rights.
- All records require a "continuum of care" throughout their life cycle. The reliance on digital record keeping has increased the complexity of this process, requiring government agencies to address education and training needs, as well as ensure that staff have the capabilities and resources to maintain the systems and infrastructure that support electronic record keeping.

Whether electronic or paper, court record systems must meet the diverse information needs of judges, court staff, litigants, the media, and the public. The creation and preservation of court records must be conducted in a way that ensures public trust and confidence in the judicial process. Public trust and confidence in the judiciary very much depends on the perception that the judicial process is transparent, that is, the processes and decisions reached as a result of those processes is visible, understandable, and accessible to citizens.

While it should be obvious that electronic records are entirely dependent upon technology, organizations often fail to realize that rapid changes in technology require continuous review and modification of electronic records management strategies. The challenges of technology, particularly relating to technological obsolescence and dependency, have complicated the long-term management of, and access to, information. At the same time there is no single solution to address and 'solve' all electronic records management issues. Often, decisions regarding electronic records management have been ad hoc or based on the promise of new technologies without due consideration to long-term impact or the impact on participation in the judicial process. Therefore, judicial leaders need to approach electronic records management with a long-term vision, commitment of resources and a regard for how decisions and strategy impact access and participation by litigants, the public and the media.

Court records are both the basis for judicial decisions and the enforcement of rights and responsibilities that these decisions address. The cornerstone to public participation and engagement in the judicial process is access. However, as the following discussion will illustrate, access is more than a matter of creating policies. The management of electronic records, in particular, involves a broad range of activities and capabilities of increasing complexity to ensure that records remain accessible and reliable for as long as needed to fulfill their purpose. For this reason, a fundamental set of principles supported by performance measures is needed to guide policy makers and practitioners.

PRINCIPLES FOR JUDICIAL RECORDS

Until recently, a unifying set of principles for application to judicial records has been lacking. Each year, the United States Conference of State Court Administrators[1] (COSCA) selects a topic of interest to address in an annual white paper. For 2013, COSCA and the National Center for State Courts[2] (NCSC) collaborated on a white paper, *To Protect and Preserve: Standards for Maintaining and Managing 21st Century Court Records*. (Linhares & Raaen, 2013) This paper sets forth a set of principles as a framework for assessing and implementing effective judicial records management practices based on ARMA International's Generally Accepted Recordkeeping Principles©. Six principles have been identified as central to judicial records management: compliance, access, integrity, preservation, disposition, and governance. Each of these principles contributes to the furtherance of an open and accessible judiciary by ensuring that judicial records are available and trustworthy throughout their life cycle for judicial decision-makers, litigants, and the public at large.

Compliance

The *Principle of Compliance* emphasizes that management practices should be in line with applicable statutes, rules of court, administrative orders, and organizational policies. The legal framework for judicial records includes not only laws and rules of procedure that apply to case-related records, but also local, state, and national laws and regulations that govern records supporting administrative activities. Compliance with the recordkeeping requirements of case records is particularly critical, as these records are the evidence of decisions and actions that create and enforce the rights of individuals and organizations. This includes adherence to statutes and rules in individual cases, as well as compliance with requirements for classes of records.

The rapid advance of technology has not always been accompanied by similar advances or revisions in laws and regulations governing digital records. As the transactions which occur in the courts and other government institutions are increasingly electronic, this disparity must be addressed. Some of the issues include the legality of e-signatures, whether an electronic document is considered the original version of a record, rules regulating public access, and requirements or standards for preservation. Laws may allow electronic images to stand in the place of original records as long as there is a reasonable assurance of integrity, but what exactly makes for reasonable assurance? Unfortunately, many laws and administrative rules are inadequate when it comes to specifying how to achieve this level of assurance.

Clearly, a legal framework must be created and maintained to support digital record keeping. Judicial agencies should utilize their governance and rule-making authority to develop appropriate guidance and standards to ensure preservation of records under their care and control, as well as work with legislative bodies to develop and harmonize the broader legal framework to ensure consistency and clarity throughout the legal system. (International Records Management Trust, 2005) The legal framework must also be sufficiently flexible to allow for the continued evolution of technology.

Access

The *Principle of Access* addresses the ability of court staff, litigants, and the public to access information to which they are entitled. The international standard for records management, ISO 15489-1, defines access as the "right, opportunity, means of finding, using, or retrieving information." Whether access is a right or opportunity depends on the particular circumstances of the record in question and whether the user is a staff member, litigant or member of the public. The right to access public information is generally based on constitutional or statutory intent to provide citizens with access to public records as a way of ensuring the right to participation in the governance process. (International Records Management Trust, 2015) Access includes policies and practices that ensure open access for the public while carrying out the business of the court without interruption, and at the same time preserving privacy rights.

Timely access to court records is fundamental to the public's perception of transparency and fairness in judicial systems. Records provide information that allows the public to follow the progress of individual cases, monitor judicial performance, and hold courts accountable for the timely and fair disposition of matters under their jurisdiction. Accessibility also applies to the ability of judges and court staff to retrieve and accurately update records within the shortest time frame possible to perform their functions and serve the public interest. Electronic record systems must be designed to ensure that information access can be tailored to the needs of users and restricts access to confidential and personal information.

The ways in which the courts provide access to records is changing profoundly. Previously, when records were limited to bound docket or registry books and paper files, public access was limited by the "practical obscurity" created by the inconvenience of going to the courthouse and waiting for staff to pull a file. (Anderson, 2011) The ready availability of court records via web interfaces, internet feed of court proceedings, and other methods of electronic access has greatly increased the complexity of managing this information as well as the burden of ensuring that information is accurate and timely. At the same time, the public is expecting the same ease and speed of accessing public information as they do other digital information.

Accessible public records have increasingly become an important part of the information economy in some countries. Private information providers accessing and distributing court information impact consumer credit, housing and employment decisions, and individual rights. The availability of large amounts of court information in electronic form has made it feasible to access and distribute court-based information on an unprecedented scale. Courts must consider the right of open access against potential invasion of privacy when granting access to records that contain personal identifying or financial information, intellectual property and commercial property rights, and information impacting state security.

Consideration must be given to how long public information should be available for publication. The "right to be forgotten" is an emerging concept that has particular application to the publication and availability of court records which have been republished by third parties. This issue is complicated by the emergence of different policies at the national level. The recent ruling by the European Court of Justice upheld the right of European users to have information removed from the Internet after a period of time "unless there are particular reasons, such as the role played by the data subject in public life, justifying a preponderant interest of the public." (Wiler, 2014)

In developing a comprehensive approach and set of policies to guide records access, judicial leaders should be able to clearly identify enforceable rights and restrictions that impact access. Systems for the creation, maintenance, and disposition of digital records should be designed to ensure that adequate controls are in place to preserve confidentiality without inhibiting timely access. The responsibility for record maintenance and control should be clearly defined as part of overall information governance, and a program of oversight or monitoring should be in place to verify compliance.

Integrity

The *Principle of Integrity* addresses the need for records to be created and preserved in a manner that guarantees the key record characteristics of authenticity, reliability, usability, and accessibility as defined by ISO 15489-1. (International Organization for Standardization, 2001) The importance of the integrity of court records was dramatically highlighted when two prison inmates, serving life sentences for murder in a Florida prison, were able to gain their release using forged court orders bearing the signatures of the State Attorney and a judge in the Ninth Judicial Circuit, as well as the seal of the Orange County Clerk of Court. Further investigation revealed at least seven cases where inmates at the same Florida correctional institution had attempted to forge court documents.

Maintaining the authenticity and accuracy of case records is critical to the credibility of our courts. In the paper world, the use of embossed seals, certification stamps, and original signatures helped ensure that documents are original and valid. In the digital world preserving trustworthiness and credibility requires a new set of tools and capabilities. Courts need to be sure that digital documents which they receive or create are complete and unaltered, and that the person who has signed the document is actually that person. An authentic and accurate court record is essential to preserving individual rights, the enforcement of laws and contracts, and in the case illustrated above, public safety.

Technologies such as digital signatures, digital rights management, electronic "stamps," metadata, and document audits are part of the new tool box for court records managers. Maintaining adequate metadata is a key to integrity as it provides information on the nature of a record, how and when it has been accessed, and whether any alteration has occurred. Interaction logs are useful for data authentication by ensuring that interactions with records are recorded, including any changes to the record. It should be possible to create an audit trail for any digital record that provides a history of changes made to the record, including who, when, how, and what.

A regime of ongoing checks of information is necessary, particularly following technological change, to ensure that any issues affecting the usefulness of information are identified in a timely manner and corrective action is taken. Integrity checks should be performed to ensure information has not been inadvertently changed. When information is converted to new formats, such as through migration to a new system or storage format, a comparison of a sample of the information should be taken to identify errors or inconsistencies. (National Archives of Australia, 2011) Once records have been created and indexed into a new technical environment they must be profiled to determine their quality and integrity. This includes the identification of key attributes that document the record's history, beginning with its creation or receipt and a full chain of custody. (Manago, 2011)

Protection of record integrity is an on-going process that is applied to records from the time of their creation through final disposition and archiving. An effective program will protect against unauthorized alteration, destruction, loss, or disclosure of information. This principle should be applied holistically to all of the information held by the judiciary, though it is particularly critical to records that impact judicial decision-making and public access to court processes.

Preservation

The *Principle of Preservation* addresses the need to maintain the integrity and accessibility of judicial records throughout their life cycle. Open justice does not end when a case is completed. Information about judicial proceedings, both individually and in aggregate, should be available as long as records are required to be retained, which in some cases is permanent.

For paper and microform-based records, preservation is a matter of storage conditions and handling. Although paper can disintegrate, ink can fade, and microfilm can experience chemical decomposition, stored under proper conditions with minimal handling, these types of records will likely last for more than a century. Long-term digital preservation, on the other hand, requires regular monitoring, frequent intervention, and the assistance of technically trained professionals. The challenge of digital record keeping is two-fold. The physical media that hold data must be preserved and protected from damage and deterioration, and the software and hardware to access and use the records must still be available. (Bollacker, 2012)

Maintaining digital records in a manner that ensures their continued authenticity and accessibility over long periods of time requires attention to factors that are unique to the digital world: (Hoke, 2012)

- **Media Obsolescence:** The options for storage and presentation of digital data continue to evolve and change, e.g., the progression of peripheral storage devices for the personal computer, and the exponential increase in storage capacity.
- **Media Failure:** Electronic media are susceptible to various levels of failure, including degradation as a result of poor storage or preparation.
- **Media Access:** Removable media such as tapes and DVDs require specific hardware to extract information from them which may become unavailable over time as manufacturers improve their products.
- **Software Obsolescence:** The continuing development of application software results in the rapid obsolescence of software to access and process digital information.
- **File Format Obsolescence:** The increasing range of formats in which data is maintained creates another challenge. Features such as "hidden text" and "change history" make digital documents more useful, but also create storage and retrieval challenges.

Preservation also includes practices and techniques that ensure data protection. These include the establishment of timely and complete backup and recovery actions that allow for the restoration of records in the event of a disaster or data corruption, as well as redundant storage of records at a location. Storage systems and software must be continually updated to ensure that the most current security measures and protocols are in place. A variety of storage management practices are available to manage information according to its lifecycle stage, such as the movement of archival records to offline storage.

The reliance on electronic records has heightened the need for dialog about approaches to long-term preservation, which may be one of the most pressing issues for governmental agencies today. The nature of some court proceedings requires preservation of these records for long periods (over ten years), if not permanently. A review of current U.S. state judicial retention schedules reveals a wide variation of policies and approaches to long-term preservation. While many states have developed guidelines and standards for long-term preservation, others have yet to address preservation beyond paper and microform formats. Electronic preservation challenges may also force jurisdictions to re-assess retention periods for many records which do not have long-term legal or historical value.

To meet the preservation challenge, judicial organizations must develop a clear preservation strategy that addresses the special needs of digital records. A preservation strategy should include greater attention to quality control, the adoption of standards, assessment of organizational capabilities, and most of all, a strategic approach that is both enterprise-wide and collaborative. A number of standards and best practices have been developed to ensure preservation of digital records throughout their life cycle. These include: (International Records Management Trust, 2015)

- Use of non-proprietary formats, software and media, and devices to access records;
- Standards that ensure the preservation of original content;
- Maintenance of backup copies;
- Provision of secondary storage/redundant servers with separate power;
- Security and environmental requirements for primary and backup media;
- Minimum metadata requirements;

- Verification of input and document quality;
- Periodic refresh of electronic records for the duration of the retention period;
- A migration strategy to prevent loss of access due to obsolete technologies; and,
- Requiring backward compatibility of new equipment and software.

For courts that are well along the way with electronic filing and document management, the time is at hand to start planning for archival storage. Planning for digital archiving is, of course, particularly important for maintaining records which have long-term retention requirements. Technology is moving so rapidly that existing data storage centers may not be able to meet future demands in terms of capacity, security, and scalability.

Two recent announcements highlight the incredible pace of technological change. Scientists at Harvard's Wyss Institute were able to successfully store nearly 700 terabytes of data in a single gram of DNA. (Anthony, 2012) Another milestone in storage capability was recently announced by the Sony Corporation, which developed a cassette tape that is able to accommodate 185 terabytes of data, equivalent to the capacity of around 3,700 Blu-ray discs. (Fashion Times, 2014) These achievements illustrate how predicting future information capability is a constantly moving target.

Disposition

The *Principle of Disposition* recognizes that all records reach a point in their lifecycle where they are committed to long-term archival storage or scheduled for destruction. Storing terabytes or even petabytes of information is no longer unusual. The decreasing cost and increasing capacity of storage technologies for electronic records has had the unfortunate consequence of making it easy for many organizations, including courts, to retain digital information well beyond its useful life. However, it has also become evident that the retention of ever-increasing amounts of information that has passed its useful lifecycle is costly. In addition to the costs for physical storage, electronic records must be periodically migrated to stay ahead of hardware and software obsolescence. Large volumes of data complicate search and retrieval. The indirect costs of managing data cannot be ignored. Further, the longer electronic records are retained the greater the risk to their integrity and accessibility.

A record retention schedule is the source of authority for records disposition and should address all records under the organization's care and control. A retention schedule should also provide for the systematic destruction of electronic records which no longer serve business or legal needs. Disposition therefore includes both records destruction and long-term preservation. A retention schedule is a formal document with executive-level approval and authority that clearly defines the life cycle of records for an agency. The schedule ensures that the court meets legal and fiscal retention requirements for all records, regardless of media, identifies records needing greater protection or control, improves records organization, and eliminates unnecessary and duplicative records.

There are four values that are generally recognized as guidelines in the records management community for assessing record retention value. In the judicial context, operational value is the period of time during which the court requires the record to perform its primary functions. This reflects only the time that records are required to meet user needs; they are not necessarily legal requirements. Legal value refers to those records whose retention is defined by statute or court rule, or those that may be needed in the event of further litigation or investigation. Legal and operational value in the courts are often concurrent. A smaller number of records have fiscal value. This refers to records that are created for administrative purposes as well as case-related transactions. Fiscal value is often determined by the time that these records must be retained for audit purposes under state or local statutes. Finally, some court records, by virtue of their exceptional age and/or connection with some significant event or precedent have historical value.

Digital systems may allow deletion of records to occur automatically or require human intervention. As the volume of digital records increases, courts will need to develop a deletion process that balances efficiency with the potential consequences of error. This may require that vital or mission-critical information not be deleted without prior review. Non-vital or duplicate information might be insignificant enough that premature or incomplete disposition would not impair the court's ability to carry out its primary functions and therefore can be scheduled for automated disposition. Regardless of the method of final disposition, the organization must establish that all legal and business needs have been satisfied prior to transfer, and appropriately document records disposal.

Governance

The growing recognition of the complexity of information management has focused attention on the *Principle of Governance*. In the context of judicial records management, effective governance contributes to the ongoing availability of court records for public access and use through consistent policies, collaboration with internal and external communities of interest, and the provision of adequate resources and capacity required to effectively sustain record-keeping systems in the face of increasing information growth and technological complexity. In the records management industry governance has been identified as one of the five most important trends that are shaping information management. (McKinnon, 2014)

The management of judicial records is unique among government institutions, as in many judicial systems records management responsibilities are shared among elected and appointed positions. For instance registrars or clerks of court are typically the individuals who have the legal responsibility for the maintenance of case-related records. The selection or appointment of these individuals, however, varies considerably. In some U.S. states, clerks of court are independently elected executive branch officials whose responsibility for court records may be in addition to other non-judicial functions such as recording property transactions, issuing passports, and maintaining marriage records. Other states provide for clerks to be appointed directly by the judiciary.

The responsibility for acquisition and maintenance of technical systems also varies. Larger jurisdictions often employ their own staff for information technology support and maintenance. However, economies of scale in smaller courts may not justify in-house staff, so that these functions are performed by information technology staff under the control and supervision of the executive branch. Even when technology support staff are employed by the judicial branch, some functions, such as state or national case management systems and networks, are managed by central administrative offices supervised by the ministry of justice or a state/provincial administrative office.

Long-term preservation and archiving of judicial records is another area where responsibility is often shared. The responsibility of governmental archives for preserving court records varies from complete responsibility for maintaining records over a certain age, preservation of historical records only, to no preservation role at all. Whatever the existing organizational structure and lines of authority are in these areas, the responsibility for management of digital court records clearly requires collaboration and coordination between elected and appointed officials, court support staff, and technology professionals to ensure that strategic decisions take into account the needs of internal and external users, are in compliance with legal requirements, meet accepted standards, and do not burden the organization with information that is no longer relevant or useful. The need for collaboration has never been greater.

SOLUTIONS AND RECOMMENDATIONS

While the principles provide a comprehensive framework for assessing records management practices and policies, their actual implementation requires the development of accompanying performance measures upon which to assess their effectiveness. Clark (2008) notes the important of performance evaluation on the judiciary's capacity to:

1. Determine whether it is meeting performance expectations;
2. Measure performance in areas important to different stakeholders;
3. Prepare, justify, and present budget requests based on performance data;
4. Focus investment to improve the provision of services to customers; and
5. Demonstrate accountability to the court's customers and community in general.

This last point, in particular, is relevant to the development of a set of performance measures to demonstrate that the judiciary is adequately performing its information stewardship role.

Current Court Performance Measures

Ongoing oversight and performance measurement is another important aspect of governance in any service organization. Records management should be part of the court's performance measurement and improvement system. The National Center for State Courts initiated the development of what came to be known as the Trial Court Performance Standards (TCPS). Over three years, the Commission on Trial Court Performance Standards engaged the court community in the development of 22 standards requiring 68 measures across 5 broadly defined areas: access to justice; expedition and timeliness; equality, fairness and integrity; independence and accountability; and public trust and confidence. (U.S. Bureau of Justice Assistance, 1993) The TCPS were intended as a tool to measure the performance of the court as an organization rather than the performance of individual judges. The standards emphasize assessing how court performance impacts court users and what steps can be taken to improve services to the public. (Schauffler, 2007)

The Trial Court Performance Standards Implementation Manual addresses court records management with measures for file integrity, access, and consistency:

Measure 1: Reliability of File Control

This measure tests whether the file control system is adequate to support timely retrieval of individual case files. The adequacy of the system is tested for each type of case file management and storage system, including pending cases, inactive cases that are stored on site, and records in off-site storage areas. Implementation of this measure requires an understanding of the file control system used by the court.

Visual inspection of the records storage areas and verification of the file control system through a records survey should be carried out prior to implementing this measure. The information gathered can be used to determine whether problems exist for a few, some, or most case or record types in the sample. This information will also reveal whether problems vary by case category or by age of the case. The court will use this information to identify what file systems or areas need corrective action.

Measure 2: Accuracy and Consistency between Case Files and the Electronic Case Management System

This measure tests whether information in paper case files and the electronic case management system (CMS) is consistent and complete. The review can be conducted by comparing entries in the CMS with contents and entries in the sample of case files. For example, the filing of documents in the case file is usually accompanied by an entry in the CMS indicating the type of document, date of filing, and other related information.

Measure 3: Case File Integrity

The purpose of this measure is to determine the integrity of individual case files. This includes determining if all documents are in proper order, the occurrence of missing documents, and the adequacy of file notations. The same cases which were pulled under measure one, reliability of the file control system, can be used as the sample for this measure. The court should have already established policies for the placement of documents in the court file.

Measure 4: Reliability of Document Processing

The purpose of this measure is to determine how well the court processes the flow of documents which are either filed with, or executed by the court, and their placement in the individual case file. The principal questions are whether documents are being processed within expected time frames and whether documents are properly filed in their respective folders.

The National Center for State Courts has developed related performance measures for records management as part of its *CourTools* suite (National Center for State Courts, 2005). *CourTool 6* addresses the reliability and integrity of case files. The measure is defined as "the percentage of case files that meet established standards of completeness and accuracy and can also be retrieved within established time guidelines." However, the shortcoming of these measures is their application to settings in which paper records, supported by electronic databases, are the primary format for record-keeping. As courts evolve into the "paper-on-demand" environment, this measurement system will become less useful, though many of the fundamental objectives, such as timely access, remain constant.

In 2008 the European Commission for Efficiency of Justice (CEPEJ) adopted a wide range of quality of justice performance measures at its plenary meeting that were "aimed at policy makers and judicial practitioners responsible for the administration of justice to improve the legislations, policies and practices aimed at raising the quality of the judicial systems, at the national system, court and individual judge levels." Although a specific category of judicial records management is not identified in the checklist, many of the performance measures are directly related to improving the accessibility, quality, and transparency of court records. What is unique about the CEPEJ approach is the attempt to address these issues at both the policy and application levels. The following are excerpts of records-related performance measures contained within the CEPEJ framework:

- **Management of Files and Archiving:**
    - Does a case management information system exist for the recording and monitoring of court files and cases?
    - Is there a specific policy concerning archiving of court files and court decisions?
    - Does an (electronic) information system for archiving court cases and decisions exist?
    - Does a court system of electronic files exist?
    - Is it possible to submit documents to the court in electronic form?
- **Information Systems:**
    - Is there a policy on the use of information and communication technologies in courts (e-justice, video-conferencing, electronic data exchange, etc.)?
    - Are the court information systems regularly reviewed and improved?
    - Are the developments of human resources-information systems in line and in conformity with the (technical) specifications of the other operational court systems (i.e. case management information systems, financial information systems, etc.)?
    - Does the information recorded in the court management information system give an overall picture of the court's performance?
    - Can the analysis of the data recorded in the court management information system be performed by all the court's staff (or authorised staff) or can only specialised staff (for example IT professionals) exploit these data?
    - Have rules been set out concerning the confidentiality of the treatment of information (for example: prohibition to enter data in the system from one's home)?
    - Is the security of the information contained in the system assured (against the risk of introducing hackers into the system)?
- **Evaluation of Means, Information Systems, Logistics and Security:**
    - Is there a system of control of financial and other risks linked to information systems and support activities?
    - Is the quality and integrity of information, in particular financial information, guaranteed?
    - Is there a history of incidents involving the security of access, people and data?
    - Is the security of information systems guaranteed?
    - Is the risk of loss and material damage covered?

The CEPEJ performance questions touch on many of the key issues, including integrity and data quality controls, policies, and adequacy of electronic systems, They are not, however, presented within a general records framework that would facilitate a comprehensive records system assessment. In comparing the current approaches to performance measurement, what is clear is that the issues of records integrity and access are an important part of the overall court performance picture. However, as noted in the beginning of this chapter, the increasing reliance on electronic record-keeping has created the need for a more robust set of standards and measures that address basic records principles in the context of digital record-keeping.

Industry Standards

There is a substantial body of electronic records standards, as well as best practice and technical guidance, available for reference and use in the general records management community that has yet to be embraced by many governmental organizations. These include the International Organization for Standardization (ISO), European Union, National Archives of Australia, ARMA International, the Association for Information and Image Management (AIIM), and the American National Standards Institute (ANSI), among others. (Jones, 2012) These organizations are a rich resource of information for ready adoption by court leadership and their technical partners for application to electronic judicial records.

Of particular relevance is the progress that has occurred in recent years to address the challenge of preserving digital assets. The Research Libraries Group (2002) has taken the lead by developing the concept of a trusted digital repository as an institution created to ensure long-term access to digital resources. At the most basic level a repository must maintain digital resources over the long term in a consistent manner, meet or exceed standards for access, management and security, and be audited for performance and quality management. The concept has continued to evolve with the development of various models and related standards. (International Records Management Trust, 2015)

The Open Archival Information System (OAIS) reference model has emerged as the principal standard for evaluating digital repositories. In addition to the reference model, other tools have been recently developed as guides for assessing the readiness of an organization to preserve digital materials. An OAIS-compliant repository should employ best practices in all areas, including: (Tilbury, 2013)

- Standards for metadata encoding, management and records description;
- Proper environmental controls for storage;
- Timely and appropriate backups;
- Emergency recovery, business continuity and contingency planning, and risk mitigation activities;
- Adequate security features, including hierarchical password access, audit trails, firewalls, virus protection and encryption.

The OAIS Reference Model has also been adopted by the International Organization for Standardization as ISO 14721. Additional standards have been developed, such as ISO 16363, which specifies auditing criteria for certifying a trustworthy repository. Building on the trustworthy repository concept, authors Lori Ashley and Charles Dollar (2014) developed the Digital Preservation Capability Maturity Model. This model provides a high level analysis of organizational capability for long-term digital preservation. Based on the Capability Maturity Model developed by the Software Engineering Institute of Carnegie Mellon University, the DPCMM defines seven components that are critical to a sustained effort to preserve electronic records. These include policies and strategies, technical components and expertise, collaboration and governance, and recognition of the user community. The model further defines eight components that are required to sustain an electronic record repository with a five level scale of capability or maturity as a metric to assess current program capability, identify gaps, and create a roadmap to achieve a higher level of organizational competency.

The National Digital Stewardship Alliance (NDSA) has also developed a framework to guide organizations in the development of digital preservations systems and activities. NDSA is described as a group of "over 140 organizations whose mission is to establish, maintain, and advance the capacity to preserve our nation's digital resources for the benefit of present and future generations." (Phillips,

2014) The *Levels of Digital Preservation Framework* defines five functional areas required for effective digital preservation. The emphasis in this model is more technical in nature, focusing on file formats and metadata, integrity and security, and storage systems. Similar to the DPCMM, the Levels of Digital Preservation framework includes four tiers or levels of compliance in each of these areas, with the goal of providing a tool to evaluate capacity to mitigate risk of information loss and identify technical steps that can be taken to improve long-term preservation of digital assets.

A Comprehensive Standards-Based Approach

The forgoing review of existing standards and performance measures illustrates the variety of approaches to addressing the need for greater accountability in the area of records and information management in the judiciary. The records management industry has made significant progress in recent years, particularly in efforts initiated by the archivist community to address concerns over long term digital continuity in the face of continuing technological evolution and change. The experience of other governmental agencies, as well as the private and non-profit sector, in addressing these challenges provides a rich source of information to guide judicial policy-makers.

As a next step, performance objectives should be associated with the principles, as shown in Table 1. The self-assessment questions are proposed as an example of a principle-based performance measurement system. The performance questions are organized in categories corresponding to the principles of effective judicial records management as adopted by COSCA, and further based on key elements associated with each objective statement. This table represents a small sample of the potential objectives and measures which can be developed in more detail based on which issues are most pressing or relevant to a particular judicial organization.

These performance objectives are just examples of a comprehensive program of digital records management, representing the beginning of a performance measurement framework adopted specifically for the judiciary but based on accepted best practices. One challenge facing court leaders is how to choose the best set of measures by prioritizing those that are most pressing or relevant given the wide range of activities covered by the principles. Performance measurement is only useful if it captures a meaningful set of consequences, can be consistently applied, and directly addresses the ability of the court to effectively perform its most critical functions. (Clarke, 2011)

Successful implementation of performance management systems relies on increasing awareness in the judicial community about the potential impact of information loss from electronic records that document the judicial decision-making process and uphold the rights of citizens and businesses. National judicial leadership should be at the forefront of efforts to raise awareness of records management strategies, in particular digital preservation, promoting discussion with experts and stakeholders, and building a business case for securing the funding and other resources necessary to sustain digital record systems. Performance measures can provide valuable information to inform policy makers and the public about the need for action in this area.

While all of the principles are important to an effective program of digital records management, the primary focus should always be on the end users of our justice systems and how they access the courts. These include not only attorneys and litigants, but the media, other public and commercial entities, and

Table 1. Sample objectives for measurable outcomes of court records management performance

Key Area	Objective	Method/Measure
Governance		
Strategy	The court has adopted a developed formal migration strategy to mitigate the risk of technical obsolescence and guarantee long-term accessibility of electronic content.	Migration plan in place for all long-term digital assets.
Training	Training programs and communication ensures that staff at all levels are aware of and able to understand applicable information and records management requirements.	Number of staff who receive training and demonstrate retention of information.
Compliance		
Compliance Auditing	Periodic audits are performed to ensure compliance with applicable statutes and court rules governing records organization and maintenance.	Frequency and results of audits.
Classification	Records are organized according to established standards for indexing and classification.	Accuracy of classification based on periodic review.
Access		
Confidentiality	Proper security controls and redaction are in place to prevent unauthorized access to confidential and restricted records by staff and the public.	Number or % of incidents of unauthorized data or information release.
Responsiveness	The court responds promptly to record requests and is able to provide information in a variety of formats for public and litigant use.	Time to retrieve and provide records in response to requests.
Integrity		
Security Control	The court has adopted privacy and information security standards that protect the confidentiality and integrity of information and information systems.	Number or % of security breaches or information loss incidents.
Media Reliability	Records media are routinely checked and steps taken to remediate loss of data due to damage or age.	Periodic sampling of media and review of results.
Preservation		
Redundancy	The court has back-up and disaster planning procedures and strategies to ensure continued availability of records and information even in a large scale disaster scenario.	Backup plan in place and periodically reviewed.
Storage	Storage conditions and facilities for records meet minimum standards and are monitored on an on-going basis.	Storage conditions meet industry standards for climate control.
Disposition		
Timely Disposition	The court identifies and eliminates redundant and duplicative records on a regular basis.	Completion of disposal pursuant to established schedule.
Documentation	The court has established records disposition processes and destruction protocols to support disposal of eligible records, including all media types.	All disposal actions recorded and verified.

the public at large. The opportunities and challenges that electronic records create in the ways people interact with the courts and the heightened impact of access policies move these issues to the top of the list. Whenever possible performance measurement design should include input from and focus on outcomes that have relevance to justice system stakeholders.

FUTURE RESEARCH DIRECTIONS

With the principles as a framework, further research is needed in several areas. First, as a comprehensive set of performance measures linked to the principles are developed, these measures should be "field tested" or validated to ensure their relevancy and suitability for practical adoption by judicial agencies. This should include a process that creates a baseline measurement for current digital capabilities, and subsequent analysis of the impact of steps taken to reach an agreed-upon level of compliance with measurement goals. It should be recognized that different jurisdictions will have unique circumstances and needs that will make some aspects of performance more pressing than others.

Long-term digital preservation may be one of the most urgent issues facing our information society today. Unless steps are taken on the front end to ensure that digital assets that have long-term value are managed properly and adequate funding is in place to sustain preservation, as some experts are predicting we may be entering a "digital dark age." This was highlighted in a 2012 the Council of State Archivists (U.S.) study which revealed that more than 60% of the U.S. states did not have an electronic records program, and that few had in place a strategy or funding to support digital preservation. What is particularly sobering about the results of the study is that if a government agency dedicated to the preservation of historical and governmental records is not prepared, then surely most other judicial and executive branch agencies are even less prepared for this challenge.

Fortunately, the Digital Preservation Capability Maturity Model provides a good assessment tool which could be easily adapted to the judicial environment. The judiciary should undertake a similar self-assessment based on existing tools and experiences learned from the archival community to determine current capabilities. A successful approach for demonstrating new concepts is for jurisdictions to select "model courts" in conjunction with field testing of the performance measures. The selection of model courts should provide for testing in a variety of settings, including first and second instance courts, for example. Based on application of the DPCMM or similar assessment tool in pilot courts, refinements should be made to the model, as needed, to improve their relevance to the judicial setting.

CONCLUSION

Although each of the principles is distinct, they are very much inter-dependent. Access is compromised if the users of court information cannot be assured that court records are maintained in compliance with applicable laws and rules, and that their integrity and content is secure over time. Preservation is a critical part of access, as without preservation, there is no access. Further, the actions taken to preserve records must include steps that ensure that their integrity is not compromised in the process. Under the principle of disposition, decisions regarding record value and their lifecycle as defined by a retention schedule provide assurance that records will remain available for as long as required to fulfill operational, legal, and if needed, historical requirements.

Overlaying all of this is the principle of governance, and the many activities that must be performed to implement the principles effectively. It is perhaps ironic that embracing technology as a path to greater efficiency and access to court processes may in fact have the opposite impact if technology is not managed and governed effectively. Among the major governance tasks for the judiciary that lie ahead are addressing long-term digital retention needs and capability, promoting greater collaboration among judicial system stakeholders, encouraging more dialog between the courts and records management communities, and providing the tools to help court leaders improve records management practices and performance.

The records management principles not only set the standard for maintaining reliable and accurate judicial records, but also help policy-makers identify actionable steps that need to be taken to ensure continuing public trust and confidence in the judicial process. For the standards to become meaningful they must be linked with a related set of performance measures that can be readily adopted by practitioners. A great deal of work has already been done in the area of court performance standards generally. But moving forward, these standards need to be refined to address the pressing challenges of the digital age in our judicial systems starting with an assessment of current capacity and capability in this area. Doing so will ensure that courts are able to perform their mission in a fully open and transparent manner as they move forward into the 21st Century.

REFERENCES

Anderson, P. H. (2011). *Court Information, Privacy, and Technology. Future Trends in State Courts*. Williamsburg, VA: National Center for State Courts.

Bollacker, K. (2012). Avoiding a Digital Dark Age. *American Scientist, 98*.

Clarke, T. (2008). *A Unifying Framework for Court Performance Measurement: Final Report*. Williamsburg, VA: National Center for State Courts.

Clarke, T. (2011). *High Performance Courts: Organizational Effectiveness and Enhanced Attorney Advocacy. Unpublished proposal to the Bureau of Justice Assistance*. National Center for State Courts.

Commission on Trial Court Performance Standards. (1997). Trial Court Performance Standards with Commentary. U.S. Department of Justice, Bureau of Justice Assistance.

Council of State Archivists. (2012). *State Electronic Records Initiative, Phase I*. Retrieved July 2, 2015 from http://www.statearchivists.org/seri/SERI%20Phase%20One%20Report%20-%20final%20review%20draft%20-%202012-06.pdf

Danish National Archives. (2013). *Strategies for Archiving Digital Records at the Danish National Archives*. Retrieved May 10, 2015 from https://www.sa.dk/en/wp-content/uploads/sites/2/2014/12/Strategy-for-archiving-digital-records-2013.pdf

Dollar, C. M., & Ashley, L. J. (2013). *Assessing Digital Preservation Capability Using a Maturity Model Process Improvement Approach*. Retrieved May 10, 2015 from http://www.nycarchivists.org/Resources/Documents/Dollar-Ashley_2013_DPCMM%20White%20Paper_NAGARA%20Digital%20Judicial%20Records_8Feb2013-1.pdf

European Commission for Efficiency of Justice. (2008). *Checklist for promoting the quality of justice and the courts*. Council of Europe. Strasbourg.

Fashion Times. (2015). *Sony Announces 185TB Tape Storage*. Retrieved June 29, 2015 from http://www.fashiontimes.com/articles/6415/20140506/sony-announces-185tb-cassette-tape-storage.htm

Hoke, G. (2012, May/June). *Future Watch: Strategies for Long-Term Preservation of Electronic Records. Information Management.*

International Organization for Standardization. (2001). *Information and documentation – Records management - Part 1: General.* Reference number ISO 15489-1:2001(E).

International Records Management Trust. (2005). *E-records Capacity Tool.* Retrieved June 2, 2015, from http://www.irmt.org/education-and-training/education-and-training-2

International Records Management Trust. (2015). *Module 4: Preserving Electronic Records. Training in Electronic Records.* Retrieved May 1, 2015, from http://www.irmt.org/education-and-training/education-and-training-2

International Records Management Trust. (2015). *Module 3: Managing the Creation, Use and Disposal of Electronic Records.* Retrieved June 2, 2015, from http://www.irmt.org/education-and-training/education-and-training-2

Iron Mountain, Inc. (2015). *Data Center for Next-Generation IT: Build v. Buy.* Retrieved June 22, 2015 from http://www.ironmountain.com/Knowledge-Center/Reference-Library/View-by-Document-Type/White-Papers-Briefs/D/Data-Centers-for-Next-Generation-IT-Build-Vs-Buy.aspx#sthash.MYHmjSQn.dpuf

Jones, V. (2012, July-August). *Standards for Establishing records and Information Management Programs. Information Management.*

Linhares, G., & Raaen, N. (2013). *To Preserve and Protect: Standards for Maintaining 21st Century Court Records.* COSCA 2013 Working Paper. Retrieved May 1, 2015, from http://cosca.ncsc.org/Policy-Papers.aspx

Manago, W. (2011, May-June). *Protect, Maintain Information Integrity to Reduce Business Risk. Information Management.*

McKinnon, C. (2014, January-February). *5 Trends reshaping Records and Information Management. Information Management.*

National Archives and Records Administration. (2015). *Disposition of Federal Records: A Records Management Handbook.* Retrieved June 2, 2015 at: http://www.archives.gov/records-mgmt/publications/disposition-of-federal-records/chapter-4.html

National Archives of Australia. (2011). *Digital Continuity Plan.* Retrieved May 2, 2015 from http://www.naa.gov.au/records-management/agency/digital/what-is-digital-continuity/plan/index.aspx

National Center for State Courts. (2005). Williamsburg, VA: CourTools.

News 13. (2013). *Judge Belvin Perry testifies about preventing escapes through forgery.* Retrieved June 22, 2015, from http://www.mynews13.com/content/news/cfnews13/news/article.html/content/news/articles/cfn/2013/11/6/judge_belvin_perry_o.html?cid=rss

Phillips, M., Bailey, J., Goethals, A., & Owens, T. (2014). *The NDSA Levels of Digital Preservation: An Explanation and Uses.* Working paper. Library of Congress, NSDA Infrastructure Working Group.

Raaen, N. (2014, January-February). Order in the Courts: RM Principles for the Judiciary. *Information & Management*.

Research Libraries Group (2002). OCLC Working Group on Digital Archive Attributes. *Trusted Digital Repositories: Attributes and Responsibilities*. Rep. Research Libraries Group.

Schauffler, R. (2007). Judicial Accountability in the US State Courts: Measuring Accountability. *Utrecht Law Review, 3*(1).

Sebastian, A. (2012). *Harvard Cracks DNA Storage-Crams 700 Terabytes of Data into a Single Gram.* Retrieved June 2, 2015, from http://www.extremetech.com/extreme/134672-harvard-cracks-dna-storage-crams-700-terabytes-of-data-into-a-single-gram

Tilbury, J. (2014). *The Active Preservation of Digital Information*. Retrieved May 2, 2015 from http://preservica.com/resources/white-papers/

U.S. Bureau of Justice Assistance. (1993). *Trial court Performance Standards and Measurement System Implementation Manual*. Washington, DC: U.S. Department of Justice.

Wiler, V. (2014, September-October). *Europe and Canada Embrace Right to Be Forgotten. Information Management*.

World Bank. (2003). *IRMT/World Bank Evidence-based Governance in the Electronic Age. Summary of Discussion Three: Legal and Judicial Reform and Record Keeping*. Author.

KEY TERMS AND DEFINITIONS

Active Record: A record that is regularly referred to and required for current use.

Archiving: For data processing usage, archiving generally means creating and managing inactive files for long-term storage.

Backing Up: Making a copy of a computer file for use in case the original is lost, damaged, or destroyed.

E-Filing: Filing of court documents in digital format.

Inactive Records: Records that have an infrequent reference rate and/or reached a stage in the case lifecycle where they are considered inactive.

Life Cycle of Records: The stages that records pass through from creation to disposition.

Long-Term Digital Preservation: A series of actions and policies required to maintain a digital record in the face of ongoing change to formats, media, software and hardware.

Metadata: Structured information about a record that describes, explains, locates, or otherwise makes it easier to retrieve, use, or manage that record.

Permanent Record: A record considered to have enduring value that it is to be permanently preserved.

Records Disposition: The final processing of records for destruction, permanent retention, or archival preservation.

Records Management: The systematic control of court records from creation, active maintenance and use, inactive storage, to final disposition.

Records Retention Schedule: A document that identifies the length of time a records series must be retained in active and inactive storage before its final disposition to permanent storage, archival preservation, or destruction.

ENDNOTES

1 Founded in 1955, the Conference of State Court Administrators is a professional association of the administrators of U.S. state courts and the courts of the District of Columbia, Puerto Rico, and Guam.

2 The National Center for State Courts is an independent, nonprofit court improvement organization founded in 1971 at the urging of the then Chief Justice of the Supreme Court, Warren E. Burger, which serves as a clearinghouse for research information and comparative data to support improvement in judicial administration in state courts.

Chapter 3

Open Judiciary in High Courts: Securing a Networked Constitution, Challenges of E-Justice, Transparency, and Citizen Participation

Jesus Cano
Constitutional Court, Spain & UNED University, Spain & IEEE eGovernment, USA

Carlos E. Jiménez-Gómez
Department of Justice of the Autonomous Government of Catalonia, Spain

Luis Pomed
Constitutional Court, Spain

Roberto Hernández
UNED University, Spain

ABSTRACT

With this work, it is hoped to offer an insight into open judiciary applied to the specific context of constitutional courts in the Civil Law system from both a legal and technological point of view. The advances in IT are now becoming the drivers of social change and new ways for citizens and public administrations to interrelate. Information technology has enabled a different way for citizens to access public services under an e-Government umbrella to a greater or lesser degree of success. In the area of e-Justice it would appear that advances are perceived in different ways, particularly in the higher courts. This chapter will set out how constitutional justice is integrated into the world of electronic justice as an example of a genuine challenge that is full of paradoxes.

INTRODUCTION

This chapter presents the electronic justice domain under the prism of the reasons behind scientific research into smart technologies that are open and close to citizens, and which, moreover, are security sensitive regarding information. From a technology perspective this involves new architectural approaches that equally effect the front-end and the back-end of public organisations, lower courts of justice and supreme courts.

DOI: 10.4018/978-1-5225-0717-8.ch003

The advances in IT are currently presented as the drivers of social change and new citizen-public administration relations. Information technologies have opened up new ways for citizens to access public services under an electronic Government umbrella within the different activity sectors. In the e-Justice area it would seem that the advances are perceived in a different way and particularly by the justice in higher courts, a proof of which is the different regulations adopted by the legislative powers of some countries.

In this chapter we will explain how constitutional justice is integrated into the world of electronic justice in the context of European law as a representation of a real challenge full of paradoxes, paradoxes that are a challenge to the design of effective and efficient technology architectures that are properly distributed and aligned with the special nature of the jurisdictional domain.

BACKGROUND

With regard to electronic justice, this shares the concepts that are applied to electronic government, although in a specific judicial context. In the case of open justice (or open judiciary as an extension of philosophy and principles of Open Government (especially transparency, participation and collaboration) applied to the justice field, innovation and currently ICTs are key items for these initiatives (Jiménez-Gómez, 2014, p. 18). The emerging applications are currently going along the lines of using transparent strategies such as citizen participation and collaboration and include the responsibility to be accountable. Finally all it rests on the classic principles of public administration such as effectiveness and efficiency.

Open Judiciary may be understood as a paradigm of legal principles that attempt to characterise the workings of justice into parameters of transparency and openness. These concepts are in line with citizens' movements in the defence of democratic regeneration since they let the application of law to specific cases and persons be seen. It also makes it easier to evaluate how the rules that those in power decide to pass are applied. To a certain extent it is a question of gaining citizens' trust in judicial institutions as well, issues that are dealt with in the chapter.

This section strives to analyse the contradictory assertions of the critical domain studied in this chapter with the intention of setting out the difficulties that this research topic means for the advance of electronic government in this sector. This is particularly so with regard to the working reality that can apparently clash with the technological approach to problem-solving and which to a certain extent requires change management to be dealt with in a special way.

CHALLENGES OF OPEN JUDICIARY

Presented herein is a perspective on the controversies or problems in relation to the constitutional position around the openness of thought of information technologies. To support the arguments we set out four challenges introducing some key aspects.

The Challenge of Legitimacy

At odds with the legitimacy of judicial review, constitutional justice has had to confront criticism of its premises: the absence of any democratic legitimacy of the members of a court to control the decisions of the representatives of national sovereignty. In Common Law, this criticism was particularly consistent in American legal literature and in those who are advocates of "popular constitutionalism" (Kramer, 2004). This criticism has been strengthened since the constitutional courts have dealt with criteria that go beyond what is strictly legal and give opinions as to the timeliness or effectiveness of legislation -courts to which the judgment of proportionality adopted by national and supranational European constitutional courts is not entirely alien (Barak, 2010). The availability of a greater amount of information is one of the beneficial effects of the constitutional courts opening up to computer technology, but it bears the risk that those very same courts will slide down the slope of "political" judgement or pass judgement on the timeliness of controversial legal regulations. Therefore, this openness may entail a risk for the very existence of constitutional justice.

The Challenge of the "Almost" Insurmountable Object

The aims pursued by the so-called "open government", that is, citizens' participation and their being given the possibility to exercise their power functions, in the case of justice, come up against an almost insurmountable obstacle. Only those who possess a right or an interest challenged in the case are entitled to take part in the judicial process. Providing access to third parties might even bring into question the very essence of the trial as an illustrated controversy between parties that are risking something in the dispute. It is not clear that direct citizen participation in legal decisions is a goal to which we must aspire. This is because the courts of justice do not assume the value of "democracy" but rather what is related to the rule of law, which is the counterpoint of the former. To put it another way: in justice in general, and in constitutional justice in particular, we must not forget that the rule of law protects minorities, a protection that could be blown into smithereens if strictly democratic criteria are introduced that call into question the survival of those very minorities. This is highly marked when basic rights are dealt with as these are simply contexts in which there is no place for discussion as they are "counter-majoritarian elements" (Jiménez Campo, 1999).

The Challenge of the Recognition of E-Openness in Justice

The above does not imply abandoning openness in Justice for improving those mechanisms that provide citizens' access to constitutional justice. But the recognition of this need must originate from the realisation that it is not so much a question of taking part in exercising judicial activity but rather ensuring there are informal mechanisms to control judges' actions. Regarding the former, openness in Justice will allow citizens to contribute their views to legal arguments that are of public interest, and there is no greater public interest than a debate on the law: citizens will thus be able contribute – albeit just as an "amicus curiae"— the opinion that the work of their representatives deserves. Regarding the latter, it is not a question of whether or not citizens endorse the decisions adopted by legal bodies but that they are aware of these decisions and are able to judge them in the light of the attendant circumstances. Rather surprisingly, the so-called "right to oblivion" or "right to be forgotten", can entail a risk for this purpose since, on occasions, it will hide data that are capital for carrying out informal control (as opposed to procedural control) of legal decisions.

We must not forget that in its ruling of 13 May 2014 the EU Court did not recognize an overwhelming individual right to oblivion (EU Court Judgment, 2014). On the contrary, in this decision the Court said that individuals have the right —under certain conditions— to ask search engines, such as Google, to remove links with personal information about them. Whether those conditions are the same that must be taken into account by the Courts when they decide to anonymize a resolution is entirely open to question.

The Challenge of Networked Justice

In Europe we live under a multilevel constitutional justice system, with different legal bodies (national constitutional courts, European Court of Human Rights and the Court of Justice of the Union), which exercise constitutional functions (Martínez-Vares García & De la Quadra-Salcedo Janini, 2014). They also apply different regulatory instruments they claim are exclusive and proclaim their supremacy (National constitutions, European Convention on Human Rights and the European Union's Charter of Fundamental Rights). Electronic justice can transform that multilevel guardianship into a networked guardianship insomuch as it will let the different bodies of constitutional justice know how their peers have resolved certain issues. Thus an authentic channel is opened up for a "dialogue between courts". A dialogue that cannot be channelled exclusively – nor even preferentially – through procedural channels, since the debate does not set out from the imposition of a single solution, as occurs by definition when citizens make use of the appeals system which procedural legislation offers them.

The Participatory Issue Enabled by the ICT of Justice

At one extreme of the considerations that can affect Open Judiciary, we can focus on the view of the players that intervene in this system. It is here that the first conflict of authority arises, which is intrinsic to the very nature of the judicial institution itself, and presents itself as the first paradox for reflection, which could be expressed as: "A group of people who have not been democratically elected take decisions regarding the decisions of democratically elected persons."

Known as a jury, this group of persons pass judgement on an accused person, a regulation or a case and then pass a ruling. The opening-up of electronic justice and its technological development represents a huge effort in the life-cycle of software development and change management in information systems. We come up against internal barriers resulting from human resistance, the tradition of operational procedures and procedural law that are difficult to transform.

Literature highlights elements that need special attention as standardisation and simplification to achieve a radical improvement in processes, eliminating "obsolete" and bad habits, a flexible structure and simplified in terms of regulatory requirements practices and identifying further accurate impacts of technological change, etc. (Jimenez-Gomez, 2013). By following we can understand that thinking only in infrastructure, computers and architectural modifications to meet modern legal office is not wise or efficient. It is important to note here that a lot of problems today are rooted in the need for business reengineering. So there could be a scenario for a comprehensive procedural change aimed at achieving rapid, efficient and guarantor electronic judicial process, especially based on the advantages of ICT tools, but as well knowledge engineering tools. Getting e-justice is reachable preventing ICTs are applied to old processes and old assumed requirements, i. e, it is relevant to think in new processes and how technological characteristics can help optimize those new processes.

Relating to Judges and Their Election

As a result, if we look at constitutional courts, there have been conflicting debates regarding the lack of democratic legitimacy of the members of a court to control the decisions of the representatives of national sovereignty - the counter-majoritarian difficulty described by (Bickle, 1962). This criticism has been particularly recurrent in American legal literature and among those who subscribe to popular constitutionalism. According to some authors, such as Pozen (2010), one of the main features of the American legal system is the election of judges to resolve constitutional issues. The differences between the work connected with the judicial review of laws and the Supreme Court's interpretation of the Constitution are highlighted in this legal thinking in a way that attempts to transmit the idea that the government belongs to the people and not the judges.

As Aragón Reyes states (Aragón Reyes, 2013) with respect to the current function of constitutional courts, "the work of judges (and particularly the constitutional court judges as the supreme interpreters of the Constitution) possess a're-creative' role that cannot be denied, but under the constraint that on making their interpretation, they can in no way make free use of the Constitution".

Although backed up by arguments that go beyond what is strictly legal, it can be seen that assessments are made on the appropriateness or effectiveness of the rules under judgement. However, this phenomenon occasionally arises in other national and supranational European courts. In spite of the fact that the publishing of a wealth of information is one of the beneficial effects of technological openness of constitutional courts, it involves the risk that those very courts will take some political aspects over controversial legal regulations. In this sense, Open Judiciary could entail a risk for the very existence of justice.

Public Participation on a Jury (Popular Jury)

Enabling citizens to participate at the heart of the legal system as one of the emerging objectives of electronic open government comes up against obstacles that are difficult to overcome. By taking matters to this extreme, it can be understood that only those who have a legitimate interest or are the holders of a right or interest, may and must take part in the process. The discussion as to whether third parties can intervene could even bring into question the very essence of the legal process in a dispute where the main parties are confronted.

It is interesting to raise the question whether direct citizen participation in legal decisions is a goal to be striven for in the conceptualisation of Open Judiciary. However, in part, the advent of the now established specific institution of the popular jury is an invitation to innovate by using communication and information technologies in the same way as indicated by the guidelines regarding the most recent contributions on electronic democracy set out with respect to smart cities (Cano, Hernandez, & Ros, 2014). In this way we could try to think of a model of "Smart Courts" borrowing the sense that inspires the concept of electronic democracy and smart cities to develop and manage resources optimally efficient, sustainable and intelligent.

Professional panels made up of legal experts pass judgement on most legal disputes compared to the option of a popular jury that is established in some countries. The Anglo-Saxon jury consists of a group of people who are not experts in law, who normally resolve the issue unanimously under the guidance of a professional judge who then decides the ruling according to the jury's decision. This is the procedure in the United States, Canada, England, Australia and Spain. However, in Scandinavia the system is to have a collegiate group of non-experts in the matter and professionals, which is the case in France, Italy, Switzerland and Portugal.

It is normal that constitutions should admit some form of citizen participation, as does the 1978 Spanish Constitution with the court jury, regulated under Article 125 in the wording "Citizens shall be able to exercise people's action and take part in the Administration of Justice through the institution of the Jury, in the manner and in line with those legal proceedings established by the Law, as well as in Customary and traditional Courts".

Although participation is recognised as a mechanism by present-day democracies, it can be considered that the courts of justice do not so much carry out the value called "democracy" but the rule of law, which is, up to a certain point, opposed to the former. To put it another way, in justice, in general, and in constitutional justice, in particular, it must be emphasised that the concept of the rule of law protects minorities. Paradoxically, this protection could fall apart if strictly democratic values are introduced that call into question the very survival of those minorities. This is very much the case when legal matters deal with basic rights, where such rights are simply contexts that admit no wide debate since they are axiomatic elements in themselves, which endows them with a counter-majoritarian significance. Obviously, openness in judicial field has to be contextualized with its special and distinctive characteristics.

Towards a Digital Amicus Curiae

Amicus Curiae is an instrument of Roman Law which makes it possible to appear in proceedings without being part of the case, with the intention of helping Justice. Etymologically, it refers to a kind of friend or collaborator of the judges. However, it is currently only applied on rare occasions and for particularly complex cases where the general interest is especially relevant. In the United States its use has been more prolific, but in other countries the figure of the Amicus is relatively limited. In Spain, it should be mentioned that the legislator incorporated this participatory figure in 2007 into the legislation referring to civil prosecution in disputes related to competition. However, this participation is restricted to public organisations, like the European Commission, the Securities and Exchange Commission (Comisión Nacional del Mercado de Valores) and the competent bodies of the regional Governments (Autonomous Communities).

The evolution of information technologies, the recognition of civil rights, particularly with respect to Electronic Administration, is not channelled towards mature proceedings that electronically could be a flexible way to implement the figure of Amicus Curiae as a mechanism that can make progress in the opening up of Justice.

Notwithstanding the above, general legislative or political decisions apart, we do not support indifferent attitudes on the part of the legal administration to improve the mechanisms for citizens to access justice and particularly constitutional justice. However, this requirement must be demanded from an awareness that it is not so much a participation in the exercise of legal actions but to guarantee some informal control mechanism over judges' decisions. This sensitivity is along the lines of Justice that is transparent and concerned about citizens by using modern technologies that enable these goals to be achieved efficiently.

Firstly, openness through technology will allow citizens to contribute their rationale to legal debates of public interest. Nothing is of greater public interest than the debate on the law: citizens will thus be able to make their contribution – albeit as "amicus curiae" – by expressing the opinion that the work of their representatives deserves.

Secondly, it is not a question of citizens endorsing or not the decisions adopted by legal bodies, but that these decisions be known and assessed in the light of current circumstances. Even here, a unique role could be played by the so-called "right to oblivion", since, on occasions, important data could be concealed so as to be able to carry out an informal check of legal decisions as opposed to a procedural check. As part of our wish for a practical conceptualisation of the opening-up of justice, protection for the weakest must be included, such as for the victims of certain crimes, minors, disabled people and those at risk of social exclusion.

Finally, although the direct participation of citizens in the decision-making process contains a dilemma of wrongdoing, opening up digital amicus curiae tools based on citizen-focused technological solutions will open up interesting and innovative paths.

NETWORKED JUSTICE

This section examines another essential aspect of Justice faced with the challenges of communication networks and the Internet. The extra-procedural connection between legal bodies and the exchange of information, may have an encouraging non-formal collaboration.

For example, let us focus on the idea of networked constitutional justice in Europe. It is presented as a multi-level constitutional justice system where different legal bodies come into play. That is, a composite of national constitutional courts, the European Court of Human Rights and the Court of Justice of the European Union; all of them exercising constitutional functions. It must also be pointed out that they apply different regulatory tools, each claiming to be exclusive and supreme, respectively, within the context of a set of national constitutions, the European Convention on Human Rights and the Charter of Fundamental Rights of the European Union.

Electronic justice openness can transform this multilevel custody into a networked custody, insofar as it permits the different bodies of constitutional justice to know how their peers have resolved matters. Thus, an authentic path for "inter-court dialogue" is opened up, a dialogue that cannot exclusively- nor preferentially- be directed by procedural channels, since the dialogue does not originate from the imposition of a single solution. A dialogue among legal operators that are part of the BackOffice that will result in enhanced management and so a better service for citizens that make use of the procedural means to appeal that the legislation places at their disposal.

TRANSPARENCY AND ICT

Infrastructures and software architectures need to be taken into account in constitutional organisation as a set of information tools and systems implemented under technical and organisational criteria. As already emphasized (Jiménez-Gómez, 2013), openness strategy in public organizations impacts in a major way directly into the back-office. An "Open Data" approach requires specific settings and characteristics in the back office and in the information systems architectures.

It is interesting to have an overview of the electronic legal initiatives in a constitutional context at an international level. We shall therefore make a technical breakdown of the information system for citizens to access jurisprudence in the case of the Spanish Constitutional Court. The key idea of the development is to take the citizen as the main player, making available not only the legal decisions but also the expert knowledge generated: synthesis, summaries, extracts, lists of laws under trial and the semantic analysis of labelled legal descriptors based on a constitutional ontology and other aspects, such as those that enable citizens to participate in the quality of the texts themselves and other information at their disposal, and so establish significant feedback in the system. This citizen-centred idea can also be seen in the technology decisions taken to design and implement: natural-responsive design presentation layers, simple HCI (Human-Computer Interaction) interfaces, a tailored option for more advanced searches, REST (Representational State Transfer) service API (Application Programming Interface), OWL (Ontology Language), JSON (JavaScript Object Notation), XML (Extensible Mark-up Language), Office Open XML formats and PDF (Portable Document Format), among others. This can be understood as a model that can inspire other supreme constitutional courts.

INFORMATION SYSTEMS AND DISTRIBUTED ARCHITECTURES OF E-JUSTICE

The transformation of society brought about by information technologies in recent years is becoming ever more evident, especially in the activism of social movements through online applications. At a legal level the use of ICT tools has not brought any radical change to the workings of procedural or decision-making processes. But this situation has now reached its limits to the extent that training in information technology is necessary for legal operators, especially judges. This need is particularly dramatic when the main issue of the legal action is about some aspect of technology, issues that are becoming more and more frequent as society becomes more reliant on technology.

The transformation in the use of ICT support tools towards an inevitable technological dependency of the Courts of Justice is as inevitable as for humanity as a whole. The acceptance of information systems for legal management and for bringing legal matters closer to citizens adds a new paradigm to the implementation of Open Judiciary.

In this unison of computer and information systems new tools are appearing in the field supported by the novelties arising out of the advance of information technology. In contrast to the Global Knowledge Society we are living in, the judiciary are often still seen as a conservative, traditional, regulated, pre-established sector where the legal players have rigid roles of interaction.

Electronic justice is an essential part of electronic Government if a modern image of legal administration is to be presented and provide the key to open up quality public services for citizens.

In the following sections it is shown the effects of the concept of Open Judiciary on an actual developed project deployed and implemented in a constitutional level Court. The basic principle is to take a citizen-centred engineering process that is close to citizens as a starting point as it has been recalling the recent literature such as (Cano, Jimenez, Hernandez, & Ros, 2015). Actual implementation experiences have served to promote research into the field of e-Justice for a wide range of audiences, expert, amateur and multidisciplinary. However, there is still a way to go and contributions to implement an innovative view of Open Justice based on these concepts of the critical domain of information systems in a legal context.

The following lines introduce the important factors of this concept, put the research into context and show how openness in justice can position itself as a technological tour to place the applications of legal databases.

Technological Evolution

This section aims to provide an idea of how the legal research under study has evolved by setting out a practical case study. The citizen-centred approach and the use of ontologies and open data guidelines from the back-office to the front-office are presented as the hubs of open judiciary systems.

For years, or rather centuries, the use of compendia on these topics has been accumulated in books and on paper that have taken over the offices of professionals. The advent of multimedia supports in the last 30-40 years has added to the vast amount of legal documents. This means inconvenient physical handling and greater complexity regarding the logical format.

As computer networks expanded legal databases appeared in legal firms and public organisations in the 90s. Evidence of the circumstances in those years is given by researchers like Páez Mañá who made a compilation of legal database systems and the incorporation of legal thesauri into the efficiency of information retrieval (Páez Mañá, 1994).

With the generalised Internet explosion of the 2000 decade, online access superseded packaged multimedia and paper and saw the spread of Web databases.

The following decade saw legal systems under the significant phenomenon of always-on ubiquitous computing. The progress in mobile technology triggered a revolution that culminated in BYOD (*Bring Your Own Devices*) devices, the spread of Cloud computing and the advent of hyper sensored cities (*Smart Cities*) as a result of the Internet of Things (*IoT*). It also brought with it the processing of enormous amounts of data requiring innovative Big Data processes.

On the other hand, government authorities are not immune to this progress. Technological capabilities brought about change in society, a large part of which was awareness and social psychology regarding the organisation of group spaces in a different way. This derived in a new impulse for electronic government and novel applications that included a general demand for transparency, a policy to make information available and for citizens to be able to understand public governance. All these phenomena have come together at present under the concept of electronic Administration to gradually shape what is now known as Smart Government.

One of the main points of research in this field has been to achieve a technological architecture that will serve as a lever to move forward in the research and study of applied legal sciences. This will facilitate an in-depth study of great volumes of legal data and find strategies for the integration and analysis of information and viewing techniques. The need to compare legal frameworks in some way, gather this information, the semantic impact of legal descriptors and their overall evaluation, is extremely complex and tedious if it is not approached from an architectural point of view. If we consider a complete overview of the legal space as a whole, it is difficult to follow since it is a dynamic domain where the changes in regulations have an impact making it almost humanly impossible to conceive in detail.

Research into the area of fundamental rights based on constitutional rules and the statutes of specific regions or states requires this kind of tool, a tool that will transform the view of ordinary citizens directly as it deals with their freedoms and rights. But if we are to reach this point, the justice systems first need to be technically designed to activate this qualitative leap.

We wish to highlight electronic justice as treating citizens as experts of everyday life. Therefore, there is now an opportunity to open the window to legal research through free access to the legal systems that were traditionally aimed at professionals and business. Using information technology for this purpose also makes it easier to offer knowledge engineering tools to be able to analyse for ourselves the result of a functional add-on that we must also fit into Open Judiciary. In this way, ICTs become the bridge by which citizens can gain access to the legal sciences.

ARCHITECTURES DESIGNED FOR OPEN JUDICIARY

Apart from examining these paradoxes set out above, here we will study the software infrastructures and architectures in constitutional organisation as a set of tools and information systems implemented under technical and organisational criteria. We will itemize a taxonomy of these kinds of systems which have one part in common with other public administrations and another part similar to standard legal administration, while a third part is exclusive to the constitutional computing used by the supreme courts. Apart from the procedural peculiarities of legal proceedings of ICT in this context, it is important to highlight the doctrine management systems that have the dual role of internal service and public access by citizens. The emerging technologies, such as social networks, the use of the cloud as a permanent store, pervasive or ubiquitous computing where the citizen is always on, the growth of hand-held BYOD devices and even the irruption of the Internet of Things (IoT), are driving e-Justice. The technology and social updating these advances represent must be properly managed if they are not to end up in conflict: the typical sensation of an evasive approach or a keep-things-as-they-are approach in a refusal to modernise.

On the other side, justice ICTs are presented as buttons of transparency for e-Citizenship. This emanates from the idea of a need for immediacy and accessibility to the data sets kept by the administration of justice regarding its own management and direct scrutiny. But to what extent is this transparency? A set of principles or guarantees come into conflict in procedural, legal or penal regulations that e-justice cannot get round.

It must be borne in mind that Justice still has an aura of formality that provides few facilities for including citizens' points of view. It is usually a field for making experts in legal matters, lawyers, attorneys and academics of Law Sciences feel at home. Most legal databases tend to be commercial ones that are available under some kind of licence or subscription where legal information is highly organised and which offer other kinds of services like legal aid or consultancy. The focus is on the client, particularly professionals and law firms, around whom the electronic services provided revolve.

Now that the Internet has come of age and the Information and Knowledge Society has been established, the public Law-related bodies are beginning to publish their trials and sentences, especially through web channels that sometimes have document text search functions. Many legal bodies and courts have some way of allowing access to the sentences and legal declarations so that lawyers and interested parties can read them. However, it is difficult to find structured information and more so understandable information written by the experts of the body that originally dictated the sentences.

Structural Parameters for Open Judiciary

To set a working framework to analyse and evaluate the distinctive aspects of information systems with respect to openness in Justice, a tool has been designed that reflects an up-to-date evaluation since the literature does not contain any universal technical position that can be adopted regarding the recent technological and social revolution. Its component parts can be linked to other aspects of similar meaning in other sectors of electronic Government inspired by Open Government philosophy. However, this is valid whenever one of the main players is considered to be at the hub of all the sectors: the citizen, and the legal systems are then built around them.

A 9-factor model has been identified that reflects the Open Judiciary information systems. The first seven items refer to vertical software features open judiciary and the two last are more horizontal nature, in the sense of implementing interoperability and innovation optimally between organizations.

1. Access,
2. Centrality,
3. Openness,
4. Transparency,
5. Semantics,

6. Management,
7. Unification (in the direction of normalizing the data and avoid islands of information),
8. Interoperability (semantic, technical and organizational dimensions, as well as governance elements),
9. Innovation.

We could discuss about adding more. However, this list has a strong pragmatic bias, based on the reality of technology solutions. However, some approaches such as open source can collaborate on the concept of Open Government and could have a key role.

Furthermore, it merges with the interoperability, which in our opinion becomes the cornerstone of eGovernment, although it may have a close relationship with the semantic dimension. Figure 1 shows a representation about that.

This list aims to provide an understanding of Open Judiciary in a technical and ICT tools context that will allow a parametric description of any open system. The empirical experience shown corroborates this model by developing and implementing an information system for constitutional jurisprudence. With its citizen-focused design, an architecture has been established that addresses legal doctrine management and citizen access under the criteria of electronic government that meets critical cybersecurity needs. The architectural structure is carefully built so as to attain a high level of openness and transparency of information. Care has been taken to design and build a legal ontology that models the domain of fundamental rights and constitutional freedoms that will offer a high consistency of the information sources and expert knowledge included in the system.

Figure 1. Factor model of pragmatic openness development

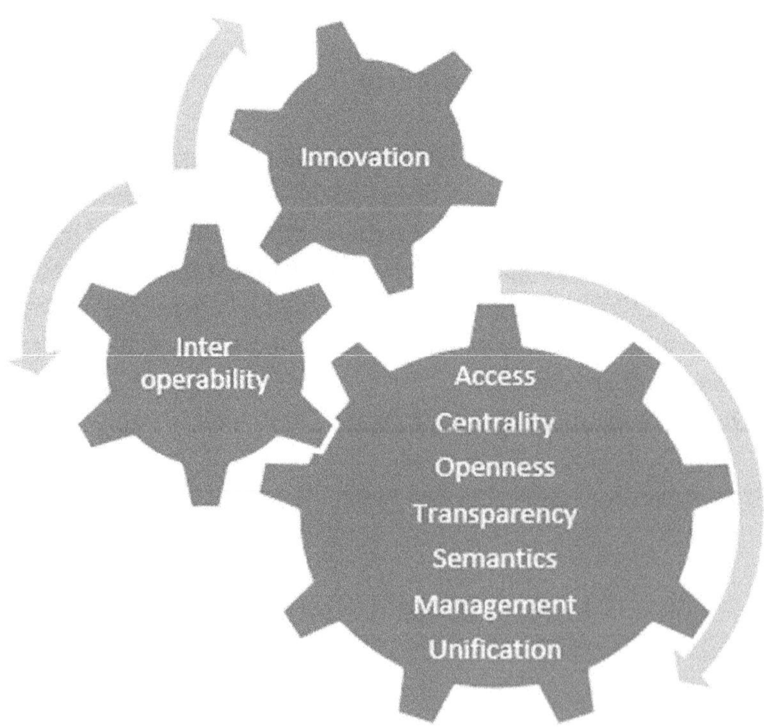

Figure 2. Ideal outline of the developed architecture

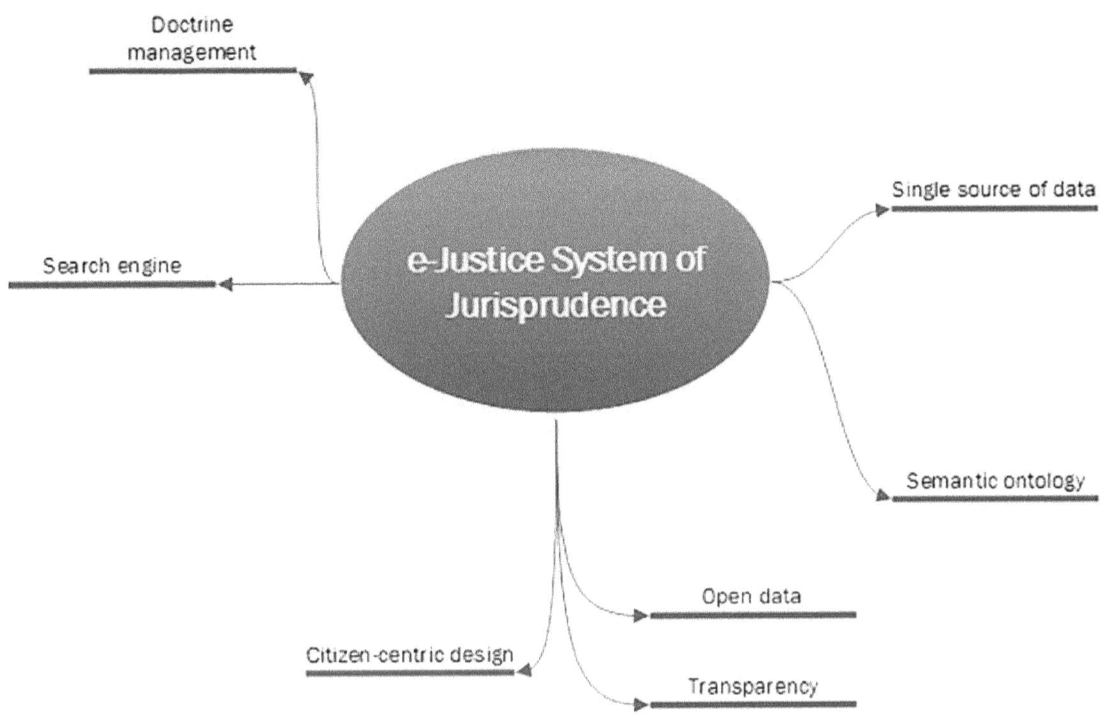

Figure 2 shows an outline of the conceptual design of the system that was implemented in the Spanish Constitutional Court.

One of the questions it is hoped to answer from the beginning is: Can any citizen gain access to the same information in the same way as a judge? Is it possible not only to have information without having expert knowledge of the know-how of the courts? Can electronic Government be performed in the legal sector where citizens, lawyers and judges are on the front line? Are there channels available for citizens to have direct participation in legal systems? And will this in itself help improve the quality of Justice? If we can give a nod of the head to these questions we can then begin to think that citizens are closer to Justice.

Developing an ICT System in the Justice Field

Coming up next it presents a tool for electronic justice focused towards openness, the aims of which are to apply the aspects already mentioned. Functionalities go in the direction of optimising access and legal knowledge searches applied to Court decisions, orders and sentences together with their semantic description.

To illustrate this, shown (Figure 3) below is the legal tool in the Internet (iHJ) that is available either on the main web of the court (www.tribunalconstitucional.es) or in the sub-domain, hj.tribunalconstitucional.es.

This system provides a database of sentences and orders as well as related information and knowledge. It is implemented over a database whose contents are exactly the same as for lawyers and judges, setting out jurisprudence for making decisions and conceiving the new judgements of the Court. These

Figure 3. Screen capture of the iHJ ICT

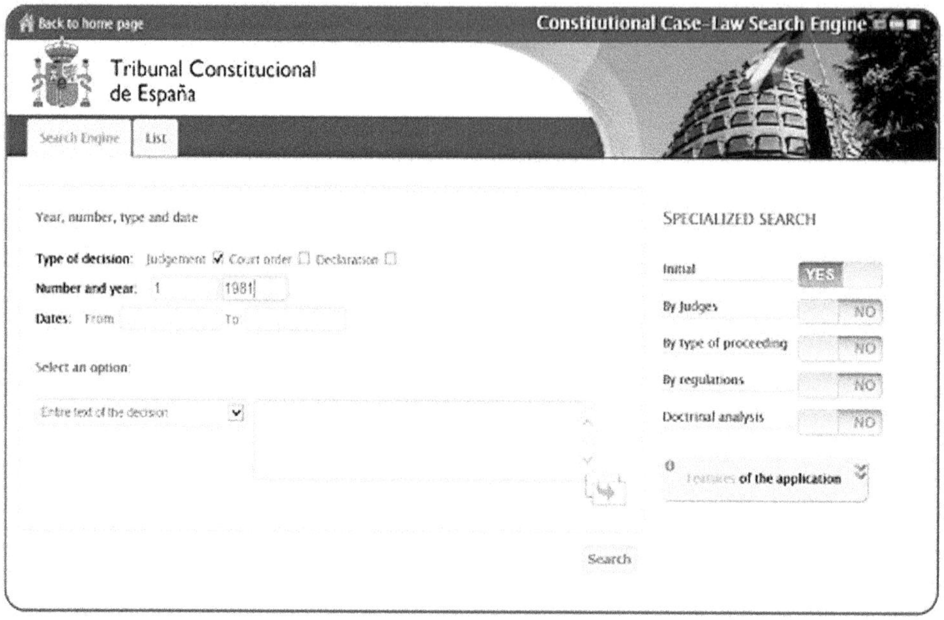

new judgements are incorporated into the system, providing information feedback and adding to overall knowledge. About privacy protection, in spite of the fact that the actors use the same contents, it does not mean a same communication architecture, or machines. That is as a result of designing a perimeter network scheme in order to add an additional layer of security.

There is a wide-ranging set of combinations for carrying out searches that allows exploring all the possibilities for accessing the jurisprudence database. For example, explore the content of a ruling, using criteria such as the type of lawsuit (appeal for protection, questions of constitutionality, constitutional complaint, or a conflict of competence between Administrations, etc). Other criteria, to give some idea, are pursuant to the Court Room (Plenary session, First Chamber or Second Chamber, and even special or temporary courts), the procedural registration number, or the individual votes of judges, among many other case studies that can be consulted directly on the Web.

However, what is particularly important is to have access to the expert know-how deriving from each previous sentence which for years has been for external consumption and which with the iHJ tool is of free access to the public. This includes doctrinal analyses, briefs, summaries, extracts, overviews, semantic descriptors, indexing, grouping related sentences, related legislation and lower ranking regulations, all of which any citizen can have access to on the Internet.

There are many options for the citizen-user, but two need pointing out. As can be seen in the figure, the first is the plurality of standards used to generate documents in an editable format. This is the case, with downloads offered in ISO/IEC 29500 or Standard ECMA-376 (ECMA International, 2012), commonly used in OpenXML formats for Mac, Windows and Linux, and user-friendly for the main office software packages on the market, either free or commercial ones. On the other hand, access can be gained in standard interoperable formats in XML and also in JSON, as it shows in Figure 4.

Figure 4. One of the interfaces for downloading in various formats

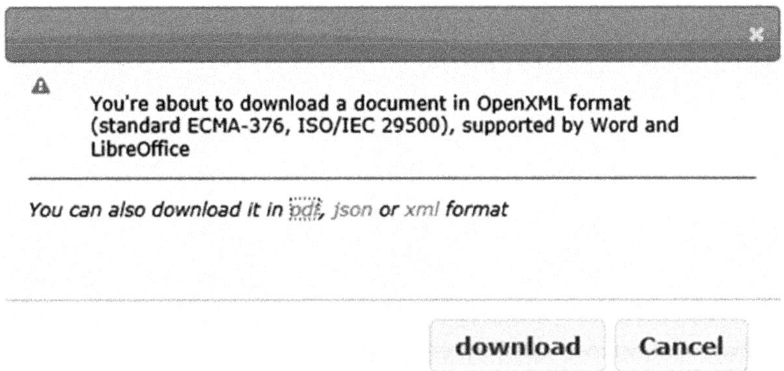

Figure 5. Citizen feedback

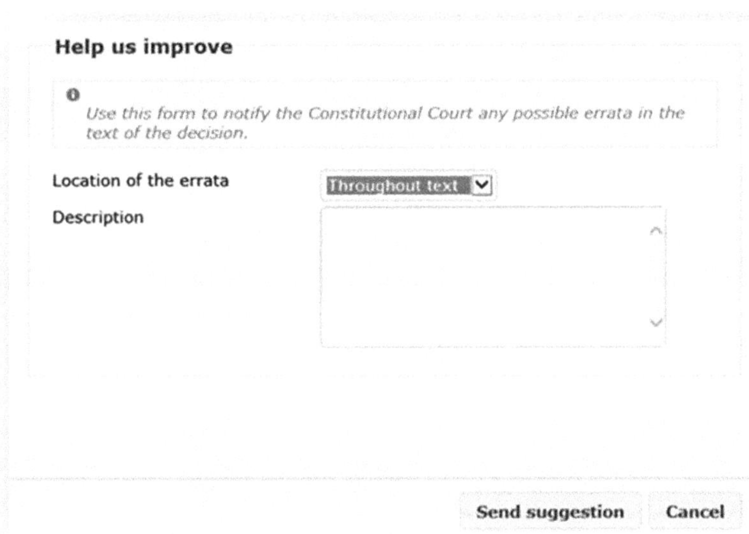

Secondly, it should be highlighted that the use scenario of a system feedback mechanism can provide information that improves or assesses the system itself. As a result, any person could point out any errata or badly referenced element to the Court, as can be seen in the Figure 5.

Along the same lines, by using another interface, suggestions can be made regarding the semantic descriptors related to a sentence. This kind of collaboration can improve and optimise the legal semantic ontology of the Court.

Deployment and Implementation

From an ICT ecosystem and implementation point of view, the developed project consists of three main sub-systems: the Web Software System, the Central Information System and the Content Cache System.

As it presented in (Cano, Jimenez, Hernandez, & Ros, 2015) the Web Software System (WSS), which is a distributed multilayer application whose users are citizens and whose basic modules are made up of citizens' views, the controller shell and the legal model:

- **Citizen Views:** This consists of the design of the presentation layers over HTML5 and jQuery, with a natural-responsive design and implementation style in ASP.NET Razor version 4 server markup syntax.
- **Controller Shell:** This consists of controllers that shape the MVC (model-view-controller) base architecture and the functions available to offer a Rest API implementation layer based on json and xml. This enables machine-to-machine (M2M) communication, or to be more precise, Court machine to Citizen machine (or group or citizens movement).
- **Legal Model:** This consists of business logic, the structure of the entities and the relationships. Worth pointing out is the use of data persistence mechanisms such as Entity Framework as well as the possibility to implement xml and json, which are widely used.
- **Central Information System (CIS):** This consists of a server database infrastructure, indexers, expert information structures and a legal ontology based on descriptors, concepts and relationships that semantically label the legal items. This system, in turn, has two clearly differentiated parts:
    - **A Knowledge Database of Jurisprudence (KDJ):** This is based on a relational database in which the information on legal decisions is interlinked with expert know-how that is externally available through the WSS citizen access system.
    - **Semantic Ontology System:** This consists of a collection of conceptual descriptors regarding constitutional justice, especially regarding fundamental human rights and civil liberties. It is organised by concept prioritisation (vertical), purely semantic relationships (horizontal) that constructs a semantic graph linked to sentences and other nodes of the ontology and the KDJ.
- **Content Cache System (CCS):** This is an electronic documentation system which enables document requests to be made from search routines and retrieve the information from the WSS system. The architecture must be based on a knowledge base system, therefore, there are no documents that initially represent jurisprudence which are gradually generated as citizens request them and have a dynamic life cycle according to the validity of the knowledge used. In addition, it is used for an optimised access with the purpose of speeding up service performance which releases Open XML editable files, which, as mentioned in the previous section are user-friendly with multiplatform office software applications. It also has another module that offers the official documents of the government gazette (BOE) as well as integrating the life cycle of the amendments published.

Figure 6 shows an outline of this architecture depicting the layout deployed by the system as a whole.

Figure 6. Developed system architecture

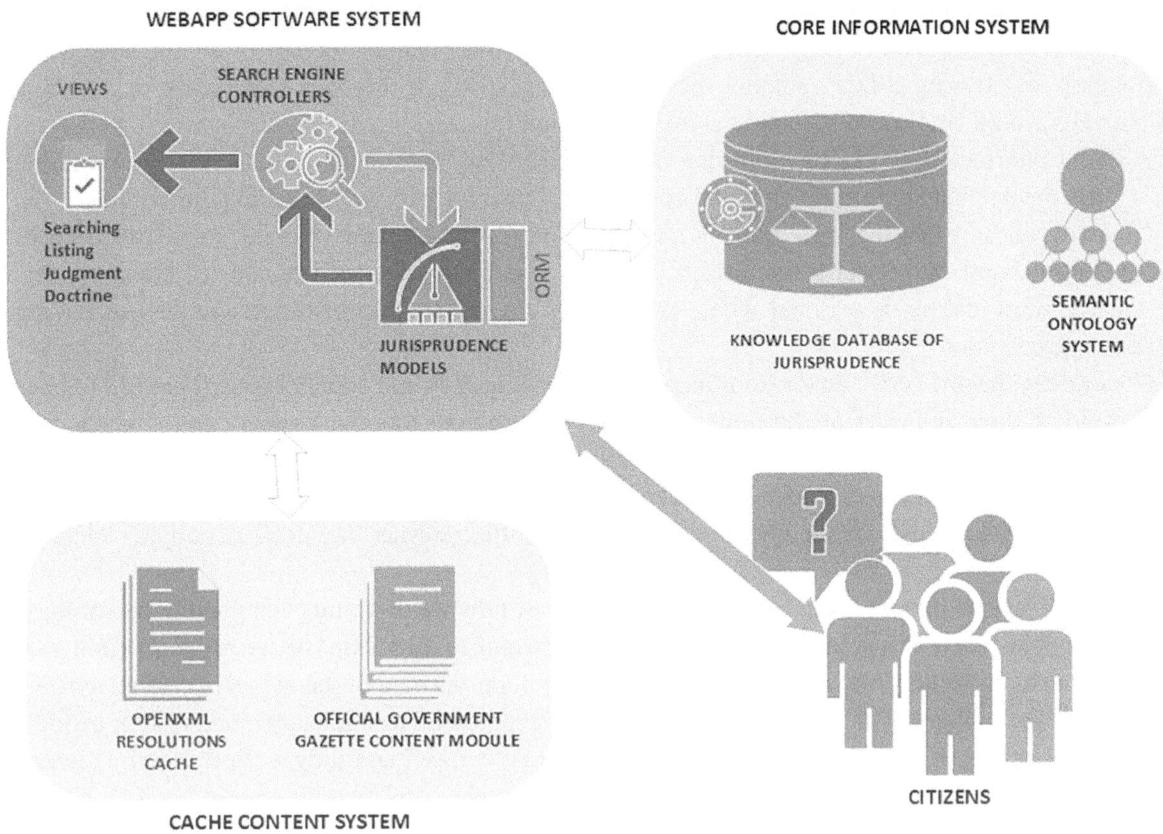

DISCUSSION

Although it is a fairly specialised field, e-Justice shares many of the approaches of electronic government. Such is the case for the highest criteria of efficiency and effectiveness as well as for the use of advanced technology and flexibility. As for its position with regard to the citizen, justice needs to run a distance alone along a different path from other public sectors because of its legal nature, as we have explained in the first section of this chapter.

Consequently, as we have been considering Justice must take on technology to become involved in more available and easily-understood services where the key design element is to be citizen-centred. This paradigm in the development of ICT in the sector is completely novel since the traditional view puts citizens' issues right at the end of the list of requirements, if there are any, and prioritises the requirements of the legal players.

Curiously, when it comes to finding solutions, the engineer is face-to-face with the legal players but not with the citizens. This means that the solutions are often focused on civil servants while citizen service is just an added or fringe benefit in the software design process. If the first requirement is a citizen-centred development cycle, this means carrying a pair of binoculars to bridge that distance so that what appears distant can be clearly seen. In short, we can interact with the legal players and continually consider its application/compatibility as part of an open judiciary plan.

Accessibility is one of the major factors in this plan to achieve the main objective of being closer to citizens. Some reports, as in (European Commission, 2008) express accessibility in terms of efficiency and effectiveness while others highlight aspects such as an easy understanding of the language used as a prior step for offering citizens a better service (Reiling, 2011). If this idea were taken up, the courts and citizens would find communication somewhat easier.

A direct interface as the factor can bring in an intermediary-free scenario to access justice through ICTs. This means that at the same time the courts could interact with non-legal expert citizens.

Cooperation between the legal players and the courts as a standard working format to achieve a transparency channelled towards the citizen. It would also encourage mechanisms of effectiveness in the legal system making it a global whole inspired by loyalty to the institutions as well as having a citizen-centred vision.

Concretely, the pro-active factors of transparency, participation and collaboration that need to be met in the field of Open Judiciary are brought to the fore. It is obvious that our society cannot be conceived without the Internet as a reference point. Its evolution has had an impact on the way the uses and customs of humanity are defined. Sociologists like Castells even speak of the Information and Knowledge Society as a bipolar phenomenon between the Being and the Internet that defines people's behaviour (Castells, 1996).

The implications for this change in the social reality of how we do things when using technology in the context of justice is of special relevance when the electronic relationships between citizens and judges are not in harmony. Indeed, in the literature there are opinions warning of the negative consequences for the courts if technology is under-used (Yáñez, 2008), the potential as a management system inside the law courts (Cerrillo & Fabra, 2009) and even to train legal counsel and judges. In this sense Jiménez-Gómez (2013) has exemplified this situation as part of the mechanisms that should become a part of the effectiveness of legal custody.

Consequently, the scientific community is approaching the need to innovate in the concept of the Administration of Justice in accord with the challenges of this century and is participating in the general progress. Making technology a part of Justice and taking advantage of its capabilities will not only help reach the objectives of the judiciary per-se but also avoid the digital divide that is sometimes felt by legal operators and the feeling of being persecuted by ICTs.

This can be achieved by incorporating new skills and capabilities on an individual and organisational level to direct the IT resources towards the challenges of Open Judiciary. To do so, awareness-raising and teaching are essential if we are to see the possibilities of ICTs as the sector undergoes the process of change.

CONCLUSION AND FUTURE RESEARCH DIRECTIONS

A great work ahead is estimated on engineering data related to Justice. New techniques and new ways of applying machine learning and artificial intelligence open paths, regardless of the theoretical approaches, to provide concrete and pragmatic solutions.

Nevertheless, interoperability remains a major challenge, not only at a technical level but especially at the organizational level, which is an effort to address the high court and constant technological investment.

We have worked in the domain of Constitutional Justice, introducing the area of research into this field from a technology point of view closely linked to cybersecurity as an enabling element for providing a continuous service to citizens. The different aspects of Open Justice have been studied as well as ICT tools and the citizen-centred approach. Although under the umbrella of the Open Government paradigm, the legal sector is of such a specifically different nature that the advances in electronic government must be applied in a different way.

For this reason, an Open Judiciary based on nine factors is presented, that allows parameterising the design and construction of an infrastructure of a legal system that is becoming open. A real architecture has been developed under these parameters and implemented in a Court, which is a highly significant contribution to this work.

REFERENCES

Aragón Reyes, M. (2013, July-December). Dos problemas falsos y uno verdadero: neoconstitucionalismo, garantismo y aplicación judicial de la constitución. *Cuestiones Constitucionales, 2013*(29), 3-25.

Barak, A. (2010). Proportionality and principled balancing. *Law & Ethics of Human Rights*, 1-16.

Bickle, A. (1962). *The Least Dangerous Branch: The Supreme Court at the Bar of Politics*. Binghamton, NY: Bobbs-Merrill Company, Inc.

Cano, J., Hernandez, R., & Ros, S. (2014, October). Distributed Framework for Electronic Democracy in Smart Cities. *Computer*, *47*(10), 65–71. doi:10.1109/MC.2014.280

Cano, J., Jimenez, C., Hernandez, R., & Ros, S. (2015). New tools for e-justice: legal research available to any citizen.*Second International Conference on eDemocracy & eGovernment (ICEDEG), 2015* (pp. 108-111). Quito: IEEE. doi:10.1109/ICEDEG.2015.7114455

Castells, M. (1996). *The rise of the network society*. Cambridge, UK: Blackwell Publishers, Inc.

Cerrillo, A., & Fabra, P. (2009). *E-Justice: Using Information Communication Technologies in the Court System*. Hershey, PA: IGI Global.

ECMA International. (2012). ECMA-376, Office Open XML File Formats - Fundamentals and Markup Language Reference (4th ed.). Author.

European Commission. (2008). *Towards a European e-Justice*. Brussels: Communication from the Commission to the Council, the European Parliament and the European Economic and Social Committee.

Jiménez Campo, J. (1999). *Derechos fundamentales: concepto y garantias*. Trotta.

Jiménez-Gómez, C. E. (2013). *Gobierno abierto y back office: reflexiones para su implementación*. Boletín Institucional e-Governa.

Jiménez-Gómez, C. E. (2013). *Impacto de la Ley Reguladora del Uso de las TIC en la Administración de Justicia*. Barcelona: Centro de Estudios Jurídicos y Formación Especializada.

Jiménez-Gómez, C. E. (2014). *Justicia Abierta: transparencia y proximidad de la justicia en el actual contexto de Open Government.* Barcelona: Centro de Estudios Jurídicos y Formación Especializada. Generalidad de Cataluña.

Kramer, L. (2004). *The people themselves: Popular constitutionalism and judicial review*. Oxford University Press.

Martínez-Vares García, S., & De la Quadra-Salcedo Janini, T. (2014). *La tutela multinivel de los derechos fundamentales. XVI Reunión trilateral de los Tribunales Constitucionales de Italia, Portugal y España.* Santiago de Compostela: Tribunal Constitucional (Spain).

Páez Mañá, J. (1994). *Bases de datos jurídicas.* Madrid, Spain: CINDOC, CSIC, Centro de Información y Documentación Científica.

Pozen, D. (2010). Judicial elections as popular constitutionalism. *Columbia Law Review*, *110*, 2047–2134.

Reiling, D. (2011). e-Justice: experiences with court IT in Europe. In J. Caballero, C. De Gracia, & L. Hammergren (Eds.), Buenas prácticas para la implementación de soluciones tecnológicas en la Administración de Justicia. Méxito.

Yáñez, R. (2008). *L'Oficina judicial a Catalunya. Mitjà d'una Justícia eficaç pel ciutadà del segle XXI.* Barcelona: Centro de Estudios Jurídicos y Formación Especializada.

Section 2

Open Justice in Asia

Chapter 4
Open Judiciary in a Closed Society: A Paradox in China?

Mei Gechlik
Stanford Law School, USA

Di Dai
Peking University Law School, China

Jordan Corrente Beck
Debevoise & Plimpton LLP, USA

ABSTRACT

This chapter examines the open government initiative and the application of open government principles to the court system in China in order to illustrate what "open judiciary"—and, ultimately, an "open state"—looks like in a relatively closed society. The authors present a comprehensive background of China's open government initiative and related court reform efforts, along with critical analysis of trends in "Guiding Cases" ("GCs"), de facto *binding precedents released by the Supreme People's Court (SPC) of China, and subsequent cases ("SCs") that cite GCs. Drawing on these theoretical and empirical studies, the authors discuss the prospects of leveraging China's open government and open judiciary efforts to develop an open state in the country and identify key factors for promoting open judiciary in other closed societies around the world.*

INTRODUCTION

In January 2009, U.S. President Barack Obama issued the *Memorandum on Transparency and Open Government* ("*Open Government Memorandum*") to announce his administration's commitment to "creating an unprecedented level of openness in Government" by "establish[ing] a system of transparency, public participation, and collaboration". The president elaborated on this commitment, stating that "[o]penness will strengthen democracy [in the United States] and promote efficiency and effectiveness in Government".

DOI: 10.4018/978-1-5225-0717-8.ch004

According to the memorandum, government should be transparent because "[t]ransparency promotes accountability and provides information for citizens about what their Government is doing". Government should be participatory because "[p]ublic engagement enhances the Government's effectiveness and improves the quality of its decisions" and, therefore, "[e]xecutive departments and agencies should offer Americans increased opportunities to participate in policymaking and to provide their Government with the benefits of their collective expertise and information". Government should also be collaborative because "[c]ollaboration actively engages Americans in the work of their Government" and, therefore, "[e]xecutive departments and agencies should use innovative tools, methods, and systems to cooperate among themselves, across all levels of Government, and with non-profit organizations, businesses, and individuals in the private sector" (*Open Government Memorandum*, 2009).

In response to this memorandum, the *Open Government Directive* (2009) was issued later in the same year to direct U.S. executive departments and agencies and set deadlines for them to take certain actions in accordance with the principles of transparency, participation, and collaboration set forth in President Obama's memorandum. To achieve this goal, the *Open Government Directive* specifically requires executive departments and agencies to publish government information online, improve the quality of government information, create and institutionalize a culture of open government, and create an enabling policy framework for open government.

As discussed in other chapters of this book, these efforts to promote open government in the United States have popularized the open government concept—a concept that can be dated to 1957 (Chapman & Hunt, 2006; Parks, 1957)—and have inspired many other countries. This chapter aims to discuss whether the People's Republic of China ("China") has also been inspired to embrace the open government concept, and, if so, whether China has extended the principles of transparency, participation, and collaboration to the court system so as to achieve "open judiciary", a term used in this chapter to express a broader concept that applies the principles of transparency, participation, and collaboration to the judiciary (Jiménez-Gómez, 2014) as distinct from the narrower, procedurally- and common law-focused concept of "open justice" (Conley, Datta, Nissenbaum, & Sharma 2012).

To this end, the authors first draw on key literature and official documents to show the extent that open government has taken root in China and analyze whether this also leads to the emergence of open judiciary in the country. Following discussion concluding that some form of open judiciary has indeed emerged in China, the authors then present a two-pronged evaluation of open judiciary in China by examining (1) the degree to which the principles of transparency, participation, and collaboration have become explicit objectives of China's court reform, as evidenced by recent court reform plans and implementation measures, and (2) the degree to which these principles have been followed in practice, as evidenced by trends in a groundbreaking system that the Supreme People's Court ("SPC") of China established in 2010, under which certain court judgments are released as Guiding Cases ("GCs"), *de facto* binding precedents. Based on this evaluation, the authors offer recommendations for addressing the limitations and challenges noted so as to help China achieve open judiciary more effectively. The authors also offer insights about the prospect of leveraging China's open government and open judiciary efforts to develop an open state in a relatively closed society. Based on China's experience in bringing the principles of transparency, participation, and collaboration to the judiciary, the authors conclude by attempting to identify key factors for promoting open judiciary in other closed societies in the world.

BACKGROUND: THE EVOLUTION OF OPEN GOVERNMENT IN CHINA

The Chinese term "open government", that is, "*kāifàng zhèngfǔ*" ("开放政府"), did not appear in China's official documents until 2014. However, Chinese scholars' discussion of "open government" started a decade earlier.

At the turn of the 21st century, Chinese scholars, like many of their counterparts around the world, were discussing the concept of "reinventing government" or "reengineering government" as the new approach to public administration (Fesler & Ketti, 1996; Johnes & Thompson, 1999; Osborne & Plastrik, 1998). They offered various models for building an "ideal government" in the future, including high-performance government, seamless government, limited government, and uncorrupt government (CHEN Zhenming, 2002; MENG, Lingmei, 2005; WANG Conghu, 2006; WANG Qian, ZHOU Zhuoru, & LI Weiyu, 2002; WANG Ying & MA Bin, 2002; ZHANG, Xin, 2005). These scholars also suggested that government initiatives should be guided by public needs and should serve to meet these needs. There was also discussion that reinventing/reengineering government meant redefining the division of labor between political state, market economy, and civil society, and that the government's overall reconstruction strategy should be (1) a return to civil society, (2) the use of a market economy, and (3) development toward public governance (ZHANG Xin, 2005).

All of these discussions, together with the government reform implemented in China at the time, led many scholars to believe that the key to the realization of different reform objectives was to have open government and that "reengineering government" was just a stage in the process of achieving this ultimate goal (WANG Conghu, 2006; ZHOU He, 2012). In his seminal text entitled *On Opening Government* (开放政府论), Professor WANG Conghu (2006) considered *kāifàng zhèngfǔ* (开放政府) to be the most appropriate Chinese translation of "open government" because the term not only suggests that the government is not closed, but also carries connotations that the government needs to be open domestically (i.e., to interact with the public, act with integrity, and protect rights) and internationally (i.e., to open the country to foreigners) (pp. 5-6). Professor WANG Conghu (2006) and Professor XIAO Jinming (2005) emphasized that the basic requirements for open government were openness and transparency, citizen participation, government integrity, and respect for human rights. They also recommended implementation of appropriate information disclosure and participation mechanisms.

Since the release of the *Open Government Directive* (2009), more scholars in China have discussed the potential impact of the directive and the principles of transparency, participation, and collaboration stated therein by examining how these principles have been implemented in foreign countries (LI Hengmin, 2014; LI Yin, 2012; LUO Bo, 2014; RAN Congjing, LIU Jie & CHEN Yi, 2013; WANG Xiwen, 2012; WU Jiannan, ZHENG Ye, MEI Hong & REN Zhiguang, 2014; ZHOU He, 2012) and making suggestions as to best steps for China to take in its attempt to establish an open government (HU Xiaoming, 2015; WANG Yaqin, 2014; ZHANG Chengfu, 2014; ZHU Cunkui & LI Yan, 2014). These scholars first generally acknowledge that, in China, open government is the latest development of e-government. As observed by these scholars, open government aims to, through network technology, actively make government information open and enable citizens to participate in the government's decision-making processes. With respect to what "open government" entails, these scholars have identified various goals, including encouraging "transparency" ("透明"), being "user-centric" ("以用户为中心"), being "open and interactive" ("开放互动"), encouraging "user participation" ("用户参与"), instilling "trust and collaboration" ("信任与协作"), and creating "social autonomy" ("社会自治"). In particular, they have emphasized the need to establish a service-oriented government, strengthen public scrutiny, government responsiveness and accountability, increase the reasonableness and accessibility of government information disclosure, create more channels for public participation, and enhance coordination among government departments.

Given that open government is built on e-government development, this section first outlines the development of e-government and then discusses how open government takes root in China.

China's E-Government Initiative

China's e-government initiative formally began with the formation of the National Informatization Leading Group in 2001. The group first stated that the aim of e-government development was to "accelerate the transformation of the government's functions, improve the quality and efficiency of government administration, strengthen the government's regulation and service capacity, [and] encourage public scrutiny" (*Guiding Opinion of the National Informatization Leading Group on the Development of E-Government Affairs in China*, 2002). Afterwards, a series of documents was released to set the foundation for the landmark regulation on open government information. These documents included the *National Informatization Development Strategy (2006–2020)* (2006), which listed e-government as a strategic priority for encouraging administrative efficiency, government efficacy, and democratic participation, and the *Overall Framework for National E-Government Affairs* (2006), which urged the enactment of government information disclosure legislation. Finally, the *Regulation of the People's Republic of China on Open Government Information* (2007) was promulgated by the State Council in 2007 to set a national standard for open government information. This regulation was the result of a series of test rules implemented in pioneering cities, including Guangzhou (*Regulation of Guangzhou Municipality on Open Government Information*, 2002), Shanghai (*Regulation of Shanghai Municipality on Open Government Information*, 2004), Chengdu (*Regulation of Chengdu Municipality on Open Government Information*, 2004), Hanzhou (*Regulation of Hanzhou Municipality on Open Government Information*, 2004), and Wuhan (*Interim Regulation of Wuhan Municipality on Open Government Information*, 2004).

In 2011, *The Twelfth Five-Year Plan of National E-Government Affairs* marked a new stage of e-government, redefining it as a "strategic initiative to deepen the reforms in the administrative system and *build a service-oriented government with which the citizens are satisfied*" (emphasis added). The plan set a number of practical directives to "strengthen [service] applications that safeguard and improve people's livelihood", such as advances in "employment, social security, medical health care, education, culture, and other application services" and accelerated extension of government service applications in townships and villages. The plan further encouraged collaboration among localities and government departments, all of which had to participate in internal and external e-government networks to promote interoperability, information sharing, and coordinated services. It also emphasized the need to improve "government-citizen interaction" by encouraging government websites to institutionalize and standardize online leaders' mailboxes for *xìnfǎng* (信访)—a petition process undertaken through letters or personal visits—and other interactive programs. Overall, the plan emphasized citizens' right to know and right to participate. Further, the principles of transparency, participation, and collaboration were embedded in the plan, even though the term "open government" was not explicitly mentioned.

The Official Recognition of the Open Government Concept in China

It is encouraging that China's e-government development has increasingly emphasized goals that are consistent with the principles of transparency, participation, and collaboration. Although none of these were officially attributed to the development of open government, recent developments, as outlined below, suggest that the vigorous discussion of "open government" among Chinese scholars has produced a positive impact on the Chinese government.

In 2014, *kāifàng zhèngfŭ* (open government), was used for the first time in an official document. When it appeared in the *Notice Concerning Speeding Up the Implementation of Work Related to the Information-for-Citizens Project* (2014). The significance of the notice is marked by the fact that it was jointly issued by a dozen ministries and important leaders' groups, including the National Development and Reform Commission, the Ministry of Industry and Information Technology, the Ministry of Finance, the Ministry of Education, the Ministry of Public Security, the Ministry of Civil Affairs, and the Ministry of Human Resources and Social Security. Among the various tasks identified as priorities in the notice were the development of open government data and open government by building systems needed for disclosing and sharing government data, treating government data resources as public resources, and promoting the transparency of the government and the interaction between the government and citizens.

In addition, *kāifàng zhèngfŭ* (open government) will likely be included in *The Thirteenth Five-Year Plan of National E-Government Affairs*, which will be released by the end of 2016. Two positive signs support this prediction. First, the State Council released the *Guiding Opinion of the General Office of the State Council on the Promotion of Coordinated Development of E-Government Affairs* in 2014, providing guiding principles that are similar to the principles of transparency, participation, and collaboration for the overall development of e-government. This, in effect, demonstrates the highest executive organ's acceptance of open government principles. The guiding principles presented in the plan include "focus on the demands for the government to perform their duties and to serve the people's needs", "promote open sharing of information resources", and "establish and improve horizontal collaboration and vertical connection at all levels of the government, as well as mechanisms for the coordinated development of e-government which the government leads and in which the society participates".

Second, China's National Information Center, which reports to the State Council's National Development and Reform Commission, has already recognized the impact of open government on the development of e-government. Two researchers of the center, YANG Daoling and WANG Jingxuan (2015), share important insights in their latest article on opportunities and challenges arising from the preparation of *The Thirteenth Five-Year Plan of National E-Government Affairs*. They first point out that governance around the world is heading toward the development of "integrated government, open government, and wise government". With respect to the importance of open government, they write, "open government emphasizes the use of a highly open approach to address social needs, the realization of transparency and openness in the course of formulating public policy and allocating public interests, and the society, market, and individual citizens being actively encouraged to participate in the entire process of public administration" (YANG Daoling & WANG Jingxuan, 2015, p. 12). These positive remarks about the open government concept in an article written by official researchers to shed light on the preparation of *The Thirteenth Five-Year Plan of National E-Government Affairs* suggest that China will likely recognize the concept in this important plan, marking another step to bring about more related changes.

THE EMERGENCE OF "OPEN JUDICIARY" IN CHINA

The official recognition of the open government concept in China prompts one to wonder whether such positive development has also inspired Chinese leaders to bring open government principles to the court system to achieve "open judiciary".

While the Chinese term for "open judiciary", that is, *kāifàng sīfǎ* (开放司法), has not appeared in China, the term *sīfǎ gōngkāi* (司法公开), which literally translates to "judicial openness", has been widely used in official documents since 2004, as illustrated below. The following analysis demonstrates how, over the course of more than a decade of development, *sīfǎ gōngkāi* has come to take on a sense broader than its literal meaning to embrace concepts consistent with the principles of transparency, participation, and collaboration. This section will then explain whether the expanded usage of *sīfǎ gōngkāi* is driven by the development of open government.

The Growth of Sīfǎ Gōngkāi (Judicial Openness)

The term *sīfǎ gōngkāi* first appeared in the *Decision of the Supreme People's Court on Further Strengthening the Basic Construction of People's Courts* released by the SPC in 2004. In this decision, the highest court emphasized the need to "further implement an open adjudication system" and "promote judicial fairness through *judicial openness*" (emphasis added). The context suggests that the term *sīfǎ gōngkāi* referred to open adjudication only and was chosen to replace *shěnlǐ gōngkāi* (审理公开; open handling) as used in, for example, Article 125 of the *Constitution of the People's Republic of China* (1982), and related terms such as *gōngkāi shěnlǐ (shěnpàn) ànjiàn* (公开审理 (审判) 案件; open handling (adjudication) of cases as used in, for example, Article 120 of the *Civil Procedure Law of the People's Republic of China* (1991); and *gōngkāi xuāngào pànjué* (公开宣告判决; open pronouncement of judgments), as used in, for example, Article 121 of the *Criminal Procedure Law of the People's Republic of China* (1979), all of which were commonly used at the time to convey the concept of openness in the judiciary.

The meaning of the term *sīfǎ gōngkāi* then broadened in 2005, when the SPC issued the *Second Five-Year People's Court Reform Plan (2004-2008)* (the "*Second Court Reform Plan*"). Apart from stating the significance of "open adjudication", the plan emphasized the need to "adopt new measures on judicial openness" and requested that "information on enforcement [of judgments] be made public". Afterwards, the SPC issued the *Several Provisions of the Supreme People's Court on Open Enforcement [Work] of People's Courts* in 2006, putting "open enforcement" within the domain of *sīfǎ gōngkāi*.

Since the release of the *Third Five-Year People's Court Reform Plan (2009-2013)* (2009) (the "*Third Court Reform Plan*") and related rules, the meaning of *sīfǎ gōngkāi* has continued to grow. The concepts embedded in the term now also include "open case registration, open trials, open enforcement, public hearings, documents made public, and adjudication affairs made public" (*Six Provisions of the Supreme People's Court on Judicial Openness*, 2009). In addition, *sīfǎ gōngkāi* also covers requirements for the "democratization of the judiciary" (*Third Court Reform Plan*, 2009, Paragraph 25), with an emphasis on "establishing and improving mechanisms for communication and expression of public opinion" and "fully safeguarding the people's right to know, participate, express, and supervise" (Paragraph 27).

In October 2014, during the fourth plenary session of the Communist Party of China ("CPC")'s 18th Central Committee, President XI Jinping and other top leaders in China adopted the *Decision on Several Major Issues Concerning Comprehensively Moving Forward "Governing the Country According to Law"* (2014) (the "*Fourth Plenum Decision*"), taking an unprecedented step toward a greater focus on the rule of law in China and noting primary goals that give support to the further expansion of the term *sīfă gōngkāi*. These goals include, among others, to "broaden *people's channels to orderly participate in the judiciary*", "ensure that *people can participate in the judiciary*", and "establish 'under sunshine' a judicial mechanism that is *open*, dynamic, *transparent*, and convenient to citizens" in order to "accelerate the construction of a rule of law government" and "guarantee judicial fairness [and] raise judicial credibility" (emphasis added).

Academics and judges in China have welcomed the enhanced coverage of *sīfă gōngkāi*. For example, Judge LI Jian (2011), Deputy Chief Judge of the Adjudication Supervision Tribunal of the Chongqing No. 3 Intermediate People's Court, stressed the significance of making adjudication affairs public, stating that "making adjudication affairs public is akin to making government affairs public. Its targets are primarily nonspecific [members of the] public and its function is to primarily reflect the courts' overall openness and transparency" (p. 7). Professors ZHANG Xinbao and WANG Weiguo have shared similar views (2013).

Main Driver for the Growth of Sīfă Gōngkāi

The expanded usage of *sīfă gōngkāi* is not officially attributed to the development of open government. Although it is possible that Chinese leaders, having been positively influenced by Chinese experts' vigorous discussion of open government since the *Open Government Directive* (2009) was issued, might have considered it appropriate to extend relevant open government principles to the court system, the *Open Government Directive* is unlikely to be the primary driver because, as shown above, the growth of *sīfă gōngkāi* began in 2005, four years before the *Open Government Directive*'s release.

In fact, the use of terms like transparency, participation, and collaboration predated the *Open Government Directive* (2009). Two examples are illustrative. First, in 2007, XIAO Yang, the then-president of the SPC, emphasized participation and collaboration. He stated that the judiciary "must act in accordance with certain rules of democracy", "accept democratic participation and supervision", and "take advantage of the supervision mechanisms to promote democratic development inside the judiciary so as to safeguard, through systems, people's broad participation in the judiciary and judicial supervision" (XIAO Yang, 2007, p. 5). In the same year, President XIAO called for "the improvement of diversified dispute resolution mechanisms" to place "citizens' effective participation and collaboration on an equal footing so as to prevent and resolve various social contradictions" (*Notice of the Supreme People's Court and the Ministry of Justice on the Issuance of the Speech by Comrades XIAO Yang, WU Aiying, and HAO Chiyong during the National People's Mediation Work Conference*, 2007).

Second, in 2008, WANG Shengjun, the then-President of the SPC, explained the importance of transparency and participation. He pointed out that, due to China's economic development and citizens' increased awareness of rights, citizens had higher expectations for the judiciary. According to Judge WANG, citizens "not only demand that adjudication results be fair, but also look forward to the judicial process's being open and transparent; [citizens] not only demand the right to know the judicial activities, but also look forward to having the right to participate in and the right to supervise judicial activities" (LIU Xiaopeng & SHI Guosheng, 2008).

The main driver for the expanded usage of *sīfă gōngkāi* is thus unlikely to be the development of open government, but rather the willingness of China's leaders to address the problems prevailing in the country's court system, which has been widely criticized inside and outside of China. Improving the court system in accordance with principles such as transparency, participation, and collaboration is a natural course taken by the ruling communist party during China's long journey toward the rule of law to show that the party can address citizens' discontent and thereby stabilize its governance. China's rule-of-law journey began as early as 1982, when China made it clear in its constitution that "people's courts independently exercise adjudication power in accordance with legal provisions" (*Constitution of the People's Republic of China*, 1982, Article 126). In 1999, a third amendment to the constitution adopted the phrase "the People's Republic of China practices ruling the country in accordance with law and builds a socialist rule-of-law country", formally enshrining the concept of "ruling the country in accordance with law" (*Amendment to the Constitution of the People's Republic of* China, 1999; *Constitution of the People's Republic of China*, 1999, Article 5).

The journey hit another milestone in 2013, when the ruling party identified "promoting the construction of a rule-of-law China and deepening reform of the judicial system" as its primary tasks in the *Decision on Major Issues Concerning Comprehensively Deepening Reforms* (2013) (the "*Third Plenum Decision*"), adopted at the Third Plenary Session of the 18th Central Committee of the CPC. The rationale behind deepening judicial reform was, according to the ruling party, to "safeguard the people's rights and interests so that the people feel fairness and justice in every judicial case" (*Third Plenum Decision*, 2013). The preceding quote was actually first put forward by President XI Jinping in early 2013 (PENG Bo, 2013). Immediately afterwards, these words became the main basis for judicial reform. ZHOU Qiang, President of the SPC, vowed to "vigorously promote judicial openness [...] through openness to promote impartiality, and through openness to make sure that each case is adjudicated to do justice" (YANG Cheng, ZHANG Yu & WANG Ze, 2013). Most recently, the *Fourth Plenum Decision* (2014) and, as discussed in the next section, *The Opinion of the Supreme People's Court Concerning Comprehensively Deepening the Reform of the People's Court—The Fourth Five-Year Reform Plan of the People's Court (2014-2018)* (2015) (the "*Fourth Court Reform Plan*"), were rolled out to provide detailed guidance on the reform of the court system.

To conclude, although the Chinese term "open judiciary" is not used in China, *sīfǎ gōngkāi* has developed in use to take on the essence of open judiciary as used in this chapter. Therefore, in the remaining parts of this chapter, any reference to the term "open judiciary" should be understood to mean *sīfǎ gōngkāi*, as broadly defined to cover the areas analyzed above.

EVALUATING "OPEN JUDICIARY" IN CHINA

This section evaluates "open judiciary" in China by first showing the extent that the principles of transparency, participation, and collaboration have guided the development of China's current five-year court reform plan, that is, the *Fourth Court Reform Plan* (2015), and the adoption of related reform measures. Since 1999, the SPC has issued four five-year court reform plans. The authors will compare these four plans to show how the SPC has gradually increased the number of reform tasks to help implement the three principles. The review of these plans will also show how the three principles are understood in China.

The second part of this section evaluates "open judiciary" in China by examining the extent to which these three principles are reflected in the implementation of the system of GCs. To this end, with support from the China Guiding Cases Project ("CGCP") of Stanford Law School, which was founded immediately after the establishment of the system in 2010 and features a unique knowledge-base of GCs and subsequent cases ("SCs") that refer to these GCs, the authors conduct their own empirical analyses of the GCs and related SCs available at the time of draft.

Court Reform Plans and Implementation Measures

In the *Fourth Court Reform Plan* (2015), the SPC identifies 65 specific tasks, without explicitly categorizing them as initiatives for promoting the principles of transparency, participation, or collaboration, but with the three terms and tasks that manifest them being written into many passages of the plan. Based on their best judgment of the essence of these three principles, as outlined in President Obama's memorandum on open government and the *Open Government Directive* (2009), the authors found that 16 of these 65 tasks involve measures related to transparency (Table 1), six related to participation (Table 2), and three related to collaboration (Table 3). The text included in the first column of each table is the authors' English summary of the Chinese description of the tasks listed in the plan. These descriptions and tabulated references help shed light on how "transparency", "participation", and "collaboration" are understood in the context of court reform.

The 16 tasks related to transparency can be further grouped under the headings of six terms explicitly used by the SPC in the plan: "open case registration", "open trials", "open enforcement", "public hearings", "documents made public", and "adjudication matters made public". As shown in Table 1, among the 16 tasks related to transparency, one involves measures related to "open case registration", five related to "open trials", three related to "open enforcement", one related to "public hearings", two related to "documents made public", and four related to "adjudication matters made public". For example, with respect to "documents made public", the SPC identified two tasks, one of which is to "establish/ improve an online platform for the disclosure of all adjudication documents unless they are withheld due to exceptional circumstances". Subsequently, as explained below, the SPC launched an official website to post court decisions.

None of the other three five-year court reform plans have identified as many tasks that involve measures related to these three principles (*Five-Year Reform Plan of the People's Court*, 1999; *Second Court Reform Plan*, 2005; *Third Court Reform Plan*, 2009), though Tables 1, 2, and 3 show that there is an increasing trend for the SPC to include more reform tasks related to these principles. For example, the above-mentioned task of establishing "an online platform for the disclosure of all adjudication documents" was not identified in the first and second reform plans, but was in the third and fourth plans. The fact that most tasks are identified in the *Fourth Court Reform Plan* (2015) is understandable because, according to the preamble of the plan, it was formulated to implement the spirit of the Fourth Plenary Session, during which, as discussed above, the *Fourth Plenum Decision* (2014) was adopted to embrace terms that help implement transparency, participation, and collaboration in the court system.

Guided by these court reform plans, the SPC has issued a series of implementation measures that help manifest the principles of transparency, participation", and "collaboration" in judicial practice. Some major measures and progress include:

1. **On Transparency:**
    a. **Open Case Registration:** In 2009, the SPC first issued the *Six Provisions of the Supreme People's Court on Judicial Openness*, requiring in its Paragraph 1, among other things, that courts promptly inform parties initiating litigation of the requirements for and processes of case registration, the procedures for reducing litigation fees, and of their rights and obligations. Later that year, the highest court sent another directive requesting that "case registration and letters-and-visits windows" be improved to provide the public with more functional judicial

Table 1. Reform tasks on transparency as identified in four five-year court reform plans

	Transparency	4th	3rd	2nd	1st
	Open Case Registration (立案公开)				
1	Set up/improve online platforms for disclosing case registration information	17, 20, 41	29	*	*
	Open Trials (庭审公开)				
1	Emphasize that any evidence used as a basis for a particular adjudication must be presented and verified in court and that judges must explain in their judgment whether a piece of evidence that is seriously contested by the parties is finally adopted by the deciding court	14	*(2)	*(3)	10, 13
2	Establish audio and video recording mechanisms for the recording of trials in their entirety	15	*(25)	*(33)	*(38)
3	Issue public notices within the court system to disclose changes made to the composition of collegiate panels that handle pending cases	18	*	*	*
4	Improve the open trial system by, if possible, giving the media priority to attend trials	37	*	*	*
5	Establish an online platform to provide parties all over the country access to information regarding the adjudication process of their cases	38	*(8, 24)	*(30)	*(8)
	Open Enforcement (执行公开)				
1	Improve mechanisms for disclosing information about property involved in a case	16	*	*	*
2	Implement an online judicial auction system (see Notes below)	24	*(6)	*	*
3	Establish an online platform to provide parties all over the country access to information regarding the enforcement process of their cases	40	*(25)	*(19)	*
	Public Hearings (听证公开)				
1	Establish an online platform for the disclosure of public hearings that handle applications for sentence reduction, parole, and temporary release for serving out-of-jail sentences	41	*(2)	*	*
	Documents Made Public (文书公开)				
1	Establish/improve an online platform for the disclosure of all adjudication documents unless they are withheld due to exceptional circumstances	39	25	*	*
2	Require that better explanations of the rationale guiding a judgment be included in adjudication documents to ensure that the reasoning of a judgment is made public	34	25	*	13
	Adjudication Matters Made Public (审务公开)				
1	Strengthen the systems that safeguard parties' and other litigation participants' right to know during the litigation process	11	27	*	*
2	Establish a database to house judicial information for all courts nationwide	22	24	*(32)	*(38)
3	Require that all information from leaders who try to interfere with an adjudication, including letters/instructions, be included in the case files, to which parties and their representatives have access	55	*	*	*
4	Promote the use of information-related applications that serve the needs of the courts and the public	65	*(24)	*	*

Table Key: In this table, as in Tables 2 and 3, columns "1st-4th" represent the *First Court Reform Plan (1999-2003)* (1999), *Second Court Reform Plan (2004-2008)* (2005), *Third Court Reform Plan (2009-2013)* (2009), and *Fourth Court Reform Plan (2014-2018)* (2015), respectively. The numbers in each of these columns signify the paragraph numbers that the reform task was identified in the corresponding reform plans. An asterisk (*) signifies that the reform task was not identified in the corresponding reform plans, while numbers in parenthesis following any asterisk indicate paragraph numbers that contain only some passing reference to the reform tasks.

Notes: A "judicial auction" ("司法拍卖") is a compulsory enforcement measure used by people's courts in civil, criminal, and administrative cases to enforce judgments that involve property (*Civil Procedure Law of the People's Republic of China* (2012), Articles 242 and 247; *Interpretation of the Supreme People's Court on Several Issues Concerning Judicial Compensation in Civil and Administrative Litigation* (2000); *Several Provisions of the Supreme People's Court on Enforcing the Property Portion of A Criminal Judgment or Ruling* (2014), Article 12). By taking this measure, people's courts can, through auction, dispose of property owned by the party subject to enforcement.

Table 2. Reform tasks on participation as identified in four five-year court reform plans

	Participation	4th	3rd	2nd	1st
1	Improve the people's assessors system to ensure that the public can participate in the judicial process (see Notes below)	33	5	27	23
2	Explore the establishment of a system that allows parties from society to participate in order to help settle disputes currently covered by the petition system	36	*(29)	*	*
3	Establish a judicial openness supervision system that enables the public to share comments and suggestions	42	*(9, 27)	*(44, 46)	*(40, 42)
4	Improve online litigation service centers to give the public easier access to the judicial process	43	*(29)	*	*
5	Reform the system for the selection of judges to allow talented lawyers, scholars, and legal professionals from other government organs to join the judiciary	50	14	37	32
6	Establish judicial disciplinary committees to welcome certain individuals from society to help formulate open and fair disciplinary rules	56	*	*(43)	*

Notes: "People's assessors" ("人民陪审员") are Chinese citizens selected to serve on the collegiate panels during the adjudication process of first-instance criminal, civil, or administrative cases (*Civil Procedure Law of the People's Republic of China* (2012), Article 39).

Table 3. Reform tasks on collaboration as identified in four five-year court reform plans

	Collaboration	4th	3rd	2nd	1st
1	Set up/improve a system for disciplinary committees and courts to jointly investigate judges who violate disciplinary rules	35	17	*	*
2	Improve coordination among different dispute resolution forums to allow all stakeholders to better collaborate with each other	46	26	7	*
3	Allow for government departmental collaboration to help reform lower level court budget management systems	63	23	49	*(45)

service platforms (*Several Opinions of the Supreme People's Court on Further Strengthening the Construction of the People's Courts' "Case Registration and Letters-and-Visits Window" (Trial Implementation)*, 2009).

b. **Open Trials:** The China Open Trial Processes Information website (中国审判流程信息公开网; http://www.court.gov.cn/zgsplcxxgkw/) was officially launched in November 2014 following the release of *Several Opinions of the Supreme People's Court on the Construction of Three Major Platforms to Promote Judicial Openness* in 2013 ("*Three Major Platforms Opinions*"). Parties to cases handled by the SPC and their representatives may follow the progress of their cases by using valid identification documents or mobile phone numbers to log into the website (The State Council Information Office, 2015). In addition, through the release of the *Provisions of the Supreme People's Court on the Broadcasting of Live or Recorded Trial Activities by People's Courts* (2010), the SPC has established a system for all the courts in China to broadcast live or recorded trial proceedings via television and Internet.

c. **Open Enforcement:** The SPC formulated another guiding document to request that the China Open Enforcement Information website (中国执行信息公开网) be accessible through courts' website portals in order to make public enforcement services information, enforcement announcements, enforcement documents, and other related information readily available (*Several Opinions of the Supreme People's Court on Making Enforcement Processes of People's Courts*

Open, 2014). Launched only in November 2014, the China Open Enforcement Information Website reportedly made significant achievements in less than a year, disclosing approximately 21 million cases that had not been enforced and allowing more than 19 million users to search information about case enforcement (The State Council Information Office, 2015).

d. **Public Hearings:** The *Six Provisions of the Supreme People's Court on Judicial Openness* (2009), in its Paragraph 4, further emphasizes the need to hold public hearings when courts in China handle applications outside of regular trial proceedings, including applications for retrials and applications involving enforcement disputes.

e. **Documents Made Public:** The *Three Major Platforms Opinions* (2013) also proposes the construction of an open platform to publish all adjudication documents. Accordingly, the "China Judgements [sic] Online" website (中国裁判文书网; http://www.court.gov.cn/zgcp-wsw/) was launched in July 2013. Detailed provisions on publishing the documents online are provided in the *Provisions of the Supreme People's Court on the Publication of Adjudication Documents on the Internet by People's Courts* (2013). As reported by the website, by the end of 2015, nearly 15 million judgments or rulings rendered by courts of different levels in China had been published on the website.

f. **Adjudication Affairs Made Public:** The *Six Provisions of the Supreme People's Court on Judicial Openness* (2009), in its Paragraph 6, mandates that adjudication management and related work be made public. The SPC, therefore, published a white paper entitled *Judicial Openness of China's Courts* (The State Council Information Office, 2015). Written in both Chinese and English and with more than 60,000 words, the white paper employs numbers, charts, and examples to demonstrate progress in judicial openness, with particular focus on progress made in promoting open trial processes, making judicial documents public, and disclosing enforcement information.

2. **On Participation and Collaboration:**

a. The SPC has not taken as many measures to promote participation and collaboration. This seems to suggest that most efforts have been directed toward achieving transparency first. Nevertheless, a few measures are worth noting. In April 2009, the SPC issued the *Opinion of the Supreme People's Court on Further Improving the Communication of Public Opinions* (2009), proposing mechanisms to improve various parties' participation in the judicial process and collaboration with the courts. These parties include people's congresses across the country, social organizations, the media, and the public. To increase public scrutiny of the judicial process, the SPC issued the *Several Provisions of the Supreme People's Court on the People's Courts' Acceptance of Public Opinion-based Supervision by the News Media* (2009), the *Work Regulation of the Supreme People's Court on Specially Engaged Supervisors (Trial Implementation)* (2009), and the *Work Regulation of the Supreme People's Court on Specially Invited Counsellors* (2009).

Using Guiding Cases to Assess Transparency, Participation, and Collaboration

Of all the efforts related to open judiciary that have been launched in recent years in China, the most significant, though least understood, is the SPC's issuance of the *Provisions of the Supreme People's Court Concerning Work on Case Guidance* (2010), which created a system for the selection and re-issuance of representative Chinese court judgments as GCs, *de facto* binding precedents. In 2015, the SPC issued the *Detailed Implementing Rules on the "Provisions of the Supreme People's Court Concerning Work on Case Guidance"* (the "*Detailed Implementing Rules*") to explicitly state that courts deciding similar cases should quote relevant GCs in their judgments (Articles 9-11) so as to let "the guiding effect of Guiding Cases fully play its role in adjudication work, to unify standards for the application of law, and to safeguard judicial impartiality" (Article 1). This is a remarkable step taken in a jurisdiction where even constitutional provisions cannot be cited in judgments.

At the time this chapter was drafted, 56 GCs had been released, the Chinese text of which, together with the CGCP's English translations, are made available on the CGCP website (http://cgc.law.stanford.edu/). Prepared as summaries of full-text judgments originally rendered by courts of various levels and from different regions of China, these GCs cover a wide range of legal areas (Gechlik, 2015). Because GCs are rather new, their subsequent developments were largely unknown until the CGCP published in early 2016 its unique analysis of 181 SCs referencing GCs (Gechlik, Zhang, & Ye, 2016). Built on this pioneering research, the authors of this chapter provide further analysis of these cases to help evaluate "open judiciary" in China, in terms of the extent to which transparency, participation, and collaboration are exemplified in practice. Readers interested in supplementing the discussion that follows with independent study should consult the CGCP's full report, which contains a list of these 181 SCs and is regularly updated (Gechlik, Zhang, & Ye, 2016).

Transparency

Table 6 (Appendix 1) catalogues the number of SCs found that explicitly reference each listed GC, along with case type. Only Guiding Case Nos. 1-45 are listed because, at the time of study, there were no SCs referring to Guiding Case Nos. 46-56, likely due to the recentness of their release. This table could not have been prepared had the China Judgements [sic] Online website not been launched to publish all judgments in accordance with the "openness is the rule, non-openness is the exception" principle (*Provisions of the Supreme People's Court on the Publication of Adjudication Documents on the Internet by the People's Courts*, Article 4), a reform measure related to transparency stated in the *Fourth Court Reform Plan*. Most notably, of the 181 SCs found, 76, 21, and 18 explicitly refer to Guiding Case No. 24 ("GC24"), Guiding Case No. 15 ("GC15"), and Guiding Case No. 9 ("GC9"), respectively. These three most frequently cited GCs involved legal issues of common nature and thus the frequent reference to them is not a surprise.

GC24—*RONG Baoying v. WANG Yang and Alltrust Insurance Co., Ltd. Jiangyin Branch, A Motor Vehicle Traffic Accident Liability Dispute* (Stanford Law School China Guiding Cases Project [CGCP], 2014)—is an automobile liability case released by the SPC on January 26, 2014. The insurance company involved sought to reduce its liability by claiming that the pre-existing physical condition of the victim, who was not at fault, contributed to the total harm that the victim suffered. The local court ruled against the insurance company on grounds subsequently summarized by the SPC as "Main Points of the Adjudication", which read:

[If] a victim of a traffic accident is not at fault, the effect of his [pre-existing] physical condition on the ramifications of the harm [he suffered] is not a type of legal circumstance that can mitigate a tortfeasor's liability.

GC15—*XCMG Construction Machinery Co., Ltd. v. Chengdu Chuanjiao Industry and Trade Co., Ltd. et al., A Sale and Purchase Contract Dispute* (CGCP, 2013)—was released by the SPC on January 31, 2013, providing the following "Main Points of the Adjudication":

1. The overlap or commingling of personnel, business, finance, and other aspects of affiliate companies that leads to the impossibility of separating out properties and the loss of independent personalities constitutes the commingling of personalities.
2. If affiliate companies that commingle personalities seriously harm the interests of their creditors, the affiliate companies bear joint and several liability among themselves for the external debt.

Similarly, GC9—*Shanghai Cunliang Trading Co., Ltd. v. JIANG Zhidong, WANG Weiming et al., A Sale and Purchase Contract Dispute* (CGCP, 2012)—helped shed light on the application of China's *Company Law*. The SPC released GC9 on September 18, 2012 with the following as its "Main Points of the Adjudication":

Shareholders of a limited liability company, or directors and controlling shareholders of a joint stock limited company, should, in accordance with law, perform liquidation obligations upon revocation of the company's business license. They cannot be relieved of the liquidation obligations on the ground that they are not de facto control persons or do not actually participate in the company's operation and management.

These 181 SCs were handled by courts located in different regions, revealing that the principle of transparency is quite widely followed (see Figure 1).

Figure 1. Geographical distribution of the courts handling subsequent cases referencing guiding cases
Authors, 2016.

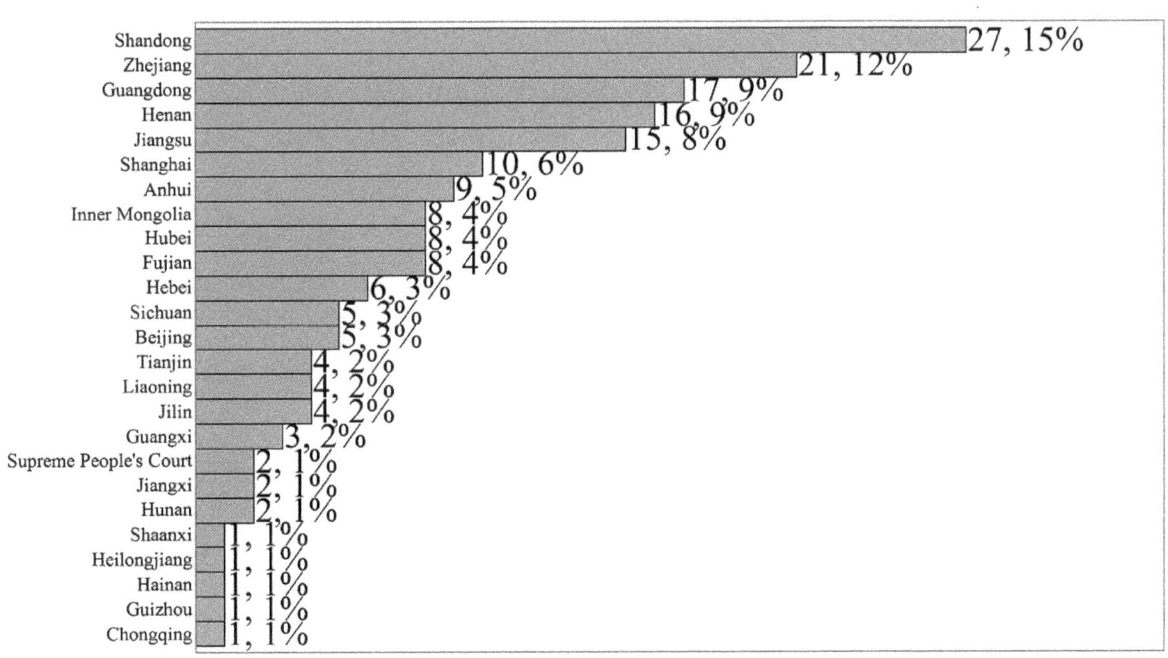

Most of the 181 SCs were handled by courts located in Shandong (27 SCs), Zhejiang (21 SCs), Guangdong (17 SCs), Henan (16 SCs), Jiangsu (15 SCs), and Shanghai (10 SCs). Five of these six places (all except Henan) are among the ten provincial-level regions that have a per capita GDP of over USD 10,000 (see Table 4), a threshold that once met is considered in China to demonstrate that the locality has the economy of a moderately developed country (Hongyu, 2016). In addition, 119 of the 181 SCs were handled by courts located in the ten wealthiest provincial-level regions in the country. These data seem to suggest that the economic development of a locality is somewhat related to the readiness of its lawyers and judges to follow SPC's instructions on citing GCs in subsequent, similar cases and posting these judgments online. This relationship is plausible as more developed regions in China can usually attract better-qualified people to join the judiciary or the legal profession there.

All 181 SCs were decided between 2013 and 2015 (see Figure 2). Seventy-six of these 181 SCs are first-instance rulings or judgments, 93 are second-instance rulings or judgments, and two are retrials that were authorized according to Article 199 of the *Civil Procedure Law of the People's Republic of China* (2012) after the original rulings or judgments had taken effect. The remaining ten SCs include procedures such as applications for retrial or applications for revoking an arbitral award. Among the 181 SCs, 151 are civil cases, while 21, six, and three are administrative, criminal, and enforcement cases, respectively.

Overall, 45% of these 181 SCs were published on the official website within 50 days after the judgments or rulings were rendered (see Figure 3) and the time elapsed between the date of adjudication and the date of publication has been decreasing (see Figure 4), showing the courts' improvements in making the judgments available sooner.

Specifically, 60% of the 93 second-instance SCs were published on the official website within 50 days after the date of adjudication, compared with 46% of the 76 first-instance SCs so published. Similarly, while 44% of the 151 civil SCs were published within 50 days after the date of adjudication, only 33% of the 21 administrative SCs were published within such a timeframe. Although it is too early to draw clear conclusions from these observations, it may serve as a reminder to courts handling first-instance cases and administrative cases that extra efforts should be made to ensure that these cases are published promptly.

Figure 2. Comparative dates of adjudication for subsequent cases referencing guiding cases
Authors, 2016.

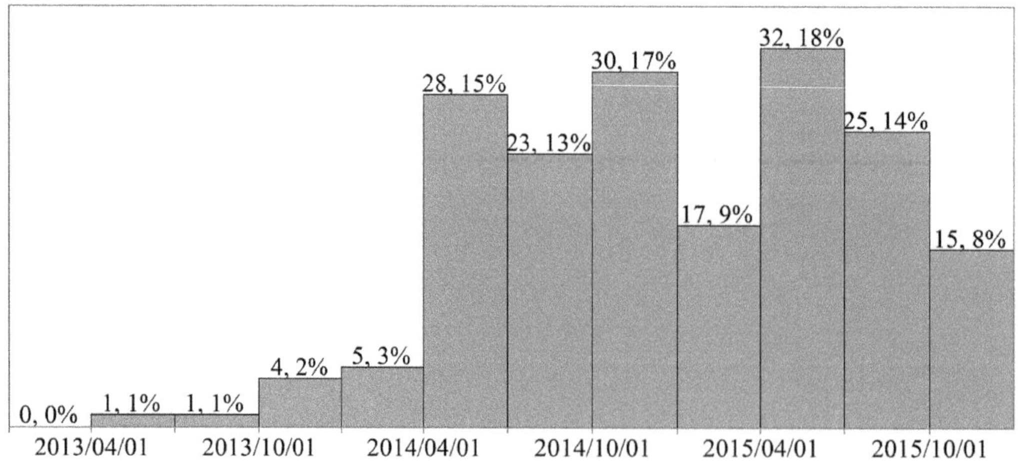

Table 4. GDP per capita of provincial-level regions vs. number of subsequent cases referencing Guiding Cases rendered by courts in those regions

Provincial-Level Regions in China	GDP per Capita (USD)**	Number of SCs
Tianjin	17,509	4
Beijing	17,143	5
Shanghai*	16,527	10
Jiangsu*	14,145	15
Zhejiang*	12,469	21
Inner Mongolia	11,561	8
Fujian	10,962	8
Guangdong*	10,903	17
Liaoning	10,511	4
Shandong*	10,335	27
Chongqing	8,439	1
Jilin	8,328	4
Hubei	8,159	8
Shaanxi	7,730	1
Ningxia	7,068	0
Hunan	6,924	2
Qinghai	6,653	0
Hainan	6,555	1
Xinjiang	6,515	0
Hebei	6,482	6
Heilongjiang	6,319	1
Henan*	6,299	16
Sichuan	5,939	5
Jiangxi	5,913	2
Anhui	5,809	9
Guangxi	5,676	3
Shanxi	5,636	0
Tibet	5,190	0
Guizhou	4,808	1
Yunnan	4,673	0
Gansu	4,209	0

Authors, 2016.
*Provincial-level regions with frequent reference to GCs in subsequent cases.
**Source: http://data.stats.gov.cn/english/.

Figure 3. Number of days elapsed before subsequent cases are posted online
Authors, 2016.

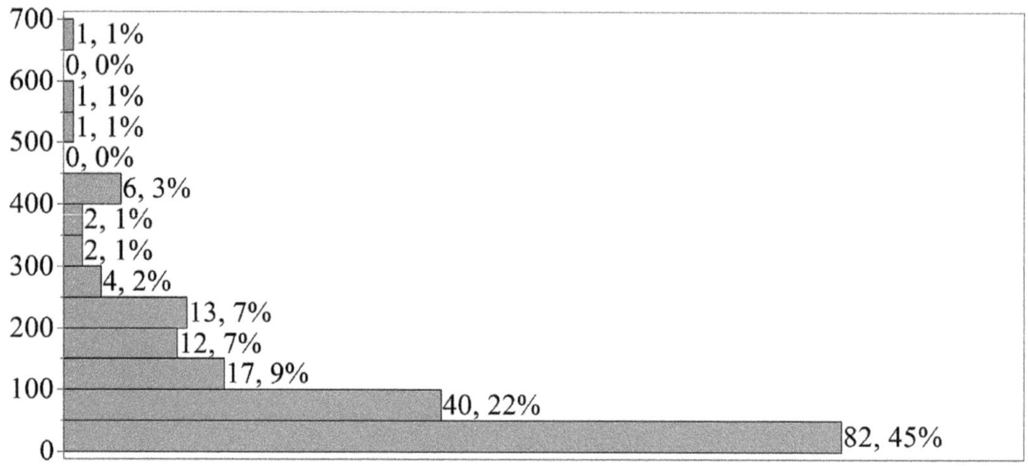

Figure 4. Number of days elapsed vs. date of adjudication
Authors, 2016.

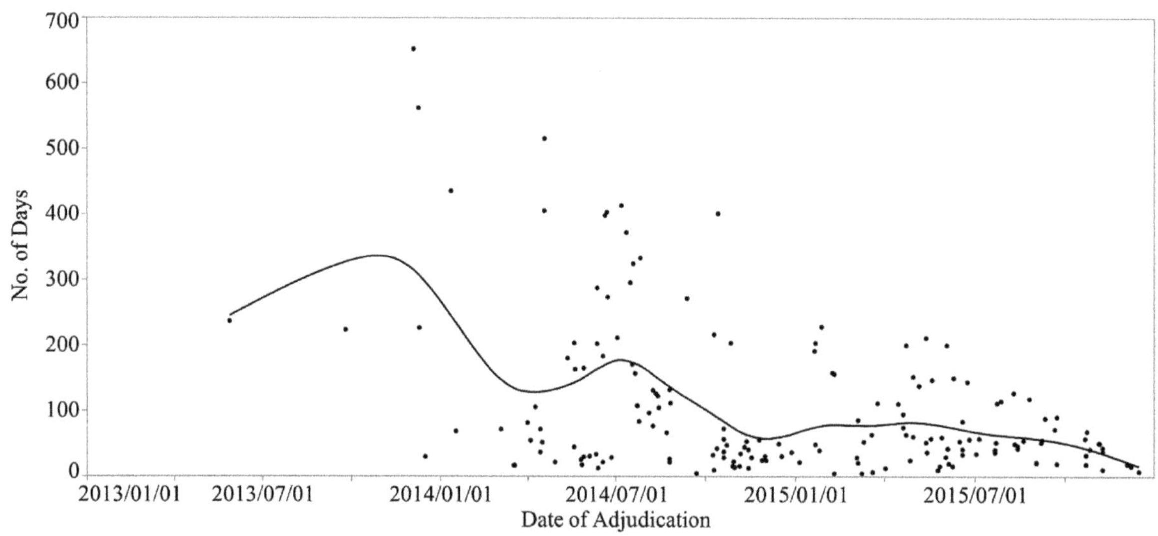

Participation and Collaboration

A closer examination of the 181 SCs referencing GCs demonstrates the extent to which the principles of participation and collaboration are reflected in the implementation of the system of GCs and reveal challenges to full achievement of these principles in the judicial context.

In 134 of the 181 SCs, at least one party involved in the dispute (or their lawyer) mentioned a GC in their arguments. In 38 of these 134 cases, the deciding courts referenced the GC explicitly or implicitly, while in the other 96 cases, the deciding courts did not mention the GC at all, let alone explain in detail whether or not the referenced GC, or any other GC, should be applied.

In the remaining 47 of the 181 SCs, GCs were not mentioned by any party involved in the dispute. Thirty-six of these cases were handled with legal representation and 11 were not. Despite the parties' failure to refer to the relevant GC, the deciding courts took the initiative to mention the GC in 44 of these 47 SCs (in the other three SCs, only the first-instance court mentioned the GC, the second-instance court did not).

Ordinary citizens and legal practitioners cannot participate in the judicial process effectively or ensure that they can represent themselves or their clients competently unless they are aware of the latest legal developments that affect citizens' interests. As shown in the above results, the presence of legal representation without proper citation to support their client's argument or mount a defense suggests that in situations where a GC should be considered, quite a few lawyers failed to provide competent legal representation. This type of poor performance weakens both their and their clients' participation in the judicial process.

Such poor performance is likely due to lawyers' inadequate understanding of GCs. The exclusion of GCs from the syllabus of the National Judicial Examination of China (*Syllabus for the National Judicial Examination in 2015*, 2015), which for Chinese legal professionals is analogous to the U.S. bar exam, wrongly signals to legal practitioners that GCs are insignificant. Another plausible explanation is that the lawyers were uncertain about whether they should explicitly refer to GCs in their arguments because, traditionally, only legislation and judicial interpretations were allowed to be cited in Chinese judgments. Now, the *Detailed Implementing Rules* clearly state that judges should quote GCs in judgments when they handle similar SCs. With these rules, lawyers should be more willing and able to cite GCs in their arguments, but, prior to their issuance, lawyers' explicit reference to GCs represented an unusual move.

Turning to the judges' handling of references to GCs, their total lack of response to parties' arguments in cases where the parties explicitly referred to a GC is a matter of concern because this affects citizens' and lawyers' effective participation in the judicial process. As revealed by related surveys of Chinese judges conducted by the CGCP, the lack of response could partly reflect inadequate understanding of GCs among judges, but may also reveal judges' uncertainty, like lawyers' uncertainty as discussed above, as to whether and how they should explicitly cite GCs in judgments (Gechlik, Philips, & Lee, 2014). Thus, the *Detailed Implementing Rules* were timely released to aid in dispelling this uncertainty.

Despite these findings that show issues of concern, it is encouraging to see that some deciding courts took the initiative to cite GCs even when the parties or their lawyers failed to do so. This signals some degree of collaboration between lawyers and judges, in the sense that judges step in when parties or their lawyers fail to effectively participate in the judicial process to protect the parties' legal rights and interests.

SOLUTIONS AND RECOMMENDATIONS

Court Reform Plans and Implementation Measures

The above evaluation shows that, although it is not explicitly stated that the principles of transparency, participation, and collaboration guided China's five-year court reform plans, the terms transparency, participation, and collaboration have become increasingly present in the plans, culminating in references in a total of 25 of the 65 tasks identified in the *Fourth Court Reform Plan* (2015) that are related to these three principles.

Explicit and clearer classification of these tasks in accordance with the principles of "transparency", "participation", and "collaboration" will help all stakeholders better understand the emphasis placed on these principles and, thereby, help achieve open judiciary. The fact that the Chinese term "open government" has already been used in an official document jointly issued by a dozen ministries and important leaders' groups and that the term will likely be included in *The Thirteenth Five-Year Plan of National E-Government Affairs* suggests that there is a real chance for the term "open judiciary" to be further included in official diction. When this happens, this would prompt leaders in the judiciary to more explicitly discuss the application of the principles of transparency, participation, and collaboration in the judiciary. This would further set a foundation for experts in China to leverage useful foreign experiences of developing "open judiciary" and find solutions that meet China's needs.

In the meantime, improvements can still be made in the name of promoting *sīfǎ gōngkāi* (judicial openness), as the term has been broadly used to convey concepts consistent with the principles of transparency, participation, and collaboration. An important improvement needed is to make the process of implementing the current *Fourth Court Reform Plan* (2015) and future court reform plans transparent, participatory, and collaborative, developing the "open" culture that the SPC essentially encourages in these plans and welcoming input from citizens and all stakeholders to ensure that the reform actions address their needs.

To achieve this goal, courts at lower levels and in different localities should formulate and publish clear *sīfǎ gōngkāi* plans to show how these courts will implement the reform tasks stated in the SPC's court reform plans. This is similar to how the Obama administration directs its agencies to formulate their own open government plans (*Open Government Directive*, 2009). The *sīfǎ gōngkāi* plans should reflect the input of the general public and experts from inside and outside of the local court system and should detail both the specific actions that the local courts will undertake in response to such input and the timeline for taking these actions. In order to illustrate how input from the general public, judges, lawyers, and other stakeholders can be easily collected, Mei Gechlik, one of the authors of this book chapter, and Carlos E. Jimenez Gomez, co-editor of this book, designed a simple questionnaire that asks its respondents to identify five factors that they consider to be most important to the development of open judiciary. The questionnaire included a list of 13 factors from which respondents could select, as shown in Table 5. The questionnaire also provided space for respondents to include additional factors of their choosing.

The trial survey was run for about 10 weeks, after it was first opened to the participants of a session on open judiciary that the CGCP organized for the Open Government Initiative Global Summit 2015. The survey was then circulated throughout the CGCP's global network, including subscribers, volunteers, advisors, donors, and affiliate groups. In the end, 146 responses were collected, 55 of which were submitted by respondents who identified themselves as individuals from countries/economies that, according to the World Bank's classification (http://data.worldbank.org/country), are "developed", and the rest by respondents from "developing" countries/economies (see Table 7 and Table 8, Appendix 2). Of the 91 respondents from developing countries/economies, 32 were from mainland China. These Chinese respondents considered the five most important factors for the development of open judiciary to be:

1. Judicial documents made public (78.1% of the 32 respondents selected this factor);
2. Set up/improve a judicial openness supervision system that enables the public to share comments and suggestions (71.9%),
3. Open registration of cases filed with courts (56.3%),

Table 5. List of factors for survey selection

Factors
1. Open registration of cases filed with courts
2. Open hearings/trials using social media, TV and/or ICT tools
3. Open enforcement of judgments
4. Judicial documents made public
5. Open data/statistics on court performance
6. Use language free of legal jargon (i.e. plain language) in promotional materials designed to foster understanding of decisions and access to justice
7. Set up/improve a judicial openness supervision system that enables the public to share comments and suggestions
8. Set up/improve a system (e.g., a jury system or a system with people's assessors) to ensure that the public can participate in the judicial process
9. Set up/improve a system for independent disciplinary committees and courts to jointly investigate judges who violate disciplinary rules
10. Improve coordination among different dispute resolution mechanisms to allow all stakeholders to better collaborate with one another
11. Collaborative tribunals (e.g. community/problem-solving tribunals; mediation conducted by courts)
12. Participatory justice (restorative justice and consensus-based justice)
13. Allow volunteering in courts

4. Open hearings/trials using social media, TV and/or ICT tools (50%), and
5. Set up/improve a system (e.g., a jury system or a system with people's assessors) to ensure that the public can participate in the judicial process (46.9%) (see Table 9, Appendix 2).

More details of the survey will be discussed in the following section, but it is helpful to note here that local courts in China could use similar methods to collect input from citizens and all stakeholders. By making the court reform process, including the formulation of related plans, transparent, participatory, and collaborative, leaders in Chinese courts can better understand citizens' and stakeholders' needs and set appropriate priorities accordingly. This further sends a strong message that courts at all levels in China are indeed committed to the principles of transparency, participation, and collaboration, as embedded in the court reform plans.

Guiding Cases and Related Subsequent Cases

The above evaluation of "open judiciary" in China, as reflected in the implementation of the system of GCs, reveals how citizens' and their lawyers' inadequate awareness of the latest legal developments, as well as legal actors' limited competence in applying GCs, have limited participation and collaboration in the judicial process, even though much progress has been made toward achieving at least the transparency prong in the court system.

To overcome these challenges, training for legal actors, as well as inclusion of GCs in the syllabus of the National Judicial Examination of China and curricula of law schools are obvious remedial measures. Another measure would be to mandate that, should a party cite a GC, even incorrectly, judges must make explicit reference to the GC and explain whether it applies in the case before them. The SPC has already taken a step toward this direction in its *Detailed Implementing Rules* (2015), which mandates that:

Where a public prosecution organ, a party to a case and his defender, or a litigation agent quotes a Guiding Case as a ground [for the] prosecution (litigation) or defence, the personnel handling the case should, in [providing] the reasons for the adjudication, respond [as to] whether [they] referred to the Guiding Case [in the course of their adjudication] and explain their reasons [for doing so] (Article 11(2) (emphasis added).

This action should be commended for heightening the efficacy and legitimacy of the use of GCs, but the mandate would be clearer if the word "should" is replaced with "must".

None of these measures address the fundamental problems arising from the fact that China's open judiciary initiative is, like other reforms in contemporary China, driven by the ruling Communist Party of China (CPC), with a top-down approach and a political agenda which dictates that only changes that do not compromise the ruling party's governance and leadership are allowed. That this is the case is demonstrated by the *Constitution of the Communist Party of China* (2012), which provides that "the Communist Party of China is the vanguard both of the Chinese working class and of the Chinese people and the Chinese nation. It is the core of leadership for socialism with Chinese characteristics" (General Program). Further, changes can occur unpredictably at the whim of current leaders, whose positions are increasingly less certain in China's ever-changing political climate. In such an environment, legal actors are likely to be guarded before they fully commit to a new reform measure, particularly one seemingly inconsistent with the country's civil law tradition, which many legal actors wrongly believe to have no place for binding precedents, as experts have pointed out (Cohen-Tanugi, 2016; HUANG Huifang, 2014; Iimura, Takabayashi, & Rademacher, 2015; LÜ Tailang, 2016).

In this regard, making the formulation and implementation of court reform plans transparent, participatory, and collaborative helps, but the real, long-range solution is to see that China evolves to be an "open state". The use of the term "open state" to describe traditional open government principles operating in the three branches of government is relatively new (Ozlak, 2013; Valenzuela-Mendoza, 2013), but the essence that it entails—accountability to the public—is not. An "open state" connotes a state in which authorities are accountable to citizens, an overarching goal that this pioneering book seeks to achieve. The authors believe that such accountability can, in turn, be fostered by the new initiatives of open government and open judiciary to capture the principles of transparency, participation, and collaboration. Based on the fact that the term "open government" has already entered into the official diction in China and that the SPC has been, in effect if not in form, pursuing "open judiciary" by prescribing measures consistent with the principles of transparency, participation, and collaboration, the prospect of leveraging these open government and open judiciary efforts to develop an open state in China, a relatively closed society, is good. However, given China's current political landscape, an "open state" would be achieved not from top-down initiatives but through bottom-up momentum generated by all of the open government and open judiciary efforts and a reform agenda that is not seen as closely bundled with political aims.

FUTURE RESEARCH DIRECTIONS

As more reform plans will be formulated in the coming years, future research should focus on how the three principles of transparency, participation, and collaboration are further integrated into the new reform plans and applied in practice. A large-scale empirical analysis of trends in SCs that refer to GCs should also be launched to seize the unprecedented opportunity presented by this new emphasis on using cases to ensure the uniform application of law. The study of Chinese law, especially Chinese law in action and related judicial dynamics, was traditionally reliant on interviews with players on the ground. That approach was obviously limited, but acceptable at a time when the Chinese legal system was completely opaque. Tracking the release of GCs and their use in SCs presents an opportunity for serious scholars to develop a wealth of knowledge about judges' reasoning and related strengths and weaknesses. Recommendations for improvements will be more convincing and clear because they are rooted in publicly available cases, instead of private interviews that are often kept confidential to protect the sources. In addition, beneficial research directions might also include similarities in trends toward openness in the executive and the judiciary to understand the interplay between open government and open judiciary.

Finally, more studies of open judiciary initiatives that have been explored and implemented around the world should be pursued. Driven by this interest, the authors complemented their understanding of China's experience with expertise from developed and developing countries to design the survey described above. Although this is a simple and preliminary step in identifying key factors for promoting open judiciary, the factors identified by respondents from developed societies, developing societies, and China, a developing but relatively closed society, have already revealed interesting similarities and differences.

As mentioned above, the 32 Chinese respondents considered the five most important factors for the development of open judiciary to be:

1. Judicial documents made public (78.1% of the 32 respondents selected this factor);
2. Set up/improve a judicial openness supervision system that enables the public to share comments and suggestions (71.9%),
3. Open registration of cases filed with courts (56.3%),
4. Open hearings/trials using social media, TV and/or ICT tools (50%), and
5. Set up/improve a system (e.g., a jury system or a system with people's assessors) to ensure that the public can participate in the judicial process (46.9%) (see Table 9, Appendix 2).

The fact that three of these factors relate to transparency, two relate to participation, and none relate to collaboration suggests an order of emphasis that is similarly seen in the decreasing number of court reform tasks related to transparency, participation, and collaboration, respectively.

The 55 respondents from developed countries/economies also identified "judicial documents made public" (67.3% of the 55 respondents selected this factor) and "open registration of cases filed with courts" (49.1%) as two of their five most important factors for the development of open judiciary. The other three factors identified by this group were: "open data/statistics on court performance" (54.5%), "use language free of legal jargon (i.e., plain language) in promotional materials designed to foster understanding of decisions and access to justice" (47.3%), and "set up/improve a system for independent disciplinary committees and courts to jointly investigate judges who violate disciplinary rules" (45.5%) (see Table 10, Appendix 2). Interestingly, these three factors were also identified by the 59 respondents from developing countries/economies (excluding mainland China), who also selected two other factors: "improve coordination among different dispute resolution mechanisms to allow all stakeholders to better collaborate with one another" and "collaborative tribunals (e.g., community/problem-solving tribunals; mediation conducted by courts)" (see Table 11, Appendix 2). Both of these factors are related to collaboration.

In order to meaningfully further what we humbly hope is the first step in identifying key factors for developing open judiciary around the world, more theoretical research and empirical studies on the ground in different jurisdictions are necessary.

CONCLUSION

Contrary to conventional wisdom that portrays China as a closed society that leaves no room for openness, the theoretical and empirical studies presented in this chapter show that much has been accomplished in the area of open government, to the extent that this term is officially used and will likely be included in a national guiding document on e-government, the development of which lays a foundation for open government in China. Equally encouraging is the development in the area of open judiciary in the name of promoting *sīfǎ gōngkāi* (judicial openness) which has been broadly used to convey concepts consistent with the principles of transparency, participation, and collaboration. Based on these analyses, the authors believe that the prospect of leveraging China's open government and open judiciary efforts to encourage the development of an open state in the country is positive. Unless major changes happen to fundamentally change China's current course, the country will likely continue pursuing paths towards open government, open judiciary, and, even open state, following its own pace in its adoption of the principles of transparency, participation, and collaboration, in a largely sequential, three-stage process.

China is a country that lacks freedom of the press and other related safeguards, as they are understood in the West, to ensure that citizens have the tools to keep state actors accountable. Given this context, transparency is the first step toward accountability. This is in line with the observations of some scholars that open data in the context of developing countries is the first step toward creating new norms surrounding openness, even if the information initially released does not display a direct link to fostering accountability (Weinstein & Goldstein, 2012). The importance of open data was also emphasized by the respondents from developing countries/economies (excluding mainland China) of our survey. They selected "open data/statistics on court performance" as the most important factor for developing open judiciary (see Table 11, Appendix 2). Once transparency takes root, authorities will gain confidence to move on to encouraging participation and, finally, collaboration.

China is basically following this three-stage approach, as revealed by the *Fourth Court Reform Plan* (2015), in which most of the reform tasks are related to transparency, less to participation, and much less to collaboration. The transparency-first approach is also reflected in a speech delivered by ZHOU Qiang, President of the SPC, who placed much emphasis on the current publication of judgments, stating that this move would help all Chinese judges develop a sense of responsibility, inspiring sophisticated judges, and motivating their less sophisticated counterparts (LI Hong, 2013). Indeed, the importance of making judicial documents public was emphasized by the mainland Chinese respondents of our survey. They selected this as the most important factor for developing open judiciary (see Table 9, Appendix 2).

The progress made by China in its incremental efforts in promoting transparency, participation, and collaboration demonstrates to other closed societies in the world that transparency could be an effective, first step to reach the high mark of open judiciary.

ACKNOWLEDGMENT

The authors thank the members of the China Guiding Cases Project of Stanford Law School for their significant contributions to this chapter, most notably: Minmin Zhang, Oma Lee, Wenjie Ou, James Yuan, Luping Zhang, and Richard Jiang for their drafting and research assistance, and Ivan Cardillo, Joseph Incalcaterra, Mengnan Li, Wen Ou, Jeremy Schlosser, Troy Song, Matthew Wells, Qin Xiao, Jeff Yau, Cynthia Ye, Pei Zhang, Shiyue Zhang, Tian Zhang, and Yifan Zhou for their assistance analyzing subsequent cases that reference Guiding Cases. These contributions were critical to the authors' discussion of issues related to the implementation of open judiciary in China. The information and views set out in the book chapter are the responsibility of the authors and do not necessarily reflect the work or views of the China Guiding Cases Project of Stanford Law School.

REFERENCES

Amendment to the Constitution of the People's Republic of China. (1999) (中华人民共和国宪法修正案(1999年)), passed and issued on and effective as of March 15, 1999. Retrieved from http://www.npc.gov.cn/wxzl/wxzl/2000-12/10/content_7075.htm

Chapman, R. A., & Hunt, M. (1987). *Open government. A study of the prospects of open government within the limitations of the British political system*. London: Routledge.

Ran, Liu, & Chen. (2013). Commentary on the progress of implementing the U.S. Open Government Initiative in the Web 2.0 environment (Web2.0环境下美国开放政府计划实践进展评述). *Information and Documentation Services*, *6*, 89–95.

Civil Procedure Law of the People's Republic of China (中华人民共和国民事诉讼法), passed, issued on, and effective as of April 9, 1991, subsequently amended in 2007 and 2012. Retrieved from http://www.npc.gov.cn/wxzl/wxzl/2000-12/05/content_4551.htm

Cohen-Tanugi, L. (2016). Case law in a legal system without binding precedent: The French example? *Stanford Law School China Guiding Cases Project: Guiding Cases Commentaries*. Retrieved from http://cgc.law.stanford.edu/commentaries/16-Laurent-Cohen-Tanugi

Conley, A., Datta, A., Nissenbaum, H., & Sharma, D. (2012). Sustaining privacy and open justice in the transition to online court records: A multidisciplinary inquiry. *Maryland Law Review (Baltimore, Md.)*, *71*(3), 772–847.

Constitution of the People's Republic of China (中华人民共和国宪法), passed and issued on December 4, 1982, effective as of Dec. 4, 1982, subsequently amended in 1988, 1992, 1999, and 2004. Retrieved from http://www.npc.gov.cn/wxzl/wxzl/2000-12/06/content_4421.htm

Criminal Procedure Law of the People's Republic of China (中华人民共和国刑事诉讼法), passed on July 1, 1979, issued on July 7, 1979, effective as of January 1, 1980, subsequently amended in 1996 and 2012. Retrieved from http://www.npc.gov.cn/wxzl/wxzl/2000-12/06/content_4373.htm

Decision of the CPC Central Committee on Major Issues Concerning Comprehensively Deepening Reforms. (中共中央关于全面深化改革若干重大问题的决定), passed by the Eighteenth CPC Central Committee on November 12, 2013. Retrieved from http://cpc.people.com.cn/n/2013/1115/c64094-23559163.html

Decision of the CPC Central Committee on Several Major Issues Pertaining to Comprehensively Promoting the Rule of Law. (中共中央关于全面推进依法治国若干重大问题的决定), passed by the Eighteenth CPC Central Committee on October 23, 2014. Retrieved from http://cpc.people.com.cn/n/2014/1029/c64387-25927606.html

Decision of the Supreme People's Court on Further Strengthening the Basic Construction of People's Courts (最高人民法院关于进一步加强人民法院基层建设的决定), issued by the Supreme People's Court October 21, 2014. Retrieved from http://www.pkulaw.com/fulltext_form.aspx?Db=chl&Gid=108953&keyword=关于进一步加强人民法院基层建设的决定&EncodingName=&Search_Mode=accurate.

Detailed Implementing Rules on the. "Provisions of the Supreme People's Court Concerning Work on Case Guidance" (〈最高人民法院关于案例指导工作的规定〉实施细则), passed by the Adjudication Committee of the Supreme People's Court on April 27, 2015, issued on and effective as of May 13, 2015. (Stanford Law School China Guiding Cases Project, English Guiding Cases Rules, June 12, 2015 Edition). Retrieved from http://cgc.law.stanford.edu/guiding-cases-rules/20150513-english/

Fesler, J. W., & Kettl, D. F. (1996). *The politics of the administrative process*. Chatham, NJ: Chatham House Publishers, Inc.

Five-Year Reform Plan of the People's Court (人民法院五年改革纲要), issued by the Supreme People's Court on October 20, 1999. Retrieved from http://www.chinacourt.org/article/detail/2013/04/id/941425.shtml

Gechlik, M. (2015). *Stanford Law School China Guiding Cases Project:* Guiding Cases *Analytics*™, Issue no. 4. Retrieved from http://cgc.law.stanford.edu/guiding-cases-analytics/

Gechlik, M., Philips, D., & Lee, O. (2014). Survey of judges in China (2013-2014). *Stanford Law School China Guiding Cases Project: Guiding Cases Surveys™, Issue No. 1*. Retrieved from http://cgc.law.stanford.edu/guiding-cases-surveys

Gechlik, M., Zhang, M., & Ye, L. (2016). Cumulative analysis of all subsequent cases referring to Guiding Cases in China (2014 Q1-2015 Q4). *Stanford Law School China Guiding Cases Project: Guiding Cases Surveys™, Issue No. 2*. Retrieved from http://cgc.law.stanford.edu/guiding-cases-surveys

Guiding Opinion of the General Office of the State Council on the Promotion of Coordinated Development of E-Government Affairs. (国务院办公厅关于促进电子政务协调发展的指导意见), issued by the General Office of the State Council on and effective as of November 26, 2014. Retrieved from http://www.yueyang.gov.cn/zcfg2/content_437921.html

Guiding Opinion of the National Informatization Leading Group on the Development of E-Government Affairs in China. (国家信息化领导小组关于我国电子政务建设的指导意见), passed by the National Informatization Leading Group and issued by the General Office of the CPC Central Committee and the General Office of the State Council on August 5, 2002. Retrieved from http://www.nacao.org.cn/publish/main/77/2009/20090114135526965360659/20090114135526965360659_.html

Hengmin, L. I. (2014). Canada's open government policy study. *Technological Development of Enterprise*, *5*, 143–144.

Hongyu, W. C. (2016, February 3). Per-capita GDP of 10 Chinese provinces exceed $10,000 mark. *People's Daily Online*. Retrieved from http://en.people.cn/n3/2016/0203/c98649-9013481.html

HUANG. Huifang (黄蕙芳). (2014). Taiwan's criminal case system and the development direction of the guiding cases system in the People's Republic of China (台湾刑事案例制度与中华人民共和国指导性案例制度的发展方向). *Stanford Law School China Guiding Cases Project: Guiding Cases Commentaries*. Retrieved from http://cgc.law.stanford.edu/commentaries/11-huang-huifang

Iimura, T., Takabayashi, R., & Rademacher, C. (2015). The binding nature of court decisions in Japan's civil law system. *Stanford Law School China Guiding Cases Project: Guiding Cases Commentaries*. Retrieved from https://cgc.law.stanford.edu/commentaries/14-Iimura-Takabayashi-Rademacher

Interim Regulation of Wuhan Municipality on Open Government Information (武汉市政府信息公开暂行规定, passed by the Wuhan Municipal Government on May 17, 2004, issued on May 31, 2004, effective as of July 1, 2004. Retrieved from http://www.hangzhou.gov.cn/main/zfxxgk/zfxxgd.shtml

Interpretation of the Supreme People's Court on Several Issues Concerning Judicial Compensation in Civil and Administrative Litigation (最高人民法院关于民事、行政诉讼中司法赔偿若干问题的解释), issued by the Adjudication Committee of the Supreme People's Court on September 16, 2000, effective as of September 21, 2000. Retrieved from http://www.law-lib.com/law/law_view.asp?id=155

Jiménez-Gómez, C. E. (2014). *Justicia Abierta: transparencia y proximidad de la justicia en el actual contexto de Open Government*. Barcelona, Barcelona, España: Centro de Estudios Jurídicos y Formación Especializada, Generalidad de Cataluña.

Johnes, L. R., & Thompson, F. (1999). *Public management renewal for the twenty-first century*. Stamford, CT: Jai Press, Inc.

Li, J. (李健). (2011, September 9). Two dimensions of judicial openness (司法公开的两种维度). *People's Court Daily (人民法院报)*, 1. Retrieved from http://rmfyb.chinacourt.org/paper/html/2011-09/09/content_33174.htm

Li, Y. (2012). Putting the U.S. National Archives and Records Administration's "Open Government Initiative" into perspective. *China Files*, *11*, 55–56.

Li, H. (黎虹). (2013, November 27). Build strong foundations for judicial openness to promote fairness and establish public trust (筑牢司法公开的基石 以公开促公正 以公开树公信). www.ChinaCourt.org*(中国法院网讯)*. Retrieved from http://www.chinacourt.org/article/detail/2013/11/id/1151559.shtml

ZhuLi., (2014). Government 2.0, open government, and construction of service-oriented government (政府2.0、开放式政府与服务型政府建设). *The Journal of Shanghai Administration Institute*, *3*, 59–66.

Liu, X., & Shi, G. (刘晓鹏、石国胜). (2008, June 23). Wang Shengjun suggests during the national meeting of presidents of higher courts: Satisfy the people's judicial needs to the largest extent (王胜俊在全国高级法院院长会议上提出:最大限度地满足人民群众司法需求). *People's Daily (人民)*. Retrieved from http://paper.people.com.cn/rmrb/html/2008-06/23/nw.D110000renmrb_20080623_3-04.htm

Lu. (2016). Review of Taiwan's Precedent System and Brief Discussion of Mainland China's Case Guidance System. *Stanford Law School China Guiding Cases Project: Guiding Cases Commentaries.* Retrieved from http://cgc.law.stanford.edu/commentaries/15-lü-tailang

Luo., (2014). Overseas open government data plan: Progress and implications. *Information Studies: Theory and Application*, *12*, 138–144.

WangMa. , 2002). Reengineering government in the view of seamless government theory. *Journal of Socialist Theory Guide*, *12*, 27–29.

Memorandum on Transparency and Open Government. (2009, January21). 74. *Federal Register*, *4685*. Retrieved from https://www.whitehouse.gov/the_press_office/TransparencyandOpenGovernment

Meng., (2005). On the relationship between government re-engineering in the information age and e-government. *Journal of Chinese Academy of Governance*, *1*, 37–39.

National Informatization Development Strategy. (2006–2020) (2006–2020 年国家信息化发展战略), prepared by the National Informatization Leading Group and issued by the General Office of the CPC Central Committee and the General Office of the State Council on March 19, 2006. Retrieved from http://www.gov.cn/gongbao/content/2006/content_315999.htm

Notice Concerning Speeding Up the Implementation of Work Related to the Information-for-Citizens Project (关于加快实施信息惠民工程有关工作的通知), issued by the National Development and Reform Commission et al. on and effective as of January 9, 2014. Retrieved from http://www.gov.cn/gzdt/2014-01/15/content_2567048.htm

Notice of the Supreme People's Court and the Ministry of Justice on the Issuance of the Speech by Comrades Xiao Yang, Wu Aiying, and Hao Chiyong during the National People's Mediation Work Conference(最高人民法院、司法部关于印发肖扬同志和吴爱英、郝赤勇同志在全国人民调解工作会议上的讲话的通知), issued by the Supreme People's Court and the Ministry of Justice on July 16, 2007. Retrieved from http://www.pkulaw.cn/fulltext_form.aspx?Db=chl&Gid=110447

Open Government Directive: Memorandum for the Heads of Executive Departments and Agencies. (2009, December 8). Retrieved from https://www.whitehouse.gov/open/documents/open-government-directive

Opinion of the Supreme People's Court on Further Improving the Communication of Public Opinions (最高人民法院关于进一步加强民意沟通工作的意见), issued by the Supreme People's Court on and effective as of April 13, 2009. Retrieved from http://www.chinalaw.gov.cn/article/fgkd/xfg/sfwj/201012/20101200330542.shtml

Osborne, D., & Plastrik, P. (1998). *Banishing bureaucracy: Strategies for reinventing government*. New York, NY: Plume.

Oszlak, O. (2013). Estado Abierto: Hacia un nuevo paradigma de gestión pública.*XVIII Congreso Internacional del CLAD.*Montevideo: CLAD.

Overall Framework for National E-Government Affairs. (国家电子政务总体框架), adopted by the National Informatization Leading Group on March 19, 2006. Retrieved from http://xxhs.miit.gov.cn/n11293472/n11295327/n11297172/11800751.html

Parks, W. (1957). The open government principle: Applying the right to know under the Constitution. *The George Washington Law Review*, *26*(1), 1–77.

Peng, B. (彭波). (2013, January 8). XI Jinping issues important instructions on properly carrying out political and legal work in a new situation, emphasizing the needs to meet the People's new expectations for public safety, judicial fairness, and rights protection, to promote the development of a safe China with rule of law and excellent team-building, to strive to make people feel fairness and justice in every judicial case (习近平就做好新形势下政法工作作出重要指示强调,顺应人民对公共安全司法公正权益保障的新期待,全力推进平安中国法治中国过硬队伍建设,努力让人民群众在每一个司法案件中都能感受到公平正义). *People's Daily (*人民日报*)*. Retrieved from http://paper.people.com.cn/rmrb/html/2013-01/08/nw.D110000renmrb_20130108_3-01.htm

Provisions of the Supreme People's Court Concerning Work on Case Guidance (最高人民法院关于案例指导工作的规定), passed by the Adjudication Committee of the Supreme People's Court on November 15, 2010, issued on and effective as of November 26, 2010. (Stanford Law School China Guiding Cases Project, English Guiding Cases Rules, June 12, 2015 Edition). Retrieved from http://cgc.law.stanford.edu/guiding-cases-rules/20101126-english/

Provisions of the Supreme People's Court on the Broadcasting of Live or Recorded Trial Activities by People's Courts (最高人民法院关于人民法院直播录播庭审活动的规定)), passed by the Adjudication Committee of the Supreme People's Court on November 8, 2010, issued on and effective as of November 21, 2010. Retrieved from http://yqcqfy.chinacourt.org/article/detail/2014/01/id/1171568.shtml

Provisions of the Supreme People's Court on the Publication of Adjudication Documents on the Internet (最高人民法院关于人民法院在互联网公布裁判文书的规定), passed by the Adjudication Committee of the Supreme People's Court on November 13, 2013, issued on November 21, 2013, effective as of January 1, 2014. Retrieved from http://www.chinacourt.org/law/detail/2013/11/id/147242.shtml

Regulation of Chengdu Municipality on Open Government Information (成都市政府信息公开规定), passed by the Chengdu Municipal Government on March 4, 2004, issued on March 29, 2004, effective as of May 1, 2004. Retrieved from http://www.chengdu.gov.cn/wenjian/detail.jsp?id=nyaEXXXWnsgW4P2lQdK9

Regulation of Guangzhou Municipality on Open Government Information (广州市政府信息公开规定), passed by the Guangzhou Municipal Government, issued on November 6, 2002, effective as of January 1, 2003. Retrieved from http://www.gz.gov.cn/gzgov/s8263/200211/595736.shtml

Regulation of Hangzhou Municipality on Open Government Information (杭州市政府信息公开规定), passed by the Hangzhou Municipal Government on April 15, 2004, issued on April 27, 2004, effective as of October 1, 2004. Retrieved from http://www.hangzhou.gov.cn/main/zfxxgk/zfxxgd.shtml

Regulation of Shanghai Municipality on Open Government Information (上海市政府信息公开规定), passed by the Shanghai Municipal Government, issued on January 20, 2004, effective as of May 1, 2004, expired on May 1, 2008. Retrieved from http://www.shanghai.gov.cn/shanghai/node2314/node12959/node12967/userobject21ai28762.htm

Regulation of the People's Republic of China on Open Government Information (中华人民共和国政府信息公开条例), passed by the State Council on January 17, 2007, issued on April 5, 2007, effective as of May 1, 2008. Retrieved from http://www.gov.cn/zwgk/2007-04/24/content_592937.htm

Wu, Zheng, Mei,Ren., (2014). National Science Foundation (NSF) information disclosure and its implications for China – using the "Open Government Data Program" (OGDP) as a research focus (美国国家科学基金会 (NSF)信息公开及对中国的启示——以开放政府指令计划 (OGDP)为研究对象). *Science and Technology Progress and Policy*, *7*, 94–99.

Several Opinions of the Supreme People's Court on Further Strengthening the Construction of the People's Courts'. "Case Registration and Letters-and-Visits Window" (Trial Implementation) (最高人民法院关于进一步加强人民法院"立案信访窗口"建设的若干意见(试行)), issued by the Supreme People's Court on December 25, 2009. Retrieved from http://www.chinalaw.gov.cn/article/fgkd/xfg/sfwj/201012/20101200330536.shtml

Several Opinions of the Supreme People's Court on Making Enforcement Processes of People's Courts Open) (最高人民法院关于人民法院执行流程公开的若干意见), issued by the Supreme People's Court on September 3, 2014. Retrieved from http://www.e-gov.org.cn/ziliaoku/news004/201503/155170.html

Several Opinions of the Supreme People's Court on the Construction of Three Major Platforms to Promote Judicial Openness (最高人民法院关于推进司法公开三大平台建设的若干意见), issued by the Supreme People's Court on November 21, 2013. Retrieved from http://www.chinacourt.org/article/detail/2013/11/id/1152225.shtml

Several Provisions of the Supreme People's Court on Enforcing the Property Portion of A Criminal Judgment or Ruling (最高人民法院关于刑事裁判涉财产部分执行的若干规定), passed by the Adjudication Committee of Supreme People Court on September 1, 2014, issued on October 30, 2014, effective as of November 6, 2014. Retrieved from http://www.chinacourt.org/law/detail/2014/10/id/148014.shtml

Several Provisions of the Supreme People's Court on Open Enforcement [Work] of People's Court (最高人民法院关于人民法院执行公开的若干规定), issued by the Supreme People's Court on December 23, 2006, effective as of January 1, 2007. Retrieved from http://www.court.gov.cn/shenpan-xiangqing-718.html

Several Provisions of the Supreme People's Court on the People's Courts' Acceptance of Public Opinion-based Supervision by the News Media (最高人民法院关于人民法院接受新闻媒体舆论监督的若干规定), issued by the Supreme People's Court on and effective as of December 8, 2009. Retrieved from http://www.chinalaw.gov.cn/article/fgkd/xfg/sfwj/201012/20101200330480.shtml

Six Provisions of the Supreme People's Court on Judicial Openness (最高人民法院关于司法公开的六项规定), issued by the Supreme People's Court on and effective as of December 8, 2009. Retrieved from http://www.chinalaw.gov.cn/article/fgkd/xfg/sfwj/201012/20101200330480.shtml

Stanford Law School China Guiding Cases Project. Shanghai Cunliang Trading Co., Ltd. v. JIANG Zhidong, WANG Weiming et al., a sale and purchase contract dispute, *English Guiding Case (EGC9)* (Nov. 9, 2012 Edition). Retrieved from http://cgc.law.stanford.edu/guiding-cases/guiding-case-9

Stanford Law School China Guiding Cases Project. XCMG Construction Machinery Co., Ltd. v. Chengdu Chuanjiao Industry and Trade Co., Ltd. et al., a sale and purchase contract dispute, *English Guiding Case (EGC15)* (Apr. 10, 2013 Edition). Retrieved from http://cgc.law.stanford.edu/guiding-cases/guiding-case-15

Stanford Law School China Guiding Cases Project. RONG Baoying v. WANG Yang and Alltrust Insurance Co., a motor vehicle traffic accident liability dispute, *English Guiding Case (EGC24)* (Apr. 4, 2014 Edition). Retrieved from http://cgc.law.stanford.edu/guiding-cases/guiding-case-24

Syllabus for the National Judicial Examination in 2015 (2015年国家司法考试大纲), formulated by the Ministry of Justice on May 1, 2015.

The Opinion of the Supreme People's Court Concerning Comprehensively Deepening the Reform of the People's Court—The Fourth Five-Year Reform Plan of the People's Court. (2014-2018) (最高人民法院关于全面深化人民法院改革的意见—人民法院第四个五年改革纲要(2014-2018)), issued by the Supreme People's Court on February 4, 2015. Retrieved from http://www.court.gov.cn/zixun-xiangqing-13520.html

The Second Five-Year People's Court Reform Plan. (2004-2008) (人民法院第二个五年改革纲要(2004-2008)), issued by the Supreme People's Court on and effective as of October 26, 2005. Retrieved from http://www.chinalaw.gov.cn/article/fgkd/xfg/sfwj/200904/20090400132177.shtml

The State Council Information Office. (国务院新闻办公室). (2015, March 10). The SPC Holds Conference to Release the "Judicial Openness of China's Courts" (White Paper) (最高法举行中国法院的司法公开(白皮书)发布会). Retrieved from http://www.scio.gov.cn/xwfbh/qyxwfbh/Document/1396210/1396210.htm

The Third Five-Year People's Court Reform Plan. (2009-2013) (人民法院第三个五年改革纲要(2009-2013)), issued by the Supreme People's Court on and effective as of March 17, 2009. Retrieved from http://www.chinalaw.gov.cn/article/fgkd/xfg/sfwj/201012/20101200330558.shtml

The "Twelfth Five-Year" Plan of National E-Government Affairs (国家电子政务"十二五"规划), issued by the Ministry of Industry and Information Technology on December 12, 2011. Retrieved from http://www.miit.gov.cn/n11293472/n11295327/n11297217/14562026.html

Valenzuela-Mendoza, R. (2013). Delimitar gobierno abierto para ampliar la colaboración con una sociedad más abierta. *Revista Estado*. *Gobierno y Gestión Pública*, *21*, 127–158.

Wang. (王喜文). (2012, June 21). The United States' "Open Government Initiative" study (美国"开放政府计划"研究). *China Economic Net (*中国经济网*)*. Retrieved from http://intl.ce.cn/specials/zxgjzh/201206/12/t20120612_23399833.shtml

Wang, , Zhou,, , & Li., (2002). An untechnical analysis of reengineering government and e-government. *Reform of Economic System*, *1*, 85–87.

Wang,, C. (2006). On opening government. *Henan Social Sciences*, *4*, 5–8.

Wang, Y. (2014). Under rule of law: Open government and public participation. *Scientific Socialism*, *4*, 75–78.

Weinstein, J., & Goldstein, J. (2012). The benefits of a big tent: Opening up government in developing countries. *UCLA Law Review Discourse*, *60*, 38–48.

Work Regulation of the Supreme People's Court on Specially Engaged Supervisors (Trial Implementation) (最高人民法院特约监督员工作条例(试行)), passed by the Supreme People's Court, issued on and effective as of October 12, 2009. Retrieved from http://www.chinalaw.gov.cn/article/fgkd/xfg/sfwj/201012/20101200330479.shtml

Work Regulation of the Supreme People's Court on Specially Invited Counselors (最高人民法院特邀咨询员工作条例)), passed by the Supreme People's Court, issued on and effective as of May 31, 2009. Retrieved from http://www.chinalaw.gov.cn/article/fgkd/xfg/sfwj/201012/20101200330544.shtml

Xiao, J. (肖金明). (2005). Administrative licensing system, as well as open government and government credibility (行政许可法制与开放政府、信用政府). China Public Administration (中国行政管理), 4, 91-95.

Xiao, Y. (肖扬). (2007). Constructing a fair, efficient, and authoritative civil trial system to provide judicial safeguards in the building of a socialist and harmonious society – speech given at the Seventh National Civil Trial Work Conference (建设公正高效权威的民事审判制度为构建社会主义和谐社会提供有力司法保障—在第七次全国民事审判工作会议上的讲话). *China Trial (中国审判), 2*, 4-8.

Xiaoming, H. U. (2015). From open government information to open government data. *E-Government*, *1*, 67–72.

Yang, , & Wang., (2015). Opportunities and challenges facing China's E-Government "Thirteenth Five-Year" Period. *E-Government*, *4*, 11–17.

Yang, Zhang, & Wang. (杨成、张雨、王泽). (2013, July 4). Zhou Qiang: Promoting impartiality by judicial openness: Openness is the rule, non-openness is the exception (周强:以司法公开促进公正,公开是原则不公开是例外). *People's Daily (人民日报)*. Retrieved from http://legal.people.com.cn/n/2013/0704/c42510-22083161.html

Zhang, . (2005). Toward alternative delivery systems of public gods and services: A critical review of reinventing government movements. *Journal of Renmin University of China*, *5*, 111–117.

Zhang, . (2014). Open government theory. *Journal of Renmin University of China*, *3*, 79–89.

Zhang & Wang. (2013). The current situation and outlook of open justice in China. *China Legal Science*, *1*, 131–143.

Zhenming, C. H. E. N. (2002). Reengineering government: Strategies and tactics of public department management reform. *Southeast Academic Research*, *5*, 16–22.

Zhou., (2010). Open government and government data disclosure strategy[Social Science Edition]. *Journal of Guangzhou University*, *10*, 11–16.

KEY TERMS AND DEFINITIONS

Guiding Cases: Chinese court judgments selected and re-issued by the Supreme People's Court of China ("SPC") due to their representative nature and utility in providing guidance for lower courts in adjudicating similar cases. The system for selecting guiding cases was established in November 2010 with the SPC's issuance of the *Provisions of the Supreme People's Court Concerning Work on Case Guidance* (2010).

Made Public (Adjudication Affairs): A reform objective stated in the *Fourth Court Reform Plan* (2015) committing the Chinese courts to disclosing documents such as court statistics related to adjudication.

Made Public (Documents): A reform objective stated in the *Fourth Court Reform Plan* (2015) committing the Chinese courts to disclosing adjudication documents.

Open Case Registration: A reform objective stated in the *Fourth Court Reform Plan* (2015) that requires courts to inform litigants of basic rights, obligations, and pertinent details of litigation as well as improved sites where parties can access information regarding their pending case.

Open Enforcement: A reform objective stated in the *Fourth Court Reform Plan* (2015) and first referenced in *Several Provisions of the Supreme People's Court on Open Enforcement [Work] of People's Courts* (2006) that put the concept within the domain of *sīfǎ gōngkāi.*

Open Government: This term dates to post-World War II, as the United States and similar jurisdictions began to act against the creation of state secrets, and gradually increasing until the emergence of legislation promoting access to government documents, such as the American Freedom of Information Act (FOIA) (Chapman & Hunt, 2006; Parks, 1957; Yu & Robinson, 2012) and, later, the E-Government Act of 2002 (Conley et al., 2012). We adopt the modern definition of open government in this chapter, namely, an open government is characterized by the three principles of focus put forward in the Obama administration's *Memorandum on Transparency and Open Government* (2009)—transparency, participation, and collaboration.

Open Judiciary: A term used in this chapter to express a broader concept that applies the principles of participation, collaboration, and transparency to the judiciary (Jiménez-Gómez, 2014) as distinct from the narrower and procedurally- and common-law focused "open justice" (Conley et al., 2012).

Open State: In the context of this chapter, the term "open state" not only includes a nation where modern open government principles operating in all three branches of government, but one in which a basic culture of openness exists, enabling citizens to hold authorities accountable.

Open Trials: A reform objective stated in the *Fourth Court Reform Plan* (2015) committing the Chinese courts to developing websites where parties can track the progress of their cases and setting up a system for broadcasting cases via audio-visual recordings.

Public Hearings: A reform objective stated in the *Fourth Court Reform Plan* (2015) committing the Chinese courts to holding public trials for cases that are outside of regular trial proceedings, including applications for retrials and applications involving enforcement disputes.

Sīfǎ Gōngkāi (Judicial Openness): The evolving concept of "open judiciary" as it exists in China at the time of this chapter's publication. This term has evolved from its literal meaning of "judicial openness" to include initiatives as various as open case registration, open trials, open enforcement, public hearings, and making documents and adjudication affairs public.

APPENDIX 1: SUBSEQUENT CASE ANALYSIS

Table 6. Subsequent cases that explicitly reference Guiding Case Nos. 1-45

GC No.	Case Name (Translated by the CGCP)	Case Type	Expl. Ref.
1	Shanghai Centaline Property Consultants Limited v. TAO Dehua	An Intermediation Contract Dispute	6
2	WU Mei v. Meishan Xicheng Paper Co., Ltd. of Sichuan Province	A Sale and Purchase Contract Dispute	3
3	PAN Yumei and CHEN Ning	A Bribe-Accepting Case	0
4	WANG Zhicai	An Intentional Homicide Case	0
5	Luwei (Fujian) Salt Industry Import and Export Co., Ltd. Suzhou Branch v. The Salt Administration Bureau of Suzhou Municipality, Jiangsu Province	A Salt Industry Administrative Penalty Case	11
6	HUANG Zefu, HE Boqiong, and HE Yi v. The Jintang Administration for Industry and Commerce of Chengdu Municipality, Sichuan Province	An Administrative Penalty Case	2
7	Mudanjiang Municipality Hongge Construction and Installation Co., Ltd. v. Mudanjiang Municipality Hualong Real Estate Development Co., Ltd. and ZHANG Jizeng	A Construction Project Contract Dispute	0
8	LIN Fangqing v. Changshu Kailai Industry Co., Ltd. and DAI Xiaoming	A Corporate Dissolution Dispute	8
9	Shanghai Cunliang Trading Co., Ltd. v. JIANG Zhidong, WANG Weiming et al.	A Sale and Purchase Contract Dispute	18
10	LI Jianjun v. Shanghai Jiapower Environment Protection Science and Technology Co., Ltd.	A Corporate Resolution Revocation Dispute	3
11	YANG Yanhu et al.	A Graft Case	1
12	LI Fei	An Intentional Homicide Case	0
13	WANG Zhaocheng et al.	An Illegal Trading and Storage of Hazardous Substances Case	1
14	A certain DONG and a certain SONG	A Robbery Case	4
15	XCMG Construction Machinery Co., Ltd. v. Chengdu Chuanjiao Industry and Trade Co., Ltd. et al.	A Sale and Purchase Contract Dispute	21
16	China Shipping Development Co., Ltd. Tramp Company	A Case of an Application for the Establishment of a Limitation of Liability Fund for Maritime Claims	0
17	ZHANG Li v. Beijing Heli Huatong Automobile Service Co., Ltd.	A Sale and Purchase Contract Dispute	2
18	ZTE (Hangzhou) Company Limited v. WANG Peng	A Labor Contract Dispute	0
19	ZHAO Chunming et al. v. The Automobile Transport Company of Fushan District, Yantai Municipality, WEI Deping, et al.	A Motor Vehicle Traffic Accident Liability Dispute	10
20	Shenzhen Siruiman Fine Chemicals Co., Ltd. v. Shenzhen Kengzi Water Supply Co., Ltd. And Shenzhen Kangtailan Water Treatment Equipment Co., Ltd.	An Invention Patent Infringement Dispute	0
21	Inner Mongolia Qiushi Real Estate Development Limited Liability Company v. The Civil Air Defense Office of Hohhot Municipality	A Civil Defense Administrative Levy Case	1
22	WEI Yonggao and CHEN Shouzhi v. The People's Government of Lai'an County	A Case About a Reply to Recover Land-Use Rights	4
23	SUN Yinshan v. Nanjing Auchan Hypermarket Co., Ltd. Jiangning Store	A Sale and Purchase Contract Dispute	3
24	RONG Baoying v. WANG Yang and Alltrust Insurance Co., Ltd. Jiangyin Branch	A Motor Vehicle Traffic Accident Liability Dispute	76

continued on following page

Table 6. Continued

GC No.	Case Name (Translated by the CGCP)	Case Type	Expl. Ref.
25	Huatai Property & Casualty Insurance Co., Ltd. Beijing Branch v. LI Zhigui and Zhangjiakou Subbranch of Tianan Property Insurance Company Limited of China Hebei Provincial Branch	An Insurer's Subrogation Right Dispute	1
26	LI Jianxiong v. Department of Transport of Guangdong Province	A Case About Open Government Information	1
27	ZANG Jinquan et al.	A Theft and Fraud Case	0
28	HU Kejin	A Case of a Refusal to Pay Remuneration	0
29	Tianjin China Youth Travel Service v. Tianjin Guoqing International Travel Agency	A Dispute over an Unauthorized Use of Another Enterprise's Name	0
30	LAN Jianjun and Hangzhou Suremoov Automotive Technology Company Limited v. Tianjin Xiaomuzhi Automobile Maintenance and Repair Services Co., Ltd. et al.	A Trademark Infringement and Unfair Competition Dispute	0
31	Jiangsu Weilun Shipping Co., Ltd. v. Miranda Rose Limited	A Ship Collision Damages Dispute	0
32	A certain ZHANG and a certain JIN	A Dangerous Driving Case	0
33	Cargill International S.A. v. Fujian Jinshi Vegetable Oil Producing Co., Limited et al.	A Dispute over Contracts Affirmed to be Invalid	0
34	Application by LI Xiaoling and LI Pengyu for Enforcement against Xiamen Marine Industry (Group) Co., Ltd. and Xiamen Marine Industry Controlling Corporation	An Enforcement Reconsideration Case	2
35	Guangdong Longzheng Investment Development Co., Ltd. and Guangdong Jingmao Auction Co., Ltd.	An Enforcement Reconsideration Case on an Entrusted Auction	0
36	Zhongtou Credit Guarantee Co., Ltd. and Haitong Securities Co., Ltd. et al.	An Enforcement Reconsideration Case on a Dispute over the Rights and Interests in Securities	0
37	Shanghai Jwell Machinery Co., Ltd. and Retech Aktiengesellschaft, Switzerland	An Enforcement Reconsideration Case on an Arbitral Award	0
38	TIAN Yong v. The University of Science and Technology Beijing	A Case of a Refusal to Award a Graduation Certificate and a Degree Certificate	0
39	HE Xiaoqiang v. Huazhong University of Science and Technology	A Case of a Refusal to Confer a Degree	0
40	SUN Lixing v. The Labor and Personnel Bureau of Tianjin New Technology Industrial Park	A Work-Related Injuries Determination Case	0
41	XUAN Yicheng et al. v. Bureau of Land and Resources of Quzhou Municipality, Zhejiang Province	A Case of a Recovery of the Rights to Use State-Owned Land	2
42	ZHU Hongwei	A Case of an Application for Compensation for Arrest without a Finding of Guilt	0
43	Haikou Binhai Avenue (Tianfu Hotel) Securities Business Department of Guotai Junan Securities Co., Ltd.	A Case of an Application for Compensation for Erroneous Enforcement	0
44	BU Xinguang	A Case of an Application for Compensation for Illegal Criminal Recovery	0
45	Beijing Baidu Netcom Science and Technology Co., Ltd. v. Qingdao Aoshang Network Technology Co., Ltd. et al.	An Unfair Competition Dispute	1

APPENDIX 2: SURVEY ANALYSIS

Table 7. Survey respondents; developed countries/economies

Developed Countries/Economies	No. of Respondents (55 in Total)	% of Total
Argentina	6	10.9%
Canada	3	5.5%
Greece	1	1.8%
Hong Kong	3	5.5%
Italy	1	1.8%
Netherlands	2	3.6%
Norway	1	1.8%
Poland	1	1.8%
Portugal	1	1.8%
Spain	21	38.2%
Taiwan	3	5.5%
United Kingdom	1	1.8%
United States	11	20.0%
	55	100.0%

Table 8. Survey respondents; developing countries/economies

Developing Countries/Economies	No. of Respondents (91 in Total)	% of Total
Brazil	1	1.1%
Colombia	3	3.3%
Costa Rica	39	42.9%
Cuba	1	1.1%
Ecuador	1	1.1%
Egypt	1	1.1%
El Salvador	3	3.3%
Macedonia	1	1.1%
Mainland China	32	35.2%
Mexico	7	7.7%
Peru	1	1.1%
Tunisia	1	1.1%
	91	100.0%

Table 9. Mainland China responses

Factors that 32 Respondents from Mainland China Consider to Be Most Important to the Development of Open Judiciary	No. of Responses	Respondents (%)
(d) Judicial documents made public	25	78.1%
(g) Set up/improve a judicial openness supervision system that enables the public to share comments and suggestions	23	71.9%
(a) Open registration of cases filed with courts	18	56.3%
(b) Open hearings/trials using social media, TV and/or ICT tools	16	50.0%
(h) Set up/improve a system (e.g., a jury system or a system with people's assessors) to ensure that the public can participate in the judicial process	15	46.9%
(c) Open enforcement of judgments	13	40.6%
(i) Set up/improve a system for independent disciplinary committees and courts to jointly investigate judges who violate disciplinary rules	13	40.6%
(f) Use language free of legal jargon (i.e. plain language) in promotional materials designed to foster understanding of decisions and access to justice	11	34.4%
(e) Open data/statistics on court performance	10	31.3%
(j) Improve coordination among different dispute resolution mechanisms to allow all stakeholders to better collaborate with one another	6	18.8%
(l) Participatory justice (restorative justice and consensus-based justice)	5	15.6%
(k) Collaborative tribunals (e.g. community/problem-solving tribunals; mediation conducted by courts)	4	12.5%
(m) Allow volunteering in courts	1	3.1%

Table 10. Developed countries/economies responses

Factors that 55 Respondents from Developed Countries/Economies Consider to Be Most Important to the Development of Open Judiciary	No. of Responses	Respondents (%)
(d) Judicial documents made public	37	67.3%
(e) Open data/statistics on court performance	30	54.5%
(a) Open registration of cases filed with courts	27	49.1%
(f) Use language free of legal jargon (i.e. plain language) in promotional materials designed to foster understanding of decisions and access to justice	26	47.3%
(i) Set up/improve a system for independent disciplinary committees and courts to jointly investigate judges who violate disciplinary rules	25	45.5%
(g) Set up/improve a judicial openness supervision system that enables the public to share comments and suggestions	22	40.0%
(b) Open hearings/trials using social media, TV and/or ICT tools	21	38.2%
(h) Set up/improve a system (e.g., a jury system or a system with people's assessors) to ensure that the public can participate in the judicial process	21	38.2%
(j) Improve coordination among different dispute resolution mechanisms to allow all stakeholders to better collaborate with one another	18	32.7%
(k) Collaborative tribunals (e.g. community/problem-solving tribunals; mediation conducted by courts)	18	32.7%
(l) Participatory justice (restorative justice and consensus-based justice)	15	27.3%
(c) Open enforcement of judgments	12	21.8%
(m) Allow volunteering in courts	3	5.5%

Table 11. Developing countries/economies responses

Factors that 59 Respondents from Developing Countries/Economies Other Than Mainland China Consider to Be Most Important to the Development of Open Judiciary	No. of Responses	Respondents (%)
(e) Open data/statistics on court performance	38	64.4%
(f) Use language free of legal jargon (i.e. plain language) in promotional materials designed to foster understanding of decisions and access to justice	36	61.0%
(i) Set up/improve a system for independent disciplinary committees and courts to jointly investigate judges who violate disciplinary rules	34	57.6%
(j) Improve coordination among different dispute resolution mechanisms to allow all stakeholders to better collaborate with one another	26	44.1%
(k) Collaborative tribunals (e.g. community/problem-solving tribunals; mediation conducted by courts)	26	44.1%
(d) Judicial documents made public	25	42.4%
(l) Participatory justice (restorative justice and consensus-based justice)	22	37.3%
(g) Set up/improve a judicial openness supervision system that enables the public to share comments and suggestions	20	33.9%
(a) Open registration of cases filed with courts	18	30.5%
(b) Open hearings/trials using social media, TV and/or ICT tools	18	30.5%
(c) Open enforcement of judgments	15	25.4%
(h) Set up/improve a system (e.g., a jury system or a system with people's assessors) to ensure that the public can participate in the judicial process	14	23.7%
(m) Allow volunteering in courts	3	5.1%

Chapter 5
An Analysis of a Lay Adjudication System and Open Judiciary:
The New Japanese Lay Adjudication System

Yumiko Kita
University of Sussex, UK

ABSTRACT

This paper presents analyses of impacts of lay adjudicators' participation in criminal matters in Japan due to the introduction of the new lay adjudication system – the Citizen Judge System [Saiban-in Seido] – in 2009. Since the late twentieth century, the introduction of the lay adjudication system seems to have been in international movement democratising the criminal justice system. This paper is devoted to an evaluation of the new system in terms of the balance between the concepts of democracy and a fair trial with consideration of the citizen judge procedures and the role of the citizen judges. In view of the closed nature of the Japanese criminal procedures and secrecy in the citizen judge system, this study will point out the challenges which prevent the fulfilment of democratic values in the practice of the citizen judge system.

INTRODUCTION

In 2001 the Japanese government announced the introduction of the new lay adjudication system, *Saiban-in Seido*, hereinafter the citizen judge system and in 2004 the National Diet passed and enforced in 2009 the law: *Saiban-in no sanka suru keijisaiban ni kansuru horitsu*, hereinafter the Citizen Judge Act. Citizens are selected randomly from the electoral register and hear and deliberate the evidence, reach a guilty or not guilty verdict, and determine the appropriate sentence with a cooperation with professional judges in a serious criminal case.

DOI: 10.4018/978-1-5225-0717-8.ch005

Democratisation in the criminal justice system appears to be a current international tendency, and the introduction of a lay adjudication system coincided with Western countries' support for democratic reform in Poland and Serbia (Carothers, 2008, p.11). The long-lasting admiration for a lay adjudication in particular in criminal trials are bolstered by a belief in democracy. Researchers, such as Vidmar, have expressed the idea that a lay adjudication system is considered as a symbol of democracy because of a focus on the significance of community standards and doubts about centralised state power (1996, p.97; 2000, Ch.1). Will a lay adjudicators' participation raise democratic values in criminal trials?

The aim of this chapter is to analyse the new Japanese lay adjudication system while considering the concepts of open judiciary and democracy. In addition, the problems of the lay adjudication system will be demonstrated in order to analyse the factors which prevent the enhancement of lay adjudicators' participation. By the introduction of the new system, the restriction of freedom of expression became even more severe. This chapter is largely divided into four sections. Firstly, the relationship between the concepts of open justice, a fair trial and democracy will be clarified. Secondly democratisation in a criminal trial will be studied with the example of the introduction of lay adjudication systems as an international movement starting in the late twentieth century. The focus of this section will be to study the international tendency towards a common law mode of criminal procedures to increase democratic values in criminal procedures. In addition, it will show the conflict between this transformation and a civil law mode, which influences the role of lay adjudicators and its openness. Thirdly, the outline of the present Japanese criminal procedure will be provided. The transformation towards adversarial modes of criminal procedure brings increased impediments to participation and openness, which are the key concepts of open justice.

BACKGROUND: THE CONCEPT OF OPEN JUSTICE, A FAIR TRIAL, AND DEMOCRACY

This section is organised in two main parts: firstly the overlapping principles between open justice, the right to a fair trial, and democracy in criminal procedures will be examined in terms of their balance; the other part will show the democratic values in a lay adjudication.

The principle of open justice requires that the courts ought to be open to the public including citizens and the media. On the one hand, the right to a fair trial is codified within the international and regional treaties such as Article 6 of the European Human Rights Convention which declares:

In the determination of his civil rights and obligations or of any criminal charge against him, everyone is entitled to a fair and public hearing within a reasonable time by an independent and impartial tribunal established by law. Judgment shall be pronounced publicly but the press and public may be excluded from all or part of the trial in interests of morals, public order or national security in a democratic society … (Section 1.)

In short, the ideal form of a fair trial will be that a judgement will be reached by impartial persons on the basis of reliable evidence fairly presented in open court (Powell, 1965, p.534). The right to a fair trial is structured by various principles such as open justice, due process, and procedural justice. A belief in due process values human rights, especially the rights of accused (Packer, 1964). All people should be equally bound by and entitled to participate, in some ways, in the administration of justice. A belief in procedural justice strongly enhances a litigant's satisfaction by the fairness of legal procedures (Thibaut & Walker, 1975). In addition, a belief in open justice means that:

... accountability and legitimacy within the legal process can be achieved through making accessible information about court procedures, court records, laws and judicial decisions. (Biber, 2014, p.73)

To sum up, open justice requires that the courts ought to be open to the public. Therefore, fairness entails a recognised balance between each party's interests, openness, and transparency (Southgate & Grosvenor, 2000) in legitimate procedures. In addition, the belief in the right to a fair trial, which is formed by other principles, is hinged on the principle of democracy. It values citizen on citizen freedom, equality, and rights (Held, 1994, p.191) in a self-governing society in which collective citizens' interests are an influence. Moreover, these features should be protected by a legitimate procedure (Huntington, 1991; Bobbio, 1994). Normatively, democracy means sharing power between citizens, and that citizens are not a subject of the government. Furthermore, in particular, the judiciary should be open to public scrutiny. The openness and the transparency of the courts are greatly connected to the principle of open justice in the contemporary world. A classical belief in open justice in England was found in the provisions of relevant institutions allowing public access to the trial and a right of public access to court files (Jaconelli, 2002, p.1-3). In this respect, the extent to which open justice requires wider permissible ranges in openness and transparency of courts including full access to court by the public, and the filming and broadcasting of cases, as well as the transparency of the criminal procedures themselves. The modern application of open justice principles can be found in diverse phrases in criminal procedures. For instance, modern applications of an open justice principle can be found in elements, such as the visual and aural elements, and the broadcasting of legal proceedings, according to the analysis in terms of England by Thompson (2011, p.220-3). The common law tradition is greatly connected with the openness and transparency of the courts and the court procedures.

Under the adversarial aspects of common law more democratic principles are emphasised than in the civil law tradition, which has more 'bureaucratic character' derived from the emphasis on written law (Stein, 1992) as well as the strong trust in the authority as a guarantor of public interest (Bradley et al. 1996, p.479). The democratic principles in the common law approach are of orality and publicity. In the common law approach, the prosecution must proof the defendant's guilt in the open court through the presentation of testimony including witness and expert testimony. A broad notion of public access to justice and transparency of the procedures provides stimulates public interest as well as being of educational value (Auld, 1935, p.99). These two common law procedural principles emphasise the importance of a lay adjudicators' participation in the procedures. In addition, as Goff claimed, the remains of judge-made law as a common law characteristic leads to the idea that one of the distinctive elements in judges is experience rather than knowledge (Goff, 1997, p.748). This perspective will also lead the willing acceptance of lay adjudicators as decision-maker in the trial.

The duty of lay adjudicators is to be present in the courtroom and to express their opinions by attending criminal procedures as a part of a political institution. Benefits of open justice appear to be the same as ones that an ideal lay adjudication system will provide. The benefits include a safeguard against corruption, and a tool for public scrutiny and promotion of citizens' trust in government. A lay adjudication is supported by the three concepts of democracy: participative, representative, and deliberative democracy, as presented by Malsch (2009). Foqué reveals that the principle of lay adjudication and democracy have a 'co-original' backbone from the historical analysis of the ancient Athens' concept of democracy, and its development shows the co-existence of principles of democracy and rule of law (2008). In addition, In a political science study, Yarez simply defined participatory democracy as institutional social reforms by means of another system of political participation, in which representative groups' preferences are presented (2004, p.820). In this respect, lay adjudication is regarded as a form of participatory democracy to express the 'voice of the people' (Fishkin, 1997) in the decision-making process of the state, and to enforce popular sovereignty.

Participatory democracy produces two main factors: it is a responsible function to show citizens' self-interests, and a concatenation between citizens in a community (Dzur, 2012, p.120). In this sense, as Darbyshire has presented, a lay adjudication system is a 'symbol of participatory democracy'(1991, p.745). In addition, as Henry has presented, participatory democracy is regarded 'as having inherent value, which complements that of representative democracy' (2005, p.11; Held, 1986). Representative democracy is based on the idea that rule and law should be governed (Eisenberg & Wells, 2002, p.1842; Casper & Zeisel, 1972) by all of the people in the legal domain. This is the idea that protects individuals, minorities' rights and freedoms and hampers the majority will (Zakaria, 2003). From this perspective, lay adjudication could be considered as a form of representative function to protect the rights and freedoms of citizens, including minorities, although it is evident that the inclusiveness of the minorities in a lay adjudicator panel has been one of central issues in the system in most countries.

Lastly, the principle of deliberative democracy, greatly developed by Jűrgen Habermas, is formulated as procedures which stimulate rational and moral issues as a consequence of 'reflection, argumentation, public reasoning and reaching consensus (Kellner, 2000, p.267). This concept stresses 'discussion, reflection, and consideration' (Raisio et al. 2014, p.79), which is possible to evaluate in procedures by means of inclusiveness of everyone, reasoned discussions, other-regarding attitudes (Chappell, 2011, p. 81-2). In this account, legitimacy in law and politics is established by the both formal and informal public discussion (Maskivker, 2010, p.865). In this respect, the meaning of legitimate law in the deliberative democratic principle is provided by fundamentally participatory democracy. Therefore, the concepts of participative, representative, and deliberative democracy, which lead procedural fairness and public satisfaction also bring one of the most considerable benefits of a lay adjudication, which is legitimacy of the verdict, laws, and legal system (Ellis & Diamond, 2003).

It is evident that lay adjudication introduced democratic values into criminal trial procedures On the other hand the enhancement of lay participation in a criminal trial appears to bring a counterthrust against the openness and transparency because of the protection of privacy and fairness. The international treaties and domestic legislation, such as the Contempt of Court Act 1981in England states that the jury room is secret, contrary to the open justice principle. For example, Article 14 of the International Covenant on Civil and Political Rights 1966 also declares a possible secrecy in the procedure in protecting reasonable 'morality, public order or national security' and privacy issues (Section 1). In England, Section 8 of the Contempt of Court Act 1981 protects the secrecy of the jury to keep the confidence in the jury deliberation. Leakages of information in lay adjudicators' deliberation can endanger 'the finality of verdicts' and damage the public confidence with not only the verdicts but also the procedures and even the existence of lay adjudication (Jaconelli, 2002, p.241). On account of this, secrecy in a lay adjudication system is recognised because of the legitimacy of the verdict and the protection of privacy including information regarding people involved the case as well as lay adjudicators.

The practice of these principles, which integrates with each other in a fair trial in a democratic society, will be seen to balance other principles in criminal justice policy. The international consensus on the issue balancing the right to a fair trial, in particular, for the accused and democratic values in particular for the participation and representativeness of the community is contested. Should the accused from a racial minority be tried in a lay adjudication panel including persons from a racial minority? Or should the panel be composed of lay adjudicators who are randomly selected from the community, even though the panel does not contain anyone from the accused's background? The examination of the balance, such as the 'balancing test' between costs and benefits and the 'balancing-of-interests' approach between liberty and order suggested by Meares and Harcourt (2000), has illustrated a clear and explanative analysis of criminal procedure. Kumm has claimed that the balancing of principles is an appropriate method to examine the relationship between the government and the law (2005, p.290). Spigelman has analysed the balance between the principle of freedom of speech and the right to a fair trial by broadcast media (Spigelman, 2006, p.158-161). Stolz has presented the four elements in a policy-making strategy: firstly to clear the problem and propose solutions; secondly if possible, encourage studies for the proposal, and consider the smaller elements which relate to the problems (1985). In this study, I will conduct a study to examine the balance between the concepts of open justice and of democracy in a lay adjudication system in decision-making procedures.

A LAY ADJUDICATION IN A CRIMINAL TRIAL AND OPEN JUSTICE

From the late twentieth century, before President Obama signed the Memorandum on Transparency and Open Government in 2009, an international movement of the democratisation in the judiciary had started by the introduction of a lay adjudication system in several countries. For example, Russia in 1993, Spain in 1997, Kazakhstan in 2007, Korea in 2008, Japan in 2009, Georgia in 2010 (re)introduced a lay adjudication system. Before the examination of the Japanese situation, which is the aim of this chapter, this section will study the current international movement which is introducing a lay adjudication system in criminal procedures and stressing common law principles, in particular, orality and publicity. Firstly, the international movement introducing lay adjudication system which started in the late twentieth century will be explained. Secondly, the secrecy in a lay adjudication system will be demonstrated with the conflicts between openness and transparency which the both principles of democracy and open justice support.

The international movement started from Russia and Spain. In particular, after the collapse of the former Soviet Union, the countries introduced a lay adjudication system. Russia introduced the new lay adjudication system, a jury system, in the inquisitorial modes of criminal procedure in the 1990 Judicial Reform. The introductory movement reached other parts of the world with a rise in democratisation in the criminal justice system. For example, the Republic of Korea introduced a new lay adjudication system, a jury system, in 2008 in order to increase 'the democratic legitimacy, the transparency, and the credibility of the judicial processes' (Park et al. 2010, p.167). This movement seem to have spread as active international research, international conferences, as well as proposals to the governments developed. The active international research regarding the new lay adjudication systems particularly in Russia (See e.g. Thaman, 2007; Esakov, 2012; Kovalev, 2014), Korea (See e.g. Lee, 2010; Park, 2010; Choi, 2014) and Japan (See e.g. Soldwedel, 2010; Senger, 2011; McClanahan, 2011), in terms of the related laws, its practice, and problems from a comparative approach has been motivationally conducted. In addition, workshops and international conferences regarding lay adjudication have been held throughout the world. For example, nine sessions and three sessions related to lay participation were held in the Law Society in 2012 and 2015. Also, several special issues of journals focusing on lay adjudication in East Asia have been published such as in the International Journal of Law, Crime and Justice in 2010 vol.38. These active movements has encouraged introducing a lay adjudication system in the Central and South American countries (Fukurai et al. 2009, p.16-7), and other countries (such as South Africa, Seligson, 2001; and Taiwan, Huang & Lin, 2014).

With the emergence of the popularity of a lay adjudication, there is also a decrease in the suspicion of a lay adjudication system, or an adherence to a bench trial system. For example, Penny Darbyshire has argued her sceptical point of view towards the English jury system throughout her research. She has claimed 'the symbolic function of the jury far outweighs its use' because the jury has been already replaced by the magistracy (Darbyshire, 1997, p.627), and has shown she doubts the jury's function as a safeguard for citizens' civil liberties because of procedural inadequacy (Darbyshire, 1991, p. 745). In addition, her collaborative research with Maughan and Stewart has pointed out thirty two issues of the jury system including unrepresentativeness of some groups of women, minorities, and some sort of occupations, public resistance to serve as a juror; concerns about the jurors' competency to judge the truthfulness of a witness, understand and remember information including the evidence and the law (Darbyshire et al. 2002). In addition, some complex serious fraud cases are exempted from a jury trial in England. Part 7 of the Criminal Justice Act 2003 states that some trials on indictment without a jury are possible for certain fraud cases (Section 43) where there is a danger of jury tampering (Section 44). In addition, there are countries which do not currently have a lay adjudication in their trials, such as Luxembourg, the Netherlands, and Turkey (Jackson & Kovalev, 2006, p. 93-4). As Gobert has demonstrated, the reasons for the decrease in lay adjudication trials and the adherence to a bench trial are concerns about complexity of cases, costs, an increase in the use of plea bargaining (1997).

Although international views about the use of the lay adjudication systems are polarised, the international emphasis on lay participation in criminal justice system is evident. The transition of the former Soviet Union countries from authoritarian to democratic market economies has encouraged other countries to develop democratic-oriented reform through criminal justice procedures by promoting 'context-specific solutions, which ensure capacity-building and sustainability at all levels (Robertson, 2005, p. 1-2). Thaman has presented in the analysis of the Russian Jury that the introduction of a lay adjudication system 'was aiming at expanding the participation of the citizenry in the administration of justice and democratizing the judicial branch of government', and also there was an educational purpose as well in the development of the public confidence both in the judiciary and criminal justice system (Thaman, 2007b, p. 360). Democratisation in criminal justice started to be stressed at the end of late 1990s, as people started wondering what the idealistic form of criminal justice was in the twenty-first century as well as starting to have concerns about the present system. Because of economic recovery, and the drastic political change in the former Soviet Union countries in the late 1990, democratisation in the political systems took place in many countries.

Legitimacy of the criminal justice system is one of the most important purposes of lay adjudication. Tyler has interpreted legitimacy as an 'acceptance by people of the need to bring their behaviour into line with the dictates of an external authority' (1990, p.25). Moreover, according to Fagan, the legitimacy of the criminal law is enhanced by the consistency with 'popular principles of procedural fairness, security and proportionality, and the legitimacy of the criminal legal institutions draws public attention to the public, the police's and elites' actions and views (Fagan, 2008, p. 126-7). Machura has demonstrated that procedural fairness and distributive justice are the key aspects for the legitimacy of legal institutions in Germany and Russian lay adjudication systems by his empirical research analysing how and what lay adjudicators evaluate and conclude from their experience (2003). In this respect, the degrees of lay adjudicators' participation in the procedures will influence the evaluations and results of what they have done, which affects the legitimacy. Open justice also requires transparency of court procedures and procedural fairness which depends on the openness of court hearings. The legitimacy of the law and system is influenced by the scope of the legitimacy of a lay adjudication panel, which is representative of the community. Therefore, legitimacy is the aim of a lay adjudication system as well as the expected outcome that a lay adjudication system can provide. The analysis of lay adjudicators' participation in terms of openness and transparency is fundamental in the sense of examining the foundation which balances open justice and democracy.

On the other hand, not only for lay adjudication trials but also for other trials there are limitations for openness and transparency. The imposed secrecy is to avoid the contempt of the courts which would interfere with the due administration of justice. For example, in England, Section 8 of the Contempt of Court Act 1981 states that 'to obtain, disclose or solicit any particulars of statements made, opinions expressed, arguments advanced or votes cast by members of a jury in the course of their deliberations' is a contempt. This releases jurors from public pressure of accusations about their decisions and moreover to avoid the situation of pre-trial publicity influencing lay adjudicators' opinions and possibly giving prejudiced ideas. As Jaconeli has presented, there are two reasons favouring secrecy in lay adjudication: no outside pressure on lay adjudicators about their verdict, and the establishment of a measure of public confidence in the verdict on the basis of the procedure (2002, p.236), and he also has presented exceptions to contempt of court on two conditions: 'the risk of prejudice to the particular proceedings is merely incidental'; or there is a debate 'in good faith' regarding 'public affairs or other matters of general public interest' (Jaconeli, 2002, p.249). The use of mass media is a useful way to obtain support from the public, and it can bring public manipulation (Takahashi, 1990, p. 111-2). Therefore, the polarised features of openness and secrecy in a lay adjudication are significant in achieving democratic criminal procedures.

The New Japanese Lay Adjudication System: Saiban-in Seido

This section will focus on the citizen judge system in light of the conflicts between openness, accessibility and closeness. First, the closed nature of the restriction in Japanese criminal procedure will be demonstrated by the lack of democratic values, in particular by the participation of lay people in the procedure. Second, the overview of the citizen judge system will be explained with its limited access to information for citizen judges. Last, secrecy in the citizen judge system will be explained. The aim of this section is to show the argument: has the citizen judge system provided openness and accessibility in criminal procedure?

Japanese judicial proceedings must be conducted in an open court which is accessible to the public and press as s stated formally, for example, in Article 24 of the Constitution of the Empire of Japan 1889 [*Dainihonteikoku Kenpo*] which states that '[N]o Japanese subject shall be deprived of his right of being tried by the judges determined by law. In addition, Article 34 of the current Constitution 1946 declares that:

No person shall be arrested or detained without being once informed of the charges against him or without the immediate privilege of counsel, nor shall he be detained without adequate cause; and upon demand of any person such cause must be immediately shown in open court in his presence and the presence of his counsel.

The Constitution also sets the right of access to the courts (Article 32) and independence of the three constitutional branches: legislative (Article 41), administrative (Article 65) and judicial (Article76 (1) as well as the independence of the judge (Article76). There is no provision in the Constitution regarding lay participation in the judiciary. Article 80(1) states 'the judges of the inferior courts shall be appointed by the cabinet from a list of persons nominated by the Supreme Court. ...' in the other words, lay participation is not prevented in the inferior courts, which is different from the Supreme Court, which is the highest authority of judicial administration. In this respect, it does not prohibit a lay adjudication panel, which is composed of the judges and lay people, in criminal procedure. However, it is argued that the lay adjudication panel can be considered as one of 'the courts', mentioned in Article 32 (Kaneko, 2012). In addition, opponents of the citizen judge system claimed that the compulsory obligation of serving as a citizen judge was a violation of the constitutional guaranteed right of freedom of thought similar to compulsory military conscription. The Supreme Court adopted the constitutionality of the citizen judge system in 2011 with Judge Takeshita saying that the system aims at criminal trials taking advantage of the combination between public viewpoints and legal professional expertise.

Japanese criminal procedures has been criticised for their closed nature. For example the secretive investigation process has been considered problematic and the Human Rights Institute (HRI) of the International Bar Association (IBA) proposed the introduction of electronically recording interviews for suspects (2015). The Japanese criminal justice system is considered a mixed system because it is a transformational mix of German and French codes as well as an American influence on the Constitution leading to similar judicial review system (See, 1982). Because of the discouragement of an emphasis on individuality, anonymity and uniformity, Foote has described the Japanese judicial system as 'nameless faceless justice' (Foote, 2007). The imbalance of power between the prosecution and the accused especially during the investigation phrase and a strong dependence on the written evidence from the investigation at the trials brings closed restrictions in the procedures (Johnson, 2000).

The Japanese Attributes: The Domination of Elites

The restriction in the criminal procedures has been supported, to some extent, by the society and culture. The long-lasting Japanese attributes, which are the domination of elites in governmental institutions and collectivism and cooperative interdependence in the community, have influenced the practice of the criminal procedures. As Ito has claimed in his study of the Supreme Court, 'judicial elitism' has dominated political institutions, part of the national bureaucracy, and local government since the Tokugawa era started in 1603. In addition, Fallows has indicated that the relationship between openness and order is different in East Asia from that in Western countries (Fallows, 1994). Dean has described the former Japanese criminal trial as an 'empty shell', where there is a formal ceremony which approves the dossier created by the prosecution (1995, p. 399). These constraints was targeted by judicial reform in 1999.

The judicial reform started in 1999 in Japan as a part of major Structural Reforms (*Kozo Kaikaku)* were the most drastic social reformation in over 60-years of post war Japanese history. Accordingly it is likely to be important to comprehend the relationship between the other social changes and judicial reform in order to understand the reform itself. The Judicial Reform Council (JRC) was established by the Cabinet in 1999 to consider fundamental measures necessary for judicial reform and judicial infrastructure arrangement by defining the role of the judicature in Japan in the twenty-first century as stated in Article 2, paragraph 1 of the Act Concerning Establishment of Judicial Reform Council [*Kaikaku Shingikai Secchi Ho*] 1999 and the main issues imposed upon the Council. The law provides fundamental principles that are 'the realisation of a more accessible and user-friendly judicial system', 'public participation in judicial system' and 'the redefinition of the legal profession and the reinforcement of its function' (JRC, 1999). This establishment was the start of massive judicial reform in many areas. Although the Japanese reforms of administrative and economic structures seemed to be necessary because of the burst financial bubble of 1991, the reforms appeared to serve as the initial trigger for wholesale social changes in attitude towards judicial reforms, and reforms to the system of administrative guidance, the electoral system in 1994 and corporate law and the amendment of the Civil Procedure Code [*Minji Sosho Ho*] in 1996. Moreover, this is what might have led to a continuing path of reforms resulting in the reintroduction of the new Japanese civil judge system. In this chapter, the background and process of the JRC will be examined considering that judicial reform started from economic restructuring, followed by details of JRC membership. The aims of lay participation will be described in terms of issues in criminal jurisdiction procedures. The examination of the process and the aims of the judicial reforms may imply an inclination for the Americanisation and Europeanisation of the Japanese criminal justice system and judicial reform in order to clarify the new system. A historical analysis of the jury system before the Second World War will be conducted to show tendencies and challenges in lay participations in Japanese criminal cases.

Judicial Reform is a series of legal reforms made since the Judicial Reform Law was passed by the Diet in November 2001. Such major reforms of the judicial system have only been conducted twice in the Japanese history. These happened after the Meiji Restoration and the Second World War. The 'Judicial Reform' is a comparable revolution to those made in those two other revolutionary histories. The reform largely consists of four parts:

1. Reform of screening and the training system,
2. The establishment of the Japan Legal Support Centre,
3. The reform of all kinds of proceeding legal systems,
4. The reform of the Lawyers Act. (Act on Promotion of Judicial System Reform [*Shihoseido Kaikaku Suishin Ho*], Chapter 1, Article 1-3, 2001)

In the series of judicial reforms, the introduction of the citizen judge system is one of the drastic changes in the criminal justice system. Citizen judges are selected randomly from an electoral list, cooperating with professional judges to reach a verdict and determine the sentence in serious criminal cases. Even if the defendant admits guilt he or she has no right to waive a hearing by a citizen judge panel. The criminal matters eligible for resolution by citizen judges consist of crimes where the maximum penalty is death or indefinite imprisonment for a criminal act, including murder, robbery-murder, rape-murder, arson, and offences against Anti-Drug Special Provisions Law 1991 [*Mayaku Tokurei Ho*].

There were 7,262 accused tried by a citizen judge trial between May 2009 and December 2014. Of the accused 1,614 were sentenced for robbery-murder, 1,597 were for murder, and 715 were for injury resulting in death. Between the same period, 41,834 lay people served as a citizen judge and the average duration of a citizen judge trial was 5.3 days (The Supreme Court, 2015b).

Japan does not allow cameras into the courtroom and the broadcasting of legal proceedings during the trials, although camera filming is allowed for two minutes after judges enter the courtroom and before the opening statement of the court, as is stated in the 1999 Application Standard of Camera Coverage in the Courtroom. This has remained in the citizen judge system, and the camera filming in a citizen judge trial is carried out before citizen judges enter the courtroom. In January 2008 the Japan Newspaper Publishers and Editors Association [*Nihon Shinbun Kyokai*] published the Prospect for Media Coverage in Citizen Judge System [*Saibanin Seido Kaishi ni atatteno Shuzai Houdou Shishin*] stating that careful consideration for reporting of testimony was needed because of the privacy of persons involved in cases, and the comments of experts because of possible prejudicial influence on readers and audiences. In history, in particular before the World War II, freedom of speech was strictly restricted by the government by Temporary Seditious Documents Order 1936 [*Fuonbunsho Rinji Torishimari Ho*], Military Secrets Law 1937 [*Gunkihogo Ho*], Military Resource Protection Law 1939 [*Gunyou Shigen Himitsu Hogo Ho*], Temporary Speech Publication Assembly and Association Order 1941 [*Genron, Shuppan, Shukai, Kesshanado Rinji Torishimari Ho*], with an administrative penalty or criminal law sanction. In addition, regarding contempt of court, there was the Act Concerning the Maintenance of Order in a Court of Law 1952 [*Hoteinado no Chitsujo ni kansuru Horitsu*] which stated an interference with the course of justice in which the courts and judges deliver the judgment, either in front of them or in a place where they experience the interference directly by verbal abuse, assault, bustle or other inappropriate behaviour, is an interference with the courts' dignity and shall be the object of the sentence of up to 20 days imprisonment or/and no more than 30,000 yen (£156.79 = £0.005 (4/7/2015)] (Article 2).

Since the introduction of the citizen judge system, a press conference has been hosted by the press club after the close of a case and citizen judges are invited to r the conference. The participation at the press conference depends on their consent. One of the reasons in favour of media coverage in the citizen judge system is to gain public attention and put pressure on citizen judges to consider the seriousness and fairness of their duties and responsibilities (Miyazawa, 2014, p. 77). The publicity and media coverage has contributed to the openness as well as the implication of the citizen judge system.

In addition, the new design of the courtroom of the District Court provides the citizen judges' seats are next to the professional judges and the citizen judges sit down with facing up to the public gallery (See Niikura, 2013). The citizen judges sit down next to professional, but citizen judges are called by number at the courtroom. The citizen judges are gained the full attention of the public gallery while they hear the evidence and ask questions to the witnesses and the accused. The Citizen Judge Acts states that citizen judges are eligible to ask questions to the accused (Article 59), the witnesses (Article 55), and the victims (Article 58). In the deliberation room, they called each other by number or by name, and this depends on the panel. The level of interactions between citizen judges in the deliberation room seem to be different from each panel. For example, some experienced citizen judges exchange their business cards and have kept in touch with co-citizen judges. On the other, some experienced citizen judges called each other by number. The architectural feature of the courtroom provides the full attention of the public gallery towards the citizen judges, and the visual impact will offer the openness to the public and a pressure of the responsible role on the citizen judges

On the other hand, from the selection of citizen judges, their deliberation process, and after the trial, secrecy is runs through the citizen judge system. Article 101(1) of the Citizen Judge Act says that:

No person shall publish the name, address and other information capable of identifying the citizen judge, alternate citizen judge, citizen judge to be appointed or candidates for citizen judge or other expected persons.

'Publish' in this context means the way in which the general public knows about the selection of a citizen judge, and media coverage includes publishing, broadcasting, and placing on the Internet. However, after the close of the case, publishing the fact that the person served as a citizen judge is not prohibited (the Supreme Court Website). In addition, to maintain the confidences of the deliberation room, citizen judges shall not expose two main kinds of information: firstly, the information in the deliberation room and the other is information which citizen judges obtained during their duties outside of the deliberation room. The first type of information includes the progress of their deliberation, opinions of members of the citizen judge panel, and details of votes.

The second type of information includes information related to privacy of victims, and people involved in the case and the names of the members of the panel. It seems to be apparent that secrecy in the citizen judge system as well as contempt of court stated in the Act Concerning the Maintenance of Order in a Court of Law 1952 focuses on the disclosure of information and the maintenance of the courts' dignity rather than the 'finality' of the verdict. Also, the desire for secrecy in lay adjudication concerns as the finality of the verdict, which bring legitimacy to the verdict, however as mentioned above, it is not applicable in the citizen judge system. The appeal against a verdict reached by a citizen judge panel is allowed and the bench trial will be held at the appellate court. The appeal by both parties the prosecution and defence, is allowed for an acquittal based on an error in legal application or fact-finding. The three professional judges in the bench trial are able to quash the original judgment reached by a citizen judge panel and 35% of citizen judge trials appeal a ruling, and the number of cases related to a drug offence in which the citizen judge panel reached a guilty verdict but in which the appellate panel reached a not guilty verdict was 13 between 2009 and 2011 (The Supreme Court, 2015b).

The restraints of the violation regarding secrecy in the citizen judge system are stated, but there is some vagueness remained in the citizen judge system. The penalties for the violation of the confidentiality in citizen judge trials has never been imposed yet since the system started. In the Japanese system, there is no strict control over citizen judges' contact with the outside world while they carry out their duties, such as staying in hotel accommodation, as they do in other jurisdictions such as England. The vagueness of the restrictions in the Japanese system causes indefinite anxiety as does the severity of s the secrecy. However, citizen judges has been bound with a strict duty of lifetime confidentiality. If it is violated there will be a fine up to 500,000 yen (approximately £2,616) or up to six months imprisonment. Moreover, the procedural challenges, such as the pre-trial arrangement process in the citizen judge system, which discuss the facts and issues between legal professionals may cast a shadow over the openness of the procedures. Therefore, it could be said that the target of citizen judge system is to enhance lay participation, openness and transparency of the procedures in order to establish accessible and user-friendly criminal procedures by injecting democratic values, while the citizen judge system introduces restricted practices.

This is considerably significant because of the two rationales in the citizen judge system: the legitimistic values and the protection of lay adjudicators' privacy. In order to stress legitimacy, which is also one of the values of the existence of the citizen judge system, there is also the stress on the enhancement of lay participation, and preserving secrecy is vital. On the other hand, it is important that the secrecy in the citizen judge system should be observed in order to maintain participation, representativeness, and deliberation, for that, improvements in the current citizen judge system will be necessary.

CONCLUSION

This chapter has argued that, the introduction of a lay adjudication system will restrict the open justice principle to some extent, although public attention by media coverage has been increased since its introduction. Since the introduction of the new lay adjudication in Japan, injecting more democratic values including open justice and an increase in public observation at trial and broadcasting programmes related to the new system, has been achieved. However, the Japanese criminal trial procedure has traditionally remained the closed, limiting access to evidence during an investigation process and weakening the position of the defendant at a trial. In addition, secrecy related to lay adjudicators participation has been brought into the citizen judge system in order to protect judicial accountability and privacy. There are two possible points for improvements on the basis of my hypothesis, which is that the form of the citizen judge system current in Japan aims to enhance e democratic values, especially participation. In order to establish the aims of the system, it will be important to clarify which principle or principles should be emphasised. From this respect, open access to the courts for serious research will be inevitable.

REFERENCES

Act Concerning Establishment of Judicial Reform [*Kaikaku Shingikai Secchi Ho*], 1999, Law no.68 of 1999.

Act Concerning the Maintenance of Order in a Court of Law [*Hoteinado no Chitsujo ni kansuru Horitsu*], 1952, Law no.286 of 1952.

Act on Promotion of Judicial System Reform [*Shihoseido Kaikaku Suishin Ho*], 2001, Law no.119 of 2001.

Ambler, L. (2007). The People Decide: The Effect of the Introduction of the Quasi-Jury System (Saiban-In Seido) on the Death Penalty in Japan, The. *Northwestern Journal of International Human Rights*, *6*(1), 1–23.

Anti-Drug Special Provisions Law, 1991, Law no.94 of 1991.

Auld, F. C. (1935). The Comparative Jurisprudence of Criminal Process. *University of Toronto Law Journal*, *1*(1), 82–103. doi:10.2307/823869

Biber, K. (2014). Inside Jill Meagher's Handbag: Looking at Open Justice. *Alternative Law Journal*, *39*(2), 73–77.

Bobbio, N. (1994). The Future of Democracy. In *The Polity Reader in Social Theory* (pp. 295–303). Cambridge: Polity Press.

Bradley, C. M. et al.. (1996). The Convergence of the Continental and the Common Law Model of Criminal Procedure. *Criminal Law Forum*, *7*(2), 471–484. doi:10.1007/BF02197174

Carothers, T. (2008). Democracy Assistance: Political vs. Developmental? *Journal of Democracy*, *20*(1), 5–19. doi:10.1353/jod.0.0047

Casper, G., & Zeisel, H. (1972). Lay judges in the German criminal courts. *The Journal of Legal Studies*, *1*(1), 135–191. doi:10.1086/467481

Chappell, Z. (2011). Justifying deliberative democracy: Are two heads always wiser than one? *Contemporary Political Theory*, *10*(1), 78–101. doi:10.1057/cpt.2010.8

Choi, J. S. (2014). Korean Citizen Participation in Criminal Trials: The Present Situation and Problems. *International Journal of Law, Crime and Justice*, *42*(2), 83–102. doi:10.1016/j.ijlcj.2013.07.003

Civil Procedure Code, 1996, Law no.109 of 1996.

Darbyshire, P. (1991). The Lamp That Shows That Freedom Lives—Is It Worth the Candle? *Criminal Law Review (London, England)*, (11): 740–752.

Darbyshire, P. 1997. An Essay on the Importance and Neglect of the Magistracy. Criminal Law Review, (Sep.), pp.627–643.

Darbyshire, P., Maughan, A., & Stewart, A. 2002. What Can the English Legal System Learn from Jury Research Published up to 2001? *Research Paper in Law*, (1), 1–84. Available at: http://eprints.kingston.ac.uk/23/1/Darbyshire-P-23.pdf

Dean, M. (1995). Trial by Jury: A Force for Change in Japan. *The International and Comparative Law Quarterly*, *44*(2), 379–404. doi:10.1093/iclqaj/44.2.379

Dzur, A. W. (2012). Participatory Democracy and Criminal Justice. *Criminal Law and Philosophy*, *6*(2), 115–129. doi:10.1007/s11572-012-9149-x

Eisenberg, T., & Wells, T. (2002). Trial Outcomes and Demographics: Is There A Bronx Effect? *Texas Law Review*, *80*(7), 1839–1876.

Ellis, L., & Diamond, S. S. (2003). Race, Diversity, and Jury Composition: Battering and Bolstering Legitimacy. *Chicago-Kent Law Review*, *78*(3), 1033–1060.

Esakov, G. (2012). The Russian Criminal Jury: Recent Developments, Practice, and Current Problems. *The American Journal of Comparative Law*, *60*(3), 665–702. doi:10.5131/AJCL.2011.0031

Fagan, J. (2008). Legitimacy and Criminal Justice. *Ohio State Journal of Criminal Law*, *6*(1), 123–140.

Fallows, J. (1994). *Looking at the Sun: The Rise of the New East Asian Economic and Political System*. New York: Pantheon.

Fishkin, J. (1997). *The Voice of the People*. New Haven, CT: Yale University Press.

Foote, D. H. (2007). *Nameless Faceless Justice* [Na mo nai kao mo nai shiho]. Tokyo: Yuhikaku.

Foqué, R. (2008). Criminal Justice in a Democracy: Towards a Relational Conception of Criminal Law and Punishment. *Criminal Law and Philosophy*, *2*(3), 207–227. doi:10.1007/s11572-008-9063-4

Fukurai, H., Knudtson, C. R., & Lopez, S. I. (2009). Is Mexico Ready for a Jury Trial?: Comparative Analysis of Lay Justice Systems in Mexico, the United States, Japan, New Zealand, South Korea, and Ireland. *Mexican Law Review*, *11*, 3–44.

Gobert, J. 1997. Justice, Democracy and the Jury, Aldershot: Aldershot.

Goff, L. (1997). The Future of the Common Law. *The International and Comparative Law Quarterly, 46*(4), 745–760. doi:10.1017/S0020589300061194

Held, D. (1986). *New Forms of Democracy*. London: Sage.

Held, D. (1994). What Should Democracy Mean Today? In *The Polity Reader in Social Theory* (pp. 304–312). Cambridge: Polity Press.

Henry, S. (2005). Shaping and Delivering Peace at the Local Level - Learning from the Experience of Peace II. In *Shaping and Deliberative Peace at Local Level?: Learning from the Experience of Peace II. Learning from Peace II* (pp. 8–13). Belfast: Community Relations Council.

Huang, K.-C., & Lin, C.-C. (2014). Mock Jury Trial in Taiwan- Paving the Gound for Introducing Lay Participation. *Law and Human Behavior, 38*(4), 367–377. doi:10.1037/lhb0000080 PMID:24707909

Huntington, S. (1991). *The Third Wave: Democratization in the late twentieth century*. Norman: University of Oklahoma Press.

Jackson, J. D., & Kovalev, N. P. (2006). Lay Adjudication and Human Rights in Europe. *Columbia Journal of European Law, 13*, 83–124.

Jaconelli, J. (2002). *Open Justice: A Critique of the Public Trial*. Oxford: Oxford University Press. doi:10.1093/acprof:oso/9780198252580.001.0001

Jiménez-Gómez, C. (2014). Desafíos de la modernización de la justicia en tiempos del Gobierno Abierto. *Revista Digital de Derecho Administrativo, 1*, 225–239.

Johnson, D. T. (2000). Prosecutor Culture in Japan and the USA. In D. Nelken (Ed.), *Constrasting Criminal Justice: Getting from here to there* (pp. 157–204). Aldershot, UK: Ashgate.

Johnson, D. T. (2012). Capital Punishment and Japan's Lay Judge System. *Aoyama Legal Research Review, 5*, 269–289.

JRC. (1999). *The Points at Issue in the Justice Reform*. Retrieved from http://www.kantei.go.jp/foreign/policy/sihou/singikai/991221_e.html

Kaneko, A. (2012). Recussation in Criminal Procedure. *Yokohama International Economic Law Review, 20*(3), 231–243.

Kellner, D. (2000). *Habermas, the Public Sphere, and Democracy: A Critical Intervention*. Perspectives on Habermas.

Kovalev, N. P. (2014). Selection of Jurors and Lay Assessors in Comparative Perspective: Eurasian Context. *Russian Law Journal, 2*(2), 9–62. doi:10.17589/2309-8678-2014-2-2-9-62

Kumm, M. (2005). The Jurisprudence of Constitutional Conflict: Constitutional Supremacy in Europe Before and After the Constitutional Treaty. *European Law Journal, 11*(3), 262–307. doi:10.1111/j.1468-0386.2005.00260.x

Lee, J. (2010). Korean Jury Trial : Has the New System Brought About Changes? *Asian-Pacific Law & Policy Journal, 12*(1), 58–71.

Machura, S. (2003). Fairness, Justice, and Legitimacy: Experiences of People's judges in South Russia. *Law & Policy*, *25*(2), 123–150. doi:10.1046/j.1467-9930.2003.00143.x

Malsch, M. (2009). *Democracy in the Courts: Lay Participation in European Criminal Justice Systems*. Surrey: Ashgate.

Maskivker, J. (2010). Participation and Rights in Athenian Democracy: A Habermasian Approach. *The European Legacy, Toward New Paradigms*, *15*(7), 855–870. doi:10.1080/10848770.2010.528902

McClanahan, J. (2011). Citizen Participation in Japanese Criminal Trials: Reimagining the Right to Trial by Jury in the United States. *North Carolina Journal of International Law and Commercial Regulation*, *37*, 725–792.

Meares, T. L., & Harcourt, B. E. (2000). Foreword: Transparent Adjudication and Social Science Research in Constitutional Criminal Procedure. *The Journal of Criminal Law & Criminology*, *90*(3), 733–798. doi:10.2307/1144276

Military Resource Protection Law [*Gunyou Shigen Himitsu Hogo Ho*] 1939, Law no.25 of 1939.

Military Secrets Law [*Gunkihogo Ho*], 1937, Law no.72 of 1937.

Miyazawa, S. (2014). Citizen Participation in Criminal Trials in Japan: The Saiban-in System and Victim Participation in Japan in International Perspectives. *International Journal of Law, Crime and Justice*, *42*(2), 71–82. doi:10.1016/j.ijlcj.2014.03.002

Niikura, O. (2013). *AGU Insite*. Retrieved from http://www.aoyama.ac.jp/research/insight/column_niikura/page2.html

Packer, H. L. (1964). Two Models of the Criminal Process. *University of Pennsylvania Law Review*, *113*(1), 1–68. doi:10.2307/3310562

Park, K., Han, Y. H., & Seong, Y. R. (2010). The Effect of Double Judgments on Public Confidence in Court Decisions for the Trial by Citizen-Participation in Korea. *International Journal of Law, Crime and Justice*, *38*(4), 166–174. doi:10.1016/j.ijlcj.2011.01.003

Park, R. Y. (2010). The Globalizing Jury trial: Lessons and Insights from Korea. *The American Journal of Comparative Law*, *58*(3), 525–582. doi:10.5131/ajcl.2009.0049

Powell, L. F. (1965). The Right to a Fair Trial. *American Bar Association Journal. American Bar Association*, *51*(5), 534–538.

Raisio, H., Valkama, K., & Peltola, E. (2014). Disability and Deliberative Democracy: Towards Involving the Whole Human Spectrum in Public Deliberation. *Scandinavian Journal of Disability Research*, *16*(1), 77–97. doi:10.1080/15017419.2013.781957

Robertson, A. (2005). Criminal Justice Policy Transfer To Post-Soviet States: Two Case Studies Of Police Reform In Russia And Ukraine. *European Journal on Criminal Policy and Research*, *11*(1), 1–28. doi:10.1007/s10610-005-2290-5

See, H. (1982). The Judiciary and Dispute Resolution in Japan: A Survey. *Florida State University Law Review. Florida State University. College of Law*, *10*(3), 339–368.

Seligson, M. (2001). Lay Participation in South Africa From Apartheid to Majority Rule. *Revue internationale de droit pénal*, *72*(1), 273–284.

Senger, D. (2011). The Japanese Quasi-Jury and the American Jury: A Comparative Assessment of Juror Questioning and Sentencing Procedures and Cultural Elements in Lay Judicial Participation. *University of Illinois Law Review*, *2*, 741–774.

Soldwedel, A. (2010). Testing Japan's Convictions: The Lay Judge System and the Rights of Criminal Defendants. *Vanderbilt Journal of Transnational Law*, *41*(5), 1417–1474.

Southgate, P., & Grosvenor, T. (2000). Confidence in the Criminal Justice System - A Qualitative Study. London: Academic Press.

Spigelman, J. (2006). The Principle of Open Justice: A Comparative Perspective. *The University of New South Wales Law Journal*, *29*(2), 147–166.

Stein, P. G. (1992). Roman Law, Common Law, and Civil Law. *Tulane Law Review*, *66*(5), 1591–1604.

Stolz, B. (1985). Congress and Criminal Justice Policy Making: The Impact of Interest Groups and Symbolic Politics. *Journal of Criminal Justice*, *13*(4), 307–319. doi:10.1016/0047-2352(85)90001-7

Takahashi, K. (1990). Contemporary Democracy in a Parliamentary System. *Law and Contemporary Problems*, *53*(1), 105–122. doi:10.2307/1191830

Temporary Seditious Documents Law 1936 [*Fuonbunsho Rinji Torishimari Ho*], Law no.45 of 1936.

Temporary Speech Publication Assembly and Association Order [*Genron, Shuppan, Shukai, Kesshanado Rinji Torishimari Ho*], 1941, Law no.97 of 1941.

Thaman, S. C. (2007a). The Good, the Bad, or the Indifferent: "12 Angry Men" in Russia, Part of Symposium: The 50th Anniversary of "12 Angry Men.". *Chicago-Kent Law Review*, *82*(2), 791–808.

Thaman, S. C. (2007b). The Nullification of the Russian Jury : Lessons for Jury-Inspired Reform in Eurasia and Beyond. *Cornell International Law Journal*, *40*(2), 355–428.

The Supreme Court. (2015a). *Q&A*. Available at: http://www.saibanin.courts.go.jp/qa/c6_6.html

The Supreme Court. (2015b). *Report: The Implications of the Citizen Judge System*, Tokyo.

Thibaut, J., & Walker, L. (1975). *Procedural Justice: A Psychological Analysis*. Hillsdale, NJ: Wiley.

Thompson, E. (2011). Does the Open Justice Principle Require Cameras to be Permitted in the Courtroom and the Broadcasting of Legal Proceedings? *Journal of Medicine and Law / Detroit College of Law at Michigan State University*, *3*(2), 211–236.

Tyler, T. R. (1990). *Why People Obey the Law*. New Haven, CT: Yale University Press.

Vidmar, N. (2000). *World Jury System*. Oxford, UK: Oxford University Press. doi:10.1093/acprof:oso/9780198298564.001.0001

Vidmar, N., & Abramson, J. (1996). We the Jury : The Jury System and the Ideal of Democracy. by Jeffrey Abramson Review by : Neil Vidmar. *Contemporary Sociology*, *25*(1), 97–99. doi:10.2307/2076992

Yarez, C. J. N. (2004). Participatory Democracy and Political Opportunism : Municipal Experience in Italy and Spain. *International Journal of Urban and Regional Research*, *28*(4), 819–838. doi:10.1111/j.0309-1317.2004.00553.x

Zakaria, F. (2003). *The Future of Democracy at Home and Abroad*. New York: Norton.

KEY TERMS AND DEFINITIONS

Open Judiciary: [*Justicia Abierta*, in Spanish] Extension of open government's philosophy and principles in the justice field (Jiménez-Gómez, 2014, pp.237).

Lay Adjudication System: The definition of lay adjudicator in this thesis is citizens who are selected as representatives of their community in order to hear, deliberate, discuss information including facts, the laws, and evidence obtaining throughout criminal procedures, and ultimately reach a verdict.

Saiban-in Seido: The new Japanese lay adjudication system will be expressed as the citizen judge system, and a lay adjudicator in the citizen judge system will be as a citizen judge in this chapter. *Saiban-in Seido* is translated as 'quasi-jury system'(Ambler, 2007), 'lay judge system'(Johnson, 2012), 'lay assessor's system' (Johnson 2012), and so on.

Section 3

Open Justice in Europe

Chapter 6
From eJustice to Open Judiciary:
An Analysis of the Portuguese Experience

Rui Pedro Lourenço
INESCC and University of Coimbra, Portugal

Paula Fernando
University of Coimbra, Portugal

Conceição Gomes
University of Coimbra, Portugal

ABSTRACT

This chapter will consider the Portuguese context, with a relatively 'traditional' eGovernment successful development, to analyse the way eJustice and open judiciary have progressed. The aim is to provide useful insights which may be considered in other contexts (countries), including a reflection on the factors that may account for differences in eJustice and open judiciary development when compared to eGovernment and open government achievements. eGovernment, eJustice, open government and open judiciary development processes are placed in dialogue, in order to discuss the factors that have contributed to differences and similarities in both generic eGovernment and open government and specific eJustice and open judiciary development in Portugal.

INTRODUCTION

Over the past decades, eGovernment development in Portugal has focused essentially on infra-structure, information and online service provision, and internal process efficiency, following the general pattern described in early eGovernment maturity models (Layne & Lee, 2001). As a result of those efforts, Portugal now exhibits good general eGovernment development indicators as well as several very successful eGovernment flagship initiatives (European Commission, 2015a).

eJustice has followed a similar path, with the development of the two main applications: CITIUS and SITAF. Both applications, although with very different layouts and procedural rules, aim at a dematerialisation of proceedings by electronically treating all information provided by the professionals, thus

DOI: 10.4018/978-1-5225-0717-8.ch006

reducing their physical form to a minimum. The implementation of this software made for significant change, mainly to the daily practice of all judicial actors, which can be classified as (1) automation; (2) process reshaping; and (3) redistribution of competences and intervention (Fernando, Gomes, & Fernandes, 2013). By achieving a full electronic procedure (with CITIUS, for civil proceedings) or a medium level electronic procedure (with CITIUS, for criminal proceedings, and with SITAF), Portugal ranks among the best performers in the benchmark results of CEPEJ and EU (European Commission, 2015b). However, despite the good scoring, there are doubts about the real impact of these eJustice initiatives on the overall efficiency of the justice system.

Having achieved some success in 'traditional' eGovernment development efforts (focused on services, processes and efficiency) over the past few years, attention has shifted to the idea of *open government*. Highly influenced by the Obama Administration Memorandum (Obama, 2009) and Directive (Orszag, 2009), open government efforts around the world embrace three main objectives: achieving *transparency*, promoting *participation*, and fostering *collaboration*.

Contrary to 'generic' eGovernment, there are no specific indicators yet that allow us to have a global picture of the development status of open government. But we can already identify some high impact open government initiatives in Portugal, particularly as regards the *transparency* dimension (such as the public contracts data portal), which may provide an interesting basis for comparison with existing (or not) similar initiatives in the administration of justice.

This chapter will consider the Portuguese context, with a relatively 'traditional' eGovernment successful development, to analyse the way eJustice and open judiciary have progressed, aiming to provide useful insights which may be considered in other contexts (countries). In particular, the analysis will look into what type (if any) of open judiciary initiatives have been launched, comparing it to other, very successful, 'generic' open government initiatives. The chapter will also reflect on the factors that may have contributed to differences and similarities in eJustice and open judiciary development when compared to generic eGovernment and open government achievements.

To provide an insight into these issues, this chapter is broadly divided into four main sections dedicated to eGovernment, eJustice, open government and open judiciary respectively. Each one of these sections begins by presenting a general conceptual framework of the specific domain, followed by a description and critical analysis of the Portuguese flagship initiatives and existing ICT systems, and of its international benchmark results concerning that domain. At the end of these sections, the above-mentioned questions will be discussed in the light of the Portuguese background, bearing in mind the importance of drawing on knowledge at national level to address similar problems in other contexts or at the transnational level.

eGOVERNMENT

Broadly defined, eGovernment refers to "the use of ICTs, and particularly the Internet, as a tool to achieve better government" (OECD, 2003). At its core, eGovernment focuses on the online delivery of government information and services (West, 2004) and seeks to improve public service efficiency and effectiveness, while taking advantage of enhanced data quality inherent to the digital world (Andersen & Henriksen, 2006).

Early eGovernment maturity/stage models reflect these core focuses and objectives. For instance, the Layne and Lee (2001) growth model for eGovernment included four stages comprising service information provision and downloadable forms (cataloguing), online forms and service provision (transaction), and internal systems and process integration to provide 'one-stop shops' for citizens and businesses.

Over the past decade, several other maturity models have been proposed (Lee, 2010) that broaden the initial eGovernment scope and reflect more sophisticated and detailed use of ICT in government operations.

As regards the scope of eGovernment, some of these models and other eGovernment conceptualisations include aspects from related concepts such as eGovernance (Dawes, 2008), eDemocracy/eParticipation (Hiller & Belanger, 2001; Siau & Long, 2005) or Open government (European Commission, 2010b).

Regarding sophistication and detail, we may look into the development of the European Commission eGovernment benchmark. In its first measurement (European Commission, 2001), the assessment framework adopted two indicators: one concerning the online availability of 20 front-end public services; the other, their degree of sophistication as measured by a four-stage maturity model (Information, Interaction, Two-way interaction, and Transaction). The latest framework abandoned the "silo view of public services – single services without connection to the overall process" and replaced it with a new approach built on the assessment of 'life events' that represent customer journeys (European Commission, 2014a). Furthermore, the framework now considers four top-level benchmarks (User centricity, Transparency, Single Market Mobility, and Key enablers) and a set of indicators under each benchmark (European Commission, 2012, 2014a).

eGovernment Flagship Initiatives and Systems

Arguably, the Portuguese eGovernment journey started in 1991 when project INFOCID - *Sistema Interdepartamental de Informação ao Cidadão* (Interdepartmental Citizen Information System) was launched to provide a unique virtual Public Administration point of contact for citizens (UMIC, 2015). In 1993 the system became available in Videotext, then it migrated to multimedia kiosks placed in key public services and finally, in 1995, it became accessible through the internet. Then, in 2004, INFOCID was replaced by a new Citizen's Portal ('Portal do Cidadão'), combining in one place different services for citizens and businesses alike and, thus, merging the portal dedicated to individual citizens and another portal intended to support businesses ('Portal da Empresa') (European Commission 2006). Already in 2007 this national government portal scored 88% while EU27+ national portals were given an average score of 75% (European Commission 2007). In 2010 Portugal was ranked 3rd (with a 94% score) with respect to portal usability, user-centric design, and service bundling (European Commission, 2010a).

Over the next decade other flagship initiatives were launched in the eGovernment area, some of them highlighted as best practice in European Commission eGovernment reports. The Portuguese online income tax service (www.portaldasfinancas.gov.pt) became available in 1999 and, since 2006, all business income tax (IRC) declarations need to be submitted online. In 2007, citizens' income tax (IRS) online declarations became pre-populated with relevant data. This online service and portal was highlighted as *best practice* in 2010, along with Social Security Online (European Commission, 2010a). The Monthly Statement of Remuneration (DMR) service, in particular, was pointed out as *good practice* by the European Commission (European Commission, 2014a). This service allows employers to deliver to Social Security statements of remuneration (DR) about their workers whose data is then used to pre-fill the employees' income tax (IRS) returns.

The Citizen's Card ('Cartão do Cidadão' – www.cartaodecidadao.pt; (AMA, 2015a)) is an electronic ID smartcard which allows for online service authentication and, as a key eGovernment enabler, it was also highlighted as *best practice* by the European Commission (European Commission, 2010a). For instance, this card may be used by a citizen in the Online Vehicle portal (which was considered *good practice* in 2014 (European Commission, 2014a)) to request the registration of his/her vehicle and receive the Vehicle Registration plate/Single Document Certificate at home, or to request the vehicle´s property transfer upon the purchase of a new or used vehicle (among other vehicle related registration acts).

On the business side, the Business Online ('Empresa Online') one-stop-shop business portal was selected as a *best practice* in 2010 (European Commission, 2010a) and 2013 (European Commission, 2013). It is now part of the broader Citizens' Portal ('Portal do Cidadão') and was renamed the Entrepreneur Desk ('Balcão do Empreendedor' – http://bde.portaldocidadao.pt). It provides access to all kinds of online services including the Simplified Business Information (IES) – *good practice* 2014 (European Commission, 2014a) – and the "Firm on the Spot" ('Empresa na Hora') service - awarded a "European Enterprise Award" already in 2006 (European Commission, 2013). The IES online service allows companies to report at a single point and in a single moment all required information on accounting, tax and statistics. "Firm on the Spot" offers entrepreneurs a totally integrated and dematerialised business creation process.

These flagship initiatives, among others, illustrate how eGovernment has evolved in Portugal over time. Apart from the identification of these individual initiatives, the European Commission eGovernment assessment exercises (since 2001) will be used the better to describe the Portuguese evolution.

EU Benchmark Results

Until 2010 (apart from 2008, year in which no assessment was performed) the assessment exercises produced two top-level (core) benchmarks (*online availability* and *online sophistication*) resulting from the analysis of twenty public services (twelve services aimed at individual citizens and eight services aimed at businesses).

The *Online sophistication* core benchmark assesses "the extent to which government services allow for interaction and/or transaction between the administration and citizens or businesses" (European Commission, 2010a). Since 2004 Portugal has scored higher in the *Online sophistication* benchmark than the average of EU+ countries, having achieved a 100% score in 2009. In 2010, both business and citizen services maintained 100% scores in comparison with 94% and 87% scores for the EU27+ average, respectively.

The *Full online availability* core benchmark assesses "the extent to which there is fully automated and proactive delivery of the 20 key public services" (European Commission, 2010a). Since 2004 Portugal has scored higher in this benchmark than the average of EU+ countries, having achieved 100% fully-online availability for businesses in 2007 (81% overall; ranking 3rd) (European Commission, 2007). Then, in 2009, Portugal scored 100% overall in full online availability with three other countries (European Commission, 2009). In 2010, the last year of this assessment period, Portugal ranked 1st out of the 32 countries measured with a 100% score, above the EU average of 82% (European Commission, 2010a).

A new benchmarking framework was established in 2011 (European Commission, 2012) which, in general, was based on a user Life Event model, that is "costumers' journeys within a particular domain. It covers both mandatory services as well as the information needs a citizen or business might have." (European Commission, 2014a). The 'stand-alone service assessment perspective' adopted previously

Figure 1. Four top-level benchmark assessment: Portugal versus EU28+ average (%)
Adapted from (European Commission, 2014b).

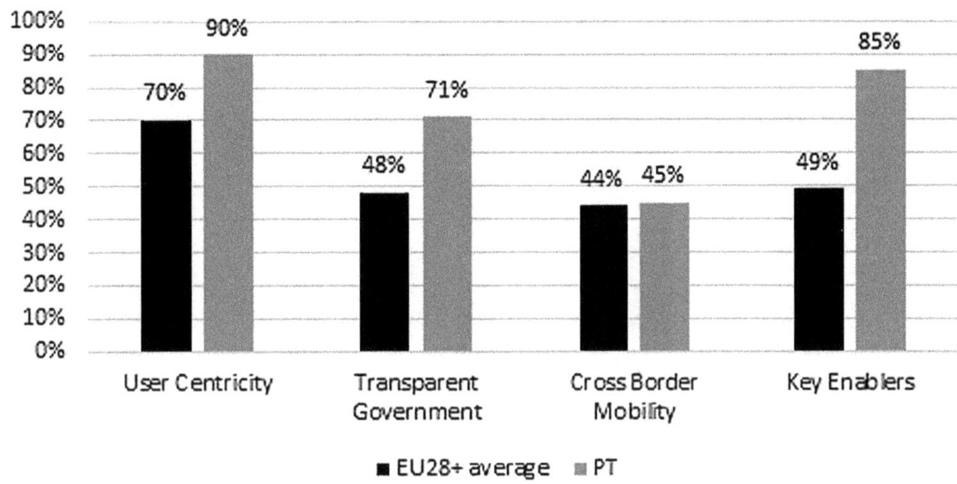

was, thus, abandoned. The current framework now comprises six top level benchmarks and seven life events, and the first complete baseline of results produced under the new framework was published in 2014 and comprises data collected over two years (2012 and 2013).

The 2012-2013 benchmark framework report (European Commission, 2014a) selected four top-level benchmarks (among the six measured) that cover important EU policy priorities. Figure 1 shows Portugal's assessment results concerning these four top-level benchmarks in comparison with the EU28+ average.

Portugal scores better in all top level benchmarks (EU policy priorities) when compared with the EU28+ countries' average, except for *Cross Border Mobility* where the scores are approximately the same. Furthermore, the Portuguese scores are well above 50% (again except for *Cross Border Mobility*). Considering these values, we might conclude that Government is well-developed in Portugal.

One important aspect of eGovernment is the existence of technical pre-conditions to foster eGovernment solution development. The European Commission benchmark framework includes one top-level benchmark (*Key Enablers* – see Figure 1) which indicates to what extent five technical pre-conditions are available online. Figure 2 shows Portugal's assessment results concerning these pre-conditions in comparison with the EU28+ average scoring.

According to the European Commission, the online availability of all chosen key enablers in Portugal exceeds the average of the other EU countries. Overall this is a good indication that Portugal removed a number of technical barriers and has already put in place some of the key enablers for eGovernment development.

More specifically, the eID (electronic identification) score reflects the impact of eGovernment initiatives such as the Citizens' Card ('Cartão do Cidadão' – www.cartaodecidadao.pt; (AMA, 2015a)), created in 2007, and, more recently, the Digital Mobile Key ('Chave Móvel Digital' – (AMA, 2015b)). These initiatives complement each other and provide secure electronic authentication mechanisms to access online public and private services, as well as digital signatures with full legal value.

Using these mechanisms, several services now accept digitally signed Electronic Documents (eDocuments) thus supporting the Portuguese score in this key enabler. The same applies to the Single Sign On (SSO) functionality which, in the Portuguese case, takes advantage of existing authoring mechanisms.

Figure 2. Key enablers online availability assessment: Portugal versus EU28+ average (%)
Adapted from (European Commission, 2014b).

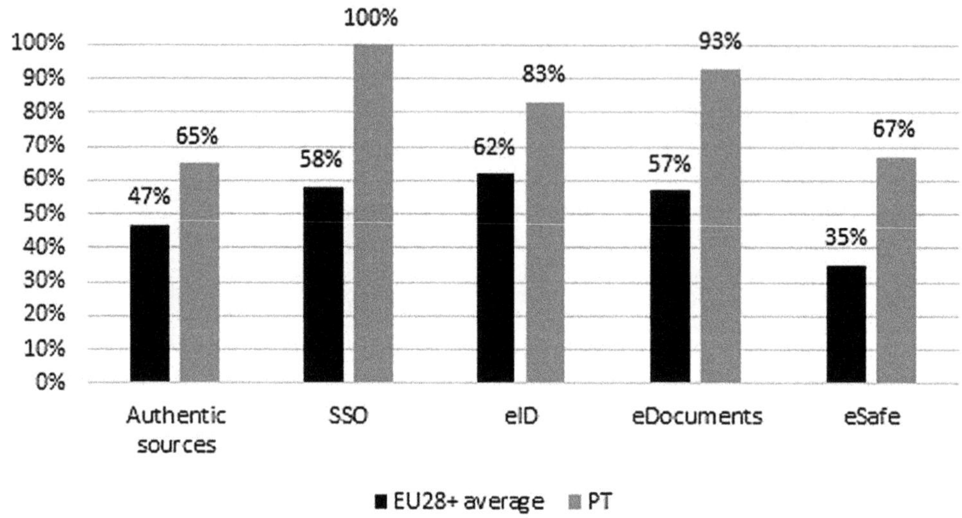

In respect of the Electronic Safe (eSafe) score, several public services (such as the Real Estate Registry) already provide virtual repository functionalities by permanently disclosing online authenticated personal documents (when requested by those involved) that can be referenced and used by interested third parties.

Finally, the Personal Income Tax Return (IRS) system provides a good example of an initiative that contributes to the Authentic Sources score (that reflects the existence of prior, base registries used to pre-fill and/or validate online form data). Nowadays, employers must provide salary information which is then used to pre-fill employees' Personal Income Tax Returns (IRS). Data from Social Security services is also used for the same purpose. Beginning in 2016, all invoices/receipts need to be automatically electronically reported by private companies to the Tax Administration services in order to be considered for individual citizens' tax deduction.

These examples, among others, illustrate some of the initiatives that implement and use eGovernment key enablers in Portugal and therefore help to better understand EU assessment scores.

eJUSTICE

Similarly to the definition provided for eGovernment, eJustice could be defined, in broad terms, as the use of new technologies in the field of justice (Inchausti, 2012). Answering the question of what is comprised in this broad definition is, however, a rather tricky task.

Fernando Gascón Incausti (2012) reduces the scope of eJustice to the activity of the courts and conceives of it as an alternative way to carry out activities that had hitherto been carried out in some other way. I. e, the changes introduced by eJustice should only be patent in the external configuration of the procedural acts.

Instead, Contini and Cordella perceive eJustice as a mechanism of "creation of new shared working practices and new 'technological artefacts' with juridical value" (Contini & Cordella, 2007), providing an infrastructure for the exchange of information within the whole judicial community (Contini & Cordella, 2007). As such, eJustice innovations should consider the "complex interplay of technological, institutional, organizational and normative components" of the judicial community (Velicogna, Errera, & Derlange, 2013). From this point of view, as an innovation effort, eJustice should not be considered just as a means to automate and replace 'traditional' paper-based procedures (process dematerialisation), and should not be concerned solely with activities occurring within the boundaries of a court (Contini & Cordella, 2007). Furthermore, eJustice initiatives should not be simply about developing technically functional systems (Velicogna et al., 2013) or merely deploying the 'right' technology to solve a 'technical problem' (Contini & Cordella, 2007).

The definition of eJustice that can be drawn from the documents produced by the various bodies of the European Union is somewhat more extensive. According to the European Commission, eJustice pursues three key goals – improvement in a) access to justice; b) cooperation between legal authorities; and b) the effectiveness of the Justice system itself. Justice or the justice system, in this sense, covers all dispute resolution fora or authorities responsible for the punishment of criminal behaviour. It, therefore, leaves behind "certain activities that sometimes involve legal institutions are themselves rather administrative in nature (e.g. land registers or the European Business Register)", but, on the other hand, include "activities such as arbitration or alternative dispute resolution (…) even when they are managed by non-legal bodies" (European Commission, 2008). For the European Commission it seems quite clear that the concept of eJustice also includes activities aiming to provide citizens with information on legal issues. One of the main projects developed under the eJustice strategy – the eJustice Portal – aims, primarily, to provide citizens with information on legislation and jurisprudence at national, European and international level (Council of the European Union, 2014).

The European Economic and Social Committee, however, seems to have a different approach. On the one hand, it excludes alternative mechanisms for dispute resolution from the scope of eJustice, arguing that "although intended to settle disputes (…) these are simply voluntary and extrajudicial processes aimed at balancing the interests of the parties concerned. On the other, it makes a distinction between eJustice and eLaw. The first "should be confined to the judicial aspects of dispensing justice in the fields of civil, commercial and perhaps administrative law – in other words, court practices and procedures, including arbitration proceedings" and the latter "which should facilitate electronic access a) to legal texts and their real-time production, be this substantive or procedural law, 'hard law' or 'soft law', b) to the case-law of the courts and c) to administrative decisions"(European Economic and Social Committee, 2009).

The difficulty of defining eJustice and of finding, among both scholars and institutions, a shared vision of the objectives eJustice should pursue is the mirror of the particular spot the justice system occupies. The relation between eGovernment and eJustice may be considered from several different perspectives. In general, eJustice may be considered as a subcategory of eGovernment ("the application of an 'e-government approach' to the judicial sector" (Contini & Cordella, 2007)), thus mimicking the relation between Justice (in particular) and Government (in general). Back in 2008, the European Commission pointed out precisely that "e-Justice is a specific field under the more general umbrella of e-Government" (European Commission, 2008). In this regard, the Strategy on European E-Justice 2014-2018 (Council of the European Union, 2014) calls for additional efforts to achieve further alignment with the general framework of eGovernment.

As a subset of eGovernment, eJustice development progress may be described and assessed by generic eGovernment maturity models found both in research literature (Lee, 2010) and official benchmarking efforts (European Commission, 2012, 2014a). Furthermore, several specific topics and terminology emerge in the eJustice field when discussing the potential role of ICTs (Cabral, Chavan, Clarke, & Greacen, 2012; Council of the European Union, 2013, 2014; Gascó & Jiménez, 2011; Jiménez, Criado, & Gascó, 2011; Reiling, 2012), such as:

- Infrastructure (internet and intranet) and basic support (office technologies, etc.);
- Communication, exchange of information within the judicial community outside court boundaries, interoperability and interconnection of registers;
- Access by the general public to information, to courts and to justice, including disintermediation and access to law and jurisprudence databases;
- Support for judicial decision-making knowledge management.
- Process dematerialisation, case registration (e-filling) and case management;
- Court administration, including personnel and financial management;
- Courtroom and hearing support tools such as videoconference.

Within the European Union some of these issues are being discussed from a cross-border perspective, including the development of a European eJustice portal, and common key enabler development oriented projects such as e-CODEX (e-Justice Communication via Online Data Exchange), STORK 2.0 (Secure Identity Across Borders Linked 2.0) or e-SENS (Electronic Simple European Networked Services) (Council of the European Union, 2013, 2014).

The fact that some activities (e.g., civil registries), while administrative in nature, involve legal institutions may cast doubt on whether the use of ICT to support them would fall into the specific eJustice or general eGovernment category. The same applies to those activities (e.g., arbitration or alternative dispute resolution) that, while considered of a judicial nature, are in fact performed by non-legal bodies (European Commission, 2008)

But, as Marco Fabri points out, "the administration of justice still seems to be considered 'a world apart' in the broad e-government debate" (Fabri, 2009), which is closely intertwined with judicial values and functions.

The Portuguese Justice System and the Use of ICT

The Portuguese justice system is divided into two different jurisdictions:

1. The administrative jurisdiction, comprising 17 first instance courts across the country ("tribunais administrativos e fiscais"), 2 appeal courts (Tribunal Central Administrativo do Norte e Tribunal Central Administrativo do Sul) and 1 supreme court (Supremo Tribunal Administrativo), which are empowered to judge administrative and tax disputes; and
2. The civil jurisdiction, that encompasses both civil and criminal disputes and comprises 30 first instance courts, 5 appeal courts (Tribunais da Relação) and 1 supreme court (Supremo Tribunal de Justiça).

Besides these two jurisdictions, there is also a Constitutional Court and a Court of Auditors. These are, thus, two different jurisdictions, totally independent from each other, with separate hierarchies and distinct judicial councils. Only the Public Prosecution Office is common to both jurisdictions. In both jurisdictions, in most cases, litigants must be represented by a lawyer. Only in civil cases where the value of the claim is lower than € 5,000 or in tax disputes where the value of the claim is lower than € 2,500 is pro se litigation allowed. Litigation in courts, in Portugal, is thus characterised by a strong intermediation process.

The implementation of ICT in these two jurisdictions was profoundly different. In Portugal, the use of ICT in justice was first mentioned in a government programme in 1987, under the XI Constitutional Government (1987-1991), associated to two fundamental goals: the shrinkage of the distance between justice and citizens and the modernisation of courts. Until 1999, however, the investment made was merely to provide courts with computers. In 2001, it became possible to examine witnesses by videoconference (Machado, Silva, & Santos, 2008).

CITIUS: eJustice Development in the Portuguese Civil Jurisdiction

In 1999, a group of court clerks and registrars started a project called GPCível (from "Gestão Processual Cível", *Civil Procedural Management*) – the ancestor of electronic procedure and dematerialisation processes in Portugal, which resulted in the application named H@bilus, that allowed court clerks to make writs of notice directly in the platform (Fernando, Gomes, & Fernandes, 2014). It was a tool mainly conceived to reduce the complexity of the workload of these professionals. It was, therefore, intended to provide court clerks with a working tool and had no intention of contributing to a wider access to justice, to an acceleration of the cooperation between legal authorities or to the improvement of the effectiveness of the Justice system itself. By 2005, all first instance courts of the civil jurisdiction were using this new tool and lawyers began to use H@bilusNet to lodge enforcement proceedings.

H@bilus was the embryo of CITIUS (meaning *faster* in Latin), the current application used by lawyers, judges and public prosecutors in the civil jurisdiction that hosts electronic pleadings. It was developed by the same team of registrars and court clerks who created and developed H@bilus and it constitutes a further development of this initial application, aiming at a procedural dematerialisation, by electronically treating all information pertaining to the proceeding, thus reducing their physical form to a minimum. CITIUS is composed of several applications designed for each category of user (the legal professionals) who communicate with each other and which allows for communication with other information systems from external entities, such as the police forces and probation service (Software, 2009). The applications used by judges (CITIUS-Judges) and public prosecutors (CITIUS-Public Prosecution) became operational in July 2007 and its use became compulsory a year and a half later.

In criminal proceedings, judges and public prosecutors use CITIUS to write and sign all sentences, court orders and judicial decisions and to send them, electronically, to the court registry. Court clerks use H@bilus to write the writ of notices and to manage the case, but have to print on paper the writ of notices and send it to both the parties involved and lawyers by post. Lawyers can consult the proceedings and related court hearings, but cannot lodge pleadings or other documents electronically. In civil cases and only in first instance courts, pleadings are lodged electronically, through CITIUS, by lawyers; judges and public prosecutors write and sign all court orders and send them, electronically, to the court registry; and court clerks use H@bilus to write and sign all writs of notice and send them to lawyers electronically. Only communication to the parties or witnesses (when needed) is made on paper through the post. The difference in the use of CITIUS between criminal and civil proceedings relies on the increased need to ensure safe communications between the court and the people involved in the proceeding. In higher courts, in all types of proceeding, communication between the court and lawyers is made on paper by post.

The implementation of case management software in civil jurisdiction courts also allowed for a change in the method of collecting justice statistics. In 2003, a new project, named Hermes, was launched and with it statistics data began to be collected, firstly, by filling in web forms, and later, when possible, by direct file transfer, via H@bilus (Machado et al., 2008).

SITAF: eJustice Development in the Portuguese Administrative Jurisdiction

SITAF is the application used by lawyers, judges, public prosecutors and court clerks in the administrative jurisdiction that hosts electronic pleadings. Unlike CITIUS, SITAF was developed so that it could begin to be used at the same time as a major procedural and judicial organisation reform of the administrative jurisdiction in January 2004. It was developed from scratch by a private company hired by the justice ministry and it allows legal professionals to perform all pleadings electronically. Once again, this is a tool developed for the use of practitioners. Nevertheless, when compared to CITIUS, SITAF has two significant limitations to achieving a full electronic proceeding: 1) the use of SITAF is not compulsory for lawyers, although there is an incentive to use the application by means of a reduction in court fees; 2) court clerks cannot electronically send writs of notice to lawyers. Although the law allows notifications to be delivered to lawyers by email, these are conducted by post.

From the beginning, SITAF revealed major weaknesses, with constant system crashes, which generated distrust among users. In 2007, one of the 17 first instance courts was affected by a crash of the computer system for more than a month, causing the paralysis of all proceedings and court hearings (Machado et al., 2008). In 2009, the Lisbon regional department of the Bar Association conducted a survey of lawyers, which generated a total of 149 answers, on the functioning of the administrative and tax courts. 70% of respondents stated they did not use SITAF to lodge pleadings, claiming that the system was too complex and that it did not work properly (Galvão, 2009). According to a newspaper article, published in May 2013, the use of SITAF constitutes, for a lawyer, a loss of two-day's work per week (Sousa, 2013).

EU and CEPEJ Benchmark Results

Although eJustice might be considered as an area within eGovernment, the EU eGovernment assessment framework used until 2010 did not include any specific justice-related benchmark, nor did it specifically consider any justice-related service. The new assessment framework (used in 2012-2013), however, does include one life event in the justice domain (*Starting a small claims procedure*). As defined by the European Commission, "this life event is part of the Justice domain, and captures the journey of someone willing to start a small claims procedure: from orientation and initiation to retrieving verdict and appeal." (European Commission, 2014b). Figure 3 presents the four top-level benchmark scores for Portugal for this life event.

When compared to the average scores of all EU28+ countries, Portugal significantly scores better in all top level benchmarks except for Cross Border Mobility including, in particular, the use of eGovernment key enablers. These results are consistent with the overall eGovernment Portuguese scores.

Figure 3. Starting a small claims procedure benchmark assessment: Portugal versus EU28+ average (%)
Adapted from (European Commission, 2014b).

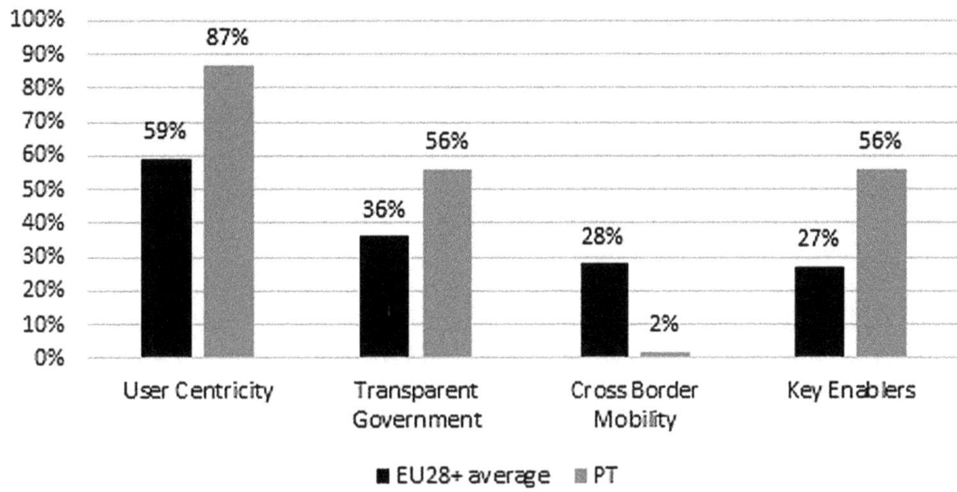

Also, the European Commission for the Efficiency of Justice (CEPEJ) has rehearsed a number of assessment exercises on eJustice. CEPEJ has categorised the ICT role in three main categories: direct assistance to judges and court clerks, support for court administration and management, and support for interaction/communication between courts and parties (CEPEJ, 2006). The benchmark reflects the dissemination of each specific ICT type (part of a specific category) across all courts: from ICT available in 100% of courts to ICT not available at all.

Since the ICT types grouped by each category have changed over the years, the benchmark data for Portugal in Figure 4 is presented in % (of the maximum value attainable in each category in each year). The data collected in 2010 and 2012 has also been used to produce the EU Justice Scoreboard (published in 2013 and 2014, respectively). The 2015 EU Justice Scoreboard is based on data from 2013, collected by CEPEJ specifically for this purpose (European Commission, 2015, p. 5). As shown in Figure 4, since 2010 all ICT considered in the benchmark has been available to all Portuguese courts.

Figure 4. CEPEJ benchmark ICT in the courts (e-justice and e-courts) for Portugal

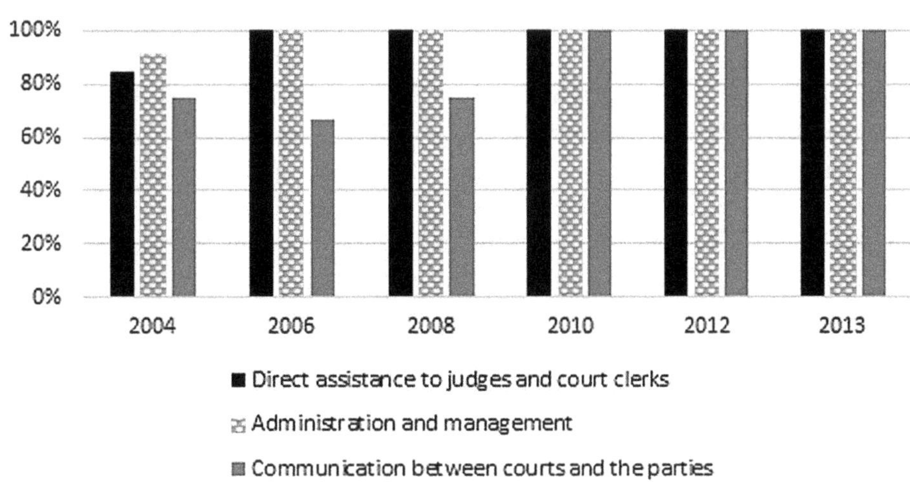

Both benchmark results (the EU benchmark and the CEPEJ benchmark) are limited to the civil jurisdiction, i. e, they only portray the use of ICT through CITIUS/H@bilus, leaving aside the administrative jurisdiction (i. e. courts that deal with administrative and tax judicial cases). On the other hand, it is only focused on first instance courts.

Paradoxically, the high scores achieved by Portugal in both EU and CEPEJ benchmarks mentioned contrast with the meagre results of the introduction of ICT regarding the efficiency of the judicial system. This disjunction highlights the lack of robustness of the indicators used to carry out the benchmark evaluation.

OPEN GOVERNMENT

The idea of promoting an open government is not new. The US Freedom of Information Act (FOIA), for instance, dates back to 1996 and illustrates the fact that "the 'open government principle' is generally linked to the public right-to-know and to issues of public access vis-à-vis government secrecy." (Linders & Wilson, 2011). Although freedom of information principles may be considered the roots of open government, nowadays the expression *Open government* encompasses the goals and perspectives of different societal stakeholders including *transparency advocates*, technology savvy *futurists*, civil engagers (eParticipation and eDemocracy activists), and bureaucrats focusing on rule compliance and accountability (Linders & Wilson, 2011). As Meijer et al put it (2012), "open government is not only about openness in informational terms [putting government information on the Internet] (vision) but also about openness in interactive terms (voice)."

This more comprehensive view on what constitutes an open government is highly influenced by the Obama Administration Memorandum (Obama, 2009) and Directive (Orszag, 2009) which list and systematise three main open government objectives: achieving transparency, that is, disclosing information held by public agencies that may be useful for public accountability purposes and/or for incentivising private companies to develop new products and services (social and economic value); promoting participation, that is, tapping into the collective knowledge of citizens to collect the best ideas to improve government solutions and decision-making (engagement and crowdsourcing); and by fostering collaboration, both between public agencies (inter-partner collaboration) and between public agencies, citizens and private companies in general (collaborative service development and delivery) (Linders & Wilson, 2011).

While in the US the Obama Administration Memorandum and Directive specifically and independently address open government principles and goals, in Europe some of these principles and goals are included in the eGovernment Action Plan 2011-2015 (European Commission, 2010b). The plan aims to support "the transition from current eGovernment to a new generation of open, flexible and collaborative seamless eGovernment services" (European Commission, 2010b) and defines several priorities and goals for that purpose. Among them, it seeks to promote 'User Empowerment' ("increasing the capacity of citizens, businesses and other organisations to be pro-active in society through the use of new technological tools") which includes several open government related issues including the 'Collaborative Production of Services', the 'Re-use of Public Sector Information', and the 'Improvement of Transparency, Involvement of citizens and businesses in policy-making processes'. After an eGovernment Benchmark Pilot on Open government and Transparency in 2010-2011 (European Commission, 2011), the new eGovernment Benchmark Framework 2012-2015 (European Commission, 2012) explicitly addressed the 'User Empowerment' ('Empowering Government') policy priority splitting it into 'User-centric Government',

'Transparent Government', 'Collaborative Government'. As a consequence, the next eGovernment assessment exercise already included the two top-level benchmarks for 'User-centric Government' and 'Transparent Government'. The 'Collaborative Government' benchmark has not yet been assessed and although it is expected to rely on 'Availability and use of social media', the actual assessment method to be used is yet to be determined (European Commission, 2014a). Traditional (core) eGovernment principles are reflected in the EU Action Plan under priority 'Efficiency and Effectiveness of Governments and Administrations', which is then translated into top-level benchmark 'Results-driven Government' (further divided into 'Effective Government' and 'Efficient Government') in the assessment framework.

The Open government approaches taken by the US and the European Commission, although addressing the same principles, illustrate two different possible perspectives on the relation between Open government and eGovernment: while the US seems to address both areas separately, in the EU the open government principles and goals are being incorporated within the broad eGovernment umbrella.

In this chapter both concepts will be considered separately in order to clarify their core underlying conceptual point of view and to facilitate analysis.

The European Union eGovernment assessment framework includes two top-level benchmarks which correspond to two of the Open government Directive's (Orszag, 2009) main objectives. But while the top-level benchmark for 'Transparent Government' is already being used (and will be analysed in the following sections), the 'Collaborative Government' benchmark has not yet been assessed. Although it is expected that this benchmark will rely on an 'Availability and use of social media' indicator, the actual assessment method to be used is yet to be determined (European Commission 2014a Figure 2.3). Furthermore, the 'Transparent Government' benchmark addresses one of the Open government Directive's transparency subgoals (*transparency for accountability*) by focusing on information disclosure on public entities' responsibilities and performance, the process of service delivery and personal data involved, while leaving out *transparency for data re-use* (the other Open government Directive transparency subgoal).

A brief analysis of Portuguese open government efforts seems to confirm the European Union eGovernment assessment framework focus and priorities, as the flagship initiatives in this area fall mostly into the *transparency for accountability* domain. Therefore, the whole open government analysis in this chapter will focus solely on this transparency subgoal.

Transparency Flagship Initiatives

As in so many other countries, in 2011 the Portuguese government created a 'data.gov' type dataset portal, Dados.gov.pt, which aims to "foster transparency and increase the visibility of Public Administration-produced information" (AMA, 2015c) while considering that "information re-usability is an essential pillar sustaining the creation of dados.gov" (AMA, 2015c). Like other 'data.gov'-type national portals, Dados.gov.pt provides a one-stop platform which allows public entities to publish their internally owned and managed datasets and ordinary citizens to access them. Despite these intentions, Dados.gov.pt is still in beta version and it has less than 700 dataset published. Furthermore, the structure and organisation characteristics of Dados.gov.pt replicates those commonly adopted by 'data.gov' type dataset portals worldwide which may not be entirely adequate for supporting public accountability (Lourenço, 2015).

A dedicated portal - GeADAP (ESPAP, 2015) was created as part of the new legal framework set up in 2008 requiring all public services to be assessed and including a provision for mandatory information disclosure requirements. The portal's purpose is to collect and disclose assessment data, including the assessment instrument defined by each public service (objectives and indicators) and quantitative and qualitative self-assessment results. However, the effectiveness of this portal, as regards open government objectives (transparency of public accountability purposes), seems to be somewhat limited by the fact that there is a very limited amount of public service assessment data actually being disclosed through the portal, possibly due to the "lack of information disclosure monitoring and public officials' accountability procedures" (Lourenço, Moura e Sá, & Veloso, 2015).

The *Municipal Transparency Portal* (Portal de Transparência Municipal - www.portalmunicipal.pt) constitutes yet another example of a recent open government (transparency) initiative. The portal was created in 2014 to "increase transparency of local public administration management with regard to citizens". It makes available a set of indicators regarding management of the 308 Portuguese municipalities ranging from *financial management* indicators (including, for instance, *outstanding arrears*) to *municipal electoral turnout* data.

Contrary to the BASE portal (see description below), the *Municipal Transparency Portal* does not disclose raw, disaggregated data. Instead, it focuses on aggregated (per entity) statistics and indicators. The base data is received from SIIAL (an integrated information system that acts as a single-access channel used by Portuguese municipalities to report mandatory, official, data to the corresponding supervising agency) and other official sources which are responsible for it. All indicators and statistics shown in the portal are also available in dados.gov.pt.

Finally, the Portuguese public tendering data portal (BASE portal - http://www.base.gov.pt) was created in 2010 to fulfill the legal requirement that public agencies must publicly disclose contract data resulting from all tendering processes. Failure to disclose data concerning a particular contract would ultimately render it legally invalid. The portal not only discloses individual contract data, but it also allows public entities to publish associated documents such as the actual contracts. The data is sent automatically from eProcurement platforms mandatorily used by public agencies, thus requiring no additional effort on their part, providing a good example of an open government (transparency) spin-off of an eGovernment initiative (the mandatory use of eProcurement platforms by public agencies). Data from the BASE portal may also be found in dados.gov.pt but aggregated in a yearly dataset.

The BASE portal is perhaps the most high-profile transparency initiative, with the highest impact on the public sphere, as the data disclosed is frequently used by journalists in their analyses, and there is even a newspaper, Jornal I, which regularly publishes a thematic analysis of the contract data published in a segment called "*Mercado da República*".

In sum, over the past few years the Portuguese government has launched several initiatives to promote transparency, particularly as regards supporting public accountability, but, apart from the BASE portal, it seems that the impact and effectiveness of these initiatives is quite limited (Lourenço, Sá, Jorge, & Pattaro, 2013; Lourenço, 2013).

EU Transparency Benchmark Results

The perception resulting from the analysis of some of the most prominent transparency initiatives, presented in the previous section, somehow seems to contrast with the results from the latest EU eGovernment assessment exercise (2012-2013) as regards the top-level Transparency benchmark (European Commission, 2014a). Figure 5 details the benchmark values for the three elements already presented in an aggregated form in Figure 1.

Figure 5. The three elements of transparent government: Portugal versus EU28+ average (%)
Adapted from (European Commission, 2014b).

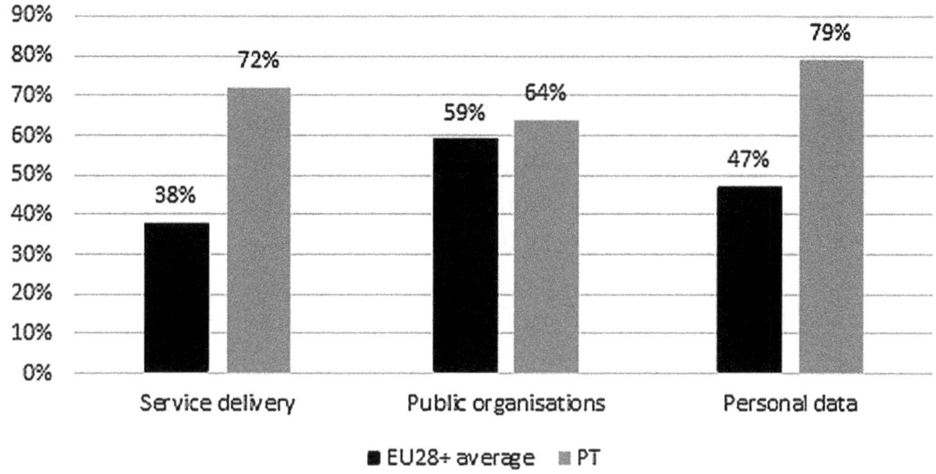

According to the EU benchmark, Portugal ranks above the EU28+ average in all three benchmark elements including service delivery (the way citizens are informed about the administrative process they have entered), public organisations (published information about their structure, activities, etc.) and personal data (the way citizens are informed about personal data held by public entities, how is it gathered, processed and stored).

OPEN JUDICIARY

Openness in justice is traditionally understood as a fundamental legal principle whereby court proceedings should be held in public as a means of granting public scrutiny of the performance of courts. The debate on the difficult relation between the judicial system and public scrutiny already has a long tradition. It has focused on distinct issues, such as the relation between courts and the media (the intermediates between courts and citizens), the grounding of judgments, discourse used during court hearings and when communicating with parties, the limits between the duty to inform and the right to privacy of the parties involved, etc. But all of these disparate issues share a common purpose: to establish how and to what extent courts should allow the public to scrutinise their rulings. Openness, in this sense, has to do with the validity and fairness of the concrete decision that was taken in a given case. It is the scrutiny of the factual case, a guarantee of an unbiased decision and of the quality of justice and a means of building public confidence in courts.

Over the past years, there has been a twist in what openness in justice should mean in this context, highlighting the fact that the scrutiny of the ruling is only a small piece of a larger puzzle and, thus, forming the concept of open judiciary. In a macro-context, the concept of open judiciary may be considered as the adoption of the basic principles of open government – transparency, participation and collaboration in the justice domain (Jiménez, 2014).

In contrast with transparency, it is more difficult to pinpoint the concept of participatory justice. Jiménez (2014) refers to this aspect of open judiciary as "a model where the parties actively participate in the search for solutions", and includes in this category institutional arrangements that deal with mediation, conciliation and arbitrage.

Collaboration seems to be even more difficult to define and characterise in the justice domain. If we consider the overall open government principles, it requires "significant (if not equal) power sharing (partnering)" (Linders & Wilson, 2011) with external entities to co-deliver public services, thus "improving effectiveness in meeting the needs of the public" (Linders & Wilson, 2011). Due to the specificity of the judiciary domain, namely concerning the legitimacy, acceptance and enforcement of legal decisions, such a power sharing requirement may be difficult to achieve ("whereas with participation opportunities the government maintains full decision-making powers" (Linders & Wilson, 2011). Jiménez (Jiménez, 2014) illustrates these possibilities using reports of community courts in the US, or different committees and commissions dedicated to tackling the root cause of social problems.

Participation and collaboration is thus frequently associated with legal reforms linked to dejudicialising which transfer the administration of justice from courts to other social actors, such as mediators, social workers, school boards, community councils, etc. The dejudicialisation movement, however, is characterised by a structural ambiguity (Santos, 1982), closely related to the duality of the legal formalism that, on the one hand, reassures as to the values of certainty and impartiality and, on the other, produces imbalances and marks the differentiation and superiority of legal professionals (Garapon, 1997). Hence, dejudicialisation is circumscribed to certain areas, answers different demands and produces different outcomes. In the sense useful for the concept of open judiciary, dejudicialisation emerges as overcoming the lack of judicial response to certain conflicts.

Faced with the inability of a univocal response from the judicial system, the bet is on a hybrid model released from limiting legal formalism, particularly visible in changes in justice issues affecting children and youth (Lauris & Fernando, 2010). Participation and collaboration in the Portuguese judicial system are prominent mainly in methods of alternative dispute resolution. Within judicial courts, the participation of citizens in the administration of justice is residual. In Portugal, the Commissions for the Protection of Children and Young People, composed of different social actors, who have the power to act whenever there is a child at risk, interacting closely with family courts, is an example. Another example can be found in some solutions adopted to deal with juvenile delinquency such as the possibility of a restorative meeting. Nonetheless, in neither of these legal reforms does ICT play a significant role.

Among the principles that comprise open judiciary, and in a similar way to what happens with open government in general, transparency is the subject most often addressed in the literature (Jiménez, 2014), primarily because it is most visible in recent experiences.

Alemanno and Stefan (Alemanno & Stefan, 2014), in a recent study that analyses the degree of openness at the Court of Justice of the European Union, start by addressing the principle of transparency in the justice domain by acknowledging the difficulty in distinguishing between the Courts' judicial ("the 'court jurisdiction'"; non-administrative tasks) and administrative ("the 'court administration', activities related to organisational functioning, human resources management and infrastructure) tasks. In a way, this effort also mimics the difficulty in defining a clear line between the eGovernment and eJustice.

Using Alemanno and Stefan's (Alemanno & Stefan, 2014) distinction, the next few pages will give a description of state-of-the-art practice in Portugal as to the adoption of transparency mechanisms and the use of ICT.

Transparency in Administrative Tasks

The top-level Transparency benchmark for the *Small Claims Procedure* life event, the one life event considered in the justice domain, provides an indication of how transparent is government in this domain, although focusing mainly on courts' administrative tasks. Globally considered, Portugal scored 56% (see Figure 3) in this top level benchmark for the *Small Claims Procedure*, above the average for the EU28+ countries for the same life event (36% - see Figure 3). However, the same *Small Claims Procedure* transparency score is lower than the average score across all life events for Portugal (71% - see Figure 1).

In sum, this benchmark, with its very limited scope, anticipates the underdevelopment of mechanisms for transparency in the judiciary that will be confirmed in the next section.

Transparency in Judicial Tasks

According to these authors, openness concerning judicial activity is divided into three areas: input, throughput and outputs. A similar distinction was proposed by Heald (2006), who distinguished between event and process transparency. While the former addresses inputs, outputs and outcomes, the latter addresses transformations (processes transforming inputs into outputs) and linkages (linking outputs and outcomes). Looking into each of these areas defined by Alemanno and Stefan (2014), state-of-the art practice in Portugal will be analysed.

Input Transparency in the Judiciary Domain

As mentioned before, the information system used by courts – both CITIUS and SITAF – was primarily designed to meet the needs of legal professionals and was thus not focused on providing transparency to the system. Legal professionals have electronic access to their legal cases (and not to the pending cases in which they do not intervene), but this is not the case for the ordinary citizen. The notice of the existence of a case is made through the assignment of the case to a judge – the first act that is performed in a new case. According to procedural laws, assignment is not only a public act, it must be publicised. Until 2004 for the administrative jurisdiction and 2007 for the civil jurisdiction, the assignment of cases was publicised by posting a list on the door of the court. With the implementation of SITAF and CITIUS, the list of assigned cases is posted online and accessible to the general public for civil jurisdiction cases (www.citius.mj.pt) and for administrative cases (www.taf.mj.pt). The information provided by these lists is scarce and different in each system. With CITIUS, the list of assigned cases is only accessible for a period of 30 days and only provides the following information: date when the pleading was lodged and assigned; parties involved; court and department to which the case was assigned; number of the case; type of process and value of the claim. This list is accessible through TribNet, also called CITIUS-Public Access - the application that offers information of compulsory publication to the general public, such as the public lists of case assignment, publicising of bankruptcies, public court sessions scheduled, edictal writ of summons, or addresses and court phone numbers. This application was not conceived to provide the general public with information, but to fulfill electronically a legal obligation to publicise a judicial act (Fernando et al., 2014).

With SITAF, the list of assigned cases has been available since its implementation (January 2004) and can be accessed at any moment. On the other hand, it provides information lacking in CITIUS: the name of the judge to whom the case has been assigned. In fact, even for legal practitioners, the name of the judge assigned to a given case in civil jurisdiction is only disclosed after the first written act of the given judge which comprises its electronic signature.

Online access to court submissions is, however, non-existent for the general public or for the parties involved. Only legal professionals, as said, have access to their legal cases. The parties involved have the right to ask the court for a copy of any document, but, for the general public, only in certain circumstances and after demonstrating a lawful interest, can the documents be handed over.

Throughput Transparency in the Judiciary Domain

As for transparency concerning the throughput phase (intermediate, oral, phase of court proceedings whereby information is generated by all parties), once again, the implementation of ICT in the justice system has not added any value to the general public. Depositions and court hearings are currently audio recorded and the recordings are integrated in, respectively, CITIUS and SITAF. Court clerks and judges have full access to such recordings, but lawyers need to provide the court with a pen drive or a DVD in order to have a copy of the audio records. The same restrictions on the general public or the parties involved pinpointed in the input phase apply to this phase. Although, in general, court hearings are public and anyone can attend these hearings, a lawful interest must be argued to request a copy of the audio record or of any document of the case.

Output Transparency in the Judiciary Domain

Alemanno and Stefan (2014) include three particular items in the output phase:

1. Publication of outputs;
2. Translation; and
3. Transparency of statistics.

As for the first item, jurisprudence of the higher courts of both civil and administrative jurisdictions is available online at www.dgsi.pt, with the redaction of the identity of the parties involved, in order to protect their privacy and personal data. First instance courts' rulings are not available online. The public database of jurisprudence, however, is mainly used by legal professionals as a working tool, namely due to the exclusive nature of legal discourse, only comprehensible to professionals. Legal discourse is still dominated by traditional rhetoric, making it impossible to be understood by external actors. In this field there is no experience that seeks to translate legal discourse into understandable language.

As for the last item – transparency of statistics – as said before, project Hermes was also conceived to provide up-to-date, electronically accessible statistics of the judicial jurisdiction courts to the general public (DGPJ, 2015a). However, due to the instability of the system, data is only made available with more than a year's delay. On the other hand, as mentioned before, there is a lack of trust in the information provided by the statistics.

If in the civil jurisdiction there are shortcomings as regards statistics, in the administrative jurisdiction statistics are almost non-existent. The Hermes project only provides statistics of higher courts of the administrative jurisdiction. As for first instance, administrative and tax courts, the available statistics are made public by its High Council annually on its website, with the indication of the number of cases lodged, pending and ruled on in a given year, per court, and the information is only available starting in 2009 (CSTAF, 2015).

DISCUSSION

The analysis of eGovernment and eJustice international benchmarking results suggest that Portugal is at the forefront of ICT usage, particularly when compared with the average of the other European countries (EU28+). Furthermore, some of these initiatives have been highlighted as 'good practice' and have had a real impact on the efficiency and efficacy of public service provision.

Although this eGovernment progress also includes a number of services in the justice domain, these are mainly of an administrative nature (registries, etc.). For instance, the *Small Claims Procedure* EU benchmarking results reflect a very specific area ('Injunções'), which is predominantly a well-defined administrative process and benefits from a specific support system (and a microsite within the CITIUS portal (MJ, 2015)). As such, it should be considered more as a general eGovernment project than as an eJustice-specific initiative.

Portugal also scores well on the CEPEJ benchmark as regards eJustice (ICT usage in the courts), but these results need to be carefully considered. To provide an overview of the efficiency development within the justice domain and the potential effect of ICT usage to support it, Figure 6 displays the *length of proceedings* in civil justice indicators from 2000 to 2013, the most recent year with statistics available, due to the CITIUS system crash in 2014 (DGPJ, 2015b).

Figure 6. Average civil process length in first instance courts 2000-2013
Source: Hermes Project/Official Justice Statistics (DGPJ, 2015a).

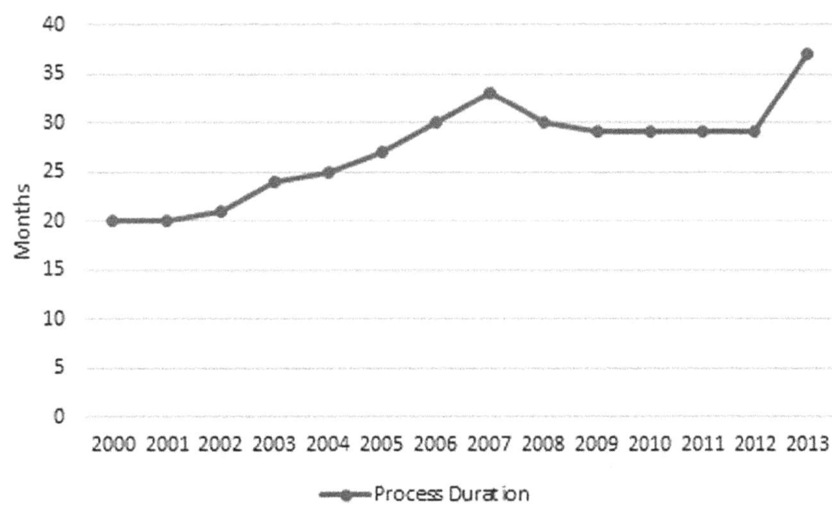

Thus, according to Figure 6, what could be said about the impact of CITIUS, the major justice system ICT support platform, in overall civil justice efficiency?

As mentioned above, CITIUS was available for judges and lawyers during the period 2006/2007 and became mandatory for civil proceedings at the beginning of 2009 (CEPEJ 2009). According to Figure 6, average *length of proceedings* did not change significantly in the 2007-2012 period (around 30 months), rising to 37 months (more than 3 years) in 2013. In fact, in 2000 only 0.49% of the cases ruled that year had lasted more than 8 years. In 2013, that percentage was of 7.9%. As for the administrative jurisdiction, due to the scarcity of statistics available, it is not even possible to conduct this exercise.

Furthermore, in September 2014, the unthinkable happened: after preparing for a change in the judicial map, the CITIUS platform became fully inoperative for several months (Veludo, 2014), revealing its instability and fragility, perhaps a consequence of its development process (described in Fernando et al (2014)). The CITIUS technical problem and consequences for the judicial system provide a stark contrast with the success of several eGovernment initiatives already presented. Furthermore, the evolution of average length of proceedings, considered a significant problem in the Portuguese civil justice system, highlights the perception that the CITIUS platform may have had limited impact on overall judicial efficiency.

One possible explanation for this lack of visible success may be due to the fact that the CITIUS platform, which was developed by registrars and court clerks, has a focus on procedural dematerialisation and does not provide enough support for judges and prosecutors. This is particularly relevant since the Portuguese judicial culture largely relies on unstructured, complex and extensive, written based legal documents which hamper judges' and prosecutors' analyses and decision tasks. Without specific support for these tasks, and perhaps a simplification of the procedures themselves, it will be very difficult to achieve important progress in overall justice domain efficiency due to ICT initiatives (eJustice). Nevertheless, as stated before, SITAF has been designed from scratch for use by all legal professionals and still reveals major weaknesses and a low impact on the efficiency of courts.

This apparent gap between eJustice benchmarking results and ICT-led actual improvement to the judicial system suggest a need to further refine the eJustice concept and revise the benchmarking framework, particularly that used by CEPEJ. This framework seems to be too simplistic when compared with existing general eGovernment assessment frameworks and maturity models, simply providing an institutional view (a single questionnaire completed by a Portuguese government official) on the dissemination of three major categories of ICT applicable to the judiciary domain (% of courts using each system type). No detailed account of the systems' sophistication, maturity or effectiveness is measured by the CEPEJ benchmark. A new, revised assessment framework is necessary and might be inspired by the EU eGovernment framework. It should consider the availability, sophistication and actual usage of infra-structure and key enabler technologies, assess integrated external 'life-events' (representing 'customer' journeys instead of single services availability), and evaluate the usage of ICT to support the different phases of diverse types of judicial process. New data acquiring methods, such as Mystery Shopper and user surveys, could be adopted to consider the viewpoint of all major judiciary stakeholders, including registrars and court clerks, judges and prosecutors, lawyers and notaries, and 'ordinary' citizens. Finally, such a framework should also take into account key elements of open judiciary such as transparency, public participation and collaboration among all stakeholders.

In the Portuguese case, some open government initiatives have benefited from these eGovernment outcomes, namely with respect to transparency for public accountability. One such successful initiative is related to public spending transparency, whereby certified tendering platforms introduced as part of an eGovernment effort to facilitate public contracting are required to automatically publish contact data in a dedicated portal. This open government (transparency for accountability) success story, although confined to a particular domain, illustrates one key point: in order to be successful and sustainable, transparency as data disclosure needs to be rooted in eGovernment automatised processes and support systems, that is, it must not depend on extra efforts (burdens) by public officials.

Similarly to open government, the success of open judiciary initiatives may depend on their connection with eJustice, and the importance of considering beforehand transparency issues and embedding them in eJustice platform development. Like other areas of governance, the judicial system does benefit from communication infra-structures (intranet, email, etc.) and basic support technologies such as video-conferencing in court rooms. Judicial operators, including judges, prosecutors and court clerks, also benefit from the widespread availability of personal productivity applications. Nevertheless, not only have these systems revealed significant technical problems that led to a partial standstill of the judicial system, they were not designed to answer any demand of scrutiny of the judicial system. If it is true that the peculiarities of the judicial system and its intrinsic values and functions might justify the absence of high impact open judiciary initiatives, it is also undoubtable, from the authors' perspective, that choices made on the eJustice development model have affected its ability to become the embryo of open judiciary initiatives and to incorporate other values, such as collaboration, participation and, at a lower scale, transparency.

CONCLUSION

The description and analyses made above provide useful clues to the issues raised at the beginning of the present chapter. Firstly, it is possible to outline the different paths travelled by eJustice and eGovernment, especially as regards the definition of a strong strategy of ICT implementation. eGovernment has benefitted from benchmarking frameworks which clearly defined the priority areas of investment and from the sophistication of such evaluation exercises that pushed for further developments. eJustice benchmarking frameworks are clearly below expectations and do not play the role of providing an incentive to investment in its development.

The lack of strategy in the implementation of ICT in the justice system is particularly visible when analysing the consequences of the technical problems of the information systems of courts in ongoing judicial reforms. Not only did the system collapse with the electronic migration process in September 2014, but some of the most emblematic issues of the judicial map reform, such as the definition of goals for the judiciary, failed to be addressed since they were dependent on the ICT system. Since the definition of goals depends on the statistics available and with the crash of CITIUS distrust in statistics became widespread, it is not foreseeable that this measure will be put in place any time soon.

As mentioned, eJustice did not succeed in becoming an embryo of open judiciary initiatives that are lacking in the Portuguese landscape. The legal reform of the Portuguese judicial organisation set up in 2014, that not only altered the geographical delimitation of courts but also introduced significant changes to the administration of courts, is a paradigmatic example. The legal reform relied on ICT mainly to provide the tools for the definition of goals for the judiciary. It did not contemplate any mechanism of public disclosure of information on court activities. It merely provides for a generic obligation to deliver a report for each court, without specifying the goals or values to be achieved by such reports.

Unlike open government initiatives, namely on transparency, that have benefited from the previous development of eGovernment, in the judiciary distrust in the information systems due to their technical problems and the over centralisation on legal professionals have contributed to the absence of open judiciary initiatives. The focalisation on legal professionals when developing and implementing information systems in courts is observable when analysing the type of information made public online. Only information of compulsory publication to the general public is published online, as a means of replacing publication in newspapers or on the door of the court, and there is no concern for providing information, namely on jurisprudence, in understandable language.

Overall, apart from some successful transparency ICT-driven initiatives, there seems to have been little to no effort in supporting the other objectives of open government and open judiciary: participation and collaboration. The reasons for such lack of attention paid to these two other dimensions can vary. For one, as stated before, it is somewhat simple to incorporate transparency mechanisms into eGovernment solutions since the data is already there in digital format. No significant extra efforts are required, as long as security and privacy concerns are properly addressed. Furthermore, transparency initiatives do not depend on external involvement (by citizens, for instance) such as participatory or collaborative initiatives. But above all, promoting transparency and public accountability (as ICT-driven data disclosure) does not require significant policy transformations in the context. Open government and open judiciary as participation and collaboration, on the contrary, demand a new contextual framework in order to be fully implemented. In the judicial domain, in particular, issues such as impartiality or the legitimacy of judicial decisions require a closer analysis and an extra effort to design ICT supported participation and collaboration venues. The Portuguese example indicates that, while eGovernment, eJustice (partially) and transparency initiatives have been successfully implemented, there is still a long way to go before significant progress can be achieved as regards participation and collaboration and, therefore, open government and open judiciary.

ACKNOWLEDGMENT

This work has been supported by the Fundação para a Ciência e a Tecnologia (FCT) under project grant UID/MULTI/00308/2013.

REFERENCES

Alemanno, A., & Stefan, O. (2014). Openness at the Court of Justice of the European Union: Toppling a taboo. *Common Market Law Review*, *51*(1), 97–139.

AMA. (2015a). *Cartão de Cidadão*. Retrieved May 28, 2015, from www.ama.pt/index.php_option=com_content&task=view&id=28&Itemid=32.html

AMA. (2015b). *Chave Móvel*. Retrieved May 28, 2015, from https://cmd.autenticacao.gov.pt/Ama.Authentication.Frontend/

AMA. (2015c). *Dados.gov.pt - Perguntas Frequentes*. Retrieved May 28, 2015, from http://www.dados.gov.pt/PT/Info/PerguntasFrequentes.aspx

Andersen, K. V., & Henriksen, H. Z. (2006). E-government maturity models: Extension of the Layne and Lee model. *Government Information Quarterly*, *23*(2), 236–248. doi:10.1016/j.giq.2005.11.008

Cabral, J. E., Chavan, A., Clarke, T. M., & Greacen, J. (2012). Using Technology to Enhance Access to Justice. *Harvard Journal of Law & Technology*, *26*, 241.

CEPEJ. (2006). European Judicial Systems. Belgium: Council of Europe.

Contini, F., & Cordella, A. (2007). Information System and Information Infrastructure Deployment: The Challenge of the Italian e-Justice Approach. *Electronic Journal of E-Government*, *5*(1), 43–52.

Council of the European Union. (2013). *Draft Strategy on European E-Justice 2014-2018 (No. 2013/C 376/06)*. Council of the European Union.

Council of the European Union. (2014). *Multiannual European E-Justice Action Plan 2014-2018 (No. 2014/C 182/02)*. Council of the European Union.

CSTAF. (2015). *Conselho Superior dos Tribunais Administrativos e Fiscais - Dados Processuais da Jurisdição*. Retrieved May 28, 2015, from http://www.cstaf.pt/Paginas/Estatistica-Processual.aspx

Dawes, S. S. (2008). The Evolution and Continuing Challenges of E-Governance. *Public Administration Review*, *68*, S86–S102. doi:10.1111/j.1540-6210.2008.00981.x

DGPJ. (2015a). *Direção-Geral da Política da Justiça - Projecto Hermes*. Retrieved May 28, 2015, from www.siej.dgpj.mj.pt

DGPJ. (2015b). *Resultados de 2014: Nota técnica*. Retrieved May 28, 2015, from http://www.siej.dgpj.mj.pt/SIEJ/PDFs/Tribunais/Resultados2014notatecnica.pdf

ESPAP. (2015). *GeADAP - Avaliação de Serviços*. Retrieved May 28, 2015, from https://www.siadap.gov.pt/PaginasPublicas/Servicos.aspx

European Commission. (2001). *Summary Report: Web-based Survey on Electronic Public Services* (Results of the first measurement: October 2001). Author.

European Commission. (2007, September). The User Challenge Benchmarking The Supply Of Online Public Services. *Measurement*.

European Commission. (2008). Communication from the Commission to the Council, the European Parliament and the European Economic and Social Committee: Towards a European e-Justice Strategy (No. COM(2008)329 final). Brussels: European Commission.

European Commission. (2009). *Smarter, Faster, Better eGovernment (8th Benchmark Measurement | November 2009)*. Directorate General for Information Society and Media.

European Commission. (2010a). *Digitizing Public Services in Europe: Putting ambition into action (9th Benchmark Measurement | December 2010)*. Author.

European Commission. (2010b). The European eGovernment Action Plan 2011-2015 : Harnessing ICT to promote smart, sustainable & innovative Government (No. COM(2010) 743). Brussels: European Commission.

European Commission. (2011). eGovernment Benchmark Pilot on Open Government and Transparency: Measuring the potential of eGovernment to foster Open Government and Transparency in Europe. Brussels: European Commission.

European Commission. (2012). *eGovernment Benchmark Framework 2012-2015: Method Paper*. Directorate General for Information Society and Media.

European Commission. (2013). *Public Services Online: "Digital by Default or by Detour?". Assessing User Centric eGovernment performance in Europe – eGovernment Benchmark 2012*. European Commission.

European Commission. (2014a). Delivering the European Advantage? "How European governments can and should benefit from innovative public services" (eGovernment Benchmark Final Background Report - May 2014). Brussels: Author.

European Commission. (2014b). *Delivering the European Advantage? "How European governments can and should benefit from innovative public services" (Portugal: eGovernment State of Play - May 2014)*. Author.

European Commission. (2015a). *e-Government factsheets. eGovernment in Portugal 2015* (No. January 2015, Edition 17.0). Brussels: European Commission. Retrieved from https://joinup.ec.europa.eu/sites/default/files/egov_in_portugal_-_january_2015_-_v_17_0_final.pdf

European Commission. (2015b). The 2015 EU Justice Scoreboard (No. COM(2015) 116). Brussels: European Commission.

European Economic and Social Committee. Opinion of the European Economic and Social Committee on the "Communication from the Commission to the Council, the European Parliament and the European Economic and Social Committee: Towards a European e-Justice Strategy"COM(2008) 329 final, 32 Organization 1–7 (2009).

Fabri, M. (2009). The Italian Style of E-Justice in a Comparative Perspective. In A. C. i Martínez & P. F. i Abat (Eds.), E-Justice: Using Information Communication Technologies in the Court System (pp. 1–19). IGI Global.

Fernando, P., Gomes, C., & Fernandes, D. (2013). Citius: the Electronic Payment Order Procedure in Portugal. In F. Contini & G. F. Lanzara (Eds.), *Building Interoperability for European Civil Proceedings Online* (pp. 215–272). Bologna: Clueb.

Fernando, P., Gomes, C., & Fernandes, D. (2014). The Piecemeal Development of an e-Justice Platform: The CITIUS Case in Portugal. In *The Circulation of Agency in E-Justice* (pp. 137–159). Springer. doi:10.1007/978-94-007-7525-1_6

Galvão, S. (2009). *Funcionamento dos Tribunais Administrativos e Fiscais*. Lisbon.

Garapon, A. (1997). *Bien juger – Essai sur le ritual judiciaire*. Paris: Odyle Jacob.

Gascó, M., & Jiménez, C. E. (2011). Interoperability in the Justice Field: Variables that Affect Implementation1. In *Proceedings of the 11th European Conference on EGovernment* (p. 272). Academic Conferences Limited.

Hiller, J. S., & Belanger, F. (2001). *Privacy Strategies for Electronic Government. The PricewaterhouseCoopers Endowment for The Business of Government. E-Government Series*. PricewaterhouseCoopers.

Inchausti, F. G. (2012). Electronic Service of Documents National and International Aspects. In M. Kengyel & Z. Nemessányi (Eds.), *Electronic Technology and Civil Procedure* (pp. 137–180). Dordrecht: Springer Netherlands; doi:10.1007/978-94-007-4072-3_8

Jiménez, C. E. (2014). *Justicia Abierta: transparencia y proximidad de la justicia en el actual contexto de Open Government*. Barcelona: Centro de Estudios Jurídicos y Formación Especializada del Departamento de Justicia. Generalidad de Cataluña.

Jiménez, C. E., Criado, J. I., & Gascó, M. (2011). Technological e-Government Interoperability. An Analysis of IberoAmerican Countries. *Latin America Transactions, IEEE (Revista IEEE America Latina), 9*(7), 1112–1117.

Lauris, É., & Fernando, P. (2010). A dupla face de Janus: as reformas da justiça e a Lei Tutelar Educativa. *Julgar*, (11), 135–146.

Layne, K., & Lee, J. (2001). Developing fully functional E-government: A four stage model. *Government Information Quarterly*, *18*(2), 122–136. doi:10.1016/S0740-624X(01)00066-1

Lee, J. (2010). 10 year retrospect on stage models of e-Government: A qualitative meta-synthesis. *Government Information Quarterly*, *27*(3), 220–230. doi:10.1016/j.giq.2009.12.009

Linders, D., & Wilson, S. C. (2011). What is Open Government? One Year after the Directive. In *12th Annual International Conference on Digital Government Research (Dg.o'11)* (pp. 262–271). College Park, MD: ACM. doi:10.1145/2037556.2037599

Lourenço, R. P. (2013). Data disclosure and transparency for accountability: A strategy and case analysis. *Information Polity*, *18*(3), 243–260. doi:10.3233/IP-130310

Lourenço, R. P. (2015). An analysis of open government portals: A perspective of transparency for accountability. *Government Information Quarterly*. doi:10.1016/j.giq.2015.05.006

Lourenço, R. P., Moura e Sá, P., & Veloso, S. (2015). Avaliação de transparência online: O caso do SIADAP das Direcções Gerais. In CISTI'2015 - 10a Conferência Ibérica de Sistemas e Tecnologias de Informação. Águeda. Academic Press.

Lourenço, R. P., Sá, P. M., Jorge, S., & Pattaro, A. F. (2013). Open Government and online transparency for accountability: One assessing model and two applications. *European Journal of Electronic Government*, *11*(1), 280–292.

Machado, H., Silva, S., & Santos, F. (2008). *Justiça Tecnológica: promessas e desafios*. Porto: Edições Ec.

Meijer, A. J., Curtin, D., & Hillebrandt, M. (2012). Open government: Connecting vision and voice. *International Review of Administrative Sciences*, *78*(1), 10–29. doi:10.1177/0020852311429533

MJ. (2015). *Ministério da Justiça - Procedimento de Injunção*. Retrieved May 28, 2015, from http://www.citius.mj.pt/Portal/consultas/Injuncoes/Injuncoes.aspx

Obama, B. (2009). *Transparency and open government. Memorandum for the heads of executive departments and agencies*. Retrieved from http://www.whitehouse.gov/the_press_office/TransparencyandOpenGovernment

OECD. (2003). *The e-government imperative: main findings*. Paris: OECD.

Orszag, P. (2009). *Open government directive. Memorandum for the Heads of Executive Departments and Agencies*. Retrieved from http://www.whitehouse.gov/open/documents/open-government-directive

Reiling, D. (2012, June). Technology In Courts In Europe: Opinions, Practices And Innovations. *International Journal For Court Administration*, 1–10.

Santos, B. de S. (1982). A participação popular na administração da justiça no Estado capitalista. In S. dos M. do M. Público (Ed.), A participação Popular na Administração da Justiça (pp. 83–98). Lisbon: Livros Horizonte.

Siau, K., & Long, Y. (2005). Synthesizing E-government Stage Models - a Meta-synthesis Based on Meta-ethnography Approach. *Industrial Management & Data Systems*, *105*(4), 443–458. doi:10.1108/02635570510592352

Software, C. (2009). *Citius. Relatório de Auditoria ao Citius*. Academic Press.

Sousa, F. A. de. (2013, May 26). SITAF faz advogados perder dois dias por semana. *Diário de Notícias*, p. 16.

UMIC. (2015). *Cronologia da Sociedade da Informação em Portugal*. Retrieved May 6, 2015, from http://www.umic.pt/index.php?option=com_content&task=view&id=3123&Itemid=477

Velicogna, M., Errera, A., & Derlange, S. (2013). Building e-Justice in Continental Europe: The TéléRecours Experience in France. *Utrecht L. Rev.*, *9*(1), 38. doi:10.18352/ulr.211

Veludo, F. (2014, October 2). Cronologia: um mês caótico na Justiça. *Jornal Público*. Retrieved from http://www.publico.pt/sociedade/noticia/um-mes-caotico-na-justica-1671700?page=-1

West, D. M. (2004). E-Government and the Transformation of Service Delivery and Citizen Attitudes. *Public Administration Review*, *64*(1), 15–27. doi:10.1111/j.1540-6210.2004.00343.x

Chapter 7
Integrating Semi-Open Data in a Criminal Judicial Setting

Mortaza S. Bargh
Research and Documentation Centre (WODC), Ministry of Security and Justice, The Netherlands

Sunil Choenni
Research and Documentation Centre (WODC), Ministry of Security and Justice, The Netherlands & Research Centre Creating 010, Rotterdam University of Applied Sciences, Rotterdam, The Netherlands

Ronald F. Meijer
Research and Documentation Centre (WODC), Ministry of Security and Justice, The Netherlands

ABSTRACT

Judiciary systems comprise various partner organizations (e.g., police, public prosecutor, courts, and rehabilitation centres) that collaboratively resolve criminal cases. These partner organizations have their own data administration and management systems, which are setup/operated separately and integrated barely. This chapter explains the approach of the authors' organization for integrating the data sets of the Dutch judiciary systems, and for opening the data integration outcomes to the public and/or to specific groups. These outcomes (e.g., data sets and reports) are meant to provide useful insights into (the performances of) the partner organizations individually and collectively. Such data opening efforts do not comply with all Open Data requirements, mainly due to the quality, (privacy) sensitivity and interoperability issues of the raw data. Nevertheless, since these initiatives aim at delivering some benefits of Open Data, the chapter introduces the new paradigm of Semi-Open Data for acknowledging such data opening initiatives.

INTRODUCTION

In recent years we have observed a surge in Open Data movements. The term Open Data refers to data that is reusable and distributable by third parties without any costs (ODef, 2015). The idea of Open Data has widely gained popularity for several good reasons. For a government, Open Data could be a means

DOI: 10.4018/978-1-5225-0717-8.ch007

to strengthen democracy. By opening up its data, a government provides transparency into its operations, meets regulatory compliance, and increases public participation and collaboration. Open Data is also expected to boost economic developments and innovations. Commercial companies and start-ups can exploit the data to develop new applications and services such as recommender apps (Choenni, Bargh, Roepan, & Meijer, 2015) and to create new types of professions such as data journalists and fact checkers. Furthermore, businesses and individuals can use Open Data to support their strategic and personal decisions. For example, individuals can use neighborhood statistics for buying houses and for implanting trees and plants in polluted areas. Scientists can reuse the data for reviewing scientific results as well as for their own evidence-based research.

Data opening, however, appears to be a tedious and almost infeasible process for many organizations. There are several impediments of Open Data identified in the literature, see for example (Zuiderwijk, Janssen, Choenni, Meijer, & Sheikh Alibaks, 2012; CoA report, 2015). These obstacles range from privacy concerns to technical issues. In this chapter, the authors argue that acting according to the current definition of Open Data (ODef, 2015) is too challenging for the judicial field. For example, three typical challenges are privacy, legacy and interoperability of judicial data. First, opening judicial data 'as it is' often contravenes the privacy law and regulations because such data pertain to real-life persons and encompass privacy sensitive attributes like names, birth-dates, crime types, and sentences. Even if these sensitive information items are removed or anonymized, there is a chance to infer such sensitive information by combining several junks of information. As an example of such inference, suppose that a school decides to publish the average exam marks of its male and female students. If we know that only two female students took part in an exam and if we are able to derive from social media that one of these female students got a 9, then the result of the other female student can be deduced.

Opening judicial data as raw as possible, as required in Open Data (OD101, 2015; Wonderlich, 2010), may put data analysts on the wrong track due to the legacy nature of judicial data. The semantics of judicial data may evolve over time since rules and regulations are subject to frequent changes. For example, crimes are categorized into different categories – the well-known categories of crimes include violent crime, theft, burglary, drugs offence, drunk driving, vandalism, and economic crime (Moolenaar, Choenni, & Leeuw, 2007). The crime categories today might be different from those categories of ten years ago. For example, ten years ago the Internet related crimes were assigned to the category of 'others' or 'economic crime', while today there is a call for a new category 'cybercrime'. If a new category is added or an existing category is deleted in a categorization system, then the objects need to be redistributed among the new set of categories. For a proper interpretation of the results obtained by analyzing or querying such data, it is of vital importance to know how the semantics of the data have evolved over time. Suppose that someone is interested in knowing how the category economic crime has developed over the last ten years, during which the objects among the categories have been redistributed due to the introduction of the new category of cybercrime. This redistribution may cause the occurrence of a trend break. For a proper interpretation of such a break in the trend, therefore, one should know how and when the redistribution was carried out.

The strength of Open Data lies in the ability of integration and combination of a data set with other data sets. Therefore, interoperable data sets are required. Unfortunately, however, many data sets in the judicial field are not interoperable and a significant amount of effort is required to process these data sets to make them interoperable. In the judicial field, there are many systems belonging to various partner organizations that collaboratively resolve criminal cases, e.g., police, public prosecutors, courts, and rehabilitation centres. Each organization has its own core business, specific rules, and regulations to meet. Furthermore, in the field of justice, it is important to satisfy the principle of 'trias politica' (i.e., separation of powers). As a consequence, these organizations have their own data administration and management systems that are setup and operated separately and autonomously. Data sets from these systems are hard to integrate or to combine since primary and foreign keys (Elmasri & Navathe, 2004) are often missing. Therefore, data processing is required before any data opening, which is against the principles of Open Data (ODH, 2015).

Given the potentials of the Open Data movement and the fundamental obstacles of judicial data opening, the goal of this contribution is to exploit the benefits whilst bypassing the obstacles of Open Data. To move towards the goal, the authors introduce the concept of Semi-Open Data paradigm. In this paradigm, the focus is on achieving some of the objectives and requirements of Open Data, for example, opening processed data, instead of meeting all Open Data objectives and requirements. The concept of Semi-Open Data paradigm is meant to encompass, acknowledge and encourage all those efforts that cannot be marked as Open Data, nevertheless these efforts push organizations in small steps in the strategically chosen direction of Open Data. This chapter also illustrates the implementation and deployment of the data opening efforts of the authors' organization, which can be characterized within the Semi-Open Data paradigm. The authors provide two example solution directions to tackle the issues with regard to, among others, privacy, legacy and interoperability of judicial data sets. Based on these two solution directions, the authors have developed two methods to deal with these (privacy, legacy and interoperability) issues. The authors will explain two cases to illustrate how they have applied these methods in practice within a real organizational setting.

The remainder of this chapter is organized as follows. The chapter starts with a problem statement section where the authors briefly describe the problem context, the motivations, and the research methodology for this study. For being self-contained, in the following section the authors provide a background on Open Data, discussing its objectives and requirements as well as a few examples of its usage. This background section discusses the challenges of judicial data opening in more detail and shortly outlines two solution directions used in practice to deal with these challenges. Adopting these practical measures pushes judicial data opening initiatives away from Open Data paradigm, therefore in a subsequent section the authors coin the new concept of Semi-Open Data paradigm to label and acknowledge these initiatives. This section also provides two example methods that are realized to tackle the challenges of judicial data dissemination and outlines two real-life judicial data dissemination cases that are deployed in the authors' organization based on these two methods. Finally, in the last three sections the authors discuss the results, provide an overview of the related work, and draw some conclusions.

PROBLEM STATEMENT

This section describes the problem context, the motivations, and the research methodology for this study.

Problem Context

The research and documentation centre (or Wetenschappelijk Onderzoek- en Documentatiecentrum in Dutch) is the research centre of the Dutch Ministry of Security and Justice. As illustrated in Figure 1, the research centre systematically collects, analyses and disseminates data about the Dutch judicial system. The data originate from various departments of the ministry like police, prosecution office and

Figure 1. An illustration of the research center's information processing and dissemination

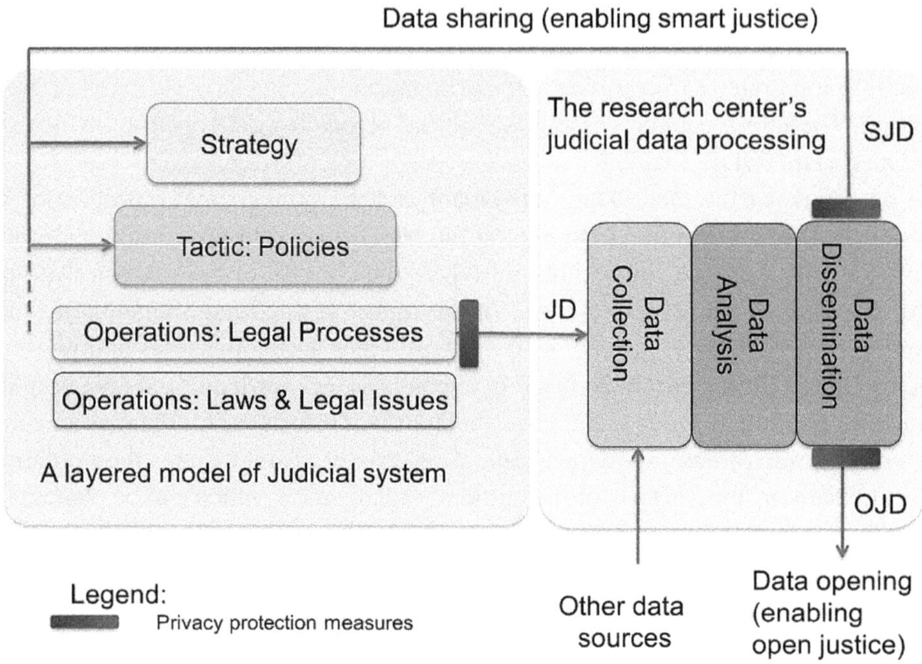

courts, where the collected data are mainly about judicial processes. In Figure 1 the link designated by JD shows the Judicial Data sets (JD) flows into our data processing system. The research centre also obtains relevant information indirectly through external sources and its partner organizations.

The collected judicial information is used for two purposes mainly: To improve the judicial system and to provide transparency. For the former purpose, the enriched information, marked by Shared Judicial Data sets (SJD), are (periodically) shared among governmental organizations, partner organizations, and policymakers to define the future research agenda, to answer the policy-related questions, and to assess the possible implications of standing policies of the ministry. For the latter purpose, the collected data or the enhanced information, marked by Opened Judicial Data sets (OJD), is disseminated to various user groups like scientists, journalists and the public. The objective of this data opening is to stimulate the open justice and open government vision. Engaging experts and the public can allow the public and experts to, for example, scrutinize the standing policies as well as the research centre's own data analysis methods and outcomes. These information sharing and information opening eventually affect and improve the judicial system directly and indirectly, respectively, thus enable the smart justice and smart government vision (Howard, 2013). Particularly, information dissemination with the public and external experts enables the public participation principle of the smart government vision.

Problem and Research Question

As a working group within the research centre, the authors have pursued the following research objective: To what extent can judicial data be opened while preventing undesired effects such as privacy violation (due to, e.g., the integration of different data sets) and misinterpretation (due to, e.g., the legacy nature of data)? This chapter limits the scope of the problem and aims at addressing the following research question: To what extent can the Opened Judicial Data sets (OJD) be marked as Open Data? In the remainder of this contribution, the authors argue that answering this question has led them to introduce the concept of Semi-Open Data.

Methodology

To answer the research question, the authors carried out a literature study about the Open Data requirements and objectives as well as about Open Data initiatives in the judicial field. The authors combined this literature study with a reflection on their own experiences to make an inventory of the major challenges that are involved in opening judicial data. For these challenges, the authors searched for possible solution directions, especially in the judicial, e-government and computer science domains. From the domain of computer science, the authors found those technical building blocks that contribute to addressing the challenges, while from the judicial and e-government domains, they found those procedural building blocks that could be used in facing the challenges. The authors have combined these building blocks in the research centre and have tailored them to the judicial field, see Figure 1 for an illustration of the scope. This chapter provides a reflection on the methods applied to the OJD output of the research centre's system, in an attempt to answer the abovementioned research question.

BACKGROUND

This section presents a background on Open Data, discusses its objectives and requirements, and provides a few examples of Open Data usage. The section discusses the challenges of judicial data opening and outlines at a high level two solution directions that are used in practice to deal with these challenges.

Objectives and Requirements

The term Open is defined in (ODef, 2015) as: *Open means anyone can freely access, use, modify, and share for any purpose (subject, at most, to requirements that preserve provenance and openness).* Open Data initiatives seek out various objectives, see also (ODRN, 2015; Verhulst, Noveck Simone, Robyn, Brown, & Paz, 2014; OGD, 2015; Meijer, Conradie, & Choenni, 2014), like:

- Improving government transparency by enabling the monitoring of the deeds of a democratic government,
- Increasing accountability and compliance through triggering of governments' accountability and democratic reforms,
- Supporting participatory governance by engaging citizens in the process of governance,
- Supporting innovation through enabling the creation of new services and products,
- Improving efficiency and cost-effectiveness by enabling the improvement of existing commercial applications and products,
- Supporting informed decisions by helping consumers, policymakers and businesses in their daily and strategic decisions, and
- Supporting for research through helping scientists with evidence-based primary research.

Open Data can be freely used, re-used and redistributed by everyone for any purpose according to the following principles (ODH, 2015):

- **Availability and Access Principle:** The data are available as a whole, as raw as possible, at no more than a reasonable reproduction cost, and in a convenient and modifiable form,
- **Reuse and Redistribution Principle:** The data are provided under terms that permit reuse and redistribution, including the capability of intermixing with other data sets (i.e., interoperability),
- **Universal Participation Principle:** Everyone can use, reuse and redistribute the data without any discrimination and restriction of the usage purpose, as well as the willingness of the owners to share their data.

Open Data requirements, as specified by Canadian government in (OD101, 2015; Wonderlich, 2010), US government in (Burwell, 2013), Dutch government in (BZK: an internal draft report, 2015), and/or organization Open Data Research Network (ODRN) from South Africa in (ODRN, 2015), can be summarized according to the following viewpoints.

- **Data Access and Usage Control:** The data should be accessible for everybody and without any discrimination or usage justification (e.g., to be license free and reusable). This is of course subject to valid restrictions like privacy, confidentiality, or security.
- **Data Access Mechanisms:** Data consumers should access data without any registration or any technological restrictions (e.g., needing a specific tool). To this end, data should be accessible free of charge, via web portal or an API (Application Programming Interface) for automatic data processing.
- **Data Formats and Types:** The data should be machine-readable and process-able (e.g., in common and standard file formats like CSV and XML). The data content or type should be timely (i.e., updated frequently and be as recent as possible), bulky (i.e., in complete form unless there are information sensitivity issues), with metadata (to convey its strengths and weaknesses) and (persistent) URIs (to locate data objects), and with primacy (i.e., published by its primary sources).
- **Post Release Support:** Data permanence is required (i.e., to remain data online with appropriate archiving).

Example Initiatives

To illustrate the Open Data concept and its challenges two example initiatives are shortly described in this section. The first example is an initiative of the Urban Management (in Dutch Stadsbeheer) department of Rotterdam Municipality. The department maintains urban infrastructures in Rotterdam, creates various products such as city maps, and provides engineering and consulting services (RotM, 2015). Directly or via its external partners, the department also collects, stores and enhances data about the public space like benches, trees, and public art. The department has released its first data set over trees in Rotterdam recently. Interestingly, the collected tree information includes also the current health status of the city's trees. But the department does not publish this data attribute due to its sensitivity. The rationale is that releasing the tree health status could lead to undesirable actions by citizens like cutting sick trees thoughtlessly or drawing wrong conclusions about the pollution status in certain areas (Conradie & Choenni, 2014). The department have published other data items such as the exact locations, the date of plantation, and type and sex of trees, which are still rich enough to make use of the data (Meijer et al., 2014).

The other example initiative of Open Data is in judicial setting, namely the website of Rechtspraak (2015). This site publishes information about, among others, the court verdicts within the Judiciary and the Supreme Court of the Netherlands. For privacy protection reasons, the website obfuscates or removes the names, birthplaces and exact birthdates of suspects, witnesses and victims. As such, the site publishes information about the investigation, prosecution and court procedures to the public.

Although in the first example the data appear to be quite innocent at a first glance, the data could not be published as it is. The data required careful preparations before being released. In the second example, it is obvious from a privacy viewpoint that the data need to be prepared before it can be published. This observation shows that opening data "as it is" is susceptible to discussion. Such examples have motivated and triggered the research of this contribution.

Challenges

Meeting all requirements of Open Data, while achieving the Open Data objectives, seems infeasible in practice for some organizations and their data sets; see for example (CoA report, 2015). The introduction section presented three typical challenges of Open Data, pertaining to privacy, legacy and interoperability of judicial data. This section elaborates further on these (and similar) challenges.

Often the data of organizations have low quality, contain potentially sensitive information, or have a proprietary/non-interoperable format. Opening such data according to Open Data requirements, for example, as raw as possible and to the public, can lead to various problems. Revealing potentially sensitive information, when one tries to open as raw as possible, can result in privacy breaches and sensitive (business) information disclosure, especially when the released data set is combined with other data sets (Kulk & van Loenen, 2012; van den Braak, Choenni, Meijer, & Zuiderwijk, 2012). For example, although the Rechtspraak site anonymizes the names of victims and offenders, in a recent case it was possible to discover the full names of victims and offenders by simply using Google to search for the keywords of the case (Bargh & Choenni, 2013). Such outcomes violate the basic principle of Open Data, namely: Not to open privacy and sensitive (business) information.

Low quality data, for example incomplete data sets, can cause misinterpretation and misleading of the public and data consumers (van den Braak et al., 2012; Wellington, 2015). Such consequences impede or violate the Open Data objectives such as transparency and decision support. Low quality and non-operable data can likely lead to low or no economic growth. Because it can be costly for data recipients (e.g., the public or non-experts) to process and make sense of the data or to create added value services from the data.

Ironically these problems are dependent and those solutions that try to address one may impact the others adversely. For example, attempts to make data interoperable (i.e., to make data integration easier) can also facilitate privacy breaches (Choenni, van Dijk, & Leeuw, 2010)! Firstly, some privacy sensitive attributes may be needed to integrate records of data sets. Secondly, the resulting integrated data sets, which often contain more attributes and information, may lead to personal information disclosure of (groups of) persons like the detailed geo-location data of groups with certain ethnic origins, political preferences, household incomes, and education levels.

Solution Directions

Enhancing data quality, reducing data sensitivity, creating sufficient metadata and/or adapting data format are some solution directions to deal with the abovementioned challenges of judicial data opening. For illustrative purposes, this section reviews two generic solution directions for coping with some of these challenges. As a consequence of adopting these solutions on achieving the Open Data ideals, a data disseminator, like the authors' research centre, inevitably moves away from the Open Data paradigm and embraces the Semi-Open Data paradigm, as introduced and defined in the next section.

Limiting Data Access Scope

Within the Open Data paradigm data should be accessible to the public without any registration or technological restrictions, e.g., via a web portal or via an API (i.e., the ease of access requirement). However, in practice the scope of recipients might get restricted for sensitive, low quality, or non-interoperable data. For instance, one can define the following access scopes for data disseminations: Data are open for the public as required within the Open Data paradigm, data are shared within a specific group like a group of scientists, data are shared among some organizations within a federation or a community, data are shared within a department of an organization, and data are shared with no one, i.e., being confidential.

Considering ease of data access, one can similarly identify various levels of access easiness. For example, data are fully accessible via a publicly known website, data are fully accessible via a website, data are only discoverable via a publicly known website (but not accessible), data are accessible on memory devices, and data are inaccessible, i.e., being confidential data.

Coping with Data Integration Issues

To integrate data from various sources, including those released in Open Data initiatives, it is important to relate data objects from these sources unambiguously. Open Data does not elaborate on this aspect, other than saying the data should be machine-readable. But in practice, there are often no standard formats for such machine-readable data objects when released from various sources. Even if the data formats are well defined, there are always data quality issues like inconsistency, incompleteness and inaccuracy among such homogeneous data sets, which make an unambiguous fusion of these data sets, i.e., to deal with data interoperability issues, an expensive and challenging undertaking.

Depending on the severity of data interoperability issues, opened data can be processed and integrated by using a specific data integration solution. These data integration solutions that are developed in practice are ordered in an increasing complexity level in the following:

- **Single Database Systems:** Data objects are fully integrated since the data objects in a database are coherent (/uniform) by definition. Note that this coherency should be created for the following approaches.
- **Data Warehouse Approach:** Data objects are integrated rather tightly, see also (Franklin, Halevy, & Maier, 2005). In this approach, one should undertake enormous amount of efforts to set up the data warehouse from various data sets. These efforts include data reconciliation activities like removing redundancies, searching for functional dependencies, and performing many joins. Recall that a join is the most costly operation in query processing (Ullman, 1988). The authors of the chapter consider this approach as a tight integration of data sets.

- **Data Space Approach:** Data objects are integrated rather loosely (Kalidien, Choenni, & Meijer, 2010). In this approach, a data space management system is used to store the relations among the databases and to serve as a communicator between the databases and the user queries. The authors consider this as a semi-tight integration of data sets, where one relies on domain-expert knowledge to lay down the relationship rules for integrating of data sets.
- **Search Based Approach:** Data objects are without any specific format. This is the case for websites in the World Wide Web where various sorts of contents can be searched and found using search engines like Google and Bing (Baeza-Yates & Ribeiro-Neto, 1999). This search-based approach differs from the other three approaches where answers for queries of users are created. In the search-based approach, unlike those query-based approaches, end-users carry out searches and receive pointers to most relevant data sources so that end-users can further investigate the retrieved documents directly. The authors of this chapter consider this as a loose integration of data sets, where one relies on end-user intelligence for integrating the search results.

Reflection

As described above, for low quality, sensitive, or legacy data it could be complex and costly for organizations to apply the solution directions and operations like data warehouse, data space, or data access and usage control. Organizations willing to open their data in this way may face unbearable and unaffordable *costs*. This may violate the *cost reduction principle* of Open Data. Moreover, the released data is *processed* data actually. As such, these solutions may violate the Open Data principle of as raw as possible data dissemination. In conclusion, it is inappropriate to regard the dissemination of such low quality, sensitive, or legacy data as Open Data.

A PARADIGM SHIFT: SEMI-OPEN DATA

Several efforts of organizations for data opening cannot be categorized as Open Data due to the reasons mentioned above. This section motivates and coins the concept of Semi-Open Data to mark such initiatives and provides a definition of Semi-Open Data paradigm. Furthermore, the section explains two methods and two cases that are realized in the authors' research centre for data dissemination in the sense of Semi-Open Data.

Motivation

Open Data objectives are genuine ideals to aspire and drive the policies, services, products, and activities of individuals, governments, and businesses. There are many organizations that are fully committed to and put efforts in (the process of) data opening; nevertheless they cannot completely fulfill all Open Data requirements due to the issues mentioned. Therefore, these efforts are not considered as Open Data initiatives although they serve or have taken pragmatic steps towards realizing (some of) the objectives of Open Data like creating transparency, enabling innovation, and/or stimulating economic growth. In order to recognize, acknowledge, and encourage these efforts, the authors coin the term Semi-Open Data for such initiatives as defined below.

Definition

Semi-Open Data concept encompasses those data dissemination solutions that aim at some of Open Data Objectives (like transparency, compliance, innovation, decision support, cost reduction, participation, and/or collaboration) but do not comply with all conditions of Open Data. This umbrella concept of Semi-Open Data is defined to mark those solutions that partially satisfy the requirements of Open Data, while trying to achieve some objectives of Open Data.

In the following the authors present two data dissemination initiatives/cases of our research centre together with two technological methods behind some of these initiatives. Hereby, the authors primarily intend to provide an overview of our Semi-Open Data initiatives to illustrate the similarities between the objectives of Open Data and Semi-Open Data. Secondly, the authors intend to illustrate the technical and nontechnical issues that influence the opening of low quality, sensitive, or legacy data because the criminal judicial data cannot be made public easily due to its sensitivity with respect to privacy, misinterpretation, and misuse.

Realized Methods

Scoped Opening of Data

Our research centre facilitates the reuse of the data processed in some of its research projects. After removing privacy sensitive data objects – unless they are explicitly needed for further research (Meijer et al., 2014) – the processed data is collected and centrally stored at the research centre. Based on the guidelines of the Dutch Privacy Protection ACT (DPPA) – which allow the (re)use of personal or privacy sensitive judicial data, under certain conditions, for scientific purposes (Meijer et al., 2014) – the research centre opens the processed data in a limited way to scientists and for scientific purposes. This limitation stems from protecting privacy and misinterpretation. The access and the use of these data sets are strongly regulated with a feedback procedure (Bargh, Choenni, Meijer, & Conradie, 2014).

To discover and retrieve the data sets of the completed research by scientists, the servers of a third party organization called DANS (Data Archiving Networked Services) are used. The control of data access is still administrated centrally at the research centre and it is based on, among others, who wants to access the data and the purpose of data access (Bargh et al., 2014). If the research centre authorizes the access, DANS delivers the data to the data requester via email.

Data Space

The data space approach has been introduced by the research centre and has widely been used for integrating the centre's judicial data sets. This section describe this approach in more depth to illustrate its capabilities and limitations. The data space is developed for integrating data sets at statistical and aggregate level (van Dijk, Kalidien, & Choenni, 2013). When data sets from multiple sources are collected and integrated, one has to take into account that redundancy, semantic changes, and dependencies in the data may occur. In the data space approach the following typical relationship rules must be maintained among databases: Maintaining data quality (for example, the plausibility and consistency of the data), handling similar data coming from different sources, dealing with missing data, allowing

Figure 2. Layered architecture of a data space

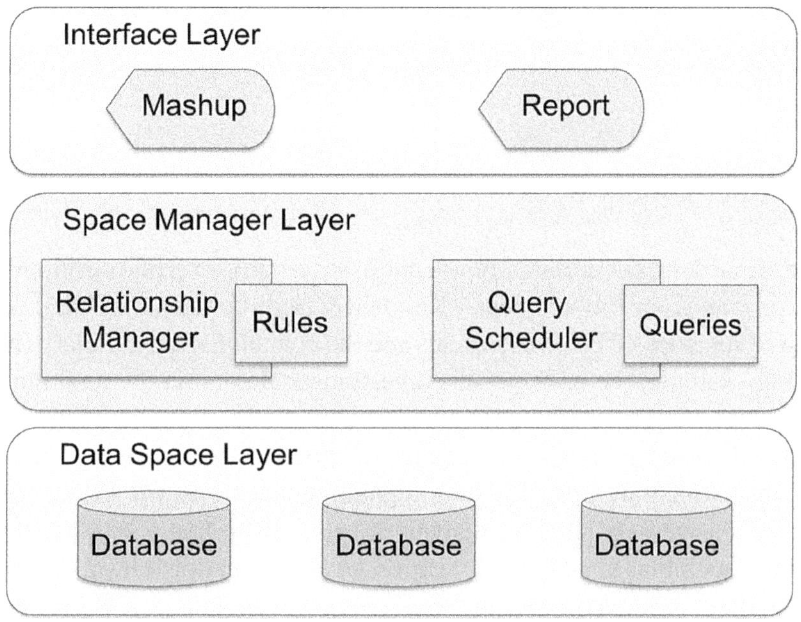

for incomplete or tentative data, recording semantic changes in attributes, filtering out the results that should not be shown to the user, and determining whether large deviations exist between past and future data or between values from the same or different databases.

Data space approach can be specified in three layers as shown in Figure 2:

- **Data Space Layer:** Contains a set of (cleaned and possibly related) databases,
- **Relationship Manager Layer:** Maintains the relations that exist among these databases as mentioned above, and serves also as a communicator between the other two layers, and
- **Interface Layer:** Enables end-users to insert queries and presents replies to users.

The Relationship Manager Layer acts as the heart of the data space approach. The maintained relationship rules enable assessing the quality and reliability of the data, alerting users when there are problems, and improving the issues found in the data sets. For example, consider two data sources where one source records the birth date of individuals and the other records the age of the same individuals. In order to complete the ages in the latter source, the birth dates in the former source may be used. In order to minimize the chances of misinterpreting of data, the history of the changes in the meaning of attributes can be used to decide on reorganizing or converting a database, particularly if the semantics of major attributes have changed considerably over the years. The Relationship Manager Layer contains also the query scheduler. Based on the question of a user at the Interface Layer, this scheduler decides which databases to query for answering the question. Once the answer is retrieved from the databases, it is displayed to the user through the interface.

The data space approach differs from the data warehouse approach. A data warehouse creates a uniform view of the data extracted from a collection of databases. In the data space approach, the related data sets are linked by some rules that are based on domain knowledge. The development of a data space system is, therefore, not only cheaper but maybe more effective for managing of heterogeneous data sets such as those in judicial settings. In data warehouse approach one should use data reconciliation by using unique identifiers, which is a costly operation to apply to such heterogeneous data sets (Kalidien et al., 2010).

Realized Cases

Crime and Law Enforcement Book

Based on collected crime data, our research centre publishes a book on crime developments in The Netherlands – called "Crime and Law Enforcement" (Kalidien & Heer-de Lange, 2014b) in collaboration with the national bureau of statistics of The Netherlands and the council for the judiciary (Kalidien, Choenni, & Meijer, 2009). For example, the book presents the statistical data on the total number of registered crimes by the police, specific crimes categorized as violent crimes, property crimes, information about victims, registered and solved crimes, and statistics of the decisions made by the Public Prosecutor. Through these figures, which are provided on a regular/annual basis, the government, policymakers and citizens can obtain a view on the development of crime (Kalidien et al., 2010). The book has an elaborate annex with data tables at a high aggregation level (i.e., national level) by sex, age categories, crime types etc. in a PDF format. All tables in the annex can be downloaded digitally in XLS format via the Internet from the site of the research centre (i.e., www.wodc.nl).

The crime statistics are based on several register databases, like the national database of the Police (abbreviated as HKS in Dutch), the police statistic of the Statistics Netherlands (abbreviated as CBS in Dutch), the databases that contain information about judicial cases (the CBS court statistic), and the Public Prosecutions Department Data (abbreviated as OMDATA in Dutch). Moreover, the register databases are used from several organizations involved in the execution of sanctions/sentences like the National Agency of Correctional Institutions (abbreviated as DJI in Dutch), the Child Care and Protection Board (abbreviated as RvdK in Dutch) being responsible for the execution of community services for juveniles, the Rehabilitation being community services for adults, and the Central Fine Collection Agency (abbreviated as CJIB in Dutch). Each of these organizations has own database. Besides, there are several other register databases (for instance, from crime surveys) that are used to create the crime statistics (Kalidien et al., 2009).

Criminal Justice Monitor

In the criminal justice domain, there are many (governmental) organizations involved that can be considered partners in a chain of events to deal with criminal cases. The term 'chain of events' implies that the input of one organization is dependent on the output of another organization in the chain. In order to deliver insightful, valid, and trustworthy management and administration information for the Ministry of Security and Justice and the government of the Netherlands, the research centre has designed and deployed a number of systems for monitoring the duration of criminal cases (Netten, van den Braak, Choenni, & Leertouwer, 2014) and for monitoring the flows within and between the chain partners in the criminal justice system (van Dijk et al., 2013). The former system may be used to obtain the statistical information on duration of criminal cases per partner organization and the duration of the whole chain of events.

The latter monitoring system provides insight into the success and possible bottlenecks of the criminal justice domain and may be used to generate management information about the criminal justice system.

The input data for the criminal justice monitors are from the information systems of many partner organizations involved in the chain of events such as the police, the public prosecution, and those organizations involved in the execution of penalties. The data obtained are of different types, ranging from comma-separated files containing aggregated data to a data warehouse with detailed information about parts of the criminal justice chain of events. The criminal justice monitors periodically receive the data sets and processes them according to the data space architecture. They offer a web interface for policymakers to query needed information (Kalidien, van Witzenburg, & Choenni, 2014a) in a user-friendly way by presenting a fixed set of variables. These variables enable policymakers to drill down the data along several dimensions such as regions and crime types (van Dijk et al., 2013).

DISCUSSION

One observes that the data opening examples mentioned in the "Scoped Opening of Data" paragraph cannot be characterized as Open Data because, for example, the data are made open for scientists not to the public, the purpose of data usage is limited to scientific objectives, the metadata of the data are publicly available not the data itself, the opened data are processed data, and data access is regulated by an authorization process. Nevertheless, some of the objectives of the Open Data are satisfied in these data opening endeavors, namely: Creating transparency, facilitating scientific research, and supporting decision making for policymakers. It is worthwhile to mention that the sketched data opening schemes are the result of about 9 years efforts to open the data according to Open Data requirements, which has been realized in a Semi-Open Data form due to the encountered problems in the course of time (Bargh, Choenni, & Meijer, 2015).

As seen in the "Data Space" paragraph above, the data space approach heavily depends on the relationship rules, which are in turn based on domain knowledge. Determining these rules can be feasible within a specific domain like criminal justice if a substantial amount of domain expertise exists and if it is applied appropriately. Applying data space approach to Open Data setting can be much more challenging due to lack of domain expertise and enough knowledge to create appropriate relationship rules. This complexity indicates the typical issues that one might expect if the data space integration method is adopted in the Open Data setting.

The Crime and Law Enforcement Book provides reliable and insightful data to policymakers and the public both digitally and on paper for government transparency and decision support purposes. Nevertheless, the initiative does not comply with the Open Data requirements completely, as it opens up processed data. The criminal justice monitors operate similarly to the Crime and Law Enforcement Book with an important difference that the policymakers and legislators are the end-users of the system, and not the public. This illustrates a main characteristic of Semi-Open Data initiatives, namely: Their similarity (i.e., proximity) to Open Data setting may differ. This signifies the importance of measuring the proximity of Semi-Open Data initiatives to Open Data initiatives. Measuring of this proximity is an important topic for future research.

RELATED WORK

Several governments have undertaken Open Data initiatives to publish public sector information, for example, governments of Colombia (Prieto & Rodríguez, 2012), Brazil (Matheus & Vaz, 2012), and the USA (Wilson & Linders, 2011). An overview of these initiatives can be found in (Yang & Kankanhall, 2013; Janssen, 2011). In judicial domain there are many (Open Data) initiatives for disseminating judicial data to citizens and/or experts as a means of government transparency and accountability. Hereby data recipients could also introduce added value services to the market. Compared to their counterparts in other public sectors, judicial data publishing initiatives have been reported less frequently in literature. In the following the authors review some of these judicial data publishing initiatives, elaborate upon some challenges they have encountered, and indicate their relevancy to the work presented in this chapter.

In the field of judiciary Open Data there are websites like (Rechtspraak, 2013) in The Netherlands and (Tribunal Constitucional, 2015) in Spain, which publish information about, among others, the proceedings and verdicts of the corresponding judiciary or supreme courts. These initiatives aim at realizing the venerable principle of open justice, which is deeply rooted in western consciousness in order to inform citizens about how justice is being rendered (McLachlin, 2014). These sites apply limited anonymization to protect privacy of individuals. For example, for suspects, witnesses and victims the website Rechtspraak (2013) removes just the names, birthplaces and exact birthdates and publishes the other information about the investigation, prosecution and court procedures. It is not the intention of the website to apply a bulletproof data anonymization and, consequently, it is possible to found out the removed information by, for example, using a simple Google search (Bargh & Choenni, 2013). This lenient and tolerant approach may stem from the open justice principle that these sites try to promote. Open justice principle has come in tension with security and privacy in an exponentially pace in recent years due to emerging information and communication technology advances (McLachlin, 2014). Nevertheless, the authors of the chapter suspect that, when a court does not mandate a closed procedure for a case, it becomes straightforward to open the corresponding procedure for the sake of the open justice principle. As shown in Figure 1, our research centre's data dissemination is concerned with judicial processes at a collective level, unlike the data dissemination in (Rechtspraak, 2013; Tribunal Constitucional, 2015) which is about the content of individual investigation, prosecution and court procedures.

Crime data, often gathered by local or national police forces, are published via web-based dashboards to inform citizens and policymakers about crime statistics and trends in their neighborhoods. Based on such information, for example, citizens can make informed decisions about needed precautions to strengthen their door locks, or to initiate or demand for appropriate actions and legislations from authorities. Examples of such crime data disseminations are 'Misdaad in kaart' (2015) in The Netherlands, Crime Spotting (2015) in San Francisco, and data.police.uk (2015) in England, Wales and Northern Ireland. The raw crime data collected from police forces contain typically information relating to identifiable entities like victims, offenders, and locations. To preserve privacy, these crime maps do not pinpoint individual crimes. For example, in (data.police.uk, 2015) the location of a crime is shown with a snap point in the centre of the nearest street with minimal 12 postal addresses (Smith & Heath, 2014). These initiatives do not satisfy all conditions of Open Data and in our opinion they can be regarded as good representatives of Semi-Open Data. Furthermore, Crime maps stem from one organization in the chain of judicial organizations, i.e., the Police, which differs from our research centre's SJD and OJD outputs (see Figure 1), which are resulted from the datasets of various organizations in the judicial chain. Furthermore, our research centre is not the owner of crime data and thus the centre cannot publish such data like the way that the crime monitoring sites do.

National and international judicial organizations publish judiciary data other than those mentioned above. Ministry of Justice of England and Wales publishes the national statistics on activities in the county, family, magistrates' and crown courts to the public at the site (Open Justice, 2015). The US Department of Justice strives to publish the underlying data of every report written by its offices and divisions via an appropriate channel (Department of Justice, 2015). When the data is of value to the general public and meets the US government Open Data requirements, the data may be released from Data.gov (2015). When the data is of value for researchers and scientists, the data may be released through other channels and access mechanisms (ICPSR, 2015; NACJD, 2015). In our opinion most of such data openings can be explained according to the Semi-Open Data paradigm as they limit the scope of data recipients and / or the access mechanisms.

The term "Semi-Open Data" is sporadically used in the literature. In the following, the authors review some of such instances. In weblog (Wellington, 2015) the author mentions: "cases where we only get partial information" are positioned in a class of issues called Semi-Open Data. The examples of Semi-Open data mentioned in the weblog are: using PDFs for data releases, providing maps without underlying data, or providing only tiny slices of stale data. As a real instance of data misinterpretation, the author mentions a report on comparing measles vaccination rates in the public and private schools in New York and the New York state based on incomplete data. "So with Semi-Open Data, we are unable to make a fair comparison" (Wellington, 2015). Open Data requires disseminating complete data to have good data utility and in order not to lead to wrong conclusions. The authors of the chapter share the same viewpoint that realizing complete data would have been better in this case, but the authors don't believe that it could have prevented all data misinterpretations. The authors of the chapter believe that in Semi-Open Data paradigm the incomplete or low quality data should be accompanied with sufficient metadata, interpreted by (domain) experts, and/or pre-processed to reach a higher quality, in order to lead to satisfactory outcomes and insights.

The Royal Netherlands Academy of Arts and Sciences has urged for careful and proper handling of research data, meaning that scientific research publications and the underlying data should be made open to enable validating research results, preventing fraudulent research, and facilitating data reuse (Hoogen, 2013). Such opening of scientific data contributes to attaining transparency, accountability, and innovations. Consequently, the School of Business and Economics of Maastricht University has considered a form of Semi-Open Data, saying "school … is thinking about a Semi-Open Data policy: raw, self-generated data are stored at the faculty level with restricted access and a careful description of the generation process, and made available for 10–15 years after generation (in case of problems). Manipulated data should be stored at a central university level, also well documented and in principle available for colleagues to use" (Hoogen, 2013). Similarly (Nosek et al., 2015; Alberts et al, 2015) requires publishing the information relevant for reproducibility of scientific experiments. Here the term Semi-Open Data is used in the specific context of preventing fraudulent academic practices. The authors believe that its scope can be extended to the public and judicial domain as outlined in this contribution.

CONCLUSION

In practice it is often infeasible for organizations to meet all requirements of Open Data in opening the data that has quality, sensitivity and interoperability issues. This chapter described the pragmatic steps that the authors and their colleagues have undertaken to deal with these issues for the judicial data within the research centre of Dutch ministry of Security and Justice in order to share or open the centre's data. These solutions include limiting the scope and means of data opening as well as using the advanced data space integration approach to enhance the quality of the opened data.

Applying these solutions, apparently, does not make these data opening efforts as Open Data initiatives. As these initiatives aim at achieving and delivering (some of) the objectives of Open Data, the chapter introduced the Semi-Open Data concept to characterize, recognize, and appreciate such initiatives. One of the future research directions is to formalize a method for measuring the level of adjacency of a Semi-Open Data initiative to the Open Data setting. Hereby one can objectively measure and monitor the distance to the desired Open Data ideals. This measurement shall enable us to evaluate those data opening efforts that push organizations in small steps in the strategically chosen direction of Open Data.

REFERENCES

Alberts, B., Cicerone, R. J., Fienberg, S. E., Kamb, A., McNutt, M., Nerem, R. M., & Jamieson, K. H. (2015). Self-correction in science at work. *Science*, *348*(6242), 1420–1422. doi:10.1126/science.aab3847 PMID:26113701

Baeza-Yates, R., & Ribeiro-Neto, B. (1999). *Modern Information Retrieval* (1st ed.). Addison Wesley.

Bargh, M. S., & Choenni, S. (2013). On preserving privacy whilst integrating data in connected information systems. In *Proceedings of the International Conference on Cloud Security Management* (ICCSM'13).

Bargh, M. S., Choenni, S., & Meijer, R., R. (2015). Privacy and information sharing in a judicial setting: A Wicked Problem. In *Proceedings of the 6th Annual International Conference on Digital Government Research* (DG.O'15). doi:10.1145/2757401.2757425

Bargh, M. S., Choenni, S., Meijer, R., & Conradie, P. (2014). Privacy protection in data sharing: towards feedback based solutions. In *Proceedings of the 8th International Conference on Theory and Practice of Electronic Governance* (ICEGOV'14). doi:10.1145/2691195.2691279

Burwell, S. M., Roekel, S., Part, T., & Mancini, D. J. (2013). *Open data policy – managing information as an asset* (White House Memorandum on Open Data Policy, May 9). Retrieved June 29, 2015, from https://www.whitehouse.gov/sites/default/files/omb/memoranda/2013/m-13-13.pdf

Choenni, S., van Dijk, J., & Leeuw, F. (2010). Preserving privacy whilst integrating data: Applied to criminal justice. Information Polity, 15(1-2), 125-138.

Choenni, S., Bargh, M. S., Roepan, C., & Meijer, R. (2015). Privacy and security in data collection by citizens. In Smarter as the new urban agenda: a comprehensive view of the 21st century city. Springer.

CoA Report. (2015). *Trendrapport open data 2015* (in Dutch). Technical Report, Court of Audit of The Netherlands (Algemene Rekenkamer in Dutch, March 31). Retrieved June 29, 2015, from http://www.rekenkamer.nl/Publicaties/Onderzoeksrapporten/Introducties/2015/03/Trendrapport_open_data_2015

Conradie, P., & Choenni, S. (2014). On the barriers for local government releasing open data. Government Information Quarterly, 31, 10–17. doi:10.1016/j.giq.2014.01.003

Crime Spotting. (2015). *Website providing crime information for San Francisco*. Retrieved June 29, 2015 from http://sanfrancisco.crimespotting.org

Data.gov. (2015). *The home of the U.S. government's open data*. Retrieved June 29, 2015 from http://www.data.gov

Data.police.uk. (2015). *Website provisioned by UK police*. Retrieved June 29, 2015 from https://data.police.uk/

Department of Justice. (2015). *Open Data*. Website of the US Department of Justice. Retrieved June 29, 2015 from http://www.justice.gov/open/open-data

van Dijk, J., Kalidien, S., & Choenni, S. (2013). Development, implementation and use of a judicial data space system. In *Proceedings of the 7th International Conference on Theory and Practice of Electronic Governance*.

Elmasri, R., & Navathe, S. (2004). *Fundamentals of Database Systems* (4th ed.). Addison Wesley.

Franklin, M., Halevy, A., & Maier, D. (2005). From databases to data spaces: A new abstraction for information management. *Special Interest Group on Management of Data (SIGMOD) Record*, *34*(4).

Howard, R. (2013). *Smart government key initiative overview*. Report Gartner G00252076. Retrieved June 29, 2015 from https://www.gartner.com/doc/2520516/smart-government-key-initiative-overview

ICPSR. (2015). *Inter-university Consortium for Political and Social Research (ICPSR) of the University of Michigan*. Retrieved June 29, 2015 from https://www.icpsr.umich.edu/icpsrweb/landing.jsp

Janssen, K. (2011). The influence of the PSI directive on open government data: An overview of recent developments. *Government Information Quarterly*, *28*(4), 446–456. doi:10.1016/j.giq.2011.01.004

Kalidien, S. N., & de Heer-de Lange, N. E. (Ed.). (2014b). Criminaliteit en rechtshandhaving 2013 (in Dutch). Justitie in Statistiek (nr. 4, CBS, WODC, Raad voor de Rechtspraak). Boom Lemma Press.

Kalidien, S. N., Choenni, R., & Meijer, R. (2009). Towards a monitoring tool for crime and law enforcement. In *Proceedings of the 3rd European Conference on Information Management and Evaluation* (ECIME'09). Gothenburg, Sweden: Academic Publishing Limited.

Kalidien, S. N., Choenni, R., & Meijer, R. F. (2010). Crime statistics online: potentials and challenges. In *Proceedings of the 11th Annual International Digital Government Research Conference on Public Administration Online: Challenges and Opportunities* (DG.O'10).

Kalidien, S. N., van Witzenburg, R., & Choenni, S. (2014a). Developing, implementing and evaluating a web interface in the field of e-government. In D. Yannacopoulos, P. Manolitzas, N. Matsatsinis, & E. Grigoroudis (Eds.), *Evaluating websites and web services: Interdisciplinary perspectives on user satisfaction*. IGI Global. doi:10.4018/978-1-4666-5129-6.ch004

Kulk, S., & van Loenen, B. (2012). Brave new open data world? *International Journal of Spatial Data Infrastructures Research*, 7.

Matheus, R., & Vaz, J. C. (2012). New perspectives for electronic government in Brazil: The adoption of open government data in national and subnational governments of Brazil. In *Proceedings of the 6th International Conference on Theory and Practice of Electronic Governance*. doi:10.1145/2463728.2463734

McLachlin, B. (2014). Openness and the rule of law. *At the Annual International Rule of Law Lecture*. Retrieved June 29, 2015 from http://www.barcouncil.org.uk/media/270848/jan_8__2014_-_12_pt.__rule_of_law_-_annual_international_rule_of_law_lecture.pdf

Meijer, R., Conradie, P., & Choenni, S. (2014). Reconciling contradictions of open data regarding transparency, privacy, security and trust. *Journal of Theoretical and Applied Electronic Commerce Research, 9*(3), 45-58.

Misdaad in kaart. (2015). *Website provisioned by Dutch national police*. Retrieved June 29, 2015 from https://www.politie.nl/mijn-buurt/misdaad-in-kaart

Moolenaar, D., Choenni, S., & Leeuw, F. 2007. Design and implementation of a forecasting tool for justice chains. In *Proceedings of the 5th International Conference on Law and Technology*.

NACJD. (2015). *Website of National Archive of Criminal Justice Data*. Retrieved June 29, 2015 from https://www.icpsr.umich.edu/icpsrweb/content/NACJD/mission.html

Netten, N., van den Braak, S. W., Choenni, S., & Leertouwer, E. (2014). Elapsed times in criminal justice systems. In *Proceedings of the 8th International Conference on Theory and Practice of Electronic Governance* (ICEGOV'14).

Nosek, B. A., Banks, G. C., Borsboom, D., Bowman, S. D., Breckler, S. J., Buck, S., & Yarkoni, T. et al. (2015). Promoting an open research culture. *Science, 348*(6242), 1422–1425. doi:10.1126/science.aab2374 PMID:26113702

OD101. (2015). *Open data 101*. Retrieved June 29, 2015, from http://open.canada.ca/en/open-data-principles

ODef. (2015). *The open definition*. Retrieved June 29, 2015, from http://opendefinition.org

ODH. (2015). *Open data handbook*. Retrieved June 29, 2015, from http://opendatahandbook.org/guide/en/what-is-open-data/

ODRN. (2015). *Open data research network*. Retrieved June 29, 2015, from http://www.opendataresearch.org/content/2013/566/early-insight-2-definitions-open-data

OGD. (2015). *Welcome to open government data*. Retrieved June 29, 2015, from http://opengovernmentdata.org/#sthash.kjB8Ex3v.dpuf

Open Justice. (2015). *Website Open Justice*. Retrieved June 29, 2015 from http://open.justice.gov.uk

Prieto, L. M., & Rodríguez, A. C. (2012). Implementation framework for open data in Colombia. In *Proceedings of the 6th International Conference on Theory and Practice of Electronic Governance*. doi:10.1145/2463728.2463732

Rechtspraak. (2015). *Website of the Dutch judiciary and the supreme court of the Netherlands*. Retrieved June 29, 2015, from http://zoeken.rechtspraak.nl/default.aspx

RotM. (2013). *Rotterdam municipality (gemeente Rotterdam in Dutch)*. Rotterdam World Port World City. Retrieved July 14, 2015, from http://www.rotterdam.nl/gw

Smith, A. M., & Heath, M. (2014). Police.uk and Data.police.uk: Developing open crime and justice data for the UK. JeDEM-eJournal of eDemocracy and Open Government, 6(1), 87-96.

Tribunal Constitucional. (2015). *The website of Spanish Constitutional Court*. Retrieved June 29, 2015 from http://www.tribunalconstitucional.es/en/Pages/Home.aspx

Ullman, J. (1988). *Principles of Database and Knowledge-Base Systems*. New York: Computer Science Press.

van den Braak, S., Choenni, S., Meijer, R., & Zuiderwijk, A. (2012). Trusted third parties for secure and privacy-preserving data integration and sharing in the public sector. In *Proceedings of the 13th Annual International Conference on Digital Government Research* (DG.0'12). doi:10.1145/2307729.2307752

van den Hoogen, H. (2013). Taking care of research data: Outcome of a seminar on managing data integrity in research. Library Connect Newsletter, Issue: Research Data Management, 1(1).

Verhulst, S., Noveck Simone, B., Robyn, C., Brown, K., & Paz, C. (2014). *Released: The open data era in health and social care*. Retrieved June 29, 2015, from http://thegovlab.org/nhs/

Wellington, B. (2015). Measles reporting and the dangers of semi-open data. *I Quant NY*. Retrieved June 29, 2015, from http://iquantny.tumblr.com/post/112113837909/measles-reporting-and-the-dangers-of-semi-open

Wilson, S. C., & Linders, D. (2011). The open government directive: A preliminary assessment. In *Proceedings of the 12th Annual International Digital Government Research Conference: Digital Government Innovation in Challenging Times* (pp. 262–271). doi:10.1145/1940761.1940814

Wonderlich, J. (2010). Ten principles for opening up government information. *Website of Sunlight Foundation*. Retrieved June 29, 2015, from http://sunlightfoundation.com/policy/documents/ten-open-data-principles/

Yang, Z., & Kankanhalli, A. (2013). Innovation in government services: The case of open data. In *Proceedings of IFIP International Federation for Information Processing*, (pp. 644–651).

Zuiderwijk, A., Janssen, M., Choenni, S., Meijer, R., & Sheikh Alibaks, R. (2012). Socio-technical impediments of open data. *In Electronic. Journal of E-Government*, *10*(2), 156–172.

KEY TERMS AND DEFINITIONS

Database: A system where data objects are uniformly and coherently maintained.

Data Space: A data integration model where multiple data sets are integrated at a statistical and aggregate level by using relational rules to deal with the redundancies, semantic changes, and dependencies in the data sets.

Data Warehouse: A data integration model where multiple data sets are integrated tightly by using data reconciliation activities like removing redundancies, searching for functional dependencies, and performing data joins.

Open Data: Open Data refers to those data disclosure initiatives where anyone can freely access, use, modify, and share the data for any purpose (subject, at most, to requirements that preserve provenance and openness).

Search Based Data Integration: A data integration model where loosely coupled data objects and contents can be searched and pointers to find most relevant data sources for further investigation by humans.

Semi-Open Data: Semi-Open Data refers to those data disclosure initiatives that partially satisfy the requirements of Open Data but certainly aim at achieving some objectives of Open Data.

Chapter 8
Digitalizing Police Requirements:
Opening up Justice through Collaborative Initiatives

Mila Gascó-Hernández
ESADE Business and Law School, Spain

ABSTRACT

In the last one or two years, the growing demand for an open state has sped up the adoption of ICT aimed at improving access to justice, making the judiciary more transparent, increasing cooperation between legal authorities, and strengthening the justice system itself. Of particular importance are interoperability initiatives since they guarantee collaboration as well as the harmonic and cohesive functioning of different existing systems, processes, and applications that, in the justice field, are many as a result of the big variety of actors that are involved: judicial institutions but, also, different public administrations, such as those responsible of police forces, and law professionals. The chapter describes and analyzes GRP (Gestió de Requeriments Policials), a project that allows for the exchange of information between the Department of Justice and the Department of the Interior in the framework of the Autonomous Government of Catalonia (Spain).

INTRODUCTION

On January 2009, President Obama signed the Memorandum on Transparency and Open Government. The memorandum declares the new administration's commitment to creating an unprecedented level of openness in government and establishing a system linking three principles: transparency, public participation, and collaboration.

Although there is agreement on the popularization of the term by the Obama Administration's Memorandum on Transparency and Open Government, the concept is not new. Despite the first written reference dates back to 1957, when Parks (1957) published "The open government principle: applying the right to know under the Constitution", its use goes back to the 70s, when the British government

DOI: 10.4018/978-1-5225-0717-8.ch008

promoted several initiatives aimed at achieving more information freedom and more access to government's activity and, therefore, at reducing opacity (Chapman & Hunt, 2006). Along time, and as a consequence of contributions from different fields[1], this first approach has been refined, giving rise to a definition related to enhancing transparency, collaboration, and participation by means of open data and open action. Gascó (2014) summarizes and operationalizes these dimensions stating that an open government is (see Table 1):

- A transparent government, that is, a government that is accountable and that delivers information to citizens about its strategies, plans, and performance.
- A collaborative government, that is, a government that involves citizens and other external and internal actors in the design, delivery and evaluation of public services.
- A participative government, that is, a government that promotes citizen engagement in political processes and, particularly, in the design of public policies.
- A government that prioritizes the use of two key tools: open data (that is, data that are available in standardized and structured formats, that are machine-readable, and that are guaranteed to be freely available over time) and open action (that is, the use of web 2.0 tools and, particularly, of social media and blogging).

During the last few years, public administrations around the world have embarked on open government initiatives and have worked to redefine their relationship with citizens and with each other. Some of them have even joined efforts and have taken part in networks such as the Open Government Partnership, which was launched in 2011 to provide an international platform for domestic reformers committed to making their governments more open, accountable, and responsive to citizens.

However, a review of the action plans undertaken in the framework of the Open Government Partnership shows that most of the initiatives have been implemented by governments (executive power), on one hand, and have focused on transparency and, to a lesser degree, on participation, on the other.

For one thing, several public institutions and agencies have designed and implemented important open government strategies and plans aimed at increasing transparency and citizen participation. This has not been the case in the justice field, despite the implementation of several initiatives world-wide, as Jiménez (2014) shows. However, the explicit recognition of the administration of justice both as a key component of the State of Law (it is one of the three powers) and as a public service has made evident

Table 1. Open government: principles, tools and related concepts

Dimensions	Tools	Related Concepts
Transparency	Open data Open action	Information access Accountability Legitimacy and trust in government
Collaboration	Open data Open action	Interoperability Co-production (Social) innovation
Participation	Open data Open action	Consultation and deliberation with citizens Participation in decision-making processes Participation in public policy design

Gascó, 2014.

the need to attain a more transparent, collaborative, and participative judiciary in order to improve access to justice and to increase society's trust towards the administration of justice. This realization has given rise to the (slow) adoption of the open government principles in this field and, as a result, to the concept of open justice/open judiciary.

At the same time, open government has mainly been about transparency and participation. It is true that, as Meijer et al. (2012) put it, in the end, everything is about vision and voice. However, Gascó (2014), respecting the popular Obama trinity, distinguishes between collaboration and participation. The author defines the former as the joint and transversal work of different actors inside and outside the public sector organization and, specifically, she refers to the collaborative work that takes place around the public services cycle. Gascó (2014) also states that participation is related to the involvement in political processes and, as a result, to initiatives of consultation and deliberation with citizens and of participation in the decision-making processes and the policy-making cycle. Participation initiatives have been at the core of governments' efforts to involve third actors.

Given this context, this chapter aims at increasing awareness and understanding regarding collaboration initiatives within the justice field and, therefore, in the framework of open justice/open judiciary strategies and plans. Our intention is to shed light on the two identified gaps and to contribute to the body of literature that tackles openness in the justice field focusing on one of the less explored topics within the open government body of knowledge: collaboration. In particular, the chapter presents the experience of GRP – Gestió de Requeriments Policials (management of police requests), an interoperability project promoted by the Autonomous Government of Catalonia, and analyzes those variables that have been key in the implementation process in order to identify common patterns that might guide future interventions and projects.

The remainder of this chapter is organized as follows. In the next section, we discuss collaboration as the second dimension of the concept of open government, with particular emphasis on the role of interoperability. The data and methods used to test this model are then explained. Subsequently, we present the case study and results of the analysis. Finally, we describe the theoretical and practical implications of our findings and what further steps are to be taken.

ON COLLABORATION

The term collaboration describes the co-ordinated approach of people or organizational units to work together to achieve commonly set goals (Von Lucke & Groβe, 2014). Ramírez-Alujas and Dassen (2012) give more details about this concept and state that a collaborative government works together with citizens and other social agents to solve national problems. This involves coordinating with citizens but, also, with private companies, associations and other stakeholders. It also implies collaboration among the different public sector organizations.

Collaboration, therefore, goes beyond the citizen as an individual and his/her right to know and participate in political processes: it takes into account other (internal and external) actors and it encourages joint and transversal work among them. Several authors have supported this idea. Márquez et al. (2013), for instance, declare that open government means transparency and participation but, also, collaboration among public agencies and between the latter and the society. Lee and Kwak (2012) propose an open government maturity model that pursues transparency, participation and internal and external collaboration with citizens, private companies and other stakeholders. Von Lucke and Groβe (2014) introduce the term open collaboration, which refers to the process of opening up to external actors and interested stakeholders. The authors list several applications of collaboration in the framework of open government such as crowdfunding, collaborative knowledge management, co-production, and open innovation.

Gascó (2014) distinguishes among three main practices related to the collaborative dimension of open government: interoperability, social innovation, and co-production of public services. The first one refers to cooperation among public agencies, and it is the concept that frames this chapter (and, therefore, it will be next further developed). The latter terms have mainly to do with interaction with external actors. In this respect, social innovation can be defined as the collective generation of new ideas (products, services, models) that work to address (social) unmet needs (Voorberg et al., 2015) while co-production is the process of planning, designing, delivering, and evaluating public services with the direct involvement of citizens, users and external stakeholders (OECD, 2011).

On Interoperability

Despite the fact that many people use the term interoperability, there is no clear consensus about what it means. Early researchers concentrated on information management and information systems and referred to the ability of ICT systems to communicate, interpret and interchange data in a meaningful way (Kubicek et al., 2011; Archman & Kudlacek, 2008; Institute of Electrical and Electronic Engineers, 1990). Interoperability had to do with the definition of rules and common standards. But the definitions have been extended along various dimensions in the years since the term was first defined (Kubicek et al., 2011).

The European Commission (2010) understands interoperability as the ability of disparate and diverse organizations to interact towards mutually beneficial and agreed common goals, involving the sharing of information and knowledge between the organizations, through the business processes they support, by means of the exchange of data between their respective ICT systems. Gottschalk and Solli-Saether (2009) round this statement off adding that "in a narrow sense, the term interoperability is often used to describe technical systems. In a broad sense, social, political, and organizational factors influencing systems and systems performance are also taken into account" (p. 6).

As a result, it is common to almost all current definitions to distinguish among three types/dimensions of interoperability (see, among others, Kubicek et al., 2011; Jiménez et al., 2011; Charalabidis, 2011; the European Commission, 2010; Criado et al., 2010; Criado, 2009):

- **Technical Interoperability:** Technological characteristics and elements that link information systems, such as interconnection services, data integration services, and communication protocols.
- **Semantic Interoperability:** It ensures that the precise meaning of exchanged information is understood and preserved throughout exchanges between organizations. It is usually associated with classification systems, ontologies, and data formats.
- **Organizational Interoperability:** It is concerned with reaching mutually agreed goals and therefore with integrating back offices and modeling business processes.

Interoperability governance adds meaning to the above dimensions. Bekker (2007) states that "back office-integration is a goal-searching process that requires the reconciliation of core values as well as sheer organizational interests through negotiating and exchanging different rationalities" (p. 396). Thus, through a negotiation process, organizations reach agreements to achieve technical, semantic, and organizational interoperability.

The specific benefits of data sharing and back office integration vary from organization to organization (Pardo & Tayi, 2007). Still, there are certain types of benefits that can be expected in almost any interoperability initiatives: increased productivity, improved decision making, reduced costs, or increased revenues (Gil-García & Pardo, 2005). However, it should be noted that achieving these benefits is not easy.

In fact, most interoperability efforts meet serious challenges and concerns (Gil-García, 2012; Willem & Buelens, 2007; Pardo & Tayi 2007). Recent works have tried to uncover the determinants of interoperability success and have assessed the influence of variables such as technology development, data quality, context, organizational performance and institutional frameworks. However, many of these studies have isolated the effect of these dimensions forgetting that interoperability is a multidimensional phenomenon (Pardo et al., 2012). Also, they have focused on information systems and technology, underestimating the role of management and network governance.

Gascó et al. (2013) and Gascó and Sierra (2015), after extensive research on the case of Catalonia in Spain, come up with a multidimensional model of interoperability critical success factors that includes six dimensions (see Table 2):

1. Factors related to data and information,
2. Factors related to technology,
3. Internal organizational factors,
4. Factors related to the governance of the network,
5. Institutional factors, and
6. Contextual factors.

Such approach stresses the importance of management and governance, also drawing on theories and research related to public management and governance.

Interoperability in the Justice Field

Investment in information and communication technologies can be considered one of the key elements to significantly improve the administration of justice. Velicogna (2007) gives a few examples of the potential of ICT in this field: "the availability of web services, the possibility of consulting on-line legislation and case law, the use of electronic filing, the electronic exchange of legal documents, are only some examples that are spurring the judicial administrations around the world to rethink their current functions and activities. ICT can be used to enhance efficiency, access, timeliness, transparency and accountability, helping the judiciaries to provide adequate services. New possibilities are emerging for the integration and automation of court procedures and practices. In addition, the use of the internet, can offer the chance to open the judiciary to the public, providing both general and specific information on its activities, thereby also increasing legitimacy" (p. 129). Other authors, such as Cerrillo and Fabra (2009), confirm his words and maintain that since the very organization of judicial systems is based on the exchange of information, the potential to be attained by the introduction of ICT is even higher in this area than in other fields.

One of the more important aspects of this technological modernization has to do with interoperability since it guarantees the harmonic and cohesive functioning of different existing systems, processes, and applications that in the justice field, are many as a result of the big variety of actors that are involved (Gascó & Jiménez, 2011).

Table 2. Interoperability critical success factors

Category	Factors
Factors related to data and information (data characteristics)	• Data digitalization • Data standardization • Data storage strategies • Security, confidentiality, and privacy
Factors related to technology	• Technological readiness • Perceived ease of use • Adjustment between available technological solutions and organizational needs • Information systems compatibility
Internal organizational factors	• Leadership • E-government interoperability management: o Planning o Resources availability and management o Change management • Environmental complexity • IT department • Organizational culture
Factors related to the governance of the network	• Perception of benefits • Power • Clarity of roles and responsibilities: o Formalization of rules and procedures o Network promoters and champions • Facilitating structures
Institutional factors	Legislation and regulation
Contextual factors	Economic situation

Gascó et al., 2013; Gascó & Sierra, 2015.

However, interoperability in the judiciary has not been paid much attention by the academic world. Only a few works have addressed ICT-enabled cooperation among judicial institutions but, also, between them and different public agencies, such as police organizations or law professionals. It is worth mentioning the works of Contini & Lanzara (2014), on the dynamic complexities involved in the design of interoperability applications that enable online trans-border judicial proceedings in Europe, and Silveira et al. (2015), on the Brazilian e-justice interoperability framework. However, it is probably Carlos E. Jiménez the author who most extensively has tackled this topic, linking it, in his first articles on the issue, to the concept of electronic justice (e-justice) and, nowadays, in his more recent works, to the open justice/open judiciary idea (for example, Jiménez, 2015; Jiménez, 2014; Jiménez, 2012; Gascó & Jiménez, 2011; Jiménez, 2010).

In his different publications, the author has drawn attention to some of the factors that play a particularly important role regarding the implementation of interoperability projects. Beyond technological and security variables, Jiménez has referred to:

1. A lack of strategy, which he links to a weak political commitment,
2. Normative barriers that have to do either with insufficient or with contradictory legislation when it comes to regulate the new situations,
3. Poor processes of collaboration and coordination among the many public administrations and governing bodies of the judicial power in the administration of justice,

4. Resistance to change, particularly experienced by those actors with plenty of power (for examples, judges) or with a lot to lose (such as intermediary bodies, like procurators in Spain), and
5. A deficient governance or institutional framework (Gascó & Jiménez, 2011).

GOALS, DATA, AND METHODS

Despite previous findings related to interoperability critical success factors, more evidence is needed regarding the role of non-technological variables in ICT-enabled collaboration initiatives within the justice field. This is precisely the goal of this chapter: to add knowledge on the determinants of interoperability in the judiciary and, therefore, on the collaboration dimension of the so-called open justice/open judiciary. In order to reach this goal the chapter explores the case of the implementation of the so-called police requirements module (GRP – Gestió de Requeriments Policials), within the wider "e-Justícia.cat" project promoted by the Autonomous Government of Catalonia in Spain.

Fieldwork was conducted during two different periods of time since we wanted to identify changes in the determinants over time. The first exploration took place during the second semester of 2010. Two qualitative methods were used during the fieldwork in order to collect the needed information. First, several documents and webpages were observed and examined. Conceptual papers about e-government, e-justice and interoperability, case studies, plans, legal measures, project presentations, indicators and performance reports were detailed studied.

Second, seven in-depth interviews were conducted: four with different people from the Catalan Department of Justice and three police officers form the Catalan police force (Mossos d'Esquadra). In the main, the interviewees were selected according to three criteria:

1. Their level of involvement in e-Justícia.cat,
2. Their seniority,
3. The degree to which they had been affected by the implementation of the GRP module.

Different interview guides were prepared to make sure that all relevant topics were covered and to keep the interaction focused. However, individual perspectives and experiences also emerged during the conversations.

Finally, during the first stage, in order to collect more information and to be able to get the insights of other actors involved, a survey was administered to 17 additional individuals who included civil servants from the Justice Administration, one person from the Information and Communication Technologies Department, two individuals from the training center of the Department of Justice and two more from the communication team, and one person from the change management unit.

The second stage of the fieldwork occurred during the months of September and October of 2013. Four additional in-depth interviews were conducted. Two of them took place with staff belonging to the Monitoring of Computer Programmes Unit of the Department of Justice of the Autonomous Government of Catalonia. Also, two police officers were interviewed. One of them had the strategic perspective of the project while the other one was the head of the Police information Systems Unit, the one in charge of the implementation of the GRP module. Finally, one focus group with different police officers from, also, the Police information Systems Unit was held.

All the interviews (the ones in 2010 and the ones in 2013) lasted between one and two hours. We did not get authorization to record them so the analysis was done taking into account the interviewers' notes. The focus group lasted for about two hours and, once more, we were not able to record it.

RESULTS

Setting

The management of the police requirements module (GRP – Gestió de Requeriments Policials) started back in 2006. It was initiated by the former Information System Service of the Department of Justice of the Autonomous Government of Catalonia in the framework of the e-Justícia.cat project (nowadays, such unit has a new name: Implementation and Monitoring of Computer Programmes).

The Spanish Constitution forces the police to assist the Justice Administration. Since the limits of this collaboration are not clear, the Justice Administration uses police forces to carry out many different tasks and the police forces have to accomplish the orders. Before GRP was implemented, paper and fax were used in order to communicate the orders. This was very bureaucratic: not only tasks were repeated (the Justice Administration faxed the requirement and, after getting it, the police had to type the data in their system again), but information was also lost. There was also the need to make the communication between Mossos d'Esquadra and the Justice Administration more agile and effective. In this respect, the project was a need for the Justice Administration and a claim for the Mossos d'Esquadra police force.

Three were, therefore, the goals of this project:

1. To reduce the number of mistakes,
2. To speed up the processes, by means of centralizing the information,
3. To build a digital database.

Digitalizing Police Requirements

As already said, the project was led by the Department of Justice although the design of the application was done jointly with Mossos d'Esquadra but, also, with other actors such as expert users, members of the provider private company or technical staff of the Information and Communication Technologies Department of the Autonomous Government of Catalonia. Therefore, since the beginning of the project, there was a need to set up coordination rules that included periodical meetings, working protocols, joint pilots, or transversal contingency plans.

Also, in order to guarantee data exchange between the Department of Justice and the Department of the Interior (in charge of the Catalan police force), an agreement between them was signed in 2008.

From a technological point of view, an application, very similar to the ones Mossos d'Esquadra were used to work with, was implemented. Within the new system, the order is received telematically once the judicial secretary signs it. Mossos d'Esquadra prove that the information is of quality and then, also telematically, delegate the order to whichever police unit has to manage it.

The information has to be of quality, it has to have a minimum set of data so the requirement can be managed. If the information is not good, the order is automatically returned/rejected by the system.

The last version of the application was finished in 2009 and a pilot was carried out between July and October of that same year. In October 2009, it was the court of first instance number 11 of the city of Barcelona the first one to send requests by means of the new system. The project was gradually implemented throughout the territory (by administrative areas) because the Justice Administration needed to implement it progressively. Currently, the system is fully working in Catalonia.

Institutional adaptation to innovation in the Spanish justice field has always been a slow process because of the poor constitutional and legal designs included in the rules and because of the huge weight carried by an organizational structure anchored in nineteenth century criteria and a very strong corporate presence. The implementation of GRP was not an exception. Thus, several activities were carried out to manage resistance to change. Of particularly interest was the training strategy, led by the Implementation and Monitoring of Computer Programmes unit and sponsored by the Training Centre of the Department of Justice: the former trained several civil servants (the so-called super-users) and these trained the rest of the employees (the users). This way of working gave rise to a high level of users' involvement which, in return, reduced reluctance to use the new system (the users were being trained by their own colleagues who were also users of the module and therefore could encounter the same types of problems and difficulties). Training sessions were also attended by police officers, who aimed at giving functional support explaining, for example, the different types of requirements or the problems they encountered with the system.

At the beginning of the project, Mossos d'Esquadra trained their officers as well, since any police unit could receive a requirement. Therefore, all of them needed to know how the system worked. They also set up a unit, which nowadays has 34 people (20 police officers and 14 administrative workers). They were very careful choosing these individuals for they needed methodical people, easy to concentrate and willing to be responsible.

Despite these change management strategies, there have been some problems. On one hand, during the implementation stage, it was hard for police officers to work with two systems (the fax and the digital one). This way of proceeding made the learning process more difficult although the predisposition of police officers towards the new system was very good.

On the other hand, civil servants from the Department of Justice were pretty reluctant to change. First, age mattered. Courts with older people were resistant to use the new application since many of them did not have good computer skills. Second, implementation coincided with the economic crisis in Spain, which was even more serious in Catalonia, and therefore with budget and salary cuts. In this context, GRP's potential users did not perceive the initiative was a priority. Last but not least, generally speaking, civil servants thought Mossos d'Esquadra were the only beneficiary of the project. They did not perceive the new system also had a lot of advantages for them. Due to this feeling, for a while, there was resistance to use the application. Thus, faxes were kept being sent. Over time, this resistance to change has been moderated. Still, there are a few cases, which is not surprising in a group of almost 4,000 users.

Finally, there are still difficulties related to the lack of information in a requirement. When this happens, police officers get in touch with civil servants from the Department of Justice and request the data/documents they need. In this respect, they also perform quality controls. If they identify a court that usually has a lot of mistakes when sending requirements, they offer training. Mossos d'Esquadra also has a phone number to manage any problems that may arise within the Department of Justice or the own police organization.

Analysis

Implementation of GRP was over by March 2012. Currently, the system is fully working. There are around 1,000 exchanges daily. Processing time has dramatically dropped. Before 2009, an urgent requirement could take up to 3-4 days. Nowadays, it usually does not take longer than an hour. Quality control has also improved. In this respect, information is homogeneous. Also, the system can be audited and mistakes can be easily identified: what and where. Finally, centralization makes communication between the two parties involved easier and faster.

According to our interviewees, the project worked well since the very beginning. The existence of an explicit plan has been one of the key factors for its success. On one hand, GRP is part of a wider program, e-Justícia.cat, which has guided its implementation. On the other hand, important tools have been used in order to detect errors in time and to solve them before general deployment. Conducting pilots have proved wise, particularly because there was not that much time to develop the application. Among other, pilots led to some changes in the technological tool, which resulted very useful in the end.

The degree of collaboration between Mossos d'Esquadra and the Department of Justice has also been very relevant for the project. Despite the formal leadership of the latter, the police force has felt involved and has taken part in the project on equal basis. The design of the application was done jointly and a functional analysis was carried out both from a technical and an operational perspective. Communication has always been fluent. The existence of coordination rules and frequent meetings has immensely helped in this respect.

The project has been managed at a technical level. This has also led to its success. Politicians have not been operationally involved and have not put obstacles in the way. However, when help has been needed (particularly when police officers and computer specialists from the Department of Justice have not been able to reach an agreement), they have showed commitment. This said, political support has changed over time. Thus, in the beginning, there was clear high-level political commitment. Gascó & Jiménez (2011) explain it, "the Councillor of the Department of Justice, Mrs Montserrat Tura noticeably promoted this electronic justice initiative to such an extent that several agreements, rules, and laws were approved (…). But other political actors, such as the General Council of the Judiciary ("Consejo General del Poder Judicial") or the Superior Court of Justice of Catalonia ("Tribunal Superior de Justicia de Cataluña"), also backed the project. In the particular case of the GRP module, political commitment was even more obvious since Mrs Tura had previously been the Councillor of the department of the Interior, which is in charge of the Mossos d'Esquadra police force. Therefore, she knew the problems both departments experienced when they had to work together" (p. 6). Nowadays, it is individuals in lower positions within the political structure the ones who give support in specific situations, particularly related to disagreement among the two main actors.

It seems that resistance to change has been higher among the Department of Justice's civil servants. For some of our interviewees, this is due to the fact that Mossos d'Esquadra is a police organization and, as such, its structure is hierarchical. Also, for them it is easier to deal with a group of 34 people than with a group of almost 4,000 users. Change management strategies work better when groups are smaller. Nevertheless, training and communication within the Department of Justice have been decisive elements to minimize the natural resistance to change within the courts.

External recognition of this project is also relevant to prove its success. The Spanish General Council of the Judiciary has awarded this initiative during three years in a row, starting in 2010. Now that the project is finished, the wider program e-Justícia.cat has been again awarded in 2013. This is important, since the implementation of GRP has resulted in lessons learned, regarding the electronic signature, the document manager, or the digital communications with external parties, which have been taken into consideration in the design of other projects or modules.

Finally, only unimportant issues remain unsolved. On one hand, there are technological improvements, which take place constantly. For the past few months, Mossos d'Esquadra have set up a small unit with capacity to solve small technological problems and to carry out relatively easy developments. Still, meetings with the Implementation and Monitoring of Computer Programmes unit of the Department of Justice are needed to expand the scope of exchanges between the two actors and, particularly, from the police organization to the Department of Justice.

On the other hand, it is important to note that the Spanish justice system has to undergo a major change if it wants to converge with the European Union. If this happens, the relationship between the police forces and the Spanish Justice Administration will change and, probably, systems like this one will have to change accordingly. Nevertheless, it is soon to predict what these changes will be and how they will take place.

DISCUSSION AND CONCLUSION

In terms of the critical success factors listed in Table 2, it seems that the success of the digital police requirements module has been driven by what Gascó et al. (2013) and Gascó & Sierra (2015) call internal organizational factors and factors related to the governance of the network. On one hand, leadership and interoperability management have played an important role. As stated, there has been political support at different levels but operational and technical leadership as well. Also, the existence of a plan to implement the project and the many activities displayed in order to tackle resistance to change have proved decisive. These findings confirm what the literature has already shown regarding the role of organizational factors in interoperability initiatives and, particularly, the role of project management (Gil-García & Helbig, 2006; Umble et al., 2003; Dawes & Pardo, 2002), goal clarity (Garson, 2006; Dawes & Pardo, 2002), and resistance to change (Gil-García & Helbig, 2006; Rocheleau, 2005; Nortrop, 2002).

On the other hand, the case has also shown the importance of those variables related to the governance of the network. Specifically, perception of benefits (which was quite different for the main two actors involved), power, and clarity of roles and responsibilities (and, in particular, formalization of coordination rules and communication procedures) have proved key, confirming previous findings in the field (among other, Gascó & Sierra, 2015; Janowski et al., 2012; Dawes et al., 2009; Pardo et al., 2009; Archman & Kudlacek, 2008; Scholl & Klischewski, 2007; Bekkers, 2007; Eynon & Margetts, 2007; Orlikowsi, 2000).

Other factors seem to have less influence than the aforementioned ones, such as contextual (the critical economic situation in Spain) or technological variables. Interestingly enough, there are hardly any references to technology other than the need for the police officers to work simultaneously with the digital and the paper-based systems and the beginning of the project and the continuous technological improvements that are required to keep the system working and updated.

These findings let us draw two main conclusions. On one hand, interoperability in the justice field is a multidimensional phenomenon. The exchange of information that takes place between different actors does not depend on one isolated factor or category of factors. On the other, these types of projects are les conditioned by technological variables than by organizational and governance of the network ones.

The works of, for example, Fountain (2001, 1995), Scholl & Klichewski (2007), Eynon and Margetts (2007), Archman & Kudlacek (2008), Gascó (2010), Yang & Maxwell (2011), and Pardo et al. (2012), also consider that multiple factors influence interoperability projects at the same time. What's more, the authors report that technological obstacles are easy to overcome. In Yang & Maxwell's words (2011), "the technological challenge is less complex when compared with challenges in organizational and political aspects (…) Overcoming technical issues in information sharing merely lays the foundation for information sharing, and more complicated challenges lie in organization and policy" (p. 169).

As a result, we can state that our conclusions are aligned with the literature on interoperability in other fields, but add evidence in the particular field of justice. However, more research on interoperability initiatives is needed, particularly because this is a field with a multiplicity of actors. Therefore, factors related to the governance of the network, which have already proved key, might even play a major role in collaboration initiatives within the judiciary than in any other fields. Thus, further work is needed in order to keep building a strong theoretical and conceptual body.

In the light of the previous results, future studies could expand the sample horizontally using data from other interoperability initiatives within the justice field. Also, future research could drill deeper vertically, in future rounds of data collection, to understand in more detail these determinants, the relationships among them, and the outputs (reduction of delays, efficiency, effectiveness,…) and outcomes (a more open judiciary and, therefore, a more trusted and legitimated justice system) they give rise to.

REFERENCES

Archmann, S., & Kudlacek, I. (2008). Interoperability and the Exchange of Good Practice Cases. *European Journal of ePractice, 2*(February), 3-12.

Bekkers, V. (2007). The Governance of Back Office Integration. *Public Management Review, 9*(3), 377–400. doi:10.1080/14719030701425761

Cerrilo, A., & Fabra, P. (2009). *E-justice: Using Information Communication Technologies in the Court System*. Hershey, PA: IGI Global.

Chapman, R., & Hunt, M. (2006). *Open Government in a Theoretical and Practical Context*. Surrey: Ashgate.

Charalabidis, Y. (2011). *Interoperability in Digital Public Services and Administration. Bridging e-Government and e-Business*. Hershey, PA: IGI Global. doi:10.4018/978-1-61520-887-6

Chesbrough, H. (2003). The Era of Open Innovation. *MIT Sloan Management Review, 44*(3), 35–41.

Chesbrough, H. (2006). *Open Innovation: The New Imperative from Creating and Profiting from Technology*. Boston, MA: Harvard Business School Press.

Contini, F., & Lanzara, G. F. (Eds.). (2014). *The Circulation of Agency in e-Justice. Interoperability and Infrastructures for European Transborder Judicial Proceedings*. New York: Springer. doi:10.1007/978-94-007-7525-1

Criado, I. (2009). Gobierno Electrónico en Latinoamérica. Aproximación Desde una Perspectiva Intergubernamental. *Estado, Gobierno, Gestión Pública. Revista Chilena de Administración Pública, 14*(December), 9–35.

Criado, I., Gascó, M., & Jiménez, C. E. (2010). *Marco Iberoamericano de Interoperabilidad*. Caracas: CLAD.

Dawes, S., & Pardo, T. (2002). Building Collaborative Digital Government Systems. In W. J. McIver & A. K. Elmagarmid (Eds.), *Advances in Digital Government: Technology, Human Factors, and Policy* (pp. 259–273). New York: Springer. doi:10.1007/0-306-47374-7_16

Dawes, S. S., Cresswell, A. M., & Pardo, T. A. (2009). From "Need to Know" to "Need to Share: Tangled Problems, Information Boundaries, and the Building of Public Sector Knowledge Networks. *Public Administration Review, 69*(3), 392–402. doi:10.1111/j.1540-6210.2009.01987_2.x

European Commission. (2010). *European Interoperability Framework for European Public Services (EIF)*. Brussels: European Commission.

Eynon, R., & Margetts, H. (2007). Organizational solutions for overcoming barriers to e-government. *European Journal of ePractice, 1*(November), 73-85.

Fountain, J. (1995). *Enacting technology. An institutional perspective*. Cambridge, MA: John F. Kennedy School of Government.

Fountain, J. (2001). *Building the virtual state. Information technology and institutional change*. Washington, DC: Brookings Institution Press.

Garson, D. (2006). *Public information technology and e-governance. Managing the virtual state*. Sudbury, MA: Jones and Bartlett Publishers.

Gascó, M. (2009). El papel de las instituciones en el desarrollo del gobierno electrónico en América Latina: Algunas reflexiones. *Estado, Gobierno. Gestión Pública, 14*, 37–59.

Gascó, M. (2010). Los retos de la colaboración. ¿A qué, si no a eso, pretendemos hacer frente con la interoperabilidad? Paper presented at the XV CLAD Conference. Santo Domingo.

Gascó, M. (2014). *Guía de buenas prácticas en gobierno abierto*. Bogota: Observatics.

Gascó, M., Esteve, M., & Fernández, Ch. (2013). *Managing e-government interoperability.Abandoning projects to develop real management models*. Paper presented at PMRC 2013. Madison, WI.

Gascó, M., & Jiménez, C. E. (2011). *Interoperability in the justice field: variables that affect implementation*. Paper presented at the 11th European Conference on e-Government. Ljubljana.

Gascó, M., & Sierra, V. (2015). *Technological innovation projects.The role of management and network governance in e-government interoperability*. Paper presented at IRSPM 2015. Birmingham.

Gil-García, J. R. (2012). *Enacting electronic government success: An integrative study of government-wide websites, organizational capabilities, and institutions*. Heidelberg, Germany: Springer. doi:10.1007/978-1-4614-2015-6

Gil-García, J. R., & Helbig, N. (2006). Exploring e-government benefits and success factors. In A.-V. Anttoroiko & M. Mälkiä (Eds.), *Encyclopedia of Digital Government* (pp. 803–811). Hershey, PA: IGI Global. doi:10.4018/978-1-59140-789-8.ch122

Gil-García, J. R., & Pardo, T. (2005). E-government success factors: Mapping practical tools to theoretical foundations. *Government Information Quarterly*, *22*(2), 187–216. doi:10.1016/j.giq.2005.02.001

Gottschalk, P., & Solli-Sæther, H. (2009). *E-Government interoperability and information resource integration: frameworks for aligned Development*. Hershey, PA: Information Science Reference. doi:10.4018/978-1-60566-648-8

Institute of Electrical and Electronics Engineers. (1990). *Standard computer dictionary*. New York: IEEE Press.

Janowski, T., Pardo, T., & Davies, J. (2012). Government information networks – Mapping electronic governance cases through public administration concepts. *Government Information Quarterly*, *29*(S1), 1–10. doi:10.1016/j.giq.2011.11.003

Jiménez, C. E. (2010). *Interoperabilidad en la administración de justicia: experiencias y buenas prácticas en un ámbito complejo*. Paper presented at the CLAD 15th International Congress. Santo Domingo.

Jiménez, C. E. (2012). Implementing interoperability in e-justice's criminal area. *Effectius*, *17*(January/February), 1–7.

Jiménez, C. E. (2013). Gobierno abierto y back office: Reflexiones para su implementación. Boletín institucional e-Governa, 27, 15-17.

Jiménez, C. E. (2014). *Justicia abierta: transparencia y proximidad de la justicia en el actual contexto del open government*. Barcelona: Centre d'Estudis Jurídics i Formació Especialitzada – Autonomous Government of Catalonia.

Jiménez, C. E. (2015). *Modernización de la justicia en el siglo XXI: la necesidad de una perspectiva de justicia abierta*. Paper presented at the CLAD 20th International Congress. Lima.

Jiménez, C. E., Criado, I., & Gascó, M. (2011). Technological e-government interoperability. An analysis of Ibero American countries. *IEEE Latin American Transactions*, *9*(7), 1112–1117. doi:10.1109/TLA.2011.6129711

Jiménez, C. E., & Gascó, M. (2012, October/November). *Y ahora... gobierno abierto. Nuevos términos en la constante búsqueda por la transparencia y la rendición de cuentas*. Paper presented at the CLAD 17th International Congress. Cartagena de Indias.

Kubicek, H., Cimander, R., & Scholl, H. J. (2011). *Organizational interoperability in e-government. Lessons from 77 European good-practice cases*. Heidelberg, Germany: Springer. doi:10.1007/978-3-642-22502-4

Lee, G., & Kwak, Y. H. (2012). An open government maturity model for social media-based public engagement. *Government Information Quarterly*, *29*(4), 492–503. doi:10.1016/j.giq.2012.06.001

Márquez, J. M., Vázquez, R., Martínez, M., & Roldán, N. (2013). *Estudio de la demanda y uso de gobierno abierto en España*. Madrid: National Observatory of Teleccommunications and Information Society.

Meijer, A., Curtin, D., & Hillebrandt, M. (2012). Open government: Connecting vision and voice. *International Review of Administrative Sciences, 78*(1), 10–29. doi:10.1177/0020852311429533

Northrop, A. (2002). Lessons for managing information technology in the public sector. *Social Science Computer Review, 20*(2), 194–205. doi:10.1177/089443930202000209

OECD. (2011). *The call for innovative and open government. An overview of country initiatives*. Paris: OECD.

Orlikowski, W. (2000). Using technology and constituting structures: A practice lens for studying technology in organizations. *Organization Science, 11*(4), 404–428. doi:10.1287/orsc.11.4.404.14600

Pardo, T., Nam, T., & Burke, B. (2012). E-government interoperability: Interaction of policy, management, and technology dimensions. *Social Science Computer Review, 30*(1), 7–23. doi:10.1177/0894439310392184

Pardo, T., & Tayi, G. K. (2007). Interorganizational information integration: A key enabler for digital government. *Government Information Quarterly, 24*(4), 691–715. doi:10.1016/j.giq.2007.08.004

Parks, W. (1957). The open government principle: Applying the right to know under the Constitution. *The George Washington Law Review, 26*(1), 1–22.

Ramírez-Alujas, Á., & Dassen, N. (2012). Gobierno abierto: la ruta hacia una nueva agenda de reforma del Estado y la modernización de la administración pública en América Latina y el Caribe. In N. Dassen & J. C. Vieyra (Eds.), *Gobierno abierto y transparencia focalizada: tendencias y desafíos para América Latina y el Caribe* (pp. 41–72). Washington, DC: Inter-American Development Bank.

Rocheleau, B. (2005). Interorganizational and interdepartamental information systems: Sharing among governments. In D. Garson (Ed.), *Handbook of public information systems* (pp. 59–82). Boca Raton, FL: Taylor & Francs Group.

Scholl, H. J., & Klischewski, R. (2007). E-government integration and interoperability: Framing the research agenda. *International Journal of Public Administration, 30*(8), 889–920. doi:10.1080/01900690701402668

Silveira, L., Wazlawick, R. S., & Rover, A. J. (2015). Assessing the Brazilian e-justice interoperability model. *Latin America Transactions, 13*(5), 1504–1510. doi:10.1109/TLA.2015.7112008

Umble, E., Haft, R., & Umble, M. M. (2003). Enterprise resource planning: Implementation procedures and critical success factors. *European Journal of Operational Research, 146*(2), 241–257. doi:10.1016/S0377-2217(02)00547-7

Velicogna, M. (2007). Justice systems and ICT. What can be learned from Europe? *Utrecht Law Review, 3*(1), 129–147. doi:10.18352/ulr.41

Von Lucke, J., & Große, K. (2014). Open government collaboration. In M. Gascó (Ed.), *Open government. Opportunities and challenges for public governance* (pp. 189–204). New York: Springer.

Voorberg, W., Bekkers, V., & Tummers, L. (2015). A systematic review of co-creation and co-production: Embarking on the social innovation journey. *Public Management Review*, *17*(9), 1333–1357. doi:10.1080/14719037.2014.930505

Willem, A., & Buelens, M. (2007). Knowledge sharing in public sector organizations: The effect of organizational characteristics on interdepartmental knowledge sharing. *Journal of Public Administration: Research and Theory*, *17*(4), 581–606. doi:10.1093/jopart/mul021

Yang, T. M., & Maxwell, T. (2011). Information-sharing in public organizations: A literature review of interpersonal, intra-organizational and inter-organizational success factors. *Government Information Quarterly*, *28*(2), 164–175. doi:10.1016/j.giq.2010.06.008

KEY TERMS AND DEFINITIONS

Collaboration: Collaboration is about different actors, inside and outside the organization, working jointly and transversally.

Critical Success Factor: It is a critical variable or activity required for ensuring the success of an interoperability project.

Interoperability: It is the ability of disparate and diverse organizations to interact towards mutually beneficial and agreed common goals, involving the sharing of information and knowledge between the organizations, through the business processes they support, by means of the exchange of data between their respective ICT systems.

Open Government: An open government is a transparent, collaborative and participative government that achieves its goals by means of the intense use of ICT tools and, in particular, of open data and open action.

Open Justice: It refers to the application of the open government philosophy and its principles and tools to the justice field, taking into account the special context and requirements of the judiciary.

Participation: It is related to the involvement in political processes and, as a result, to initiatives of consultation and deliberation with citizens and of participation in the decision-making processes and the policy-making cycle.

Transparency: Transparency is about access to information.

ENDNOTE

1 Such as the open innovation perspective (Chesbrough, 2003, 2006) or the evolution of ICT adoption by public administrations approach (Jiménez, 2013; Jiménez & Gascó, 2012; Gascó, 2009).

Chapter 9
Openlaws.eu:
Open Justice in Europe through Open Access to Legal Information

Thomas J. Lampoltshammer
Danube University Krems, Austria

Clemens Wass
BY WASS GmbH, Austria

Andres Guadamuz
University of Sussex, UK

Thomas Heistracher
Salzburg University of Applied Sciences, Austria

ABSTRACT

Legal texts represent a fundamental building block in all democratic states. As such, legal information must be accessible to all members of society to the widest possible extent, to aid inclusiveness and to enable participation in public decision-making. In recognition of this, the EU and its Member States work to make laws, court decisions, etc. publicly available online. The sheer mass of legal norms, instruments, and interpretations in court decisions, commentaries and other sources, makes it increasingly difficult for citizens, civil society, businesses, and all involved stakeholders in legal practices to locate the relevant law. The challenge is to interlink local legal information and to have structures in place to enrich this information through aggregation and mass customization. The technological possibilities to achieve this goal do exist. The European project openlaws.eu aims for initiating a platform and to develop a vision for Big Open Legal Data (BOLD): an open framework for legislation, case law, and legal literature from across Europe.

INTRODUCTION

Legal texts represent a fundamental building block in all democratic states. As such, legal information must be accessible to all members of society to the widest possible extent, to aid inclusiveness and to enable participation in public decision-making. In recognition of this, the EU and its Member States work to make laws, court decisions, etc. publicly available online. Much has been achieved locally already. However, the sheer mass of legal norms, instruments, and interpretations in court decisions, commentaries and other sources, makes it increasingly difficult for citizens, civil society, businesses, and all involved stakeholders in legal practices to locate the relevant law.

DOI: 10.4018/978-1-5225-0717-8.ch009

The challenge is to interlink local legal information and to have structures in place to enrich this information through aggregation and mass customization. The technological possibilities to achieve this goal exist. The European project openlaws.eu aims for initiating a platform and to develop a vision for Big Open Legal Data (BOLD): an open framework for legislation, case law, and legal literature from across Europe. This contributes to better access to legal information and ultimately to better governance, both of which support higher social welfare goals and in the long run build the foundation for *Open Justice*.

The remainder of this chapter is structured as follows: after an introduction to important key terms and concepts, the evolution of *Open Justice* in Europe is presented. After that, the authors show the current legal framework across Europe including initiatives regarding legislation and case law. Next, viewpoints of various stakeholders are presented followed by ICT-related challenges to be solved in governmental environments. Afterwards, the openlaws.eu project is introduced in detail and how the project aims to overcome the before-mentioned open challenges. The chapter closes with the conclusions and recommendations towards future directions.

DEFINITION OF KEY TERMS

When reaching out to the topic *Open Justice* and the associated environment, the reader is confronted with a plethora of key terms and their definitions can vary depending on their origin or the crispness/fuzziness intended by the defining body. In order to set the direction of this chapter and to present the reader with the views of the authors, this section introduces important key terms and how they contribute to the overall theme of *Open Justice*. Alongside with the definition of terms, the authors present the reader with a visualization, showing the interdependencies and complimentary nature of all concepts involved (see Figure 1).

Figure 1. Visualization of key terms in the Open Justice environment

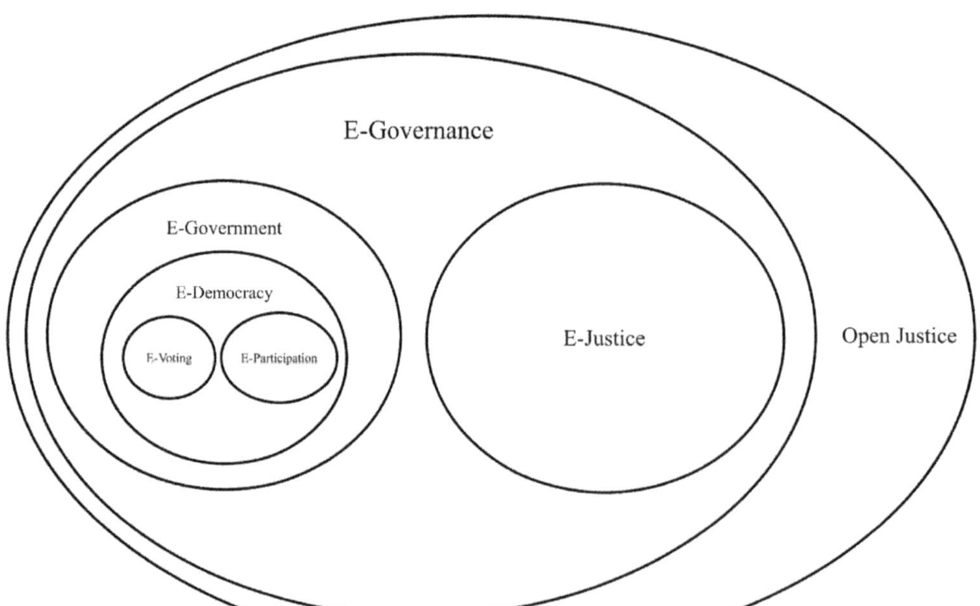

The first term to present is *E-Governance*. This term is often used interchangeably with the term *E-Government*. Yet, the terms describe, while being strongly related, different aspects of the same concept. This can lead to confusion regarding the extent of each term within the governmental environment (Palvia & Sharma, 2007). The definitions the authors of this chapter use go along-side with the definitions by Palvia and Sharma (2007): *E-Governance* is representing the environment for *E-Government*, setting its course to the conceptualization and implementation of information and communication technologies (ICT) within organizational or governmental bodies, while *E-Government* is the actual use of this infrastructure for all actions within the government as well as within the interaction with external stakeholders.

Embedded within *E-Government* is the concept of *E-Democracy*. The idea of this concept is to change existing structures of representatives towards a direct influence of citizens in the governmental processes and decision-making (Mahrer & Krimmer, 2005). As this definition can be approach from different angles, in this chapter, the authors see it rather as a complementary movement than as an entire replacement. Within the *E-Democracy* movement, three major sub-processes can be identified (Parycek, 2003):

1. Acquisition of information,
2. Formation of an opinion, and
3. The decision itself.

These three processes demonstrate the exchange of information between citizens and the government as well as decisions from citizens, based on the information available. Therefore, the authors identify two major concepts, namely *E-Participation* and *E-Voting*.

E-Participation describes the idea of involving citizens in democratic processes via the use of ICT. It can be seen as a kind of electronic bridge between citizens and the administration as well as citizens and politics in general (Sanford & Rose, 2007). E-Voting on the other hand goes even one step further, by not only using ICT for information flows, but to empower citizens to take actions electronically in the decision-making process. This way of opinion expression can reach from current societal questions, up to the selection of representatives in the government (Zissis & Lekkas, 2011).

At this point, the alert reader will recognize that the concept of *Open Justice* is not included as sole entity within the *E-Governance* concept (see Figure 1). This is due to the fact that *Open Justice* represents a kind of a metaconcept, which reaches throughout all the before-mentioned concepts. Therefore, the authors will explain their understanding of *Open Justice* in more detail in the following dedicated section.

THE EVOLUTION OF OPEN JUSTICE

While the constant evolution of the Western concept of justice falls outside of the remit of a work such as this, it may suffice to say that the authors see justice more towards the context of the justice system (and access to such system in the sense of the substantive justice system as described by Posner (1993)) than with the concept of justice itself, masterfully explained by authors such as Rawls (1999). With that in mind, the justice system consists not only on the courts that make interpretive decisions, but it is better understood as the entire apparatus of law, from legislative texts to judicial decisions. Access to justice in this context would be understood not in the sense of being able to go to court (Rhode, 2000), but more about having access to the corpus of law (Woolf, 1996).

The traditional approach to access justice in Western countries has been through the authoritative publication of legislation in official journals, and the publication of case reports. The advent of information technologies, and in particular the Internet, made wider dissemination of legal documents possible, in what is called generally legal information systems (Zeleznikow & Hunter, 1994).

Susskind (1996, p.78) comments that in the previous paradigm lawyers acted as an interface between the public and legal information, but with digital technologies this role disappeared. The logical evolution with enabling technologies is for the creation of models of sharing legal information.

Access to knowledge in general is now recognized as a key driver of social, cultural, and economic development, with tangible economic advantages to be gained by sharing (Weiss & Pluijmers, 2004; Kapczynski, 2008). Legal information then becomes just another part of the wider progress towards wider dissemination of knowledge, and in particular becomes an important element of the open access and open data movements.

Specifically, the concept of *Open Justice* can be best encapsulated in a quote from the case of *R v Sussex Justices* as follows: "It is not merely of some importance but is of fundamental importance, that justice should not only be done, but should manifestly and undoubtedly be seen to be done." (Müßig, 2007, p.13). The idea is that the public should not only have access to legal proceedings in an open manner (Spigelman, 2006), but that there should also be have access to legal information in the shape of legislation and rulings.

Bearing this discussion in mind, it is obvious that *Open Justice* is "not just another concept" in the legal realm, but an essential part of all aspects involved. It stands for transparency and access to information. Demands, that are vital for all legal concepts discussed in the section before (see Figure 1). Therefore, the authors are going to frame a picture of the current situation in Europe regarding transparency and access to information and its implementation.

THE CURRENT EUROPEAN FRAMEWORK

For many years, the European Union has been at the forefront of the provision of legal information to the public (*Note: It is not the remit of this paper to act as an introduction to European Law. Those interested in learning more about European integration see:Dinan, 2004;Cini & Borragan, 2013;McCormick, 2014)*. Since 1952, the European Union has been publishing its Official Journal (OJ), first as a joint report (A and P series), and then releasing two separate publications, legislation (L series) and Information and Notices (C series). While many other countries publish similar reports and official journals, what makes the European effort unique is the scope of the task at hand. The Official Journal needs to be published in all of the 24 official languages, and must also be made available in all 28 Member States. It comprises both the continental system of law and common law, as well as mixed legal systems. It must publish a complex legislative framework comprising of directives, regulations, and national implementation. It must also respond to a complex regulatory framework that includes various legal regimes, such as data protection (European Commission, 1995) and public sector information (European Commission, 2003), just to name a couple.

Adding to the complex issue is the matter of case law, which encompasses national courts, each with their own languages and reporting mechanisms, but also the subject of European case law, which is made up of the Court of Justice and General Court of the European Union. One should also note the decisions of the European Free Trade Area (EFTA) court and European Court of Human Rights (ECHR) have a strong interaction with the main European Courts as guardians of the treaties (see Defis (2000) for further details).

Given the massive amount of legislation and case law, it becomes evident that the issue of reporting and providing access to the European legal corpus requires a robust system in place. The European Union has therefore undertaken a considerable enterprise to implement a system of *Open Justice* that makes available legal information to the European public. The authors must state clearly that they use the term open in this paper following the Open Definition established by the Open Knowledge Foundation (OKFN), which defines openness as follows: "Open means anyone can freely access, use, modify, and share for any purpose (subject, at most, to requirements that preserve provenance and openness)." (Open Definition, 2016).

Open Justice then could be defined as providing free access to legal information, which can be shared for any purpose. As a result of the growing need for openness, at the moment, most of EU law can be found in the European database called EUR-Lex, but there remains a need for greater access to both European legal process and implementation at member state level.

But legal information is just part of a growing push towards openness in general. The EU's open agenda is mostly implemented by the public sector information regime, this has been created by the EU legislature to stimulate wider use of public sector information in the shape of the Public Sector Information Directive, which was updated by the Directive 2013/37/EU (European Commission, 2013), henceforth referred to jointly as the PSI Directive for convenience.

The objective of the PSI Directive is to harmonize various national practices on the re-use of public data. The Directive does not mandate the sharing of public data, but rather concentrates on the economic aspect of such sharing by establishing conditions in which public entities will be able to release information. An important over-reaching element to be found is a desire to encourage the cross-border sharing of public information to enable other organizations to make use of the data to produce value-added products, making sure that the sharing does not act as a distorting force for existing players in the market.

One key element of the PSI Directive is that it mandates Member States to allow re-use of public sector information, and that terms of use must be transparent. There is a shift towards the use of open licenses, particularly when taking into consideration the guidelines on recommended standard licenses, datasets and charging for the reuse of documents (European Commission, 2014), which explicitly favours the use of standard open licenses such as Creative Commons in the release of public sector information.

Another element of note contained in the PSI Directive is to establish limits on the charges to the public for re-use, which has to be shared with a ceiling calculated on the basis of actual costs of managing and extracting the information. In particular, public sector bodies need to calculate charges per re-use in a way so that the total income from charging does not exceed marginal costs incurred to produce and disseminate the information, together with a reasonable return on investment. Some exceptions to this rule have to be calculated with objective, transparent and verifiable criteria.

In addition, PSI Directive is to establish conditions for re-use that are non-discriminatory for comparable categories of re-use. This is one of the biggest concerns of the Directive, which aims to create a level playing field for the private sector. Without a provision on equal treatment of re-users, the legislator feared a serious potential for public sector bodies to distort markets and engage in unfair competition. While it is permissible for public bodies to re-use their data for the provision of (commercial) value-added services, it is made clear that there is a prohibition of cross-subsidies. If a public sector body re-uses its documents to offer added-value information services on the market outside the scope of its public task (i.e. acts as a re-user), it has to be subject to the same charges and other conditions that apply to re-users engaged in similar activities. Public sector bodies are also in principle prohibited from entering into exclusive arrangements with re-users. Exclusive deals can only be authorized in exceptional circumstances if they are necessary to provide services in the public interest, and only if they do not disturb the market negatively.

As a result of the PSI Directive framework, one is continuously encountering a strong incentive to publish all sorts of information to the public, be it as software and data.

With regards to software, the Commission has continued to implement a policy of fostering free and open source software (FOSS) at all levels of the EU (see also Guadamuz, 2009; Vasudeva, 2014).

The Commission has identified the use of FOSS in five areas (OSS Strategy, 2016):

1. Running FOSS to run its servers and data centres.
2. Using open source to run participation and social media tools.
3. Using FOSS in the desktop machines.
4. Using open source to develop tools.
5. Releasing software using FOSS licenses.

The above is part of the Commission's published strategy plan for the years 2014-2017, which promises to formally adopt and encourage the deployment of open source tools throughout the whole EU.

But some of the most interesting developments in the EU's openness agenda are taking place in the open data camp. The European Commission generally defines open data as data that should be freely available for use and re-use (European Commission, 2011). As part of the PSI Directive framework, the Commission has been implementing a very strong open data strategy at an internal level. The main example of this is the creation of an open data portal for the EU (Open Data Portal, 2016), where datasets from all EU institutions are released to the public under very permissive permission for re-use, which mostly requires attribution to the source material (OSS Strategy, 2016).

The Commission has also been encouraging member states to release data:

[...] Member States should formulate and implement open data policies, taking up good-practice examples from across the EU. Support should for example be given to open data pilots and open data competitions, in particular those targeting the development of cross-border products and services. (COM, 2011)

This is because member states usually have their own arrangements for the release of open data in place. The Commission is trying to create a large database that will aggregate national datasets under one portal (COM, 2011).

LEGISLATION AND CASE LAW INITIATIVES IN THE EU

End of 2013 the Justice and Home Affairs (JHA) Council of the EU adopted the new Strategy on European e-Justice 2014-2018. This Strategy defines the general principles and objectives of European e-Justice and sets out general guidelines for the establishment of a corresponding new multiannual European Action Plan on e-Justice. This second multiannual European Action Plan on e-Justice aims to build upon the work already undertaken and to continue this positive development at national and European level. The plan includes activities in the following areas:

1. Access to information in the field of justice (information through the e-Justice Portal, registers, semantic web),
2. Access to courts and extrajudicial procedures in cross-border situations (general aspects, cooperation with the judiciary and legal practitioners),
3. Communication between judicial authorities,
4. Horizontal issues.

A high priority is given to the area of semantic web development and the enhancement of communication between legal experts. A few research projects have already been launched on a European or national level, trying to make progress in this direction (Council of the European Union, 2014).

There are several on-going projects and initiatives around legislation and case law in Europe. A few selected projects should be mentioned:

- **EU Cases:** EUCases is a collaborative research project supported by Seventh Framework Programme (FP7) funding. The project will develop a pan-European law and case law Linking Platform transforming multilingual legal open data into linked open data after semantic and structural analysis. The web based EUCases Linking Platform will provide services linking EU law and case law with legislative acts and court decisions of six EU member states: Austria, Bulgaria, France, Germany, Italy and United Kingdom (EUCases, 2016).
- **Building on ECLI:** BO-ECLI is a research project the will be funded by DG Justice. The objectives of the project are: Further implementation of ECLI and integration with ESE-EEJP (in: Belgium, Italy, Germany, Estonia, Czech Republic, Greece, Croatia, Netherlands); improving accessibility to case law by creating linked open data; a 2.0 version of the ECLI standard, which is aligned with other semantic web standards as well as backwards compatible with the 1.0 version; to have EU wide policy guidelines on the publication of case law, specifically addressing the issues of selection criteria, data protection and open data; to have ECLI widely used for citing of case law in all legal and academic writings and for interoperability in (legal) IT applications. The project is supposed to start in October 2015 (BO-ECLI, 2016).
- **LAPSI/Share PSI:** Share-PSI 2.0 is the European network for the exchange of experience and ideas around implementing open data policies in the public sector. It brings together government departments, standards bodies, academic institutions, commercial organizations, trade associations and interest groups to identify what does and doesn't work, what is and isn't practical, what can and can't be expected of different stakeholders. The impetus for the Share PSI 2.0 Thematic Network is the revised European Directive on the Public Sector Information. This revises and increases the obligations on European Union member states to make their publicly funded data available at zero or, at most, marginal cost. Noting the work of the LAPSI project, which is concerned with legal aspects of Public Sector Information, this project focuses on the practical and technical challenges (Share-PSI 2.0, 2016).
- **Big Data for Law:** The National Archives has received 'big data' funding from the Arts and Humanities Research Council (AHRC) to deliver the 'Big Data for Law' project.
- **Big Data Research:** Big data research is perfectly possible with legislation if only the basic ingredients - the data, the tools and some tried and trusted methods - were as readily available as the computing power and the storage. The vision for this project is to address that gap by providing a new Legislation Data Research Infrastructure at research.legislation.gov.uk. Specifically tailored

to researchers' needs, it will consist of downloadable data, online tools for end-users; and open source tools for researchers to download, adapt and use. There are three main areas for research, i.e. understanding researchers' needs, deriving new open data from closed data, and Pattern language for legislation (Big Data For Law, 2016).

- **Innovating Justice:** The Innovating Justice Accelerator is about making justice work and innovating justice delivery as it has traditionally been organised. To promote innovation in the rule of law and to find the best innovations across the world, the Innovating Justice Accelerator issues challenge competitions. Innovating Justice is a creative approach to promote and support new projects in an open innovation way. Even though not limited to legislation and case law projects (Innovating Justice, 2016).
- **Openlaws.eu:** Openlaws.eu is funded by DG Justice with the aim to make access to justice easier by using open data (legislation and case law), open innovation (bringing together the stakeholders), and open source software (using the latest state-of-the-art technology). As this project is the example project onto which the authors of this chapter are introducing their conceptualization and improvement of Open Justice, details further details are given in a dedicated section of this chapter.

Having drawn the picture of the current "open" landscape within Europe, the authors are going to discuss in the following part of the chapter, who is effected in what way by the before-described situation at hand.

STAKEHOLDERS IN EUROPE

Open Justice is a broad field and as such impacts and affects numerous stakeholder groups in Europe. Each group has different interests in *Open Justice* and open access to legal information. Yet, openness manifests itself as a bi-directional phenomenon. While the motivation of some stakeholder groups might be to adopt legal information that is available, other groups might be interested in providing and sharing existing and new legal information. In many cases it is a combination of both. For example, a lawyer has an interest in using the legal contents that are available; nevertheless, this lawyer might also be willing to publish some legal information in form of open commentary. The motivation behind this act might be to show expertise or to increase reputation.

The following matrix (Table 1) is a model to categorize legal stakeholders by their expertise and by their individual/institutional size. Legal expertise is rated from A to C - where level A indicates a very high level of legal expertise, B indicates a medium level of legal expertise, and C indicates a low level of legal expertise. The individual and institutional size is categorized from 1 to 3 - where 1 indicates a small size including individuals, 2 indicates a medium size, and 3 indicates very large institutions, including society as a whole. The authors would like to note that it is intended to provide a general classification with this matrix. However, in specific cases, this general classification might not apply. Also, this matrix is not intended to be exhaustive.

Group A1 represents legal professionals, featuring a high level of expertise. This expertise is acquired through a special legal education in combination with practical experience. Due to the complexity of law, a layperson will often have to contact a professional to answer legal questions appropriately. How-

Table 1. Stakeholder matrix

Legal Expertise (Lower to Higher)	**A1** Judges Lawyers Notaries General counsels Legal scholars	**A2** Judiciary Legislative authorities Large law firms Universities	**A3** Vision: Stakeholder collaboration meets Big open legal data
	B1 Law students Semi-professionals Small enterprises	**B2** Legal publishers Medium enterprises Governmental administrations	**B3** Legal publishers Large enterprises Media
	C1 Citizen (Individual)	**C2** Citizens (Groups/associations/etc.)	**C3** Society (as a whole)
	Individual/Organizational Size (Smaller to Larger)		

ever, even these professionals are affected by this complexity, which results in specialization - although there are generalists as well with a broader background (who might have to consult a specialist for very specific questions).

For them, legal information is a valuable asset while for layperson such information typically represents costs. This distinction is important to understand the motivation behind *Open Justice* and open access in a modern sharing economy within a legal context.

Within Group A2, legal professionals work together in groups, law firms, universities or within the judiciary or legislative authorities. Here the expertise of individuals is bundled. Teamwork helps to set up the European legal framework and to solve complicated legal questions. Legislatures on a EU and on a Member State level have the power to enact, amend and repeal laws. They need to have an excellent legal qualification to do that. Accordingly, they have a strong political influence. Following the Public Sector Information (PSI) directive, documents held by public bodies shall be made available for re-use. Legislative acts are such documents and have always been meant to be available for everybody so that people know the law. This is also one reason why laws are often exempt from copyright protection in many EU Member States.

Group A3 can be seen rather as a vision than reality at the moment. With reference to the CILFIT case of the ECJ and the *acte clair doctrine*, the role of EU-wide cross-boarder legal information systems becomes more and more important. The focus of professional legal organizations in Europe is still rather inbound than outbound. Open innovation may help to reach A3, where the entire legal professionals community meets Big Open Legal Data.

Group B1 includes for example law students, semi professionals and small enterprises. The vast majority in the EU are micro companies with less than 10 employees. Such companies can hardly ever afford to hire an internal legal professional. Accordingly they have to consult external experts. Dealing with legal questions and risks is highly important for small enterprises even if it is cumbersome. A lawsuit (e.g. based on the infringement of intellectual property or competition law) or violations of public law (e.g. for the protection of the environment or workers) can be costly and even threaten the whole business. With a maximum of 250 employees and higher financial thresholds, medium sized enterprises may already be considerably larger than micro enterprises or small enterprises. On this level companies may start to insource legal expertise and to introduce more formal processes to limit their legal risks. It is also more likely that they expand their business to different countries, meaning that they will be active in different jurisdictions where they have to deal with different national laws and several local legal professionals. Legal publishers take a specials position in the model. Legal publishing is the process of production and dissemination of value-added legal information like literature and commentaries, but includes also the publication of 'primary sources' like legislation and case law.

Publishers as medium or large enterprises are located in Group B2. Based on the legal expert content that they possess, their legal expertise is well above average companies. Still, publishers depend on the input from legal experts on level A. Traditionally publishers have been selling books, printed journals and legal text collections. But even if legal professionals still like hard copies, there is a clear transition phase towards electronic publication and distribution of legal information via the Internet. Open access publication is on the rise in Europe, especially in projects that are financed under the Horizon 2020 funding scheme.

When it comes to *Open Justice* and open data, media and data-driven journalism in Group B3 will be empowered. With better access to legislation and case law and the right tools to view, analyse and understand legal information, journalists will be enabled to explain the concepts of European and national law much better. With open data, media can be a catalyst and bring law closer to the citizen on Group C.

Group C represents the average citizen. There are over 500 million people living in 28 Member States of the European Union, speaking 24 official languages. Each citizen has rights and obligations according to national and European laws. People are surrounded by law, while often without thinking about it, for example, when respecting the property of another person or when driving a car. However, sometimes people become more aware of the law and it's consequences, for example when signing a contract to acquire property or when receiving a ticket for speeding. Not knowing the law is no excuse for breaching the law. Unfortunately, knowing and understanding the law has become more complicated, in particular for citizens. This is the point where open access to legislation and case law in combination with collaboration and transparency tools can transform the legal system, as we know it today.

So far, issues and demands regarding the current framework as well the user base respectively have been discussed. In the following part, the authors will move to the next step, namely, the ICT-related aspects within *Open Justice* that are necessary to fulfil all these requirements and to tackle upcoming associated challenges.

ICT AND WEB 2.0 CHALLENGES TO OPEN JUSTICE

Information and communication technology (ICT) has a significant impact on public administration.

The exchange of digital data within jurisdiction, enabled by the rapid evolvement of technologies and associated possibilities, triggered a rethinking within the authorities about their function, activities, and development chances. The benefits of ICT-enabled environments are manifold and reach from increasing efficiency and accessibility to accountability and demanded transparency. By connecting this infrastructure to the Internet, the public sector enables the participation of the public, which in return supports the authority in distributing information about legislation, activities as well as providing feedback from the people represented by the government (Velicogna, 2007). However, in order to fulfil all demands and requirements, various issues and challenges have to be solved (non comprehensive list).

A major group of challenges originates from the legal data sources. Availability of free access is a huge problem. At this point, the authors do not refer to licensing issues, but to access to the service infrastructure that holds legal data. Often, these services have a strict limit regarding pull rates on their APIs, which means that building additional services on the existing services becomes difficult. Furthermore, there is no guarantee that theses services are available 24/7. This results in another "uncertainty factor", which adds to potential issues for platforms building on these APIs. The severity of such a situation becomes even more obvious, if critical decision-making processes are relaying on this kind of interface infrastructure.

Another issue is related to the high volume of data. Providing access is not the only issue a BOLD infrastructure has to handle. The community expects more than pure data. The support of analysis process is necessary to generate additional value. However, this comes at high computational costs, which in return can negatively influence the performance of the entire system, and as such the overall user experience. A slow reacting system is not only tedious to work on, but nearly unusable on mobile devices.

Furthermore, the infrastructure must support scaling mechanism to grow with its data and its users. This includes as well replication of data to different locations – not only to provide load balancing for better performance, but also to reduce the risk of loss of information.

In current developments, where regulations regarding data in the cloud have dramatically changed (see Schrems, 2016), it is more important than ever to carefully engage private user data, its storage, analysis, and potential distribution as anonymized data. This does not only affect the logical geographic extent of services but also their physical locations, which in return can have potential backslashes on replication and backup plans.

An issue not to be neglected comes in form of heterogeneous data sources. Each member state does not only provide its own database (if even available), but also its own data schema. This leads to an enormous demand of resource allocation regarding the process of data aggregation and data fusion. In addition, while on the one hand the existing platforms do provide APIs, they are often not very stable and changes are not always communicated to potential developers nor aligned with the community.

Still many governmental institutions relay on closed software and single vendor solutions. This comes with several severe issues. One issue is related to possible restrictions the vendor can put onto the organizations in terms of licensing agreements. Furthermore, price rises after the implementation of the software could be possible, pushing running costs to a level not foreseen within the initial forecast. Another issue can be found within the fact that a certain vendor could become bankrupt and no support is available anymore. This danger of course also exists for open source software; however, with huge supporters such as the Apache Foundation and the open source community it is unlikely to happen soon and with enough time to react to it.

Having presented the most prominent challenges, the authors are going to introduce the openlaws.eu project and its concept to address the before-mentioned aspects towards the road of an *Open Justice* environment.

OPENLAWS.EU: OPEN ACCESS TO LEGAL INFORMATION

OpenLaws.eu (Note: While this the official title of the project, the authors will refer to it by its abbreviated form "openlaws", see http://openlaws.eu) is an ambitious legal information project that is built on open data, open innovation, and open source software. Openlaws will help users find legal information more easily, organize it the way users want and share such information with other users (Clemens Wass et al., 2013). The Internet platform is adding a "social layer" to the existing "institutional layer" of legal information systems. Together with the different stakeholders the project will create a network between legislation, case law, legal literature, and legal experts - both on a national and a European level, leading to better access to legal information. The openlaws core team will also create a "BOLD" Vision 2020 about what Big Open Legal Data (BOLD) can do in the future and propose a roadmap to the European Commission.

Today, a huge amount of legal information remains published and administered by a limited number of organizations, typically in closed structures in public authorities and public-private partnerships. This includes the management of legal metadata, which is the basis for automated processing. Legal scholars and practitioners publish mainly through traditional highly specialized commercial publishing or isolated websites. Back-channels are limited, and there is little space for contributions from wider communities. Fully automated processing of legal data is not yet possible. Strikingly, whereas in many domains such as statistics, spatial information, and life sciences, research data and open information infrastructures are rapidly developing, this is not the case for legal information. The project's aim is to help build and promote an open ICT environment (including tools and sources like EUR-Lex, the European e-Justice System, e-Codex, national databases, etc.) so that all stakeholders (individuals and businesses, legal experts, and public bodies) can benefit from it (e.g., additional metadata, data curation). Mass customization will make it possible to define individual bookmarks, folders, create highlights, tags, comments, alert functions, and share these with others via a newly introduced social layer.

The vision of openlaws is to provide access to legal information and legal experts in the user-friendliest way possible, both on a national and on a European level. Legal information means primary sources of the law, i.e. legislation and case law, as well as secondary sources, i.e. literature and commentary. These two categories of sources will be complemented with a social layer, i.e., the legal community in its broadest sense (see Figure 2).

Figure 2. Information sources of openlaws

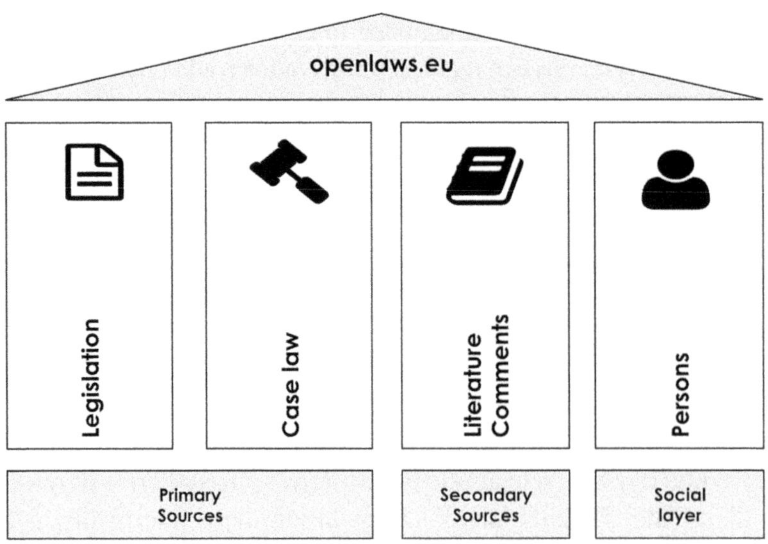

Citizens will learn more about their rights. For companies it will be easier to act in accordance with the law. Legal experts can demonstrate their knowledge and intensify the customer-relationship. Publishers can integrate their premium legal content via open interfaces. Governments can support openlaws and the creation of a community-driven legal knowledge base by making even more data sources available as open data. For this purpose, openlaws is building a cloud-based online service, where users can search for legal information, organize it the way they need it (e.g., by creating personalized folders, by adding tags, highlights and comments, etc.), and share it with others, either entirely openly or in private groups.

Openlaws is built on open design principles:

- **Open Data:** Legislation and case law that are made available by governments are integrated into openlaws.
- **Open Innovation:** Users can contribute data and metadata in the form of summaries, user-generated collections, links, tags and highlights, which will lead to a community generated legal information system.
- **Open Source Software:** Openlaws is built on top of open source software components. It will provide open interfaces, so that third parties can join the open innovation process.

The use of open source software as a significant positive impact on the other two design principles as well. Within ICT environments, open source software takes a leading role. This is due to the fact that organizations and institutions have to think outside of the box and have to reach beyond hardened process-related structures and boundaries (West & Lakhani, 2008). Lakhani & Panetta (2007), i.e., argue for a hybrid approach by combining in-house expertise with external community-driven knowledge, matching perfectly the concept and idea of openlaws.

Some main features and advances the project will realize:

- A legal meta-search across multiple databases will make it possible to search in different databases at the same time, also cross-border.
- The quantity of publicly available legal information can be increased. More legal metadata will help structure the content and will enable big data analysis. Open access publication (in combination with quality control mechanisms) will enable experts to easily publish comments, full papers, or translations – which would have been too complicated to do in the past – increasing their visibility and reputation.
- The quality of legal information can be increased. By involving the legal expert community, metadata can not only be generated, but also curated. Ambiguities can be presented to the community for correction. The quality of papers can be increased through review processes.
- The legal network within and between the target groups will help find experts and exchange information and best practices.
- Input from individuals and businesses in law-making, the analysis of case law (#goodlaw) promises a better knowledge and understanding of law, more direct democracy, and better policy-making.

The platform will aggregate legislation and case law from different open data repositories from the EU.

In addition, user-generated content and metadata will be collected. This information will be stored in the Big Open Legal Database (BOLDbase) and is the basis for the services described above (Wass, Sageder & Lampoltshammer, 2015). The core of this BOLDbase is formed by an innovative approach based on a graph database (Lampoltshammer, Sageder, & Heistracher, 2015). In accordance with open innovation principles, the *BOLDbase* will be also made available to third party projects. Such third parties can then build their own services on top of it. Rather than having to aggregate the legal data themselves, third parties can immediately use the entire database or parts of it (e.g., the EU and all integrated Member States or the EU and only one Member State). This will reduce risk, costs, and time to market and in return boost the establishment of micro-services, which are very flexible and can interact based on technology-independent ways.

The openlaws platform successfully addresses several of the before-mentioned issues regarding the utilization of ICT in the open legal data domain. Availability and scalability is achieved by building the platform on Neo4j (Miller, 2013), which represents on of the biggest and most powerful graph database provider worldwide. The openlaws platform is EU-based and is therefore liable to the strict EU data privacy and data protection laws, ensuring the right treatment of sensitive user-related data. By implementing distinct connectors in a close corporation with the actual member states, the openlaws platform provides a powerful and unique set of homogenous and enriched (meta) data of open legal data in Europe. The open innovation based principles, including the heavy use of open source software as well as the intensive involvement of the community, promises a prosperous future community ecosystem.

CONCLUSION

Better access to legal information is imperative to ultimately enable better governance, both of which build the foundation for *Open Justice*. Interoperability between legal applications is still in an experimental stage. There is, however, a high level of structural similarity between various legal functions all over Europe, thus the prerequisites for a systematic interoperability are given in principle. Based on the fact that open software systems have a high acceptance within Europe, open standards for interoperability have best chances to be established.

But it is not only the interaction of governments and public sector institutions with citizens that is impacted by ICT. The interaction between governmental organizations within and between countries benefits from this empowerment as well. The leading role here can be seen in data-driven approaches. The collecting process of data includes classical data sets as well as spatial data. It is imperative to already put high efforts in a sustainable data infrastructure at this point. There is also the necessity for high quality metadata.

By maintaining this quality, the analysis of these data sets, paired with relevant search tasks can be sped up. This leads, amongst other aspects, to a high level of accessibility within the governmental institution. To cover all these aspects, fast and flexible database solutions have to be employed as demonstrated by the openlaws.eu project.

The combination of public administration and governmental organizations form a critical mass regarding their technical requirements, demands, and licensing issues regarding software vendors related to the arising tasks. Furthermore, these tasks are specific to each single institution and therefore demand for highly customized solutions that are hardly available from off-the-shelf products. In addition, while as many data as possible should be available for citizens, the privacy of person-related information has to be guaranteed. This requires open software architectures as well as open standards to be the core of governmental ICT solutions. Proprietary software struggles with openness regarding its source code due to intellectual property issues. Open source software provides here the required level of flexibility, adaptability, and re-usability.

From the viewpoint of the European Commission, open source software is a crucial driving force for building a momentum regarding the empowerment towards openness and interoperability of software and ICT infrastructure across Europe. There are several positive aspects in conjunction with Open Source Software that support this ambitious goal: OSS can foster political commitment at a high level to support sustainable decision making processes. Furthermore, specification based on OSS on a European level can establish open standards regarding features and functionalities as well as compatibility. In addition, the high level of transparency provides the opportunity for a permanent bi-directional talk between the governmental organizations, citizens, and industrial partners. Finally, the newly build interoperability enables maintenance and support across Europe. As a consequence, the evolution of existing solutions and ICT infrastructures towards a European role model becomes possible. The EU project openlaws.eu is one example of such a role model.

ACKNOWLEDGMENT

The openlaws.eu project is funded by the Civil Justice Programme of the European Union under grant no. JUST/2013/JCIV/AG/45.

REFERENCES

Angles, R., & Gutierrez, C. (2008). Survey of Graph Database Models. *ACM Computing Surveys*, *40*(1), 1–39. doi:10.1145/1322432.1322433

Big Data for Law. (2016). Retrieved February 22, 2016, from http://www.legislation.gov.uk/projects/big-data-for-law

BO-ECLI. (2016). Retrieved February 22, 2016, from http://www.ittig.cnr.it/progetti/bo-ecli/

Cini, M., & Borragan, N. N. P. (2013). *European Union Politics*. Oxford, UK: Oxford University Press.

COM. (2011). *Communication From The Commission To The European Parliament, The Council, The European Economic And Social Committee And The Committee Of The Regions Open data An engine for innovation, growth and transparent governance*. COM/2011/0882 final.

Council of the European Union. (2014). *Multiannual European e-Justice Action Plan 2014-2018, 2014/C 182/02*. Author.

Defeis, E. F. (2000). Human Rights and the European Union: Who Decides-Possible Conflicts between the European Court of Justice and the European Court of Human Rights. *Dickinson International Law Annual*, *19*, 301–531.

Dinan, D. (2004). *Ever closer union: an introduction to European integration* (3rd ed.). Boulder, CO: Lynn Rienner Publisher.

EUCases. (2016). Retrieved February 22, 2016, from http://www.eucases.eu/

European Commission. (1995). *Directive 95/46/EC of the European Parliament and of the Council of 24 October 1995 on the protection of individuals with regard to the processing of personal data and on the free movement of such data, OJ L 281/31*. Author.

European Commission. (2003). *Directive 2003/98/EC of the European Parliament and of the Council of 17 November 2003 on the re-use of public sector information, OJ L 345/90*. Author.

European Commission. (2011). *Open data: An engine for innovation, growth and transparent governance*. COM(2011) 882.

European Commission. (2013). *Directive 2013/37/EU of the European Parliament and of the Council of 26 June 2013 amending Directive 2003/98/EC on the re-use of public sector information, OJ L 175/1*. Author.

European Commission. (2014). *Guidelines on recommended standard licences, datasets and charging for the reuse of documents* (2014/C 240/01). Author.

Guadamuz, A. (2009). Free Open Source Software. In L. Edwards & C. Waelde (Eds.), *Law and the Internet* (3rd ed.; pp. 359–391). Oxford, UK: Hart.

Innovating Justice. (2016). Retrieved February 22, 2016, from https://innovatingjustice.com/en/

Kapczynski, A. (2008). The access to knowledge mobilization and the new politics of intellectual property. *The Yale Law Journal*, *117*(804), 804–885. doi:10.2307/20455812

Lakhani, K. R., & Panetta, J. A. (2007). The principles of distributed innovation. *Innovations*, *2*(3), 97–112. doi:10.1162/itgg.2007.2.3.97

Lampoltshammer, T. J., Sageder, C., & Heistracher, T. (2015). The Openlaws Platform - An Open Architecture For Big Open Legal Data. In E. Schweighofer, F. Kummer, & W. Hötzendorfer (Eds.), *Proceedings of the 18th International Legal Informatics Symposium IRIS* (*Vol. 309*, pp. 173–179). Vienna: Österreichische Computergesellschaft.

Lewis, J. A. (2007). *Government open source policies*. Washington, DC: Center for Strategic and International Studies.

Mahrer, H., & Krimmer, R. (2005). Towards the enhancement of e-democracy: Identifying the notion of the 'middleman paradox'. *Information Systems Journal*, *15*(1), 27–42. doi:10.1111/j.1365-2575.2005.00184.x

McCormick, J. (2014). *Understanding the European Union: A Concise Introduction*. London: Palgrave Macmillan.

McLachlin, B. (2003). Courts, Transparency and Public Confidence-To the Better Administration of Justice. *Deakin Law Review*, *8*, 1.

Miller, J. J. (2013). Graph database applications and concepts with Neo4j.*Proceedings of the Southern Association for Information Systems Conference*.

Müßig, U. (2007). *Gesetzlicher Richter ohne Rechtsstaat? Eine historisch-vergleichende Spurensuche*. Paper presented at the Juristische Gesellschaft zu Berlin, February 2006 (No. 182), Berlin, Germany.

Open Data Portal. (2016). Retrieved February 22, 2016, from https://open-data.europa.eu/en/data/

Open Definition. (2016). Retrieved February 22, 2016, from http://opendefinition.org/

OSS Strategy. (2016). Retrieved February 22, 2016, from http://ec.europa.eu/dgs/informatics/oss_tech/opensource/ossinec_en.htm

Palvia, S. C. J., & Sharma, S. S. (2007). E-government and e-governance: definitions/domain framework and status around the world. In A. Agarwal, & V. Venkata Ramana (Eds.), *Proceedings of the Fifth International Conference on e-Governance (ICEG)* (pp. 1–12). Sonning Common: Academic Conferences Ltd.

Parycek, P. S. (2003). Electronic democracy: Chances and risks for municipalities. In A. K. Prosser (Ed.), *E-Democracy: Technology, right and politics (paper #174)*. Vienna: OCG.

Posner, R. A. (1993). *The Problems of Jurisprudence*. Cambridge, MA: Harvard University Press.

Rawls, J. (1999). *A Theory of Justice*. Cambridge, MA: Belknap Press of Harvard University Press.

Rhode, D. L. (2000). Access to justice. *Fordham Law Review*, *69*, 1785.

Sanford, C., & Rose, J. (2007). Characterizing eparticipation. *International Journal of Information Management*, *27*(6), 406–421. doi:10.1016/j.ijinfomgt.2007.08.002

Schrems. (2016). *Judgment in Case C-362/14 Maximillian Schrems v Data Protection Commissioner.* Retrieved February 22, 2016, from http://curia.europa.eu/jcms/upload/docs/application/pdf/2015-10/cp150117en.pdf

Share-PSI 2.0. (2016). Retrieved February 22, 2016, from http://www.ercim.eu/activity/projects/390-share-psi-2-0

Simon, K. D. (2005). The value of open standards and open-source software in government environments. *IBM Systems Journal*, *44*(2), 227–238. doi:10.1147/sj.442.0227

Spigelman, J. (2006). The Principle of Open Justice: A comparative perspective. *The University of New South Wales Law Journal*, *29*(1), 147–166.

Susskind, R. E. (1996). *The Future of Law: Facing the Challenges of Information Technology*. Oxford, UK: Clarendon Press.

Vasudeva, V. N. (2014). *Open source software and intellectual property rights*. New York, NY: Kluwer.

Velicogna, M. (2007). Justice Systems and ICT-What Can Be Learned from Europe. *Utrecht Law Review*, *3*(1), 129–147. doi:10.18352/ulr.41

Wass, C., Dini, P., Eiser, T., Heistracher, T., Lampoltshammer, T. J., Marcon, G., . . . Winkels, R. (2013). OpenLaws.eu. In E. Schweighofer, F. Kummer, & W. Hötzendorfer (Eds.), *Proceedings of the 16th International Legal Informatics Symposium IRIS* (*Vol. 292*, pp. 21–23). Vienna: Österreichische Computergesellschaft.

Wass, C., Sageder, C., & Lampoltshammer, T. J. (2015). openlaws.eu - Offene Rechtsinformation. *Proceedings of the 4.OGD D-A-CH-LI Conference Open X*.

Weiss, P., & Pluijmers, Y. (2004). *Borders in cyberspace: conflicting public sector information policies and their economic impacts*. Cheltenham, UK: Edward Elger Publishing.

West, J., & Lakhani, K. R. (2008). Getting clear about communities in open innovation. *Industry and Innovation*, *15*(2), 223–231. doi:10.1080/13662710802033734

Woolf, S. H. (1996). *Access to Justice: Final Report*. London: HM Stationery Office.

Zeleznikow, J., & Hunter, D. (1994). *Building Intelligent Legal Information Systems: Representation and Reasoning in Law*. Amsterdam: Kluwer.

Zissis, D., & Lekkas, D. (2011). Securing e-Government and e-Voting with an open cloud computing architecture. *Government Information Quarterly*, *28*(2), 239–251. doi:10.1016/j.giq.2010.05.010

Chapter 10
Consumer "Access to Justice" in EU in Low-Value Cross-Border Disputes and the Role of Online Dispute Resolution

Inmaculada Barral-Viñals
University of Barcelona, Spain

ABSTRACT

This paper examines consumer access to justice in the EU by analysing how Alternative Dispute Resolution (ADR) and Online Dispute Resolution (ODR) can improve this access, especially in the case of low-value cross-border disputes, which constitute the majority of consumer contract complaints. The discussion is based on a widened concept of open justice that not only seeks to provide greater transparency, but also greater participation and collaboration as a means to improve consumer access to justice. The approach deals with the subjective and objective obstacles to accessing justice and the role of participatory justice. Finally, the paper examines the decisions taken by the EU in its attempt to foster both ADRs and ODRs for consumer disputes and determines which obstacles have been eliminated in promoting access to justice.

INTRODUCTION

From Openness to Participation

The traditional meaning of open justice is based on the common law concept concerned with public access to trials where transparency plays an essential role. The best picture is related to the 'open court principle' (Harris, 1995), which implies trials materially open to public scrutiny that are able to maintain public confidence in the justice system (Dyson, 2013). This first approach to open justice implies that both public and media can attend the trials, thus guaranteeing transparency in justice. This concept has been broadly developed and limited by other valued concepts, namely privacy and security –two limitations that are currently being rethought given the impact they can have on the principle of openness (McLachlin, 2012).

DOI: 10.4018/978-1-5225-0717-8.ch010

Following this, Jiménez (2014) makes a difference between the traditional, limited concept of open justice based on transparency and a new and broader approach through which cooperation and participation have a place next to transparency in the so called "open judiciary". In that sense, open justice needs to be understood in this much broader sense, and recent developments in the field of e-government should be employed to achieve this goal. Jiménez's position on the coordination between these three principles is supported by relevant studies on open government. Without this combination, if only transparency is taken into account but not participation, justice will keep being alien to citizens.

Harris (1995) distinguishes between material access to trial (traditional and basic concept of open justice) and participatory access. The latter allows citizens to access the justice system, that is, not only the courtroom but also the whole system of administration of justice. As a consequence, open judiciary does not only imply transparency but also participation.

Participation has grounds to become an elemental dimension of the justice system together with the much needed transparency. The access to the justice system upon which participation is based means the possibility for citizens to find effective ways to resolve their conflicts in accordance with due process of law. Participation entails the development of access to justice. Access to justice is the expression of fundamental rights in the field of conflict resolution. This dimension is recognized by the Universal Declaration of Human Rights adopted by the UN General Assembly in 1948, as well as by the Convention for the Protection of Human Rights and Fundamental Freedoms (or European Convention on Human Rights, Art. 6) drafted by the Council of Europe in 1950 and which entered into force in 1953.

This Chapter, however, does not aim to set the conceptual basis for the inclusion of the concept of participation within that of open judiciary. The aim of this Chapter is instead to analyze a specific kind of conflict in which participatory access to justice is especially not guaranteed: consumer conflicts. But as these conflicts do not usually reach the judicial stage, the problem is not solved through the increase of transparency in the judicial process. What needs to be conceived is a way for citizens to participate in the resolution of these conflicts.

For the purpose of this Chapter the characteristics of consumer conflicts established in the results of the White Book on Mediation in Catalonia (Barral-Suquet, 2010, p. 157 ff.) will be taken as a reference. Such disputes are typically low-value and high-volume (Cortés-Esteban de la Rosa, 2013, p. 408 ff), which means that a great amount of small, almost identical claims need to be resolved. Many of the cases do not go to court, for consumers are usually reluctant to get involved in a judicial process for such claims, as many studies carried out in the EU confirm (Barral, 2014, p. 50). The first consequence is that, unless there exists a swift, cheap resolution mechanism, these claims are unlikely to reach court for reasons of cost effectiveness. The second consequence is even worse: although the redress sought by each consumer might be of little value, if all consumers are considered as a unity the total amount claimed becomes a very large sum, reason for which not solving the dispute is far from being fair.

This problem illustrates the limits of open justice when understood following its traditional sense: if no means of access are provided, justice cannot be participative, nor can it be open. One solution that has been applied in the recent years, especially in the EU, is the use of Alternative Dispute Resolution (ADR) mechanisms as they constitute a clear example of participative justice. For this reason, this work aims to analyze the improvements in consumer access to justice through tools that promote participation, mainly, ADR. In that sense, ADR allow consumers to play an active role in the resolution of their conflicts through participative justice. Then, in specific situations technology eases their access to justice, so we turn to Online dispute resolution (ODR).

The methodology applied is based on studies of the Canadian doctrine of consumer access to justice, the obstacles that arise and the proposed solutions based on empirical research studies (Section 2). These studies clearly demonstrate that the main positive results in this field are achieved through ADR mechanisms which, despite presenting some disadvantages as well, are strongly connected with participatory justice (Section 3). Section 4 analyzes a specific case: the treatment of customer complaints in the EU, where ADR and Online Dispute Resolution (ODR) mechanisms have been used for some years. Indeed, the EU has fostered the use of technology and developed ODR mechanisms especially designed for consumer complaints. Section 4 studies their main achievements, in particular with respect to the interactive platform for the management of consumer conflicts set forth by EU Regulation 524/2013 (hereinafter, the RODR) which will become accessible to consumers and traders in February 2016. This work aims to maximize the dynamics of ADR through the use of ODR. In these kinds of processes, technology can improve citizen access to, and thus participation in, justice even more.

MAIN FOCUS OF THE CHAPTER

Consumers Access to Justice

While any attempt at defining 'access to justice' lies outside the scope of this paper, an overview of the main assumptions made in this area constitutes a useful starting point. First, the different problems of access to justice will be described (a) and, secondly, the specific obstacles in the field of consumers will be analyzed in a deeper manner (b).

The Many Faces of a Problem

The first analysis of access to justice was undertaken by Cappelletti and Garth (1978, p. 3 ff.) who described 'three waves' of increasing access to justice. The first wave originated in Europe in the sixties and was led by scholars of procedural law who sought to reform the excessive formalism that had hitherto characterized the structures of civil procedure; thus, access to justice meant access to a lawyer and to legal representation in the courts. The second wave in the seventies was a movement to reform the institutions in order to facilitate access, that is, a new, user-oriented access to justice. This wave ushered in the small claims courts and class actions, but access remained closely tied to access to courts. The third wave went further in the so-called demystification of the law and took a more general approach being guided by the prevention of conflicts, out-of-court mechanisms and changes in the legal systems, personnel and processes of dispute resolution.

In the case of Canada, Macdonald (2010, p.5-7) has undertaken an in-depth analysis of access to justice and has distinguished a further two waves. The fourth is the recognition of ADR, and especially of the so-called preventive law, which also implies the normative power of non-state-owned bodies. The fifth wave is concerned with the proactive access to justice that has emerged in all legal systems and institutions. Macdonald also describes a broader concept of access to justice (and not one limited solely to access to legal institutions) and examines the general conditions of justice in society. In this sense, the principle of access to justice has, he claims, evolved and become the idea that underpins access to law. As Macdonald points out, what is needed is a comprehensive approach which, rather than asking about access to courts, takes into account access to the law as a multidimensional strategy (2010, p. 11).

Yet, these objectives are more challenging as far as consumer access to justice is concerned, since the many specific problems that can arise act as a constant hindrance. As Macdonald stresses, a major problem with a broader access to justice is that consumers are a heterogeneous group and, while they share the same legal status, they cannot face the legal institutions in the same way (2010, p. 15). The so-called 'vulnerable consumer' is merely a new division in an attempt to understand this heterogeneity. This is the same opinion as that expressed by Ramsay (2003, p.19): access to justice and consumer protection are two sides of the same problem, as the access to justice is not only to give new and more efficient tools to seek for redress. Ramsay (2003, p. 22-25) claims that many socio-legal studies have been undertaken in the field of consumer behavior showing how simple assumptions about such behavior based on a rational weighting of costs and benefits may need to be modified. He warns that too little empirical research into the effectiveness of consumer law exists for a proper answer to be given to the many attempts at achieving access to justice. By way of a solution, he opts for the self-enforcement of the law, as a new way of ensuring access to justice.

In short, access to legal institutions may constitute an important first step, but it should be borne in mind that this needs to be considered part of a wider plan for consumer access to law. Access to justice is primarily access to the prevention and the resolution of the conflict by any means; however, it also means access to the resources, access to the institutions of creation and administration of law, and access to power (Macdonald, 1990). Although such a situation would represent the perfect achievement of meaningful access to justice, it is far from being achieved in practice. For this reason, it is worth analyzing what steps have been taken to date in reference to consumer access to justice, examining whether they have been appropriate and successful and determining what remains to be done.

Challenging Obstacles to Consumer Access to Justice

Consumers usually encounter a set of obstacles as they seek access to justice, which can render it impossible, or at least, very difficult to attain. As such, consumer access to justice depends on the removal of those obstacles that act as a hindrance. This study adopts the approach taken by Canadian scholars drawing a useful distinction between objective and subjective obstacles to access to justice –above all Giard Proulx, 1985, p. 244; Macdonald, 1990, to show the narrowness of this approach; Macdonald (2010, p. 25) and Lafond (2010, p. 125). This distinction was also used by the *Groupe de travail sur l'accessibilité à la justice* (1991) to analyze civil justice. It should be noted that these obstacles can affect any party to a conflict and, as such, should be considered general, but many acquire even greater significance when they affect consumers.

As discussed, the obstacles to access to justice can be either objective or subjective. The former are concerned mainly with the constraints imposed by the legal system for the resolution of disputes and include the costs of litigation and the lengthy, formal procedures that typically overwhelm consumers. These obstacles are structural failures in the system that tend to be more consistently present in court than in out-of-court proceedings. But even in this case, they are likely to be reproduced because the model is the judiciary, even if the latter call for a less formal structure and for a reduction in ritualism (Iavarone-Turcotte, 2012, p. 8). Subjective obstacles, on the other hand, are related to consumer perceptions throughout the process of bringing a complaint and seeking a resolution. First and foremost, consumers are typically unaware of their rights and do not know the best course of action to take in bringing their complaint. They are usually ignorant of their rights in a specific situation and, those who have the information will often find the legal language impenetrable. Additionally, they are typically uncomfortable during the procedures, which differ markedly from anything they encounter in everyday life, and are strongly affected by the formality of the whole scenario (Lafond, 2010, p. 70 ff.).

The first attempt at providing consumers with more opportunities of individual redress was introduced with the so-called "small claims procedures" (SCP). These judicial procedures are additional to the ordinary civil procedure and the costs incurred and the time involved in reaching a resolution are allocated in proportion to the value of the settlement. Cortes (2011, p. 118) outlines the main features of SCP in EU countries in the following list: more informal and simplified procedures; legal representation of litigants is usually discouraged; judges play a more interventionist role at oral hearings; procedural rules are more relaxed and litigants pay only their own legal costs. While this legal design seems to target primarily the objective obstacles described above, the practice has been somewhat different. Macdonald and McGuire (1996) undertook an empirical study of SCP in Quebec 25 years after their introduction. Their study clearly shows that it is largely professionals and the self-employed that use this procedure in order to recoup the fees for their services (75%); as such the consumer problems solved are often quite different from expectations and the structure does not achieve its objective of improving consumer access to justice (Lafond, 2015, p. 396-397). Similarly, and based on a legal and economic perspective, Duggan (2003, p. 66) reaches the conclusion that SCP are uneconomical because of the fixed nature of legal fees, which cannot be circumvented. In response he proposes developing legal-aid mechanisms or even seeking consumer agency mediation or industry-specific dispute resolution arrangements as a cost-avoidance measure.

For these reasons, the removal of obstacles to consumer access to justice has been carried out through extrajudicial conflict resolution mechanisms. ADR is usually considered more flexible than courts and allows for greater participation of the parts in the process. Consequently, a priori ADR meets some of the characteristics that improve consumer access to justice. The following Section analyzes this possibility.

ADR AND CONSUMER ACCESS TO JUSTICE: TOWARDS PARTICIPATORY JUSTICE

As has been said, the problems that encounter small claims to be settled by short procedures have led to the need for dispute resolution mechanisms outside of the judiciary. The second step is the search for out-of-court dispute resolution procedures based on ADR. Based on the US tradition developed in the seventies, ADR incorporates a neutral third party that imposes (as an arbitrator) or facilitates (as a mediator or conciliator) the resolution of the conflict. Negotiation, even without this neutral party, can also be considered ADR, as can other consultative schemes such as those led by an ombudsman. ADR has expanded greatly across Europe, especially with regard to consumer claims, where this would seem to be the correct path.

This Section analyzes the pros and cons of ADR mechanisms with respect to consumer access to justice based on empirical research carried out in Canada (a). The concept of participatory justice that arises from the ADR tradition will also be presented (b).

Can ADR Solve the Problem?

The positive effects that the use of ADR has had on consumer access to justice are undeniable. Lafond (2010, p. 132-138) has tested them empirically in a study that compares small claim procedures and a set of different ADR mechanisms used in Quebec. The author concludes that ADR clearly overcomes some of the aforementioned objective obstacles. They are cheaper, and sometimes free of charge. They are swifter in terms of providing an answer or solution. They attach greater importance to equity as opposed to the strict application of the law. Finally, the informal nature of the process is also positive as it allows solutions that take into account the interests of the parties and offer more imaginative resolutions. All in all, ADR mechanisms appear to be the solution for some of the objective obstacles, insofar as they involve less formal processes in which consumers should feel more at ease and, more especially, they can play an active role in the resolutions (proactivity). This also relieves some of the subjective obstacles as well, because the aim of the system is to involve consumers in the process and to empower them to find a solution. All of this should have a direct effect on lowering the psychological fear of dispute resolution.

It is nevertheless true that ADR mechanisms also suffer a number of threats that should not be silenced. They can, it is said, lead to second-class justice (Nader, 1998) where neither individual positions nor collective rights are upheld. In the case of individual interests, concerns have been expressed about the skills and competences of the neutral party and the way in which these experts are recruited. Likewise, concerns have been expressed about the partiality of the latter, especially when they are paid by a private dispute resolution system. Finally, there is evidence that at best these schemes reduce but do not eliminate the unequal bargaining power between businesses and consumers.

In the case of collective interests, concerns have been raised about the marginalization of small disputes that are resolved outside the judicial system; the sacrifice of the rights of consumers even in tailored ADR agreements that can be harmful to the consumer (Demeulenaere, 1987, p. 123 -124); and, last but not least, the unsolved problem of privatization of justice, and the end of justice as a public service in the current wave that is seeing the deconstruction of the pillars of the welfare state (Esplugues, 2014, p. 357-359).

The negative effects of ADR have gone largely discussed and, logically, they are far from being solved. However, when dealing with consumer dispute resolutions, ADR mechanisms are really no longer an "alternative", instead they are the only way of seeking redress. In any consumer dispute where the amount involved is low, ADR is the only way of complaining, the only real and effective means of accessing the system (Barral-Suquet, 2010, p. 159; Lafond, 2010, p. 150-152). Thus, ADR helps ensure consumer access to justice and so policy-makers should try to minimize any negative side effects. The EU, the case study in the following Section, has clearly opted for these mechanisms as a means for dealing with consumer complaints. The EU has developed a quality assessment process that can be deemed reliable, but the choices regarding a public/private system, recruitment and the role of neutrals have to be given more serious consideration.

Having said this, in seeking to draw a provisional conclusion, access to justice can be defined in line with Lord Woolf (1996), who claims that an accessible system should be just in the results it delivers, be fair in the way it treats litigants, offer appropriate procedures at a reasonable cost, deal with cases with reasonable speed, be understandable to those who use it, be responsive to the needs of those who use it, provide as much certainty as the nature of particular cases allows, and be effective, adequately resourced and organized. This comprehensive list of characteristics identifies virtually all concerns about access to justice. In these terms, ADR is better placed to achieve these goals than the courts when handling consumer disputes because of the low value of the complaints and their ability to reduce subjective obstacles, since they circumvent many of the disadvantages of the formal court process, especially in the case of a non-imposed solution, be it through mediation or conciliation.

To end with a warning remark, the above definition presents a traditional approach to the access of justice from an institutional perspective. The idea is focused on legal normativity, disregarding other social sources of norms, and is based solely on the expertise of the actors (Roberge, 2011, p. 24). In this sense, access to justice is equivalent to access to a judge or a third party which applies the legal framework leading to a solution that is fair by definition. This is why two sets of problem arise: first, the system is greatly challenged by issues of independence, impartiality and the quality assessment of neutrals; second, there are concerns about the correct application of the law, even if equity is gaining increasing importance in these cases. This is major issue because it seems to provide a direct report between the participation of the parties that could increase fairness throughout the process and the privatization of justice (Barendrecht, Gramatikov, Verdonschot & Porter, 2012).

ADR and Participatory Justice

The second concept to take into consideration is participatory justice, which takes ADR further in developing some of the ideas discussed above in terms of a party's involvement in the dispute resolution process. It needs to be analyzed because it represents a reformulation of the main concerns about access to justice based on a variety of remedies –both in and out-of-court– that seek to find the best solution for all parties concerned.

Participatory justice is based on the parties' involvement in the resolution of the conflict. In private law this is called consent justice, and in criminal law it is related to restaurative justice that puts the compensation for the victim in the arena of the criminal case.

Coming back to private law, participatory justice is a concept born in the shadow of the traditional concept of justice, i.e., 'legal justice', so its chief characteristics are drawn in opposition to it. It is not easy to define the complete approach to legal justice, as many concepts and definitions exist depending on previous choices made within the general theory of law. However, this study opts for the positivist state-owned concept of justice (Green, 2009) where justice means having access to an enforcement system that protects individual rights granted by the law.

In this sense, participatory justice relies, according to Roberge (2011, p. 12 a 24), upon three main concepts: first, the idea of a complementary view on the issue that will either prevent or solve the conflict; second, the participation of the parties, which leads to a solution to the conflict, and, third, an integral approach to the conflict that will lead to the best solution. To achieve these goals, participatory justice is based on three values, respect, creativity and proactivity, that underpin three main dimensions of the proceedings: the interaction between the parties, the content and the process. Thus, participatory justice aims to achieve respect in the interaction, creativity in the content and proactivity in the process of achieving the best solution to the conflict. This almost certainly implies the need for a new breed of legal professionals who are capable of dealing with such concepts in any conflict and can propose the best means of reaching a solution either via the judiciary or having recourse to some form of ADR: the process being a continuum and the choice in the hands of the parties. In the field of access to justice, participatory justice can bring legal pluralism to conflict resolution and challenge the model of access to justice.

Participatory justice, however, is not concerned with the institutional perspective of access to justice, rather it adds the parties' perception of fairness to accessibility. In so doing, it takes a contextual –case-by-case– approach that provides the necessary social regulation that underpins legal pluralism. The multi-disciplinary nature and the parties' proactivity aim to find a better solution which satisfies the expectations and feelings of the parties. This might, be, for example in the design of new ways of solving disputes, such as crowdsourcing, where the dispute is open to a large number of participants who act in a collaborative way.

It is undoubtedly a new approach to access to justice, the first representation of which might be the multi-door courthouse where parties are offered a variety of courts and out-of-court procedures to resolve the dispute (National Action Committee on Access to Justice in Civil and Family Matters, Canada, 2013); and it is one that can also be applied to consumer access to justice. Although EU policies tend to take into account only the institutional perspective (as we show in the following section), new remedies and new processes, they also pay considerable attention to ADR and especially to mediation. So, the key concept of participatory justice can be easily adopted in this context.

IMPROVING CONSUMER ACCESS TO JUSTICE IN THE EU: FROM ADR TO ODR

The EU has promoted consumer access to justice in response to concerns about the effectiveness of mechanisms of redress for consumers around Europe. In conjunction with decades of EU Directives unifying the rights of the Member States' consumers, EU consumer protection policies have striven to provide solutions for the enforcement of these rights. Indeed, this would seem to represent the best way forward, as the new remedies provided by European consumer law are now well established, while their enforcement remains at an early stage.

The following Sections present an overview of the choices made by the EU in terms of consumer access to justice when developing the use of ADR (a), as well as an overview of the use of technology and ODR in this type of conflict in order to improve access to justice (b).

The Use of ADR in Consumer Disputes in the EU

In 1993 the EU launched an ambitious program for consumer access to justice with the publication of the Green Paper entitled 'Consumer access to justice in the internal market'. This initiative was in fact taken before the Green Paper on access to justice in civil and commercial matters, which was not published until 2002. The 1993 Green Paper established a legal framework in which mechanisms should be developed to safeguard the effectiveness of the legal framework providing consumer protection. The approach provided tools of enforcement to ensure the effectiveness of the legal system:

[…] If The Rights Recognised By The Legal Order Thus Created Are Infringed Through A Breach Of One Of These Norms, A Procedure (Judicial Or Administrative) Must Exist In Order To 'Render Justice' To The Victim And At The Same Time To Redress The Balance Of Interests As Required By The Legislator. If Such A Procedure Did Not Exist Or Was Not 'Accessible' To The Holders Of The Interest Protected By The Legal Order, There Would Clearly Be A Gap Between The Legislator's Designs And The Reality Experienced By Citizens. The Problem Summarised Here Under The Rubric 'Access To Justice' Is Nothing Other Than That Of This Gap Between Law And Reality.

It is readily apparent that this document is based mainly on the concept of redress, understood as access to tribunals or other decision-making bodies, in which access means equality in the search for legal redress when the law is not applied; in other words, it provides a very clearly institutional perspective. Consumer access to justice is thus given a global approach where the remedies provided by the judiciary are also taken into account, including, for example, the settlement of collective actions in civil law countries for some specific consumer conflicts, the promotion of legal advice and legal aid and the strengthening of cross-border cooperation (Art. 6 of the European Convention on Human Rights, 1950; and Art. 47 of the European Chart of Fundamental Rights). Besides this, ADR for consumer complaints is also considered a form of access, and, for this reason, the development of ADR for this purpose is linked to consumer access to justice and to the set of actions that aims to strengthen possibilities of redress in cases of dispute. This position is based on the fact that most of the Member States had already developed out-of-court systems for consumer complaints based on the assumption that they provide more flexible and cheaper proceedings than the courts.

The next step in this process was the presentation in February 1996 of the Commission's Communication entitled "Action plan on consumer access to justice and the settlement of consumer disputes in the internal market" (COM(96) 13 Final). This second text was a clear step forward in the promotion of ADR, as opposed to the more general approach advocated by the Green Paper. The Action Plan argued that consumer access to justice can be achieved with a variety of instruments, yet that access to justice does not always mean access to the courts. In this sense, it establishes quite clearly that alternative extra-judicial processes also constitute a means of access. Thus, this broader concept of access to justice was promoted, together with ADR, across the EU for dealing with consumer complaints. This underlying assumption was made even more evident in the Commission's Communication of 4 April 2001, "Widening consumer access to alternative dispute resolution" (COM(01) 161 Final), in which the Commission affirmed that ADR mechanisms for resolving disputes have a key role to play in improving access to justice for individual consumers. This Communication is also of great interest because as well as clearly favoring ADR because of the nature of their proceedings, it also links the development of these instruments to the use of information and communication technologies. From this point on, the development of ADR in the EU framework was to serve these two ideas.

In this sense, the EU has clearly opted for an ADR system for individual consumer redress, and EU policy instruments need to be understood in the light of this task. The first regulation in this regard was the Recommendation of the Commission, 98/257/EC of 30 March 1998 on the principles applicable to the bodies responsible for the out-of-court settlement of consumer disputes. This text regulates any alternative dispute resolution that involves the intervention of a third party who proposes or imposes a solution; that is to say, arbitration – where the third party *imposes*, or a consultative body such as the ombudsman *proposes* a solution with no binding outcome. This was followed by Recommendation 2001/310/EC of 4 April, which is applicable to any facilitative process that aims to bring parties together to convince them to find a solution by common consent, which is the essence of mediation or negotiation (Art. 1). These two texts established a wide range of principles that ADR mechanisms for consumers have to comply with.

Additionally, the EU has carried out an important task of classification of consumer ADR, registering those ADR mechanisms that satisfy the principles established in the above two recommendations. Two studies promoted by the Commission highlight the heterogeneity of consumer ADR within the EU, with Member States opting for different mechanisms that often do not sit easily with those of another country.

Moreover, existing consumer ADR not only differs in design and effectiveness, but also in the use of comparable legal mechanisms: conciliation, mediation, arbitration, ombudsmen, etc., where some kind of harmonization is needed, which presumably will have to constitute the next step forward (Barral, 2012).

The line established by the two Recommendations has been confirmed by Directive 2013/11/EU of the European Parliament and of the Council of 21 May 2013 on alternative dispute resolution for consumer disputes (Directive on consumer ADR -DADR-). This text was to be transposed by all Member States no later than July 2015. This text is a not a recommendation but a legislative act that allows Member States to organize their own systems of ADR, although they have to undertake to comply with a set of principles and quality standards. A system of national accreditations is applied in each country that registers its processes and a list of qualified entities has to be given to the EU.

Via the different ADR schemes operated by the Member States, the EU has learnt to deal with consumer access to justice. Nevertheless, specific achievements in terms of removing obstacles to access are, in most cases, left up to the individual regulator. In fact, the DADR lays down the efficiency principle when it states that ADR procedures should be free of charge or available at a nominal fee for consumers (Art. 8.c.) or at a rate that does not discourage consumers. It also provides that the parties should have access to he procedure without being obliged to retain a lawyer or legal advisor (Art. 8. b). The procedures should also be swift, an outcome having to be made available within a maximum period of 90 days from the date on which the entity received the complete complaint file (Art. 8.d.). Thus, it is clear that a competent ADR, in the terms established by the Directive, needs to be cheap and swift, but because of the legal requirements, not simply because of the fact that they are ADR mechanisms. Yet, it should be stressed these constraints in terms of costs and delays are better suited to a low-value claims oriented system which corresponds most closely to consumer disputes. Thus, this choice of law is to be welcomed.

The obvious advantage of the choice of ADR is that the litigants are exposed to less formal procedures, thus removing one of he subjective obstacles to justice. Moreover, some of the disadvantages of the ADR system that might advise against its use can be limited by the quality assessment undertaken by the Member States. This means that only those entities that comply with the quality requirements of the text (Art. 20), namely, in relation to their expertise, independence and impartiality (as provided for under Art. 6 of the DADR), can operate as ADR entities.

In short, in the field of consumer disputes, the EU clearly opts for alternative forms of resolution, while leaving it to the Member States to ensure they have in place the necessary procedures while guaranteeing a minimum standard of quality. As such the system is designed to foster consumer access to justice, especially in the case of low-value complaints. However, the results of empirical studies need to be examined before we can vouch for its effectiveness.

Online Dispute Resolution: The Way Forward

EU policies regarding the enforcement of consumer rights and consumer access to justice have been governed by a second approach in addition to that of ADR analyzed just now. The new approach has tackled consumer access to justice through resorting to Information and Communication Technologies (ICT) to the existent ADR systems. At this moment, technology offers a wide range of emerging procedures that may be used to communicate or to resolve disputes. For this reason, following the Commission Communication in 2001 discussing ideas to boost growth and strengthen confidence, the EU launched an initiative to implement ODR in consumer disputes.

As has been said, the low value of many consumer disputes justifies the adoption of ADR in this field which, at least in Europe, seems to represent part of the solution. ICT can be useful in this regard in lowering costs, at least those of direct payments (Gramatikov, 2012, p. 125 to 133). But, there is a second issue of considerable importance in our analysis. The cross-border dimension of many consumer disputes adds a further deterrent, namely, the difficulty in knowing which law is applicable to the case and in identifying the competent jurisdiction, which serve to emphasize the deficiency of traditional justice for such conflicts, raising the costs and impeding a swift resolution (Pecherzewski & Rodziewicz, 2012, p. 45 ff). The EU has shown a particular concern for cross-border consumer contracts, since this is a clear embodiment of its internal market, which constitutes the main objective of EU consumer legislation. Thus, it is readily apparent that the term 'cross-border' refers to an area without frontiers and, therefore, the primary concern is to provide new commercial practices with alternative methods for dealing with disputes. It is this shift in practices that is instigating the change from ADR to ODR.

The following Subsections analyze the concept of ODR (a) and provide an overview of the different steps that have been followed to introduce ODR in consumer disputes within the EU and how they have enhanced access to justice (b), as set forth by EU Regulation 524/2013 of the European Parliament and of the Council of 21 May 2013 on online dispute resolution (RODR) that creates an ODR platform accessible to consumers and traders from 15 February 2016 on.

Evolving ADR: Online Dispute Resolution

ODR, as a part of ADR, takes advantage of the information-processing mechanisms of computers and the long-distance communication methods offered by the Internet (Hörnle, 2009). Conley-Tyler (2004) describes ODR as dispute resolution processes conducted with the assistance of information and communications technology, particularly the Internet. Similar terms are 'online ADR', 'eADR', 'iADR', 'virtual ADR', 'cyber mediation' and 'cyber arbitration'. Nevertheless, according to the author of this study, cyber mediation and cyber arbitration are some examples of the broader term ODR that focus on the interaction between alternative conflict resolution and technology. The term was coined originally in 2001 by Ethan Katsh and Janet Rifkin (2001) to refer to the application of ICT in the resolution of disputes between parties (Poblet, 2008). Even if no restriction exists, ODR is related to ADR inasmuch as it improves ADR through the use of technology.

ODR mechanisms, under constant and extraordinary evolution to facilitate conflict resolution, use technology in several different levels. Firstly, this use of technology might refer to communication between the parties, that is, to long-distance communication techniques that already exist, such as e-mails or chats. Secondly, it might be related to interactivity, since the process may be propelled by a combined use of websites, blogs, wikis and other web 2.0 tools, for instance. Finally, the use of technology might take place in the process of resolution itself through specific tools such as web forms, automatic flow control, information organization and algorithms that cross proposals (as the basis of automatic negotiation systems) (Poblet, 2011). In the latter case technology facilitates the dispute resolution itself.

The use of technology is constantly growing and web 2.0 and 3.0 technologies offer real possibilities for the development of the three main ODR areas: communication, cooperation and interactivity (Suquet, 2012). As Benyekhlef (2005) states, nowadays technology allows for the creation of mechanisms that automatize specific functions, model the process of dispute resolution and offer an interface that allows for the achievement, documentation and filing of the different steps of the resolution process. One of the most extended uses are interactive platforms based on a computer with internet and a set of websites with information and instructions. Interactivity allows the parties to send documents, see those sent by the other party and respond to them. They usually have communication features like e-mail, chat and audio or videoconference as well (Hörnle, 2009). These tools allow for an automatic flow control which determines the parties' participation and the process sequence according to the phase in which they are. They might also contain a database and a digital register of the cases. This is the model adopted for the EU ODR platform that will be analyzed in depth in next Subsection.

Finally, second generation ODR is already a reality. In this case, technology does not play a secondary role in supporting communication, management and interactivity. It is now used to generate the strategy, the definition and the decision-making. In these processes where the use of technology is indispensable for the resolution of the dispute, autonomous and intelligent software systems provide the essential tools (Poblet, 2011). There are many possibilities for artificial intelligence in this field and they will need to be taken into account in the future: this is what is known as agreement technologies (Ossowski-Sierra and Botti, 2013).

When used in ADR, ICT reduce the travel and accommodation costs incurred in a cross-border dispute (Vermeys, 2013, p. 10 ff). Conley-Tyler (2004, p. 8), in a 2004 study of 115 ODR services all over the world, states that services offering techniques such as automated negotiation and facilitated negotiation can be delivered at a very low cost whereas services relying on third party human intervention are not so cheap. This means that, regarding consumer disputes, ODR may offer cost savings in almost every case because are suitable for automated or facilitated negotiation. However, it is true that ODR is not always a low-cost option when using third party human intervention. Other impacts of ICT in terms of reduction in delays, enhanced accessibility or the elimination of the subjective obstacles depend on the type of ODR chosen.

Indeed, it is not easy to assess the improvements in access to justice without referring to a specific ODR system. Therefore, the following Subsection focuses the attention on the interactive platform created by the EU and set forth in the RODR. This legal text is the latest legal application of ICT to consumer dispute resolution in the EU for now.

The ODR Platform in EU Regulation 524/2013

The RODR creates a claim management system that derives claims to the competent national institution, as well as a case management online platform that should have been available in the EU on 9 January 2016; it was finally available on 15 February 2016.

The RODR emphasizes the close link between e-commerce and ODR, since only online disputes can be solved using this platform (Preamble, nº. 15, art. 2.1), which is an irrational limitation. Moreover, this limit is not consistent with the DADR, as the latter takes a broader approach in its dealings with consumer disputes in general, not being confined solely to e-commerce. In fact, ODR is also suitable for offline disputes as the real problem consumers face in accessing justice concerns the enforcement mechanism for any kind of dispute, whether it involves e-commerce or not, provided the dispute is cross border (Bényekhlef, 2012). Therefore, providing consumers with a means for seeking redress, even if the contract is offline, would equally improve access to justice. In short, consumer cross-border conflicts are hard to deal with if we continue to think in terms of traditional dispute resolution, but the response can be quite different if technology is employed.

In terms of cost, ODR is the best option as it avoids the consequences of the conflict of laws in a cross-border dispute. Across Europe, the substantive law regulating consumer disputes is largely harmonized, especially following the Directive on Consumer Rights (2011/83/EC), which promotes the idea of maximum harmonization; and the Rome I and II conventions that provide consumer friendly examples of applicable law. However, when this somewhat homogeneous piece of legislation is enforced in another member state it raises a number of concerns (Cortés, 2010, p. 25-39). In this regard, the EU has been exploring the possibility of interactive platforms to deal with consumer complaints until the approval of the ODR regulation, which can exploit ICTs in resolving such disputes. The extent to which this is happening is what we analyze here.

The first step was a complaint form designed to facilitate communication, created by the European Commission's communication on the out-of-court settlement of consumer disputes (COM (1998) 198), which sought to facilitate access to extrajudicial resolution procedures and help consumers, through a series of questions, to establish the points of dispute and the exact nature of the problem. Subsequently, the Council's Resolution of 25 May 2000 on a "Community-wide network of national bodies for the extra-judicial settlement of consumer disputes" urged the Commission to build a network of centers to help consumers bring their complaints using ICTs, particularly the internet. This heralded the start of the European ExtraJudicial Network (EEJ-NET) connecting a centre in each of the EU Member States, to help consumers resolve their disputes. This project was started in 2001 and enjoyed a relative degree of success. Later, FIN-NET for disputes involving financial products was established along similar lines. However, their role was updated when the EU started to construct its own electronic dispute resolution platform, ECODIR, which in turn was replaced by the management tool in the ODR Regulation (Bényekhlef, 2010, p.103 ff). Arguably, ECODIR provided a better solution than that offered by the RODR: ECODIR was designed as a tool for the management of complaints and, at the same time, as a platform for conflict resolution through direct negotiation between the parties and the introduction of a mediator if no agreement was reached. This second aspect is not included in the RODR. Yet, some of the revitalized structure of the EEJ-NET underpins the new regulation.

In fact, the RODR provides for a "Network of ODR contact points" (Art. 7), where each Member State's contact point is responsible for receiving complaints from consumers and for directing them to the competent entity for resolution. The network represents an obvious example of case management, relying on the existing centers in the Consumer Centers Network, as specifically stated under Art. 7. The second main innovation was the establishment of the ODR platform (see Art. 5) to be developed, operated and maintained by the Commission. This ODR is designed as an electronic access to an interactive Internet site via a "single point of entry" (Art. 5.2.), conceived primarily as a case management platform.

According to Art. 5.4. the platform should comprise four main technical tools: an electronic complaint form; a translation system that does not rely solely on automated translation tools; a case management tool to identify the competent ADR entity to conduct the dispute resolution procedure; and a system providing general information about consumer rights and details about competent ADR and ODR contact points, as well as guidelines for submitting complaints through the platform (Art. 5.4.h.). Initially, the platform is designed only to channel claims to the national competent authority (Article 5.4.c.) and to serve as a reference point for communication between the parties during the process as provided for under art. 5.4.d. Thus, it would serve as a 'meeting point' for the consumer and the ADR entity, where the complaint might be addressed to the competent resolution system.

The Factsheet published by the European Commission in January 2016 summarizes the functioning of the platform in four (easy) steps:

1. The consumer fills in an online complaint form and submits it.
2. The complaint is sent to the relevant trader, who proposes an ADR entity to the consumer.
3. Once consumer and trader agree on an ADR entity to handle their dispute, the EU ODR platform transfers automatically the complaint to that entity.
4. The ADR entity handles the case entirely online and reaches an outcome in 90 days.

At this stage, the ODR is not yet solving the dispute; it merely redirects it. This means that the eventual resolution mechanism will be a competent ADR system, as defined under Art. 20 DADR, which should constitute one of the possible legal forms to this effect (mediation, arbitration, ombudsman, etc.). It should be stressed that the platform does not resolve the disputes; rather, this is the competence of the ADR entity whose rules govern the process.

The platform offers electronic case management online, via the ODR platform (Art. 5.3.d.), but once an electronic complaint form has been submitted and this has been channeled to the competent ADR, this entity is under no obligation to use the ODR platform (Art. 10 d). This means that new developments in the platform expanding the technical possibilities for case resolution (including videoconferencing and automated negotiation tools) are not compulsory.

Despite these technical shortcomings, the platform can promote access to justice. As such, redirecting the consumer complaint to the competent entity to resolve cross-border disputes can be considered the first step in encouraging consumers to enforce their rights. Further, the information provided by the platform should reduce the main subjective obstacles concerning the lack of knowledge about the corresponding legal system and about where and how to complain (Barral-Suquet, 2010, p.). However, the platform does not remove the obstacles to the access of justice imposed by the ADR entities since it redirects all claims to the competent dispute resolution entity.

In short, the EU ODR platform should improve consumer access to justice, especially in the case of cross-border disputes because, even if it continues simply to channel the complaints to the competent resolution entity, it will provide access to the system for a large number of low-value cross-border disputes. In this way, the platform will ensure a resolution which in other circumstances would not be possible. Yet, the opportunity to use interactive tools for conflict resolution, which is a technical possibility, appears to have been lost for the time being. The combination of a channeling tool and a case resolution system would have been highly positive for consumer redress, because the speed of the resolution process is likely to be challenged in a system where the complainant has not only to identify a competent entity, but also deal with the problems presented by each ADR. Thus, better consumer access to justice via ODR awaits the development of more effective case-resolution ODR platforms.

CONCLUSION

Access to justice should be put at the core of the new concept of open justice, which is concerned not only with transparency but also participation and collaboration. Open justice is, then, calling for participatory access to justice. In this new concept participation means, in the first place, having access to the legal institutions, but also having recourse to a complete set of actions that guarantee justice.

ADR is able to remove some of the objective obstacles to access to justice in that it can reduce costs and delays. Yet, because for low-value claims, ADR mechanisms are the only cost effective mechanism available to consumers, such dispute resolution schemes have ceased to be truly "alternative". However, an overview of EU policies shows that the development of ADR schemes has succeeded in improving consumer access to justice, especially in the case of low-value claims. Additionally, because they use less formal procedures and are able to give greater priority to equity, ADR has been able to remove some of the subjective, psychological barriers to a more participatory, open justice.

As well as providing full access, participatory justice helps litigants in terms of promoting creativity in the resolution of disputes and the proactivity of the parties in a multi-door system based on ADR, where the best solution is sought in providing redress. Consequently, ADR schemes confirm an improvement of consumer access to justice and also take a clear step in the link between open justice and participation as participatory justice lays in the concept of ADR.

ADR schemes, however, have also generated a new set of problems, most notably in relation to the independence, impartiality and quality of the neutral parties, which can result in a second-class justice, especially when provided by private schemes. In response the EU has instigated ADR quality assessment by its Member States in an attempt at ensuring the independence and impartiality of these entities; yet, threats regarding the privatization of law remain.

Even consumer protection cannot be understood without contemplating the technical possibilities of electronic platforms to offer a cheap and swift dispute resolution system that can enhance efficiency. The specific ODR scheme chosen by the EU Commission is an interactive platform as presented in the RODR. This platform is set to be of great use in promoting access to justice. First, in helping consumers seek redress, the platform is able to forward the consumer complaint to the entity with the necessary competence to resolve cross-border disputes. Second, the information that the platform makes available serves to reduce some of the main subjective obstacles related to the litigants' lack of knowledge about the legal framework, and where and how they should complain. However, the platform does not remove the obstacles to access of justice inherent to ADR since the platform merely redirects claims to a competent ADR entity. In short, the platform is a somewhat basic case management tool, but one that offers a wide variety of technical possibilities which should have a marked impact on access to justice.

Thus, the EU's policy aimed at promoting ADR and ODR is clearly having a positive impact on consumer access to justice in the case of low-value cross-border disputes, since the schemes offer a means to redress that is not so readily accessible via the judiciary. Yet, much work has still to be done in facilitating consumer access to justice.

REFERENCES

Barral-Viñals, I. (2011). E-consumers and effective protection: the online dispute resolution system. In M. Kenny & J. Deveney (Eds.), *European Consumer Protection. Theory and Practice* (pp. 82–98). Cambridge, UK: Cambridge University Press.

Barral-Viñals, I. (2014). Reclamaciones de consumo y ODR: Procesos automáticos, small claims y plataformas interactivas. *Revista Aranzadi de Derecho y Nuevas Tecnologías*, *34*, 43–65.

Barral-Viñals, I., & Suquet Capdevila, J. (2010). La mediación en el ámbito del consumo. In P. Casanovas, E. Lauroba & J. Magre (Eds.), *Libro Blanco de la mediación en Cataluña* (pp. 301-450). Barcelona: Huygens. Retrieved from www.llibreblancmediacio.com

Benyekhelf, K., & Gélinas, F. (2005). Online Dispute Resolution. *Lex Electronica*, *10*(2), 1-129. Retrieved from http://www.lex-electronica.org/articles/v10-2/Benyekhlef_Gelinas.pdf

Bényekhlef, K. (2010). La résolution en ligne des différends de consommation: un récit autour (et un exemple) du droit postmoderne. In *L'accés des consommateurs à la justice* (pp. 89–119). Cowansville, Canada: Éditions Yvon Blais.

Canada, National Action Committee on Access to Justice in Civil and Family Matters, Access to Civil and Family Justice: A Roadmap for Change, Ottawa. (n.d.). Retrieved 23, June, 2015, from http://www.cfcj-fcjc.org/sites/default/files/docs/2013/AC_Report_English_Final.pdf

Cappelleti, M., & Garth, B. (1978). Access to justice: The wordlwide movement to make rights effective- A general report. In Access to justice (pp. 1-30). Alpenn aan den Rhijn: Sijthoff and Noordhoff.

Commission's Green Paper, 16 November 1993, on access of consumers to justice and the settlement of consumer disputes in the single market - COM(93) 576 Final.

Cortés, P. (2011). *Online Dispute Resolution for Consumers in the EU*. Oxon, UK: Routledge.

Cortés, P., & Esteban de la Rosa, F. (2013). Building a global redress system for low value cross-border disputes. *The International and Comparative Law Quarterly*, *62*(2), 407–440. doi:10.1017/S0020589313000109

Demeulenaere, B. (1987). La médiation et les droits du consommateur. *Windsor Yearbook of Access to Justice*, *7*, 118–128.

Duggan, A. (2003). Consumer access to justice in common law countries: a survey of the issues from a law and economics perspective. In C. Rickett & T. Telfer (Eds.), *International perspectives on consumers' access to justice* (pp. 66–90). Cambridge, UK: CUP.

Dyson, J. (2013). *Advances in open justice in England and Wales. Hong Kong, China,* Retrieved 14, June 2015, from https://www.judiciary.gov.uk/wp-content/uploads/JCO/Documents/Speeches/mr-speech-hong-kong-lecture-18102013.pdf

Espluques Mota, C. (2013). Hacia una nueva noción de "Acceso a la justicia" en la EU a través del fomento del recurso a los mecanismos de ADR: la Directiva 2008/52/CE y su transposición en los diferentes estados miembros. In J. Forner, C. González, & R. Viñas (Eds.), *Estudios sobre la unificación internacional y regional del Derecho internacional privado, Liber Amicorum Alegria Borrás* (pp. 351–376). Barcelona: Marcial Pons Editores.

Giard, M., & Proulx, M. (1985). *Pour comprendre l'appareil judiciaire québequois.* PUQ.

Gramatikov, M. (2012). Measuring costs of ODR. In M. Gramatikov (Ed.), Costs & quality of Online dispute resolution (pp. 125-133). Maklu.

Green, L. (2009). Legal Positivism. In *The Stanford Encyclopedia of Philosophy*. Retrieved 06, June, 2015 from http://plato.stanford.edu/archives/fall2009/entries/legal-positivism/

Groupe de travail sur l'accessibilité à la justice. (1991). *Jalons pour une plus grande accessibilité à la justice*. Sainte Foy, ministère de la Justice.

Harris, B. V. (1995). Equal Access to Justice: A Constitutional Principle in Need of a Higher Profile. *N.Z. L. Rev.*, *282*, 282–309.

Hörnle, J. (2009). Cross-border internet dispute resolution. *Lex electrónica*, *17*(2), 1-14.

Jiménez, C. E. (2014). *Justicia Abierta: transparencia y proximidad de la justicia en el actual contexto de Open Government*. Barcelona: Centro de Estudios Jurídicos y Formación Especializada del Departamento de Justicia. Generalidad de Cataluña.

Katsh, E., & Rifkin, J. (2001). *Online dispute resolution: resolving conflicts in cyberspace*. San Francisco: Jossey-Bass.

Lafond, P. C. (2010). Les modes alternatifs de règlement des différends en droit de la consommation: d'un progrès né du chaos à l'optimalisation. In *L'accés des consommateurs à la justice* (pp. 119–180). Cowansville, Canada: Éditions Yvon Blais.

Lafond, P. C. (2015). *Droit de la protection du consommateur: théorie et pratique*. Comwansville, Canada: Éditions Yvon Blais.

Law Commission of Canada. (2003). *Transforming Relationships through Participatory Justice*. Ottawa, Canada: Law Commission of Canada.

Macdonald, R. (1990). Access to justice and law reform. *Windsor Yearbook of Access to Justice*, *10*, 287–337.

Macdonald, R. (2010). L'accès à la justice et le consommateur: une "marque maison? In P. C. Lafond (Ed.), *L'accés des consommateurs à la justice* (pp. 4–10). Cowansville, Canada: Éditions Yvon Blais.

Macdonald, R., & Mc Guire, S. (1996). Small Claims Courts Cant. *Osgoode Hall Law Journal*, *34*(3), 509–530.

McLachlin, B. (2014). *Openness and the rule of law*. Remarks of the Right Honourable Beverley McLachlin, P.C. Chief Justice of Canada at the Annual International Rule of Law Lecture. London, United Kingdom. Retrieved 06, June, 2015 from http://www.barcouncil.org.uk/media/270848/jan_8__2014_-_12_pt.__rule_of_law_-_annual_international_rule_of_law_lecture.pdf

Nader, L. (1988). The ADR explosion -The implications of rhetoric in legal reform. *Windsor Yearbook of Access to Justice*, *8*, 269–291.

Online dispute resolution for cross-border electronic commerce transactions: draft procedural rules, Working Group III (Online dispute resolution) de la UNCITRAL, Viena, 18-22 November, 2013.

Ossowski, S., Sierra, C., & Botti, L. (2013). Agreement Technologies: A Computing Perspective. In S. Ossowsky (Ed.), *Agreement Technologies. Law, Governance and Technology* (pp. 1–16). Berlin: Springer. doi:10.1007/978-94-007-5583-3_1

Pecherzewski, P., & Rodziewicz, P. (2012). ODR and trans-border dispute. In Costs and quality of Online dispute resolution (pp. 39-50). Maklu.

Poblet Balcell, M. (2008). Introduction: Bringing a new vision on online dispute resolution. In M. Poblet (Ed.), *Expanding horizons of ODR,Proceedings of the 5th International Workshop on online dispute resolution*. (pp. 1-8). Firenze: Springer.

Poblet Balcell, M., et al. (2011). Tecnologías para la mediación en línea, estado del arte, usos y propuesta. In Libro Blanco de la mediación en Catalunya (pp. 943-1008). Barcelona: Huygens.

Ramsay, I. (2003). Consumer redress and access to justice. In C. Rickett & T. Telfer (Eds.), *International perspectives on consumers' access to justice* (pp. 17–45). Cambridge, UK: CUP.

Suquet Capdevila, J. (2012). Exploring online consumer mediation in Catalonia: principles and technological uses. *International review of Law and Information Technology*, *20*(2), 124-146.

Tang, Z. (2007). An effective dispute resolution system for electronic consumer contracts. *Computer Law & Security Report*, *23*(1), 42–52. doi:10.1016/j.clsr.2006.11.002

Vermeys, N. W. (2013). La cyberjustice et l'espace OHADA: Des outils virtuels pour une avancée réelle. Journal Africain de Droit des Affaires, 102- 135.

Wolf, R. (1996). *Access to justice, Final report to the Lord Chancellor on the Civil Justice System in England and Wales*. Lord Chancellor's Department. Retrieved 06, June, 2015 from http://www.dca.gov.uk/civil/final/index.htm

Section 4
Open Justice in Latin America

Chapter 11
Open Data for Open Justice in Seven Latin American Countries

Sandra Elena
Coordinator of Open Justice Program, Ministry of Justice, Argentina

François van Schalkwyk
University of Stellenbosch, South Africa

ABSTRACT

The study focuses on the openness of judicial data in seven countries in Latin America. The judiciary continues to be among the least willing institutions to implement policies on transparency and access to information, generally because of their conservative tradition and lack of accountability practices. The study adopted an exploratory design in order to analyze enabling country and judicial contexts for open data, as well as whether judicial data publication meets open data standards of accessibility, sustainability, re-usability and non-discrimination. Study results show that even though access to judicial information is increasing and that there is also an increase in transparency policies for the judiciary, the publication of judicial data in open formats is still infrequent. This research seeks to build a baseline for an initial measurement that can be compared with future measurements, so as to be able to evaluate progress made in Latin American judiciaries.

INTRODUCTION

According to Transparency International's Global Corruption Barometer 2013, the judiciary is the third most corrupt institution in the world (after political parties and the police). In recent years, numerous initiatives have been undertaken globally to promote open governments, access to information and transparency (Naser, 2012). Nevertheless, the judiciary continues to be among the least willing of the public institutions to implement policies supporting openness, generally because of their conservative values and a general absence of a culture of accountability (Elena, Aquilino, & Pichón Riviere, 2014).

Institutions such as the judiciary play a critical role as stable, enduring social arrangements that provide the rules, practices and structures that shape the public agencies in which society trusts to disburse their public service responsibilities. However, we are living at a time in which trust between society and

DOI: 10.4018/978-1-5225-0717-8.ch011

public institutions is strained. Citizens are wresting control from public institutions to improve their daily lives and, as they do so, it is critical to restore and maintain trust between citizens and public institutions (Castells, Forthcoming) (Castells, Chacón, & Himanen, 2014).

Open data is often touted as having the potential to increase transparency and, in so doing, to enable citizens to hold public institutions more accountable for their decisions and actions. Open data also holds the promise of increased public participation in the governance of public institutions.

In others words, instead of being confronted by and potentially being immobilized by a fearful and frustrated citizenry, public institutions can restore trust by becoming more open as a means of engaging with citizens.

Dyson, for example, suggests that public trust in the justice system can be achieved through public scrutiny. Dyson regards the principle of open justice as essential and emphasizes the importance of new technologies as an enabler: "We now live in a technological age. We have the means to enhance public access to the courts. If we want justice to be truly public, for the courts to be properly open, we will have to continue to build upon recent advances and utilise that technological [sic] as far as we can, as far as is consistent with our commitment to making sure that justice is done" (Dyson, 2013). According to Velicogna the new needs of a system that delivers justice generates "(…) a growing need for the capability of finding viable solutions, based on a basic understanding of the many levels of complexity of ICT implementation in the courts" (Velicogna, 2010). The Berkman Center for Internet and Society of Harvard University has further emphasized the need of taking advantage of new technologies in order to improve the efficiency of this branch of the state (Malone, et al., 2010).

Open justice therefore appears to be strongly linked to the modernization of the judiciary. The judiciary must have access to new technologies and through the innovative deployment of such technologies improve public participation in judicial processes.

Public participation in open governments generates a two-way relationship between the citizenry and the state. This new mode of communication, through the application of new technologies, facilitates multiple interactions between society and the state, and this translates into a more transparent, participative and collaborative relationship (Kaufman & Ozlack, 2014).

Direct communication between the judiciary and citizens also allows for the removal of intermediaries, generating a more direct relationship between the public and judges (Reilling, 2011). Public participation may also help in finding new solutions to existing challenges, including how to reimagine current judicial systems (Lenaola, 2011).

To assess possible degrees of participation, the International Association for Public Participation (IAP2) proposes a spectrum of participation. This spectrum (see Table 1) describes and provides examples of participation in the justice system. To achieve open justice, judiciaries are expected to move upwards through the spectrum using open data to improve the quality of public participation in decision-making processes.

In terms of transparency as a core principle of open justice, Alemanno and Stefan suggest that transparency implies more than access to public documents. They consider transparency to be an opportunity to achieve legitimacy, accountability and good governance (Alemanno & Stefan, 2014). One of the major challenges of the transparency principle, however, is that initiatives that promote a more transparent judiciary must overcome the inherent resistance for greater openness from within. Political will and strong judicial leadership from supreme courts and judicial councils are key to success (Vargas Vianco, 2006).

Table 1. Public participation spectrum

	Inform	Consult	Involve	Collaborate	Empower
	Level 1	**Level 2**	**Level 3**	**Level 4**	**Level 5**
Public Participation Goal	To provide the public with balanced and objective information to assist them in understanding the problem, alternatives, opportunities and/or solutions.	To obtain public feedback on analysis, alternatives and/or decisions.	To work directly with the public throughout the process to ensure that public concerns and aspirations are consistently understood and considered.	To partner with the public in each aspect of the decision including the development of alternatives and the identification of the preferred solution.	To place final decision-making in the hands of the public

(IAP2, 2014)

The availability of judicial data is an indispensable instrument to materialize transparency as it allows for greater participation by an informed public (Hammergren, 2011). If reliable and complete data are not available, it is impossible to identify judicial failures and areas for improvement. The publication of judicial data is essential to enable the modernization of justice (Hammergren, 2011).

The advances in digital technologies and the openness of judicial data have two immediate effects. First, the distance between the judiciaries and the citizenship narrows, allowing the latter to participate in addressing problems, solutions and challenges faced by the former. Second, it promotes accountability by allowing citizens to monitor and hold the judiciary to account (Asociación por los Derechos Civiles, 2009).

The integration of new technologies into the justice administration that allows for greater openness by making data on the judiciary openly available requires a constant effort in order to achieve considerable levels of efficiency (Velicogna, 2010). Velicogna highlights that if the dissemination of these technologies do not go hand-in-hand with new practices of work, they are likely to have a very limited impact on administrative efficiency and, by implication, openness (Velicogna, 2010). In line with this caution offered by Velicogna, a potential barrier that may be impeding the publication of open data in the judiciary are the institutional dynamics at play in government as a complex organization.

Given the promise of open data – that is, the potential of open data to increase the credibility of institutions in the eyes of citizens through greater the transparency and greater accountability – the open data movement needs to develop a more nuanced understanding of the institutional context (Luna-Reyes & Gil-Garcia, 2014), particularly if open data practice is to become an enduring and taken-for-granted course of action in government in general and in the judiciary in particular.

OBJECTIVE OF THE CHAPTER

The research presented in this chapter focuses on the openness of judicial data. Its starting assumption is that openness and judicial transparency can lead to improvements in the delivery of justice, and that this will affect the lives of citizens positively. Moreover, openness can have a beneficial impact on judicial accountability, that is to say, the responsibility and the capacity to provide an effective response from the judiciary to society and to other branches of state.

The objective of this chapter is to present the findings of two pieces of research conducted by the Center for the Implementation of Public Policies Promoting Equity and Growth (CIPPEC) on judicial open data and its impact in seven Latin American countries (Argentina, Brazil, Chile, Costa Rica, Mexico, Peru and Uruguay). This will make a contribution to the corpus of case studies on openness in the judiciary. The study provides evidence to inform the debate on the role of open data in the judiciary in the region as well as globally. In addition, the findings provide guidelines for decision-makers and practitioners to implement effective, evidence-based open data policies in the judiciary.

These findings will also be discussed briefly with reference to institutional theory and how it explains organizational behavior and change. While the empirical research presented in this chapter was not conducted within this theoretical framework, it is hoped that a reflection of the empirical findings in relation to institutional theory may nevertheless provide some value in terms of assessing the probable success of promoting open data practice in the judiciary. In particular, the extent to which progress is being made in embedding enduring practices of openness in an institution that is perceived to be both ultra conservative and corrupt, should reveal insights in terms of how institutions respond to and begin to integrate openness initiatives, including the release of open data, with the purpose of becoming more transparent and, ultimately, more accountable and participatory.

FEATURES OF OPEN DATA IN THE JUDICIARY

Even though the concept of open justice is new, it is possible to apply some of the general principles of open government and to adjust them to the justice sector (Jiménez, 2014). The distinctive features of open data include:

- **Accessibility:** The data generated by the judiciary must be available as a whole, at a reasonable reproduction cost, preferably available for download over the Internet.
- **Non-Discrimination**: There should be no discrimination against fields of endeavor or against persons or groups in the use, reuse and redistribution of data. Access to data must not be restricted to certain purposes or subject to copyright.
- **Reusability:** Data must be in formats that enable reuse, redistribution and intermixing with other datasets, to enable interactive use of the information.
- **Sustainability:** It is of particular significance to consider whether the benefits of an activity or program are able to be extended into the future regardless of who implements them. Data must be kept updated; the frequency for the loading of data should be set, and there should be standardized processes for the forms and timing of the publication of the data.
- **Relevance:** Data must be of interest and of use to data users so that the data may contribute to solving real world problems to improve the lives of ordinary people.

In terms of the types of data that the judiciary should publish, the following are suggested as the minimum requirements (Elena, Aquilino, & Pichón Riviere, 2014):

- **Court Rulings:** All rulings should be published. rulings are the decisions by the court that bring cases to an end. other court resolutions ending processes or that are relevant to their resolution, and those ordering their dismissal, should also be published. ideally, judiciaries should publish court decisions of all instances: district courts, courts of appeals and supreme courts.

- **Statistics on Operations**: Quantitative data that describe the structure and activity of the courts, and specifically reflect their performance. Among others, indicators to be included are caseloads, cases solved, congestion rates disaggregated by type of case, type of court, presiding judge, etc.
- **Budget and Administrative Data:** Data related to budget allocation and its execution. This category also includes data related to procurement and contracting, human resources and infrastructure, among others.

COUNTRY BACKGROUND

Latin America is a region of political, economic and social diversity. It is also the region with the greatest social inequality (Munoz, 2013). Rising social inequality is closely related to the deterioration in institutional quality in Latin American democracies over the last two decades, although some signs of improvement have recently begun to be seen in several countries.

Countries in Latin America show differing levels of implementation of open government and transparency policies. Significantly, most Latin American countries are signatories of the Open Government Partnership (OGP). Coincidentally, those countries that are not members of the OGP – such as Bolivia and Venezuela – are those that record the poorest results on international institutional quality indicators.

To provide a snapshot of the contextual conditions in each country, the following economic, social and institutional data for the relevant countries are provided:

- **Argentina**: Argentina's human development and per capita income levels are among the highest in the region. Per capita GDP is USD 12,568 (World Bank, 2015). According to Transparency International 2014 ranking, Argentina ranks 106 out of a total of 177 countries surveyed with a score of 34 out of 100 on the Perception of Corruption Index (Transparency International, 2015). Argentina's political system is a federal one which generates two levels of judicial courts: (1) national with the Supreme National Court of Justice as the highest court in the country, and (2) 24 subnational judicial systems.
- **Brazil:** Brazil is considered to be a high-development country with a per capita GDP of USD 11,384 (World Bank, 2015). The country is ranked 72 in the Perception of Corruption Index 2014 with a score of 42 out of 100 (Transparency International, 2015). Brazil has federal political system with the country divided into 26 states and a federal district. The judicial branch is divided in two sections: federal and regional. The regional judiciary is divided into five divisions that are further subdivided into a different number of geographical areas of jurisdiction.
- **Chile:** Chile is considered to be a mid- to high-income country. Its quality of life, economic growth and human development indicators are among the highest in Latin America. Per capita GDP is USD 14,528 (World Bank, 2015). Chile scores of 71 out of 100 on Transparency International's Perception of Corruption Index for the year 2014, placing it 22nd among the 177 countries surveyed (Transparency International, 2015). Chile is a unitarian country divided into 15 regions. The judiciary is made up of a Supreme Court of Justice, Courts of Appeal and first instance tribunals.
- **Costa Rica** is considered to be a medium-income country. Its per capita GDP is USD 10,415 (World Bank, 2015). According to Transparency International 2014 ranking it ranks 49th out of a total of 177 countries surveyed, with a score of 53 out of 100 on the Perception of Corruption

Index (Transparency International, 2015). Costa Rica is a democratic unitarian republic. Its Constitution establishes the judiciary as having the obligation of reinforcing the rule of law and administrating justice.

- **Mexico:** Mexico's per capita GDP is USD 10,230 (World Bank, 2015). Transparency International ranks Mexico in 106th place out of a total of 177 countries surveyed, with a score of 34 out of 100 on the Perception of Corruption Index 2014 (Transparency International, 2015). The country is a federal country organized into 32 federative entities and a federal district. Each district has its own judicial branch that coexists with the federal one.
- **Peru:** Peru per capita GDP in Peru is USD 6,550 (World Bank, 2015). Transparency International ranks Peru in 83th place out of a total of 177 countries surveyed, with a score of 38 out of 100 on the Perception of Corruption Index 2014 (Transparency International, 2015). Peru is a unitarian state, divided in 24 departments and a constitutional province. The judicial branch in Peru is composed by a Supreme Court, 29 Superior Courts that generally are correspondent with the geographical departments, specialised and mixed tribunals, and peace judges.
- **Uruguay:** Uraguay ranks well on quality of life, economic growth and human development indicators, and is positioned as one of the countries with the highest standards of living in the region. Per capita GDP is USD 16,806 (World Bank, 2015). According to 2014 Transparency International's Perception of Corruption Index, Uruguay scores of 73 out of 100, placing it 19th out of the 177 countries surveyed (Transparency International, 2015). The Judiciary is integrated by a Supreme Court of Justice, Courts of Appeal and courts of first instance.

While the above list provides a brief macro-level picture of the context in each country, Table 2 presents relevant contextual conditions specific to open data implementation. The simplified data presented in Table 2 is extracted from the 'Country Context' section of the evaluation matrix described in the Methodology section of this chapter. This simplified version is included here because it provides insight into the contextual conditions at country level.

METHODOLOGY

This study focuses on the existence of open data within the judiciaries. Therefore, the questions that oriented this research are whether the seven judiciaries publish data, and whether this data is published according to standards of open data. In addition, in order to broaden the study beyond the supply of open data by judiciaries, the following two questions were included: (1) Who are the users of judicial data? and (2) What are the uses of judicial data?

In order to have a consistent data collection and analysis framework across the countries, it was decided to create an evaluation matrix. The matrix was used to analyze the dimensions attributed to open data linked to specific judicial processes (court rulings, operations, budgeting and administrative processes).

The matrix was based on a tool designed by CIPPEC to evaluate the level of compliance with principles for active transparency, data production, ethical principles, administration of human resources, transparency in public tendering processes and citizen participation. This tool was presented in Public Policy Document 113: Impartial, but not invisible: Justice, Transparency and Open Government (Elena

Table 2. Country and judiciary context on open data and access to public information

	Argentina	Brazil	Chile	Costa Rica	Mexico	Peru	Uruguay
Country Context							
1. There is a law on access to public information.	Somewhat	Yes	Yes	Somewhat	Yes	Yes	Yes
2. There are mechanisms to sanction breaches of the law on access to information.	No	Yes	Yes	Somewhat	Yes	Yes	Yes
3. There is an independent body responsible for ensuring compliance with the law on access to public information.	No	Yes	Yes	No	Yes	No	Yes
4. There is an initiative in the country on open data led by the National Executive Branch.	Yes	Yes	Yes	Yes	Yes	Somewhat	Yes
5. There is a public data portal.	Yes	Yes	Yes	Yes	Yes	Yes	Yes
6. The State is a member of the Open Government Partnership (OGP).	Yes	Yes	Yes	Yes	Yes	Yes	Yes
Judiciary Context							
7. The judiciary has a web page.	Yes	Somewhat	Yes	Yes	Yes	Yes	Yes
8. There is an office or body responsible for publishing the information.	Yes	Yes	Yes	Yes	Yes	No	No
9. There is a systematic open data policy in the judiciary.	No	Yes	No	Yes	Yes	Yes	No
10. Supreme Court rulings are published.	Yes	Yes	Yes	Yes	No	Yes	Somewhat
11. The Supreme Court case agenda is published.	No	Yes	Yes	Yes	No	Yes	No
12. Statistical data is published on incoming caseload.	Yes	Yes	Yes	Yes	Somewhat	Yes	Yes
13. Statistical data is published on pending caseload.	Yes	Yes	No	No	Somewhat	No	Somewhat
14. Indicators are published based on the information.	Yes	Somewhat	No	Somewhat	No	No	Yes
15. Budget information is published on the judiciary.	Yes	Somewhat	Yes	Yes	Yes	Somewhat	Yes

& Pichón Rivière, 2012). The tool was used to analyze the National Judiciary Branch, the National Public Prosecutor's Office and the Public Defense Service in Argentina. The analysis was published in Public Policy Analysis Document 118: Access to Information and Transparency in the Justice System: A Road that is Just Beginning (Elena & Pichón Rivière, 2012).

To assess the openness of judicial data, the matrix drew on a report prepared for the Exploring the Emerging Impacts of Open Data in Developing Countries Project (Elena & Pichón Rivière, 2013).

The matrix consists of seven components:

- Two on the general context of the country and the judiciary,
- Four in relation to the characteristics of the open formats, and
- One on the relevance of data published.

These seven components were divided into 44 variables that measure concrete aspects of judicial data such as the use of free formats, ease of search, use of licenses, among others.

The results obtained for each country in each of the categories is scored on a scale of 0 to 120.5. Given that the study is aimed at analyzing open data, it was decided to give a weighting of 1.75 to the intrinsic dimensions of open data (accessibility, non-discrimination, reusability and sustainability), whereas the dimensions of relevance, country context and judiciary context were weighted by a factor of 1.00.

Data was collected by means of a review of the current information available on the seven countries, by means of visits to the web pages of the judiciaries in question, and c) interviews with key players, including officials of the various judiciary branches and intermediaries and users of judicial information.

While the evaluation matrix provided a more structured and comparable approach to understanding open data in the judiciary, the interviews conducted with users, intermediaries and producers of judicial data provided more detailed and nuanced insights into open data practice in each of the judicial systems in the seven Latin American countries.

The producers of information are the judiciaries, including the supreme and other courts, the office of the public prosecutor and defense, judicial councils and ministries of justice. The intermediaries are the users that recycle, share or modify data, generating information for end-users: "An open data intermediary is an agent positioned at some point in a data supply chain that incorporates an open dataset, is positioned between two agents in the supply chain, and facilitates the use of data that may otherwise not have been the case" (Van Schalkwyk, Cañares, Chattapadhyay, & Andrason, 2015). Examples of intermediaries in the judicial system are civil society organizations (CSOs) specializing in justice, gender, crime prevention, etc.; judicial data journalists, and political science and law schools. These intermediaries play a substantive role in disseminating judicial information. The users are those that use the information, but not necessarily circulate, share, or modify it, for example, the Ministry of Justice, Parliaments and citizens.

The research questions on the users and uses of open judicial data were included in the interviews. Insights gained from these interviews are included in "Findings on the perceptions of judicial open data actors" section as well as in the discussion sections of this chapter.

In total, interviews were conducted with 26 producers, intermediaries and users of judicial data in the target countries. Two structured questionnaires were developed to collect interview data: one for judicial data user and intermediaries that asked questions about data availability and quality; and a second questionnaire for members of the judicial branch that included questions how data was used in the management of the judicial process, dedicated resources for the publication of data, attitudes to open data, and the quality of their data.

FINDINGS

Figure 1 shows the results of the seven countries, as calculated using the evaluation of open data in the judiciary matrix. Scores have been recalibrated from a score out of a possible maximum of 120.5 to a score out of 100 for ease of reference and comparison.

Brazil

Brazil scored 107.5 out of a possible 120.5, equivalent to 89 out of 100. Brazil has a law on access to public information, promulgated in 2011, that includes sanctions in cases of non-compliance, and guarantees the publication of data on budget, projects and activities of three branches of government (legislative, judicial and executive).

Brazil has an open data portal that allows users to access information freely. However, the judiciary is a step behind the executive in this regard; it is still has to centralize and publish all available data on a single web page.

Information on budget, judgments and statistics are freely available; this allows data to be exported and facilitates its reusability.

Brazil has a systematic judicial policy on open data. It has a specific regulation for the collection and publication of data. There are rules for the publication of Supreme Court judgments and judges' meeting registries. Unfortunately, this is not the case in the courts of appeal; some resolutions and the registries are not available. Brazil is the only country that has a judicial officer designated exclusively to reply to requests or enquiries relating to judicial data.

The above findings show efforts to increase transparency in the Brazilian judiciary; nevertheless data still needs to be centralized, completed and available on a single website.

Figure 1. Open data in the judiciary

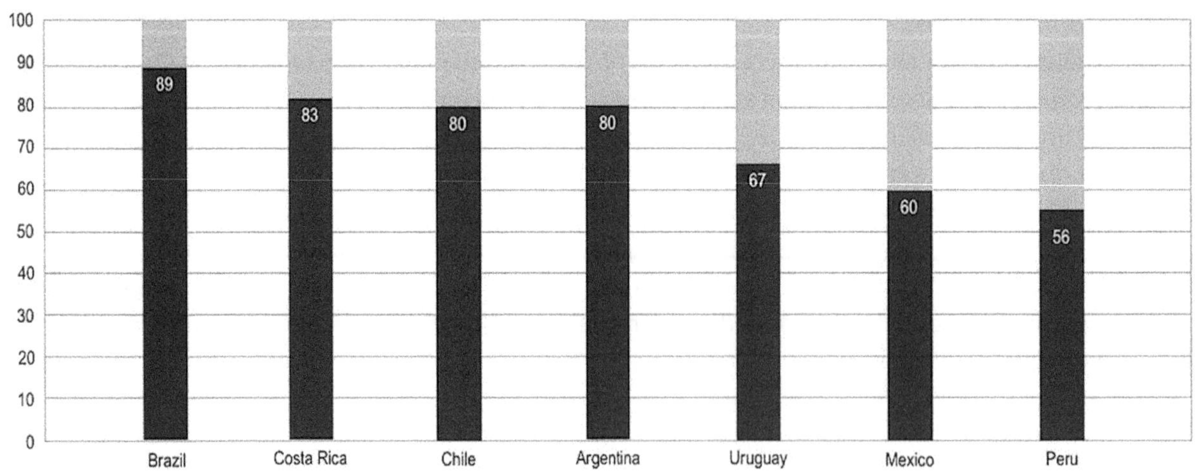

Costa Rica

Costa Rica scored 99.86 out of 120.5 or the equivalent of 83 out of 100. Although Costa Rica does not have a law on access to information, there are many related regulations that are working effectively. Even if there are no specific sanctions for failing to provide access to information, government officials, and in particular judicial ones, are keen to provide public access.

Costa Rica implemented an Inter-Institutional Transparency Network that includes the judiciary making efforts to ensure easy and free flow of information. The judiciary through its own internal policies and regulation dictates that data should be accessible to the public.

Budget data, judgments and statistics are published and are accessible on-line. Data are in general terms complete, and can be reused and exported. Data can also be downloaded without any authorization and use is not restricted by copyright.

Costa Rica publishes Supreme Court and courts of appeal rulings as well as their judges' meeting registries, but does not publish judgments of the first instance courts and those tribunals' registries. It only publishes statistical data on filed cases. This data are disaggregated only by instance and not by jurisdiction. Owing to this, Costa Rica does not obtain a good score in terms of statistics.

To keep data updated, two offices have been set up: the finance office, in charge of the budget, and the judicial investigation bureau that focuses on publishing other types of judicial data.

Costa Rica has a dedicated web page for the judiciary with complete data on budgets, an organizational chart and legal rulings, amongst other data. The page has an internal search option, with several sections. It also provides a tool to assist users in locating relevant data.

Chile

Chile scored 96.25 out of a possible 120.5, equivalent to 80 out of 100. Chile has in place a state policy on transparency and the publishing of information, and has a law on access to information that includes disciplinary mechanisms and a body responsible for its implementation. The judiciary is no exception. It has adopted significant measures to increase its transparency. It has in place a transparency committee, a body that ensures compliance with the law on access to information.

Chile publishes its decisions, budget data and statistics in formats that can be easily exported.

Statistical information is limited; only the data regarding new filed cases, pending cases and cases solved by jurisdiction, type of court and instance are published. Data are available as spreadsheets, in small datasets. It is possible to generate a database of filed cases and solved cases by year (for 2012 and 2013), which can be exported to an Excel document.

In Chile, the reusability of data is limited. The Administrative Corporation for the Chilean judiciary authorizes users to use, print, reproduce and store the information on its website exclusively for personal or academic purposes, which excludes the possibility of commercial use, among other uses. This is counter to one of the fundamental tenets of open data.

Argentina

Argentina scored 95.9 out of a possible 120.5, equivalent to 80 out of 100. This score is comparatively high, particularly given the fact that in the "Country Context" category it received the lowest score because of the absence of an access to information law in the country. Nevertheless, in an effort to improve transparency, the judiciary in Argentina has increased the publication of information in reusable and accessible formats.

In Argentina, there is not a systematic strategy for promotion of access to information and data publication. Nevertheless, the Executive Branch has implemented the Digital Agenda Forum which promotes open data, open source software, open government and interoperability. These efforts do not constitute a uniform public policy, and have not yet permeated the actual practice of government agencies, including the judiciary.

However, the Supreme Court has implemented some policies to promote access to information and open data. Argentina has a policy for publication of information consistent with a judicial transparency policy. Supreme Court decision 14/2004 promotes the use of new technologies to improve justice service delivery: "Within the process of change and modernization of services provided by the system of justice (…) the Supreme Court of Justice of the Nation proposes to establish and implement the use of management tools applying information technology." The Supreme Court has also created the Center of Judicial Information (CIJ), a web page devoted to the dissemination of judicial information. Information and data are updated and well presented at the CIJ.

Published data includes the rulings of the National Supreme Court, courts of appeal and some trial courts in PDF format, sometimes as scanned images. Because PDFs are not open, it prevents the reuse of documents.

Uruguay

Uruguay scored 80.87 out of 120.5 or the equivalent of 67 out of 100. In Uruguay there is an explicit transparency policy led by the legislative and executive branches of government. There is a national law on access to information in place and a public data portal. The law does not include sanctions for the administration but there are sanctions for public officials. However, the judiciary is not subjected to sanctions. The executive also has an aggressive open data policy but the judiciary is a step behind. It has not adopted a specific policy on transparency and data publication. At the time of collecting data, most judicial officers did not know about open data and appeared overprotective of judicial data.

The judiciary in Uruguay has dedicated personnel responsible for collecting and publishing judicial data. However, both statistics and budget data are published in PDF format. This limits its reuse and prevents machine readability. Rulings and other significant decrees are also published in PDF format as scanned images.

The judiciary in Uruguay has made significant progress in the publication of data following the requests of civil society organizations working on specific agendas.

Mexico

Mexico scored 72.1 out of 120.5 or the equivalent of 60 out of 100. While this score reflects a lack of open data in the judiciary, Mexico obtained the maximum score in the "Country Context" category.

Mexico has implemented transparency policies at a national level that include a freedom of information law and the creation of a data portal. The *Instituto Federal de Acceso a la Información Pública y Protección de Datos* (IFAI) is one of the most well-known agencies for the protection of access to information in Latin America. It is responsible for enforcing the access to information law. However, the IFAI does not have jurisdiction over the judiciary.

The publication of judgments of district and appeals courts is limited. Statistical data are incomplete. Data are not disaggregated by jurisdiction or instance. However, the publication of the judicial budgetary information is complete.

Even though there is an entity in charge of publishing information there are not existing regulations on the publication of judicial data.

A factor hindering the re-use of data is that even though the information can be downloaded without requiring authorization of any type, it remains subject to copyright.

Peru

Peru scored of 67.15 out of 120.5 or the equivalent of 56 out of 100. In 2011, the Government of Peru joined the Open Government Partnership, committing to increase government transparency. Peru has a public access to information law passed in 2002.

The judiciary in Peru does not have specific regulations for the publication of information and does not have an office responsible for judicial data. Nevertheless, the judiciary publishes data including a directory of officials and on laws, rulings and other legal dispositions on the Transparency Portal run by the government.

Budget data are not published in the judiciary's official website, although, it is possible to find some budget data on the Transparency Portal.

The judiciary publishes judgments from courts of appeal and the Supreme Court, but not from first instance courts. The registries of the Supreme Court are online. Statistics are not available online. Peru returned the lowest score on the "Accessibility" dimension related to statistics.

COMPLIANCE WITH OPEN DATA STANDARDS

The evaluation matrix was structured around four key characteristics of open data: no discrimination, accessibility, sustainability and reusability. This allows for an assessment of whether the data published by the judiciary in each country comply with accepted criteria on what constitutes *open* data. This analysis helps to identify which dimensions of open data are stronger in the countries analysed and, conversely, where countries are experiencing difficulties in complying with specific dimensions that characterize open data. In general terms, the criteria of sustainability and no discrimination returned higher scores compared with the criteria of reusability and accessibility.

Sustainability

This criteria considers whether the benefits of an activity or program can be extended into the future regardless of who implements them. In this case, it assesses whether open data policies are likely to be kept in place over time. In particular, this criteria evaluates whether published data is updated, the frequency for loading of data, and the existence of standardized processes for the formats and timing for the publication of the data.

This criteria includes five variables: if data is regularly updated (the most recent data was no more than a year old); if there is a rule that specifies the way data should be gathered and published; if there are rules on data publication policy; if there is an office responsible for collecting and publishing data; and if there is was a person responsible for responding to users enquiries.

Brazil returned the best score for this category. The substantial difference between Brazil and the other countries is that Brazil is the only country that has a public office with the specific mandate to respond to enquiries and claims related to data.

Brazil, Mexico and Chile have an information publication policy accompanied by a transparency policy in the judiciary outlined in laws and judicial regulations. Peru has made advances in this area but still lacks a specific transparency policy for the judiciary.

No Discrimination

Access to data must not be restricted to certain purposes or be subject to copyright. There should be no discrimination against uses of data or against persons or groups in the use, reuse and redistribution of data.

This criteria includes five variables: if data could be accessed without the need to request authorization of any kind; whether access to data is without registration or mandatory provision of personal information; if data access is easy (requiring only basic computer knowledge); if information is restricted by copyright or use restrictions.

Mexico and Peru score lowest because of copyright restrictions which prevent data reusability. Chile has a specific restriction on the use of data for business purposes which constitutes a discriminatory measure.

Accessibility

The degree of accessibility assesses whether the information produced by the judiciary is available as a whole, at a reasonable reproduction cost and available for downloading over the Internet.

This criteria includes four variables: if information is available online; if information is complete and comprehensive; if the content could be found in less than three clicks; and if data is accessible without monetary payment.

Judiciaries scored lower in this dimension due to the poor quality and quantity of information online. In particular, Mexico and Peru do not publish or publish very little data online regarding judicial statistics and court rulings. On the other hand, no country with the exception of Peru requires a fee to obtain judicial information.

Reusability

This criteria assesses if data is published in formats that enable reuse, redistribution and interoperability with other datasets, and allows interactive use of the information.

This criteria includes four variables: if there are restrictions on data reproduction; if data is published in a computer-readable format (not as a scanned image, for example); if data could be exported; and if information is available in bulk (if it could be obtained with a single request).

Costa Rica returns the highest score for reusability, closely followed by Brazil and Argentina. In Costa Rica and Brazil data from rulings as well as statistical and budget data can easily be exported, downloaded and are accessible online. Mexico returned the lowest score as most of the judgments are scanned images difficult to reuse.

FINDINGS ON THE PERCEPTIONS OF JUDICIAL OPEN DATA ACTORS

In addition to the scores and relative positions of the countries according to the evaluation matrix, are the findings from the interviews conducted with producers, intermediaries and users of judicial data.

Producers

Some judicial officers were unaware of the concept of open data. Those who knew about open data, considered it too alien to the judicial environment. Among those familiar with the concept of open data, there was no consensus on whether the judicial data they publish meet the criteria required for data to be considered open. Almost half of the officials say their judiciaries publish data in open formats; a large proportion of the remaining half say that data is partially open, while the remaining minority does not consider their data to meet requirements for openness. In particular, this minority corresponds to the Peruvian judiciary.

All officials indicated that they use judicial data in some way in their work. And 70% indicated that the judiciary uses the data to improve the management of the courts. In Argentina, officials said the lack of communication among offices in charge of producing data and those in charge of designing judicial policy negatively impact efficiency.

With regard to the quantity of data that the judiciary produces, a minority of officials consider the amount of data published to be sufficient. The vast majority, however, in Argentina, Uruguay and Chile in particular, believe that there is a need to publish more judicial data. Officials pointed out that there is still a need to publish data on intermediate judicial resolutions (hearings and notifications), costs of the judicial process and gender indicators, among others.

Most judicial officials interviewed indicated that in addition to the importance of supporting laws, it is important for there to be authoritative leadership within the judiciary that provides a clear directive to publish information. One judge said: "We can have the best regulations but if we don't have the order from the Chief Justice or the President of the Judicial Council, the information will not be properly produced, or will 'sleep' at the computer of the officer in charge of statistics."

All seven countries agreed on the importance of open data to improve transparency and accountability. However, as producers of data, officials could not yet see any economic impact of judicial open data, other than the reduction of judicial process costs.

Judicial officials consider that the use of datasets and even spreadsheets to publish data is not frequent although it is increasing. In all seven countries, officials affirmed that the most frequent users of judicial data are academic institutions. Officials indicated that PDF format is still the rule, and paper copies are gradually being eliminated, although 10% of the information is still published in hardcopy.

Intermediaries and Users

Almost all users and intermediaries of judicial data say they are aware of the concept of open data.

The most used format for judicial information according to users is PDF, while the second is spreadsheets (XLS, XLSX, etc.).

Sixty per cent of users and intermediaries say they used judicial information more than ten times in the previous year. The remaining 40% used judicial information from 1 to 10 times in the same period.

Almost all users say they have also used data produced by other organizations or individuals that reused judicial information published by the judiciaries. These intermediaries are mostly judicial centers of study, universities and the media.

Most users and intermediaries agree that the quality of information is very good or good. They consider that both quality and quantity have improved during last three years. Regarding the quantity of published information, the scores are a bit lower with an average rating of 3 out of 5. Users in Peru, in particular, believe their judiciary needs to publish more information.

Representatives of civil society organizations and academics all agreed that the judiciary produces more information than it publishes. They also said that even though the quantity and quality of information have improved, they are still poor. An additional problem pointed to is the level of disaggregation of the information. Even though judiciaries have information by gender, type of cases and other variables, in some cases they do not publish the data with this level of granularity.

Of the interviewees that have requested unpublished information, around half resorted to non-official channels, such as a contact person within the judiciary. This could be an indicator of the informality of access to information mechanisms in the judiciary.

Users and intermediaries usually present collected judicial data in narrative reports, data tables and infographics. The use of judicial data to produce open datasets is still rare in the region. Only 20% of the users say that they produce primary judicial information.

Users and intermediaries do not agree with the producers of data in that judicial data is used to improve court management or to design evidence-based judicial policy. This could indicate higher expectations around the use of data among users as compared with producers.

Finally, users and intermediaries consider that open judicial data may have a positive impact on court management efficiency, judicial monitoring and evaluation, transparency and accountability. In particular, they believe that open data will help to improve oversight and control over judicial budgets.

DISCUSSION

The discussion presented in this section draws from both the analysis of the quantitative data (the evaluation matrix) and the qualitative data collected from the interviews with key actors in the judiciaries. While the results of the application of the matrix reveal how the judiciaries are publishing their data, the interviews and the survey provide insight to why judiciaries are publishing data in a particular way, and to what the gaps are between the available judicial data and the expectations and needs of users, both internal and external to the judiciary.

While the application of the matrix shows a positive trend in terms of an increase in open data practice, the qualitative results of interviews show a less positive context – they point out gaps, unsatisfied needs, lack of regulation and barriers to publishing more and better data.

The findings show that openness and transparency in the judiciary are not yet standard practices in the region. Even though the judiciary provides a public service, data production, disclosure and publication are not yet considered a priority.

In cases where judiciaries publish data, the publication of data does not meet desired quality, volume and frequency requirements. This means that despite the efforts made, there is still a gap between the supply and demand of judicial data.

Although there are transparency and access to information initiatives in the seven countries, systematic open data policy and practice is still infrequent. With considerable variation among countries, none publishes all its judicial data in open formats. Most still publish data protected by copyright laws and in formats that do not facilitate reuse.

This finding is not reflected in the relatively high scores for most of the countries using the evaluation matrix. This may be due to the limits inherent in an approach that emphasizes the technical over the social simply because the technical aspects of open data practice are easier to measure. It is for this very reason that this study included a qualitative dimension in its data collection as an acknowledgement of the importance of considering not only the technical but also the social dimension of government agencies, in particular the institutional context in which civil servants function, when thinking about how to open government to its citizens.

Research results from the interviews conducted show that leadership within judicial branches is equally important for judicial openness as the enabling regulatory and technical conditions captured in the evaluation matrix. This combination of regulative context in the form of a public access to information law (combined with sanctions) and policies both internal and specific to the judiciary as having a bearing on a country's openness ranking, is shown in Table 3.

All seven Latin American countries are members of the Open Government Partnership and five have access to information laws. However, there are underlying differences reflected in Table 2 that provide clues as to the differences in the degrees to which the countries' judiciaries can be described as open.

For one, the enforcement of openness differs across countries. It seems that the existence of enforcement bodies with disciplinary powers such as in Brazil is key for compliance with access to information laws.

Mexico, Uruguay and Peru have clear open access to information laws but their judiciaries are lagging because there are no sanctions to give teeth to the legal provision and there are no internally formulated policies on openness. On the contrary, the Argentine judiciary is moving towards openness faster than other branches of state, despite the lack of a public access to information law, indicating that internal policies may carry a greater weighting in determining openness. However, it is in those countries (Brazil

Table 3. Laws, sanctions, policies and recourses in relation to open data in seven Latin American judiciaries

Rank	Country*	Country Context		Leadership Within the judiciary	
		Public Access to Information Law	Includes Sanctions	Policy on Data Publication Specific to Judiciary	Resources to Support Publication of Open Data
1	Brazil	✓	✓	✓	✓
2	Costa Rica	×	×	✓	✓
3	Chile	✓	✓	✓	✓
4	Argentina	×	×	✓	✓
5	Uruguay	✓	×	×	✓
6	Mexico	×**	×	×	✓
7	Peru	✓	×	×	×

* Listed in descending order according to evaluation matrix score.

** Mexico has a public access to information law but its enforcing agency, the *Instituto Federal de Acceso a la Información Pública y Protección de Datos* (IFAI), has no jurisdiction over the judiciary.

and Chile) where there is both a supportive legislative framework (with sanctions) and evidence of support internally at leadership level within the judiciary, as indicated by internal policies and regulations, that the judiciary is most open.

Costa Rica appears to be an outlier – it ranks second but does not have a public access to information law. However, of the seven countries, only Costa Rica appears to be systematically geared to developing open justice. It has in place open judicial government directives and its National Open Government Action Plan includes specific commitments applicable to the judiciary. It also includes commitments on open data. Costa Rica also has in place an Inter-Institutional Transparency Network that includes the judiciary. This Network is again both supported by the executive and inclusive of the judiciary. In this sense, despite the fact that Costa Rica does not has a public access to information law, it has in place what appear to be effective mechanisms for promoting openness in the judiciary and a judicial leadership responding positively to the executive.

This research was not conceptualized or framed within an institutional theory framework. Therefore any inferences from the results are necessarily tentative. Nevertheless, there is value in attempting some linkages between these results and a theory of organizational change, if only to reveal areas where further research may convert the tentative into the concrete.

The findings reveal a *possible* interplay between what Scott (2014) describes as the regulative pillar of institutions and the institutional logics perspective (Thornton & Ocasio 2013) that emphasize agency in institutional settings. Scholars who emphasize the regulative pillar give prominence to the effects of rule-setting, monitoring and sanctioning activities as influencing the behavior of institutional actors. Individuals conform to rules and laws as a means of seeking reward for conforming and of avoiding sanctions (Scott, 2014). However, individuals in public agencies may take a critical 'mindful' stance towards imposed policy and/or executive sanction, and work out locally appropriate responses and practices. This speaks to a development in the theory of organizations on institutional logics (Thornton & Ocasio 2013; Scott 2014). This perspective suggests that organisations constitute multiple institutionalised norms, and change occurs at the intersection of multiple external as well as internal established beliefs, structures and practices.

Overall, these relatively recent updates to the institutional theory of organizations suggest that government agencies and departments are not just the receivers of pressures for change from their environments, including the regulative environment. Their members are capable of agency, which is manifest in their capacity to take initiatives vis-à-vis developments in their environment (Scott, 2014).

What seems evident from this research is that in the case of the judiciary, a regulative approach, one that is external, top—down and that relies on sanctions to ensure open data practice, is effective. Table 3 shows that those countries that have public access to information laws with sanctions in place, score better on the open data evaluation matrix. At the same time, the existence of a supportive leadership within the judiciary, as evidenced by policies drafted by the judiciaries themselves and the provision of internally-determined resources, is also a factor that predicts a higher score on the evaluation of openness in the judiciary matrix.

One may therefore want to venture that in the case of an institution as established and conservative as the judiciary, external regulation combined with self-regulation within the judiciary, form a harmonious point of intersection, enabling effective organizational change within the judiciary. What this study shows is that when the judicial leadership does promote open data practice within their own organization, and when this takes place in a context where external provisions and sanctions are in place, then openness is more likely to follow.

CONCLUSION

All the Latin American countries in this study have, to a certain degree, implemented access to information and data policies within their judiciaries. However, the findings of the research presented in this chapter show that the information made available by the judiciaries in the seven Latin American countries do not yet meet most of the requirements of open data, and there is still an imbalance between the supply and demand of judicial data.

Change within the judiciary is slow and such change is not only driven by external demands or a changing environment. Based on the findings presented in this chapter, the combination of both regulative provisions with sanctions external to the judiciary combined with internal leadership, appear to be critical factors in enabling change within the judiciaries of Latin American countries.

The findings presented in this chapter provide a snapshot of openness in Latin American judiciaries using open data practice as an indicator. It is hoped that the research will be replicated in the future in additional and more diverse contexts, and that future findings will reveal greater insights into how to create more open and transparent judiciaries in Latin America and globally.

REFERENCES

Abrahamson, S. S. (2002). *Involving individual citizens with courts and tribunals: Initiatives in the United States and Canada*. Montreal, Canada: Editions Thémis.

Alemanno, A., & Stefan, O. (2014). Openness at the Court of Justice of the European Union: Toppling a taboo. *Common Market Law Review*, *51*(1), 97–139.

Asociación por los Derechos Civiles (ADC). (2009). *Acceso a la información y transparencia en el poder judicial. Guía de buenas prácticas en América Latina*. Buenos Aires, Argentina: ADC.

Bertot, J., McDermott, P., & Smith, T. (2012). Measurement of open government: Metrics and process.*45th Hawaii International Conference on System Sciences* (pp. 2491-2499). IEEE Computer Society. doi:10.1109/HICSS.2012.658

Calderón, C. (2012). Por qué un Gobierno Abierto. In A. Naser & G. Concha (Eds.), El desafío hacia el gobierno abierto en la hora de la igualdad (pp. 27–47). Santiago, Chile: CEPAL. Retrieved from http://www.cepal.org/es/publicaciones/3969-el-desafio-hacia-el-gobierno-abierto-en-la-hora-de-la-igualdad

Castells, M. (Forthcoming). Rethinking development in the global information age. In J. Muller (Ed.), *Higher education and development*. Cape Town, South Africa: African Minds.

Castells, M., Chacón, I., & Himanen, P. (2014). Toward a Welfare State 2.0? The Crisis and Renewal of the European Welfare State. In M. Castells, I. Chacón, & P. Himanen (Eds.), *Reconceptualising development in the global information age* (pp. 89–115). Oxford, UK: Oxford University Press. doi:10.1093/acprof:oso/9780198716082.003.0005

Cohendet, P., Creplet, F., & Dupouët, O. (2002). *Communities of oractice and epistemic communities: A renewed approach of organisational learning within the firm*. Strasbourg, France: Universitè Louis Pateur.

De los Ríos, N. (2010). Los nuevos liderazgos. In C. Calderón & S. Lorenzo (Eds.), *Open government* (pp. 185–197). Granada: Algón Editores.

Dyson, J. (2013). *Advances in open justice in England and Wales*. Hong Kong: Master of the Rolls.

Elena, S. (2015). *Datos Abiertos para una Justicia Abierta: Un Análisis de caso de los Poderes Judiciales De Brasil, Costa Rica, México y Perú.* Buenos Aires, Argentina: Iniciativa Latinoamericana por los Datos Abiertos (ILDA).

Elena, S., Aquilino, N., & Pichón Riviere, A. (2014). *Case Study: Emerging Impacts in Open Data in the Judiciary Branches in Argentina, Chile and Uruguay*. Buenos Aires, Argentina: CIPPEC.

Elena, S., & Pichón Rivière, A. (2012). *Imparcial, pero no invisible: justicia, transparencia y gobierno abierto*. Buenos Aires, Argentina: CIPPEC.

Elena, S., & Pichón Rivière, A. (2013). *Acceso a la información y transparencia en la justicia: un recorrido que recién comienza*. Buenos Aires, Argentina: CIPPEC.

Estrella, R. (2010). Diplomacia Abierta - Nueva Diplomacia. In C. Calderón & S. Lorenzo (Eds.), *Open government* (pp. 143–163). Granada, Spain: Algón Editores.

Exploring the Emerging Impacts of Open Data in Developing Countries (ODDC). (2013). *Researching the emerging impacts of open data*. Washington, DC: World Wide Web Foundation. Retrieved from http://www.opendataresearch.org/sites/default/files/posts/Researching%20the%20emerging%20impacts%20of%20open%20data.pdf

Gavelin, K., Burall, S., & Wilson, R. (2009). *Open Government: Beyond Static Measures*. Paper produced by Involve for the OECD. Retrieved from http://www.oecd.org/gov/46560184.pdf

Granickas, K. (2013). Understanding the impact of releasing and re-using open government data. Topic report no. 2013/08. European Public Sector Information Platform. Brussels, Belgium: European Union. Retrieved from http://www.epsiplatform.eu/sites/default/files/2013-08-Open_Data_Impact.pdf

Hammergren, L. (2011). Judicial governance and the use of ICT. In J. A. Caballero, C. G. De Grácia, & L. Hammergren (Eds.), Buenas prácticas para la implementación de soluciones tecnológicas en la Administración de Justicia. Mexico City, Mexico: Instituto de Investigación para la Justicia. Retrieved from http://www.iijusticia.org/docs/Linn.pdf

Iglesias, C. (2015). *The Benefits and Challenges of Measuring Open Data*. Retrieved from http://opendatacon.org/the-benefits-and-challenges-of-measuring-open-data

International Association for Public Participation (IAP2). (2014). *IAP2's public participation spectrum*. Retrieved from http://www.iap2.org.au/documents/item/84

Jiménez, C. E. (2014). *Justicia Abierta: Transparencia y proximidad de la justicia dentro del actual contexto de open government*. Barcelona, Spain: Generalirar de Catalunya, Departament de Justícia.

Jolías, L., & Prince, A. (2013). *Las fuentes conceptuales de Gobierno Abierto y el Open Data*. Madrid, Spain: Telos.

Kaufman, E. (2012). *Aportes para el Gobierno Abierto y la Entrega de Servicios: Experiencias canadiencer*. ASAEC y la Embajada de Canadá de Argentina y Paraguay.

Kaufman, E., & Ozlack, O. (2014). *Teoría y práctica del gobierno abierto: Lecciones de la experiencia internacional.* OAS: Red GEALC-IDRC.

Lenaola, I. (2011). Public participation in judical processes. Kenya Annual Jusges Colloquium, Mombasa, 14-19 August. *Kenya Law*. Retrieved from http://www.kenyalaw.org/kl/index.php?id=1934

Luna-Reyes, L. F., & Gil-Garcia, J. R. (2014). Understanding the co-evolution of institutions, technology, and organizations: The enactment of the state government portal of Puebla.*14th Annual International Conference on Digital Government Research*. Quebec, Canada: Digital Government Society.

Malone, P., Cheuk, A., Rowe, S., Kriegman, I., Wong, S., & Fein, D. (2010). *Practices in the use of technology to facilitate access to justice initiatives*. Boston, MA: Berkman Center for Internet and Society.

Munoz, H. (2013, July 10). *Lessons from the world's most unequal region.* Retrieved from UNDP: http://www.latinamerica.undp.org/content/rblac/en/home/presscenter/speeches/2013/07/10/lessons-from-the-world-s-most-unequal-region.html

Naser, A. (2012). *Datos abiertos: Un nuevo desafío para los gobiernos de la región*. Santiago, Chile: CEPAL.

Nemirovsci, O. (2010). Un cambio cultural. In C. Calderón, S. Lorenzo, C. Calderón, & S. Lorenzo (Eds.), *Open government: Gobierno Abierto* (pp. 87–101). Granada, Spain: Algón Editores.

OECD. (2010). *OECD guiding principles for open and inclusive policy making. Building an open and innovative goverment for better policies and service delivery*. Paris, France: OECD.

Ortiz de Zárate, A. (2010). Por qué esta obsesión con la participación? In C. Calderón & S. Lorenzo (Eds.), *Open government* (pp. 29–49). Granada, Spain: Algón Editores.

Ozslak, O. (2013). Estado abierto: Hacia un nuevo paradigma de gestión pública. Trabajo presentado en el panel "Gobierno abierto en Iberoamérica: promesas y realizaciones". *XVIII Congreso Internacional del CLAD*, Montevideo, Uruguay.

Pastor, S. (2005). *Cifrar y descifrar volumen 1: Manual para generar, recopilar, difundir y homologar estadísticas e indicadores judiciales*. Santiago, Chile: CEJA.

Ponce, A. (2015). *A new way to measure open government.* Retrieved from http://worldjusticeproject.org/blog/new-way-measure-open-government

Rajevic, E. (2012). Transparencia: qué están haciendo los gobiernos. In A. Naser & G. Concha (Eds.), *El desafío hacia el gobierno abierto en la hora de la igualdad* (pp. 101–113). Santiago, Chile: CEPA.

Ramírez Alujas, Á., & Dassen, N. (2012). Gobierno Abierto: la ruta hacia una nueva agenda de reforma del Estado y modernización de la administración pública en América Latina y el Caribe. In N. Dassen & J. C. Vieyra (Eds.), *Gobierno abierto y transparencia focalizada. Tendencias y desafíos para América Latina y el Caribe* (pp. 41–71). Banco Internacional de Desarrollo.

Ramírez-Alujas, Á. V. (2011, December15). Gobierno abierto y modernización de la gestión Pública. Tendencias actuales y el (inevitable) camino. *Revista Enfoques: Ciencia Política y Administración Pública*, *9*(15), 99–125.

Reilling, D. (2011). E-justice: experiences with court IT in Europe. In J. A. Caballero, C. G. de Grácia, & L. Hammergren (Eds.), Buenas prácticas para la implementación de soluciones tecnológicas en la Administración de Justicia. Mexico City, Mexico: Instituto de Investigación para la Justicia. Retrieved from http://www.iijusticia.org/docs/REILING.pdf

Sandoval-Almazán, R. (2015). Gobierno abierto y transparencia: Construyendo un marco conceptual. *Convergencia. Revista de Ciencias Sociales*, 68.

Scott, W. R. (2014). *Institutions and organizations: Ideas, interests, and identities* (4th ed.). Thousand Oaks, CA: Sage.

Subirats, J. (2012). Preámbulo. In A. Hofmann, R. A. Álvaro, & J. A. Bojorquez Pereznieto (Eds.), La Promesa del Gobierno Abierto (pp. 13–17). Academic Press.

Transparency International. (2015). *Transparency International Corruption Perception Index*. Berlin: Transparency International.

Valenzuela Mendoza, R. (2013). Delimitar Gobierno Abierto para ampliar la colaboración con una sociedad más abierta. In *Revista Estado, Gobierno y Gestión Pública Nº 21* (pp. 127-158). México City, Mexico: ITAP. Retrieved from http://inicio.ifai.org.mx/Publicaciones/La%20promesa%20del%20Gobierno%20Abierto.pdf

Van Schalkwyk, F., Cañares, M., Chattapadhyay, S., & Andrason, A. (2015). *Open data intermediaries in developing countries*. Ottawa, Canada: ODDC. Retrieved from http://figshare.com/articles/Open_Data_Intermediaries_in_Developing_Countries/1449222

Vargas Vianco, J. E. (2006). *Gobierno judicial: La organización y el rol de las Cortes Supremas*. Santiago, Chile: CEJA.

Velicogna, M. (2010). ICT within the court in the e-justice era. *Effectius*. Retrieved from http://www.effectius.com/yahoo_site_admin/assets/docs/ICT_within_the_court_in_the_e-Justice_Era_by_Marco_Velicogna.207234735.pdf

World Bank. (2015). *World Bank*. Retrieved from http://data.worldbank.org/country/

World Justice Project. (2015). Retrieved from http://worldjusticeproject.org/open-government-index

KEY TERMS AND DEFINITIONS

Civic Participation: Refers to a condition in which every citizen has the means to actively engage in the public sphere, including political processes.

Institution: An institution is an enduring collection of rules and organized practices, embedded in structures of meaning and resources, for example, the church, the military, the judiciary.

Judiciary: The judges and associated personnel of a country or a state, socially constructed as an enduring collection of rules and organized practices, responsible for the delivery of justice according to the law.

Open Data: Data that can be freely used, re-used and redistributed by anyone, subject only, at most, to the requirement to attribute and share alike.

Open Data Intermediaries: An open data intermediary is an agent positioned at some point in a data supply chain that incorporates an open dataset, is positioned between two agents in the supply chain, and facilitates the use of data that may otherwise not have been the case.

Open Justice: A justice system that is open to citizens in the sense that it is transparent, participatory and collaborative.

Open Government: The transparency of government actions, the accessibility of government services and information, and the responsiveness of government to new ideas, demands and needs.

Chapter 12
Open Justice in Latin America?
An Assessment Framework for Judiciary Portals in 2015

Rodrigo Sandoval-Almazán
Universidad Autonoma del Estado de México, Mexico

ABSTRACT

The new trend of information technology and communications has been adopted by court systems. A similar path follows other powers in the republics: executive branches with e-government portals and legislative branches with informative and participatory portals. Despite the fact that technology has reached the judiciary branch, we know very little about the changes, advantages or disadvantages of this adoption. The purpose of this chapter is to explore the use of technology, especially in the websites portals in the Latin America region. An assessment model, which has been developed by Sandoval and Gil-García (2015) and that has four components: information, interaction, integration and participation, has been implemented on a sample of 25 countries during the month of July, 2015. Findings reveal a great disparity among the different countries in the region.

INTRODUCTION

Currently, most agencies, departments, and government offices have some integration with technology. This Internet-centrism trend explained by Morozov, (2014) has induced judicial branches to adopt technology in order to become more effective. Also, the open government worldwide trend creates new needs to manage information and to open their processes and data to the public, being this another reason to use information technology in judiciary information.

It is commonly accepted that government offices in the executive branch use ICT's which includes both, services and policies (Deb, 1999). This e-government trend has been studied at national and local levels. Many scholars have promoted efforts to assess electronic government implementation and uses with different perspectives and indicators; most of them having been developed in the last decade (Scholl, 2010).

DOI: 10.4018/978-1-5225-0717-8.ch012

The e-government assessment evaluation has been implemented to differentiate between executive portals, judiciary portals and legislative portals. A first attempt was made by Sandoval and Gil-García (2010) in order to produce a distinction among these as shown in Table 1.

However, there have been just a few previous attempts to research judicial branch websites (JSCA, 2012; Gorham, 2012; Tonn et al., 2012). More research is needed and this study attempts to start filling this gap. This paper explores the characteristics of judicial websites in Latin America and highlights some differences between regions. Using an assessment model previously tested and developed in México (Sandoval-Almazán & Gil-García, 2015), the instrument was refined and updated with new questions to evaluate judiciary websites in 25 countries in the region.

In order to achieve this goal, this chapter is divided into six sections including this introduction. The second section describes the theoretical background of the judiciary branch and technology. The third section describes the method and the assessment model; the fourth section describes the research design and studied model; the fifth section discusses the main findings and the last section presents solutions and recommendations related to this topic.

THEORETICAL BACKGROUND

The purpose of this section is to review recent literature on judicial websites and provide an overview of similar research on judicial websites evaluations. For such purpose it has been divided into two main sections: the first one will address the literature review on judicial websites and the second one will focus on the examples and similar studies in order to integrate a solid state of the art.

Evaluation and Assessment of Public Sector Websites

Government websites can be considered communication systems that operate via a computer and the Internet (Sandoval-Almazán & Gil-García, 2010). A portal definition of Gant and Gant (2002) states: "A Web portal serves as the integrated gateway into the state government websites and provides visitors

Table 1. Distinction on e-government portals

	E-Government Portals (Federal and Local)	Legislative Websites	Judicial Websites
Objective	Sharing information and transactional	Information and interaction	Information
Usefulness	Reduction of time and transactions	Precise information and legislative debate of bills	Timely information
Relationship with the citizen	Integral	Bidirectional	Bidirectional
Value Added	Efficiency and image	Social participation and public image	Image and openness
Offered Services	Payment of taxes, discussion forums, training, videos, information about procedures, training, information sharing among agencies, collaboration, citizen interaction	Laws updating, congressman interaction with citizens; civic culture, online debates	Updated laws, lawyers interaction, training, online debates, legal actions, updated legal information. Legal interaction
Citizen participation	Interactive, payments, collection of information	Debate and discussion, overview of information	Passive role, accountability of information

Source: Sandoval-Almazán and Gil-García (2010) page 100.

with a single point of contact for online service delivery within the state." Most government portals contain an interesting mixture of applications (Sandoval and Gil-García, 2008). E-government portals have evolved during the last few years, from unidirectional sharing of information and data with citizens to more interactive engagement. Judiciary portals have evolved too, from information delivery to interaction.

Recent technological innovations such as Web 2.0 applications, social media platforms and tools have caused, at least partially, this evolution. E-government portals need to continuously evolve and adapt to new technological features. This constant evolution has also transformed the main functions that websites can perform and the way citizens and other social actors can interact with them (Sandoval-Almazán & Gil-García, 2012). There are different models that explain the development and evolution of government websites (Sandoval & Gil-García, 2008; Layne & Lee, 2001; Soon et al., 2010; Elling et al., 2007).

One of the most frequently used approaches to assess e-government portals is the evolutionary perspective, which creates stages and analyzes e-government initiatives according to the characteristics and technical features found in these stages (i.e., presence, interaction, integration). The evolutionary approach is useful to understand government websites because it attempts to measure the degree of innovation and provides guidance for developments and improvements. The assessment model for this research (Sandoval-Almazán & Gil-García, 2015) is based on the evolutionary approach to build its components and allow frequent updates.

Using only an evolutionary approach to evaluate e-government initiatives, including Web portals, is difficult because it can have characteristics and features identified with multiple stages. Nevertheless, we used this approach for our research because we think it is one of the best developed options so far to measure government portals.

Other scholars have also assessed websites. Abanumy et al., (2005) contributed on Saudi Arabia and Oman e-government website, defining accessibility direction points in the field of assessing e-government portals. Henriksson et al., (2007) on e-government websites evaluation; Büyüközkan, (2009) using multi criteria methods for assessing e-government sites. Also Huang, (2007) contributed to the usability on e-government sites. Economides and Terzis, (2008) evaluated tax sites, the same as Saha et al., (2012) but focusing on different quality system's approaches. On the other hand, Assimwe and Lim, (2010) evaluated the usability of websites in Uganda. Donker-Kuijer et al., (2010) focused in producing some guidelines for e-government websites. Yücel and Ozok, (2010) directed their research on what they considered the "ergonomic quality of government websites". Kopackova et al., (2010) focused on two important characteristics: accessibility and fundability in Czech Republic Websites.

On the municipal perspective, Chatzopoulos and Economides, (2009) contributed in the assessing of Greek municipalities. Van den Haak et al., (2009) has the same orientation; Becker (2004) focused on the visual accessibility for older adults. This overview of different perspectives of assessment on e-government websites describes more trends on visual and usability aspects rather than usefulness or information quality. Most of this research was made focusing on executive-level websites, not on legislative or judicial websites. This is the gap that this investigation intents to contribute, focusing on judiciary websites.

Judiciary Portals

Since 1971, Baca et al., (1971) promoted the use of technology and information systems from the private sector into court systems. Most recently, with the advent of the personal computer era, Arial's research (2001) about the federal judicial website in the U.S. described the main changes and transformations for that website over time. Other studies in the judicial information systems of Norway, Netherlands, Italy, Australia, Venezuela and Singapore, provided novel ideas, best practices and advantages of their use (Oskamp et al., 2004). Diez and Prenafeta researched the case of communication registries on judicial notices in Europe (Diez & Prenafeta, 2002). Glassey and Gordon (2005) introduced the concept of the legal knowledge system to manage the legal process in a German county.

Velicogna and colleagues (2006) studied the Italian experience of introducing websites into the judicial system and the related impact on legitimacy and trust. In another case study, Schmidt (2007) analyzed the computerization of judicial processes in the Netherlands. Trochev (2007) showed some preliminary examples of the use of websites in Russian courts. A different ICT adoption perspective is the implementation of information management systems in courts. Another example is Gordon (2007) who suggested legal knowledge based-systems (LKBS) to support the implementation of technology in the life cycle of legislation. Satola (2007) proposed a framework approach to understand legal regulations on Internet.

Several scholars have researched different courts in Latin America. For example, Andrade and Joia (2012) analyzed the role of different actors involved with strategic planning and the definition of ICT strategies in the Brazilian justice system, particularly focusing on the central role of the National Council of Justice (NCJ).

Judiciary websites research also has been oriented on automated process and bureaucratic tasks that can be updated with information systems (Gorham, 2012; Tonn et al., 2012). For example, research from the Court of Neuquén, Argentina, has proposed a pilot project to allow electronic court notification documents (Luzuriaga & Cechich, 2011). Gorham, (2012) supported this idea and proposed a framework of analysis based upon a theory of innovation and diffusion, seeking to identify those factors that contribute to state courts' adoption of e-filing process.

Another research by Zuniga and Murillo (2014) compared the implementation of Quality Management Standards for district courts and courts of appeal in Costa Rica and Panama through a process-performance tracking and improvement tool being the most recent example of this trend in court systems. Jimenez (2014) has a pioneer study linking open justice adoption and online network in Cataluña, Spain, which is the first of its kind looking at the open justice with the focus of how social networks influence in the achievement of such strategy. A complementary path of research on judicial branches are the governance or policies among courts that use ICT's. An Argentinean study from Lezcano and Oliveira (2009) discusses the electronic ombudsman as a legal institution that regulates people and their links with technology in the information society era.

Correa et.al (2014) evaluated transparency websites through a survey with 20 municipalities. The Brazilian law requirements were used as evaluation criteria for their findings and showing a gap between local transparency portals and the effective implementation of the OGD principles.

The most similar research to this study comes from the Justice Studies Center of the Americas (JSCA), which conducted an investigation using the Accessibility Index of Judiciary Information to assess and rank 34 nations of the OCDE using variables such as schedule for sessions, sentence communication, rules, statistics and basic information (including judges' wages, curriculum vitae, and background); in 2010, Chile was ranked first (JSCA, 2010).

In Mexico, research about judiciary websites addresses how they differ from e-government implementation for local and state executive websites. This study was made by Sandoval-Almazán and Gil-García, (2010). In this exploratory research of 32 local government judiciary websites, their findings reveal a lack of organization of judicial information and websites, focusing mainly in providing information to the general public rather than services for judges or lawyers. A more recent study was held in Mexico in 2014, assessing 20 local judiciary websites. The judicial website of the state of Puebla rank first in this measure, (Sandoval-Almazán, & Gil-García, 2015).

METHODOLOGY

The purpose of comparing judiciary websites is to promote open justice. This idea of openness in the government will affect all government branches, nor just the executive power. In order to support this idea of openness, the aim of comparing judicial web sites will help to introduce the competitiveness aspect and provide more information to citizens through open websites. These two arguments - openness in all branches and improve citizen information - will be foster with a possible comparison among open judiciary websites in different countries.

In order to achieve such a goal, this research instrument was developed using two previous studies. The first one was the e-government assessment model for web sites, developed by Sandoval-Almazán and Gil-García (2008) mostly used for assessing e-government portals in Mexico since 2005. The main components for this assessment model were: presence, information availability, interaction, integration, transaction and political participation (See Table 1).

The second research held by Sandoval-Almazan & Gil-Garcia (2010) was an exploratory research on judicial websites held in Mexico in 2010 which analyzes 32 local judicial websites using a mixed methodology. Findings of this research were common topics among web sites, weaknesses and gaps to be studied and the focus of the websites more related to internal processes rather than providing information to citizens.

The lessons from these previous studies define the components of the model as follows:

- Eliminate the component of transactions, because none of the studied judiciary websites have something similar;
- Include a section for internal information like education, courses or updates;
- Include more tools related to citizens participations. Most of the websites have different kind of tools, some of them related to government 2.0;
- Include information related to privacy or secrecy of personal information;
- Include information related to budget or financing from judiciary websites.

The next step in the design of the instrument was to pilot the new instrument into the Mexican judiciary websites and improve it. This test was held on 2014 and published in a conference paper in 2015 (Sandoval-Almazán & Gil-García, 2015). The actual instrument for Latin American Judiciary websites is the most updated instrument and is the result of this research process during the last five years.

Data Collection and Variables

The data collection was held in two stages. During the first stage, 25 countries that belong to the OCDE and that have a valid URL of a national level judiciary web site were selected. Table 3 presents this sample. The second stage was conducted during July 2015. Each website was visited by one researcher in a 30-50 minute session to collect data according to all the items in the questionnaire. Each item was measured using a dichotomous variable (1, 0) and all the items within each component were added to generate an overall score for the component. The final data was reviewed and coded by the research team before the analysis was performed. Our ranking was obtained by finding the average of the grades from each component (information + interaction + integration + participation/4).

Research Design

This section presents the research model to assess judiciary websites, describes its components and explains how the model was built. It also describes the sample and the research design followed to obtain this data.

The purpose of this research is to test an assessment model for judiciary websites in Latin America. Prior testing was made on Mexican judiciary websites (Sandoval-Almazán & Gil-García, 2014). The model was developed through an experience of five years, starting on 2009 on judiciary websites in Mexico.

The main focus on the judiciary website assessment was to consider the user perspective, in the sense of the general public since it was difficult to have information from the internal users - judges, minister of justice - on each Latin American Country. Accordingly to this limitation of focus and the previous research on assessing e-government portals (Sandoval-Almazán & Gil García 2008, 2013), we selected four main components for the research model. The items for each component were selected accordingly to the purpose of each one. The next step was to build a more comprehensive questionnaire to measure the technology use of judiciary websites. In order to pursue this goal, we followed the next steps:

1. Literature review of different assessments models in e-government and judiciary websites;
2. Verify each question and its relationship with the components;
3. Match new questions with components and review the questions from related research, like JSCA (2010);
4. The final outcome was an instrument of 86 questions that was tested on Mexican judiciary portals in 2014.

Based on the review of existing literature presented in the previous two sections and our previous experience assessing e-government portals, the Sandoval-Almazán and Gil-García (2015) model was developed to assess judicial websites. It has four components (see Figure 1). The main orientation of the

Table 2. Components and variables for the 2015 ranking

Component	Variables
Information	Published statistics; news, updated information; frequent cases, online library, last update; internal rules; budget; wages; phonebook, help information; performance indicators, site map, online services catalogue; accessibility; open data section; financial information from the court
Interaction	Webmaster email present; chat 24/7; search engine; alternate search; information request form; download formats; online track of cases and appeals; one-stop portal; intranet presence
Integration	Mobile integration; link for municipalities and federal judiciary; portal access with password; homogenous design; information from edicts, sentences and bills online by date
Participation	Presence of blogs, forums, chats and social media platforms. Online activity on forums and chats; information sharing possibility to different social media platforms, email or other devices

Table 3. Sample of Latin American countries and URLs

Country	URL
Antigua and Barbuda	http://www.eccourts.org/
Argentina	http://www.pjn.gov.ar/
Bahamas	http://www.courts.gov.bs/
Barbados	http://www.barbadoslawcourts.gov.bb/
Belize	http://www.belizejudiciary.org/web/
Bolivia	http://www.boliviajudicial.com/
Brazil	http://www.tjdft.jus.br/
Chile	http://www.pjud.cl/
Colombia	http://www.ramajudicial.gov.co/
Costa Rica	http://www.poder-judicial.go.cr/
Ecuador	http://www.funcionjudicial.gob.ec/
El Salvador	http://www.csj.gob.sv/idioma.html
Guatemala	http://www.oj.gob.gt/
Guyana	http://www.caribbeancourtofjustice.org/
Honduras	http://www.poderjudicial.gob.hn/Paginas/Iniciocortesuprema.aspx
Jamaica	http://supremecourt.gov.jm/
Mexico	http://www.cjf.gob.mx/
Nicaragua	http://www.poderjudicial.gob.ni/w2013/default.asp
Panama	http://www.organojudicial.gob.pa/
Paraguay	http://www.pj.gov.py/
Peru	http://www.pj.gob.pe/wps/wcm/connect/CorteSuprema/s_cortes_suprema_home/as_Inicio/
Dominican Republic	http://www.poderjudicial.gob.do/
Trinidad and Tobago	http://www.ttlawcourts.org/
Uruguay	http://www.poderjudicial.gub.uy/
Venezuela	http://www.tsj.gob.ve/

assessment instrument is an objective perspective. If the evaluated item is found on the judiciary website it is valued as 1. If the item is not found, it gets a 0. There could be subjective considerations or ranges for the assessments, but this model tries to avoid partial or misunderstanding data of the measurement. The components are described below and variables are listed in Table 2:

1. **Information (INF):** The objective of this component is to assess the organization of information on the website, the type of information provided, whether information is up-to-date, transparency and open data, and finally accessibility;
2. **Interaction (INT):** The aim of this component is to evaluate the different methods available to contact public officials (judges, ministers, and website managers). The site's information search capabilities and whether information is dynamic (e.g., if the website is open or restricted to certain stakeholders);

Figure 1. Assessing judiciary websites model
Sandoval-Almazán & Gil-García, 2015.

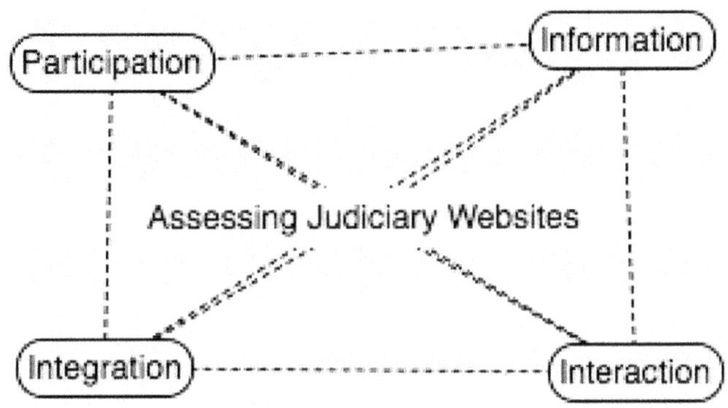

3. **Integration (INTG):** This component assesses the extent to which information is vertically integrated (content is of the same type but from different agencies or different levels of government) or horizontally integrated (different content from different units within a single agency or government);
4. **Participation (PART):** The purpose of this component is to assess what kind of participation tools the website provides for its users - lawyers, citizens, etc. - in the form of blogs, forums, chats, social media and tags among others.

There are two other components which are assessed in this study: design and performance. These are complementary assessments for the websites portals. It is more important to evaluate the citizen perspective of the government information - including judiciary information - from the perspective of the legal user - or any citizen - focusing on quality content and the information sharing capacity of the judiciary website rather than speed (performance) or usability (design). This is why we didn't consider these two last components as a part of the ranking, but because of their usefulness for the purpose of comparison, they will be described in the findings section and explained as follows.

Performance (PRF) - this component measures three variables: 1. Download speed; 2. Alexa website ranking and 3. Performance without errors. In order to achieve this measurement, the best option is to use external websites and consider their results in the questionnaire. For example, PingDom and Alexa Ranking evaluates performance and the World Wide Consortium (W3C) assesses the performance of the websites without mistakes like broken links.

Style and Design (S&D).- the purpose of this component is to measure several variables related to letter size, relationship picture-text, breadcrumbs navigation, buttons format, organization. All of them measured through different items on the subjective perception of the evaluator.

Just for the performance, the Alexa Ranking is measured by the following formula:

Speed or Alexa Number minus (Max Number Speed or Alexa Ranking)

divided by

Minimum (Speed or Alexa Ranking) - Maximum (Speed or Alexa Ranking)

This generates a number between 1 and 0 that is placed on the assessment just for these two kinds of measurement.

In the case of the W3C, we run the test over the website and if it has no mistakes - i.e., no broken links - the number is 1. If any mistake appears after running the test, the grade will be zero.

FINDINGS

Research findings are divided into three parts. The first part presents the ranking of judiciary websites along the four main components (information, integration, interaction and participation), while the second part analyzes the performance and designed components of the websites. Third section compares the ranking position of this research with the JSCA report that measured the same countries in 2010.

Latin America Judiciary Portals Ranking 2015

According to our results, the Latin American judiciary portals that obtained the highest integrated average were Colombia (62.16), Costa Rica (61.14) and Argentina in third place (58.45). While Uruguay and El Salvador had the lowest scores in the ranking (27.7 and13.60, respectively). Costa Rica had the highest score in Information, Interaction and Integration, but a very poor score in Participation (30), which places it in the second place of the ranking. The differences among the top three are not prominent and could be from one or two items that were not present from the evaluation requirements (see Table 4).

The total average obtained in this sample was 44.79 points which is below the Mexican judiciary websites averages in 2014 (50.30). Half of the analyzed judiciary websites are above this average (50%), which is an important trend for Latin America's legal system. However, 50 percent of the websites are below average, suggesting important gaps to be filled. Maybe the most important issue is the participation section, which for example, in Panamá, Brazil, Jamaica and Barbados has no tools for allowing users' participation.

Judiciary Portals by Component

A closer look on each component of the model reveals interesting patterns. For example, there is a tie for the second place in the information component between Nicaragua and Colombia, with 87.10 points each one. This could be interpreted as if the two state judiciary websites have more quality information or better-organized data than other judicial websites in the country. In this component the average was 64.77, and only Costa Rica gets the highest points with 90.32, a considerable gap with El Salvador 29.03 points. The rest of the judicial websites have some lack or absence of this fundamental section that organizes all of their website activity.

The interaction component allows users to communicate with public officials, in this case judges, ministers or the website managers. This component had an average of 34.80, being the highest score 55 points and several countries reached this point (Costa Rica, Argentina, Mexico, Chile, and Antigua and Barbuda). The lowest was Bahamas and El Salvador with zero. This lack of interaction tools could be normal for these kind of websites because they are normally not citizen centered. However it is also linked to the lack of opportunities for participation.

Table 4. Evaluation of judicial portals in Latin America 2015

Ranking	Country	Total	INF	INTER	INTEG	PART
1	Colombia	62.16	87.10	40.00	61.54	60.00
2	Costa Rica	61.14	90.32	55.00	69.23	30.00
3	Argentina	58.45	74.19	55.00	84.62	20.00
4	Chile	58.22	70.97	55.00	76.92	30.00
5	Mexico	55.72	70.97	55.00	76.92	20.00
6	Ecuador	55.09	74.19	40.00	46.15	60.00
7	Nicaragua	51.58	87.10	30.00	69.23	20.00
8	Guatemala	50.86	74.19	40.00	69.23	20.00
9	Honduras	50.32	77.42	50.00	53.85	20.00
10	Antigua and Barbuda	50.30	67.74	55.00	38.46	40.00
11	Dominican Republic	45.11	51.61	35.00	53.85	40.00
12	Belize	44.82	67.74	40.00	61.54	10.00
13	Panamá	43.26	74.19	45.00	53.85	0.00
14	Guyana	42.09	64.52	30.00	53.85	20.00
15	Bolivia	42.08	54.84	35.00	38.46	40.00
16	Paraguay	41.76	61.29	25.00	30.77	50.00
17	Brazil	40.52	45.16	40.00	76.92	0.00
18	Peru	40.03	61.29	15.00	53.85	30.00
19	Trinidad and Tobago	39.23	58.06	25.00	53.85	20.00
20	Jamaica	38.65	58.06	35.00	61.54	0.00
21	Barbados	37.19	64.52	15.00	69.23	0.00
22	Venezuela	37.16	45.16	35.00	38.46	30.00
23	Bahamas	33.21	61.29	0.00	61.54	10.00
24	Uruguay	27.29	48.39	20.00	30.77	10.00
25	El Salvador	13.60	29.03	0.00	15.38	10.00
Average		44.79	64.77	34.80	56.00	23.60

Judiciary Websites: Performance and Design

The performance and design of judiciary websites are complementary, but also relevant individually. The main results are organized by performance (PRF) in Table 5. Mexico's judiciary portal rank 1st position on performance, followed very closely by Costa Rica in 2nd place and followed by Peru in 3rd place. Despite the fact performance is an important characteristic, content, development and services are more important. Costa Rica has these two characteristics because of its position in the general ranking and the position of performance.

On the other hand, the average of performance points reached 78.69 points and the large majority of the Latin American websites are above this average. Just a few of them - Uruguay, El Salvador, Guatemala, Guyana, Belize and Barbados - are below this average. An interesting case is Bolivia with 9.71 points, the lowest of all countries that can be studied closely to understand the problems of performance.

Table 5. Performance and style and design components, ordered by performance

Ranking	Country	PRF	S&D
1	Mexico	99.93	66.67
2	Costa Rica	97.20	88.89
3	Peru	95.76	66.67
4	Dominican Republic	95.32	55.56
5	Ecuador	94.09	88.89
6	Argentina	93.96	88.89
7	Venezuela	93.62	66.67
8	Brazil	93.57	100.00
9	Trinidad and Tobago	92.39	55.56
10	Panama	92.37	77.78
11	Colombia	91.50	77.78
12	Paraguay	90.88	66.67
13	Jamaica	90.73	66.67
14	Antigua and Barbuda	89.54	100.00
15	Honduras	89.46	88.89
16	Nicaragua	87.46	66.67
17	Chile	84.14	100.00
18	Uruguay	75.37	77.78
19	Bahamas	64.29	77.78
20	El Salvador	63.58	11.11
21	Guatemala	52.32	88.89
22	Guyana	49.35	88.89
23	Belize	43.92	77.78
24	Barbados	36.67	66.67
25	Bolivia	9.71	77.78
Average		78.69	75.56

Regarding style and design, which gathers usability, appearance and feelings of the website and accessibility in general terms, the average was 75.56 points and just some portals reached this number. Brazil, Chile and Antigua and Barbuda are interesting exceptions reaching 100 points.

These two components are not the most important ones for any judiciary portal. It seems that the website design is more important for the webmaster rather than for other components such as service and information for the users.

Judiciary Websites by Regions

In general terms, there is not a clear pattern in terms of any geographical region. Findings were divided into three regions: central, northern and southern countries in order to compare results within regions.

Table 6. Ranking by regions: Central America

Ranking	Country	Total	INF	INTER	INTEG	PART
2	Costa Rica	61.14	90.32	55.00	69.23	30.00
7	Nicaragua	51.58	87.10	30.00	69.23	20.00
8	Guatemala	50.86	74.19	40.00	69.23	20.00
9	Honduras	50.32	77.42	50.00	53.85	20.00
12	Belize	44.82	67.74	40.00	61.54	10.00
13	Panama	43.26	74.19	45.00	53.85	0.00
25	El Salvador	13.60	29.03	0.00	15.38	10.00
Average		12.62	20.00	10.40	15.69	4.40

Table 7. Ranking by regions: North America

Ranking	Country	Total	INF	INTER	INTEG	PART
5	Mexico	55.72	70.97	55.00	76.92	20.00

The Central American region gathers a second place. Costa Rica could be the best portal except for the participation component, and three countries in the top 10 of the general ranking. However, its regional average is impacted by El Salvador's low qualifications.

This region gathers the best and the worst judiciary portals at the same time.

On the other hand, Mexico was located in the North American region, despite the fact that other measurements place it in South American region. But for explanatory purposes of this study, we decided to exclude Mexico from this table in order to have a more integrated look over the South American region. There is no other country to compare to Mexico. Canada and the US were not part of this sample, so that these country numbers were just for reference with the other two Latin American regions (see Table 6).

The South American region reached a 29.94 point regional average which is more than the double of Central America. It has 5 countries in the top ten of best judiciary portals in this study, including the first place - Colombia. However, the overall results are completely mixed in the region (see Table 7). Most of the countries are in the middle and bottom of the general ranking with different results of the components. Some judiciary portals of certain countries are better in Information, other in Integration. A constant is the lack of participation tools in the portals. At least in the Central American region there is a consistent lack of tools, and the South American region is completely disperse with Colombia and Ecuador with great tools and the rest of the countries with other points (see Table 8).

It is important to mention that there isn't a common strategy or impact among the different portals considering this comparison among the three different Latin American regions of judiciary websites. There's not even communication among them to share experiences or best practices. The overview of this analysis describes completely different strategies to approach judiciary portals for every region.

Table 8. Ranking by regions: South America

Ranking	Country	Total	INF	INTER	INTEG	PART
1	Colombia	62.16	87.10	40.00	61.54	60.00
3	Argentina	58.45	74.19	55.00	84.62	20.00
4	Chile	58.22	70.97	55.00	76.92	30.00
6	Ecuador	55.09	74.19	40.00	46.15	60.00
10	Antigua and Barbuda	50.30	67.74	55.00	38.46	40.00
11	Dominican Republic	45.11	51.61	35.00	53.85	40.00
14	Guyana	42.09	64.52	30.00	53.85	20.00
15	Bolivia	42.08	54.84	35.00	38.46	40.00
16	Paraguay	41.76	61.29	25.00	30.77	50.00
17	Brazil	40.52	45.16	40.00	76.92	0.00
18	Peru	40.03	61.29	15.00	53.85	30.00
19	Trinidad and Tobago	39.23	58.06	25.00	53.85	20.00
20	Jamaica	38.65	58.06	35.00	61.54	0.00
21	Barbados	37.19	64.52	15.00	69.23	0.00
22	Venezuela	37.16	45.16	35.00	38.46	30.00
23	Bahamas	33.21	61.29	0.00	61.54	10.00
24	Uruguay	27.29	48.39	20.00	30.77	10.00
Average		29.94	41.94	22.20	37.23	18.40

Comparison with JSCA

The last comparison of these findings is with the Index of Judiciary Online Services (IJOS), developed by the Justice Studies Center of the Americas (JSCA) (2010), considering similar countries. Table 9 presents them in alphabetic order.

The comparison was only made with the position in the ranking because both instruments don't have the same components; even though they share similar questions and variables when compared in detail. However, this comparison could give us some ideas about the maturity or the improvements of each portal since 2011 after the publication.

For example, Belize and Honduras' judiciary portals have dramatically improved in four years, climbing 18 positions from one ranking to the other. More important is the case of Ecuador that climbed 22 positions obtaining the highest place in this comparison.

It is also important to observe the consistency of both measurements in the top countries of the rankings. Costa Rica was in the seventh position in 2011 and reached now the second place. Colombia was in the third place and reached the first place in 2015. Chile was in the sixth place and is now in the fourth position. These examples show that similar countries of the top ten maintain their achievements in the actual model.

Despite the fact that this assessment model (Sandoval-Almazán & Gil-García, 2015) cannot be validated with the JSCA (2012) model because of their differences in structure and samples, this comparison can be a starting point to better understand relations and changes among the top ten countries or the last ten

Table 9. Difference between IJOS ranking 2010 and RSA ranking 2015

Country	Ranking RSA 2015	Ranking IJOS 2011	Difference
Antigua and Barbuda	10	19	9
Argentina	3	14	11
Bahamas	23	29	6
Barbados	21	32	11
Belize	12	30	18
Bolivia	15	18	3
Brazil	17	4	-13
Chile	4	6	2
Colombia	1	3	2
Costa Rica	2	7	5
Ecuador	6	28	22
El Salvador	25	26	1
Guatemala	8	12	4
Guyana	14	31	17
Honduras	9	27	18
Jamaica	20	5	-15
Mexico	5	15	10
Nicaragua	7	13	6
Panama	13	16	3
Paraguay	16	11	-5
Peru	18	10	-8
Dominican Republic	11	9	-2
Trinidad and Tobago	19	25	6
Uruguay	24	8	-16
Venezuela	22	17	-5

countries. Countries with negative numbers like Jamaica, Uruguay and Brazil and countries with good numbers like Ecuador. What do they do? Which changes have been made over these four years? These are some questions that can be answered with future research.

SOLUTIONS AND RECOMMENDATIONS

In order to implement an open justice in Latin American courts, the first step could be opening the data. Because of this reason, Internet portals are so important. A portal could become the outlet for this effort and be the best promoter of an open judiciary system.

This Latin American ranking of judiciary portals allow us to understand the actual position in which countries of the region are located and become a starting point for further development in certain areas. For example, most of the judiciary portals have important lacks in the participation component, that is one of the key elements for open justice which allows collaboration and peer production. Countries listed with these absences are able to introduce efforts to reduce this lack.

On the other hand, most of the Latin American assessed countries have a strong presence with information. This means that judiciary portals focus on this perspective that belongs to the first era of Internet. It is important to transform such portals into a web 2.0 era allowing more tools to interact and to integrate information.

It is important to mention that promoting open justice through Internet portals in Latin America will foster other changes inside courts in order to update information, respect privacy and promote efficiency in internal processes. Such changes will create new regulations and specific laws that establish the correct boundaries between what is possible to become open and what must be closed to safe personal guarantees and allow a fair and fast trail of any matter. One example in such direction is the Constitutional Court of Justice in Spain that allows the citizen participation and openness of their process (Cano et al., 2015).

Another recommendation derived from this study is to create an open justice system. Judiciary portals in Latin America will create changes in the data but also in the organizational field in order to maintain the data updated and valid. This creates a necessary open justice system that includes the technology adoption for courts, but also the institutional arrangements such as laws and regulations that regulate actions and stages for the openness.

Finally, the comparison analysis among regions and also between the JSCA's prior study (2012) and the actual ranking allow some recommendations for the regional purposes. Many of this countries have a very low budget for technology adoption in their courts. Because of this reason, it would be important to share expenses and strategies among them. Although they do not have the same laws and internal regulation, it is feasible to develop Internet portals with similar characteristics, functions and security measures that foster collaboration, interaction and reduction of costs for national and local courts.

Some of Central American countries have many problems regarding justice and urgently need systems and technologies that allow faster processes, cost lowering and corruption controls, enabling internal systems for accountability. A regional strategy could help to solve some of these needs and promote internal changes that endure different political administrations.

FUTURE RESEARCH DIRECTIONS

Open Justice for Latin America Judiciary portals is an emerging topic. There are too many paths for future research but I will focus only on the assessment perspective. The lack of ranking or indexes in the area is an important gap that needs to be filled in the short term.

If we do not know where the efforts of openness in justice are heading, then we would not know which actions or directions to take. This research establishes a comparison between the JSCA, Justice Studies Center of the Americas index and the model proposed by Sandoval-Almazán and Gil-García (2015). Although comparison only took place in the ranking, many other comparison items can be considered for each variable or even component with similar variables that allow a more detailed and precise effort. That's why it is necessary to develop an assessment model for judiciary websites that standardizes fundamental or basic variables that must be considered in any study of this kind.

Another path of future research is to complement this quantitative exploratory research with a qualitative research. The necessity of understanding expectations, needs and process of the open justice's implementation through Internet portal directly from citizens, webmasters, judges, lawyers and even court staff will be very interesting and it will be very important to have an overall picture of this new trend.

A qualitative research will also help to understand corruption and accountability problems that Latin American courts face and will help to introduce changes in technology in order to reduce or solve some these problems. This idea leads to another research path: the open justice system.

Judiciary portals are just the most visible part of the open justice system. This kind of system involves customer relationship, management for cases, resolutions and sentences, but also to manage personnel and private data. The need of an integrated system, reliable, easy to administrate and to update, which allows all sort of different kinds of stakeholders - users, lawyers, judges, etc. - to make consultations of precedents or actual cases, must be developed simultaneously in an Internet portal.

The judiciary portal will be the visible face of the transformation and modernization of courts that allow information sharing, data collection and security of the data that flows around the whole system.

In sum, at least three research paths are important to explore in the following years: developing assessment model for research over judiciary portals; qualitative research to deeply understand motivations, causes and expectation of the adoption of technology and ways to implement and to develop the open justice system.

CONCLUSION

The aim of this chapter is to report the Latin America Judiciary portals ranking of 2015, and to describe the Sandoval-Almazán & Gil-García (2015) assessment model and its implications on the open justice trend. The findings reveal some absences of the judiciary portals in some countries. The information component of the model was the strongest one of the basic variables. This is consistent with the idea of informational portals of the web 1.0 but do not align with the openness concept that fosters participation and collaboration. This is one of the important aspects that the majority of the assessed portals lack and need important development.

The majority of the judiciary portals obtain good scores for style & design and performance. This part can be considered as solved and positive but does not reach the objective of openness for an informational portal.

On the other hand, the regional comparison - north, central and south - seems not to have a direct relation to the development of judiciary portals. There are mixed results for each region and what we can appreciate is the common lack of participatory tools.

This research is consistent with the former assessment held by the Justice Studies Center of the Americas (JSCA). The comparison of the two rankings shows consistent results for the top ten countries and some other country variables. More studies are needed for better understanding the causes and functions of these variations in the ranking.

The absence of assessments for the open justice field, particularly on the judiciary portals, was one of the main reasons to develop this first effort in order to provide all kinds of stakeholders a systematic approach to understand the direction of the different kinds of efforts to implement information technologies in courts.

This study, analyzing 25 countries in the region of Latin America, was compared to a previous study in Mexico (2010) using the same instrument. This instrument is perfectible and requires constant changes to become more effective and valid for further research, but the contribution of having this kind of tool for the open justice field is a starting point for future research in this area.

Judiciary portals are just the front-end of a radical transformation in courts. The need to create an open justice system will be developed in the near future to implement more technology in the courts around the globe. However, these technological changes need simultaneously legal changes that allow the adoption and functioning of these technologies inside the courts.

One of the problems that open justice faces is precisely these legal changes, because opening data will change processes in courts, reducing corruption and promoting accountability almost immediately. Because of this, there is much resistance from the different stakeholders - politicians, judges, policemen – in order to implement technologies in the court. However, this is a worldwide unstoppable trend that is part of the modernization of the information society. An open justice system will not occur suddenly but step by step, according to the needs of the users and the political will.

REFERENCES

Abanumy, A., Al-Badi, A., & Mayhew, P. (2005). e-Government Website Accessibility: In-Depth Evaluation of Saudi Arabia and Oman. *Electronic. Journal of E-Government*, *3*(3), 99–106.

André, A., & Joia, L. A. (2012). Organizational Structure and ICT Strategies in the Brazilian Judiciary System. *Government Information Quarterly*, *29*(1), S32–S42. doi:10.1016/j.giq.2011.08.003

Arial, D.L. (2001). History of the Federal Judiciary Website: Washington, DC: The Federal Judicial Center. Accessed May 2000. *Journal of Government Information*, *28*(3), 351–353.

Asiimwe, E. N., & Lim, N. (2010). Usability of Government Websites in Uganda. *Electronic. Journal of E-Government*, *8*(1), 1–12.

Baca, R. L., ... (1971). Automated Court Systems. In *Proceedings of the Fall Joint Computer Conference*. New York, NY: ACM. Available at: http://doi.acm.org/10.1145/1479064.1479120

Becker, S. A. (2004). E-government visual accessibility for older adult users. *Social Science Computer Review*, *22*(1), 11–23. doi:10.1177/0894439303259876

Büyüközkan, G. (2009). Evaluating Government Websites Using a Multi-Criteria Decision Making Approach. In *9th European Conference on e-Government*. London, UK: Academic Publishing Limited.

Cano, J., Jiménez, C. E., Hernández, R., & Ros, S. (2015). New Tools for E-Justice : Legal Research Available to Any Citizen.*Second International Conference on eDemocracy & eGovernment (ICEDEG)*. doi:10.1109/ICEDEG.2015.7114455

Chatzopoulos, K.-C. & Economides, A.A., (2009). A holistic evaluation of Greek municipalities' websites. *Electronic Government, an International Journal*, *6*(2), 193–212.

Chun, S. A., Shulman, S., Sandoval, R., & Hovy, E. (2010). Government 2.0: Making connections between citizens, data and government. *Information Polity*, *15*(1-2), 1–9.

Corrêa, A. S., Corrêa, P. L. P., & da Silva, F. S. C. (2014, November 23). Transparency Portals Versus Open Government Data: An Assessment of Openness in Brazilian Municipalities. *Proceedings of the 15th Annual International Conference on Digital Government Research (dg.o 2014)*. http://doi.org/doi:10.1145/2612733.2612760

Deb, G. K. (1999). Electronic governance - A vehicle for the new world order. *Electronics Information & Planning*, *27*(1), 29–33.

Diez, C., & Prenafeta, J. (2002). E-Government Applied to Judicial Notices and Inter-Registrar Communications in the European Union: The AEQUITAS Project. In *Electronic Government: Proceedings of the 1st International Conference, EGOV 2002*. Retrieved from http://www.springerlink.com/openurl.asp?genre=article&id=N6KCG770FN7795V5

Donker-Kuijer, M. W., de Jong, M., & Lentz, L. (2010). Usable guidelines for usable websites? An analysis of five e-government heuristics. *Government Information Quarterly*, *27*(3), 254–263. doi:10.1016/j.giq.2010.02.006

Economides, A.A. & Terzis, V., (2008). Evaluating tax sites: an evaluation framework and its application. *Electronic Government, an International Journal*, *5*(3), 321–344.

Elling, S., Lentz, L., & de Jong, M. (2007). Website Evaluation Questionnaire: Development of a Research-Based Tool for Evaluating Informational Websites. In *6th International Conference, EGOV 2007*. Regensburg, Germany: Springer Berlin/Heidelberg. doi:10.1007/978-3-540-74444-3_25

Gant, J. P., & Gant, D. B. (2002). Web portal functionality and State government E-service. In *Proceedings of the 35th Annual Hawaii International Conference on System Sciences (HICSS'02)*. Waikoloa, Hawaii: IEEE Computer Society. doi:10.1109/HICSS.2002.994073

Glassey, O., & Gordon, T. F. (2005). Feasibility Study for a Legal Knowledge System in the County of Herford. In *Electronic Government: 4th International Conference (EGOV 2005)*. Berlin: Springer.

Gordon, T. F. (2007). Legal Knowledge Systems. In A.-V. Anttiroiko & M. Mälkiä (Eds.), *Encyclopedia of digital government* (pp. 1161–1166). Hershey, PA: Idea Group Reference. doi:10.4018/978-1-59140-789-8.ch175

Gorham, U. (2012). State Courts, e-Filing, and Diffusion of Innovation: A Proposed Framework of Analysis. In *Proceedings of the 13th Annual International Conference on Digital Government Research*. New York, NY: ACM. doi:10.1145/2307729.2307767

Henriksson, A. T., Yi, Y., Forst, B., & Middleton, M. R. (2007). Evaluation instruments for e-government websites. *Electronic Government: An International Journal*, *4*(2), 204–226. doi:10.1504/EG.2007.013984

Huang, C. J. (2007). Accessibility of E-Government Web Sites. In *Encyclopedia of digital government* (pp. 11–15). Hershey, PA: Idea Group Reference. doi:10.4018/978-1-59140-789-8.ch002

Jiménez, C. (2014). *Justicia Abierta: transparencia y proximidad de la justicia en el actual contexto de Open Government*. Barcelona: Centro de Estudios Jurídicos y Formación Especializada del Departamento de Justicia. Generalidad de Cataluña.

Justice Studies Center of the Americas (JSCA). (2010) *Índice De Accesibilidad A La Información Judicial En Internet 2010 (IACC)*. Retrieved from http://www.cejamericas.org/index.php/areas-de-trabajo/tecnologia-de-la-informacion-y-transparencia/transparencia-rendicion-de-cuentas-y-acceso-a-la-informacion-judicial/indice-de-accesibilidad-a-la-informacion-judicial-en-internet.html

Kopackova, H., Michalek, K., & Cejna, K. (2010). Accessibility and findability of local e-government websites in the Czech Republic. *Universal Access in the Information Society*, *9*(1), 51–61. doi:10.1007/s10209-009-0159-y

Lanvin, B., & Lewin, A. (2006). *The Next Frontier of E-Government: Local Governments May Hold the Keys to Global Competition.* Global Information Technology Report.

Layne, K., & Lee, J. W. (2001). Developing fully functional E-government: A four stage model. *Government Information Quarterly*, *18*(2), 122–136. doi:10.1016/S0740-624X(01)00066-1

Lezcano, J. M., & Olivera, N. (2009). The Electronic Ombudsman. In *Proceedings of the 3rd International Conference on Theory and Practice of Electronic Governance (ICEGOV).* Bogota, Colombia: ACM. doi:10.1145/1693042.1693086

Luzuriaga, J. M., & Cechich, A. (2011). Electronic Notification of Court Documents: A Case Study. New York, NY: ACM. doi:10.1145/2072069.2072077

Morozov, E. (2014). *To Save Everything, Click Here: The Folly of Technological Solutionism.* New York: Public Affairs.

Oskamp, A., Lodder, A. R., & Apistola, M. (2004). *IT Support of the Judiciary*. Asser Press. doi:10.1007/978-90-6704-659-6

Saha, P., Nath, A. K., & Salehi-Sangari, E. (2012). Evaluation of government e-tax websites: an information quality and system quality approach. *Transforming Government: People, Process and Policy*, *6*(3), 300–321.

Sandoval, R., & Gil-García, J. R. (2008). Limitations of Evolutionary Approaches to E-government. In D. Garson & M. Khosrow-Pour (Eds.), *Handbook of Research on Public Information Technology* (pp. 22–30). IGI. doi:10.4018/978-1-59904-857-4.ch003

Sandoval-Almazan, R., Gil García, J. R., Luna Reyes, L. F., Luna, D. E., & Rojas Romero, Y. (2012). Open government 2.0: citizen empowerment through open data, web and mobile apps. In *Proceedings of the 6th International Conference on Theory and Practice of Electronic Governance*. New York, NY: ACM. doi:10.1145/2463728.2463735

Sandoval-Almazan, R. (2013). *La larga marcha del Gobierno Abierto. Teoría, medición y futuro. In The Long Walk of the Open Government: Theory, Metrics and Future*. Mexico City: INAP.

Sandoval-Almazan, R., & Gil-Garcia, J. R. (2010). Evaluating Websites in the Judicial Branch: An Exporatory Study. In Electronic Government and Electronic Participation: Joint Proceedings of Ongoing Resarch and Pojects of IFIP eGOV and ePart 2010. Lausanne, Switzerland: Trauner.

Sandoval Almazan, R., & Gil Garcia, J. R. (2015). Understanding Judicial Websites: An Exploration of Portals in the States of Mexico. IEEE Computer Society. doi:10.1109/HICSS.2015.253

Satola, D. (2007). Legal Aspects of Internet Governance Reform. *Information Polity: The International Journal of Government & Democracy in the Information Age, 12*, 49–62. Retrieved from http://iospress.metapress.com/app/home/contribution.asp?referrer=parent&backto=issue,6,9

Schmidt, A. (2007). IT and the judiciary in the Netherlands – A state of affairs. *Computer Law & Security Report*, *23*(5), 453–460. doi:10.1016/j.clsr.2007.03.006

Scholl, H. J. (2010). Electronic Government: A study Domain Past Its Infancy. In *E-Government: Information, Technology, and Transformation* (pp. 11–32). Armonk, NY: M.E. Sharpe.

Tonn, B., Dorian, S., Scheb II, J. M., Glennon, C., & Sharma, H K. (2009). Future of the Courts: Fixed, Flexible, and Improvisational Frameworks. *Futures of Governance, 44*(9), 802–11. doi:10.1016/j.futures.2012.07.005

Trochev, A. (2007). Courts on the Web in Russia. In A.-V. Anttiroiko & M. Mälkiä (Eds.), *Encyclopedia of digital government* (pp. 260–265). Hershey, PA: Idea Group Reference. doi:10.4018/978-1-59140-789-8.ch039

Van den Haak, M. J., de Jong, M. D. T., & Schellens, P. J. (2009). Evaluating municipal websites: A methodological comparison of three think-aloud variants. *Government Information Quarterly*, *26*(1), 193–202. doi:10.1016/j.giq.2007.11.003

Velicogna, M., & Ng, G. Y. (2006). Legitimacy and Internet in the Judiciary: A Lesson From the Italian Courts' Websites Experience. *International Journal of Law and Information Technology*, *14*(3), 370–389. doi:10.1093/ijlit/eal009

Villeneuve, J.-P. (2014). Transparency of Transparency: The pro-active disclosure of the rules governing Access to Information as a gauge of organisational cultural transformation. The case of the Swiss transparency regime. *Government Information Quarterly*, *31*(4), 556–562. doi:10.1016/j.giq.2013.10.010

Yücel, G. & Ozok, A.F., (2010). Quantifying ergonomic quality of governmental websites. *Electronic Government, an International Journal*, *7*(3), 233 – 251.

Zuniga, R., & Murillo, R. (2014). Draining the judiciary bottleneck: A quasi-experiment in improving a government service. *Journal of Business Research*, *67*(6), 1267–1276. doi:10.1016/j.jbusres.2013.04.003

KEY TERMS AND DEFINITIONS

E-Government: The World Bank conceives e-government as the use of ICT, such as the Internet and mobile devices, to transform relations with citizens and businesses, and between branches of government (Lanvin & Lewin, 2006).

E-Government Web Site: Organized collection of government data, entry points and process to share information and provide transactional gateways for citizens and public officials from different government areas.

Information: This component could be understood to assess the organization of information on the website, the type of information provided, whether information is up-to-date, transparency and open data, and finally accessibility.

Integration: This component could be understood to assesses the extent to which information is vertically integrated (content is of the same type but from different agencies or different levels of government) or horizontally integrated (different content from different units within a single agency or government).

Interaction: This component could be understood to evaluate the different methods available to contact public officials (judges, ministers, and website managers). The site's information search capabilities and whether information is dynamic (e.g., if the website is open or restricted to certain stakeholders).

Judiciary Web Site: Organized collection of judiciary information available for general public and for the purpose of management disclosure legally approved in order to promote citizen participation and collaboration to help judiciary officials.

Open Government: "Is a technological and institutional platform which transforms government data into public data, in order to allow use, protection and collaboration from citizens on the public decisions, accountability and the improvement of public services" (Sandoval, 2013: p.40).

Participation: This component could be understood to assess what kind of participation tools the website provides for its users - lawyers, citizens, etc. - in the form of blogs, forums, chats, social media and tags among others.

Portal: "A Web portal serves as the integrated gateway into the state government websites and provides visitors with a single point of contact for online service delivery within the state." Gant and Gant (2002)

Transparency: Conduct public affairs in an open manner or otherwise be the subject of public scrutiny Villeneuve (2014) p. 557.

Compilation of References

Abanumy, A., Al-Badi, A., & Mayhew, P. (2005). e-Government Website Accessibility: In-Depth Evaluation of Saudi Arabia and Oman. *Electronic. Journal of E-Government*, *3*(3), 99–106.

Abrahamson, S. S. (2002). *Involving individual citizens with courts and tribunals: Initiatives in the United States and Canada*. Montreal, Canada: Editions Thémis.

Act Concerning Establishment of Judicial Reform [*Kaikaku Shingikai Secchi Ho*], 1999, Law no.68 of 1999.

Act Concerning the Maintenance of Order in a Court of Law [*Hoteinado no Chitsujo ni kansuru Horitsu*], 1952, Law no.286 of 1952.

Act on Promotion of Judicial System Reform [*Shihoseido Kaikaku Suishin Ho*], 2001, Law no.119 of 2001.

Alberts, B., Cicerone, R. J., Fienberg, S. E., Kamb, A., McNutt, M., Nerem, R. M., & Jamieson, K. H. (2015). Self-correction in science at work. *Science*, *348*(6242), 1420–1422. doi:10.1126/science.aab3847 PMID:26113701

Alemanno, A., & Stefan, O. (2014). Openness at the Court of Justice of the European Union: Toppling a taboo. *Common Market Law Review*, *51*(1), 97–139.

AMA. (2015a). *Cartão de Cidadão*. Retrieved May 28, 2015, from www.ama.pt/index.php_option=com_content&task=view&id=28&Itemid=32.html

AMA. (2015b). *Chave Móvel*. Retrieved May 28, 2015, from https://cmd.autenticacao.gov.pt/Ama.Authentication.Frontend/

AMA. (2015c). *Dados.gov.pt - Preguntas Frequentes*. Retrieved May 28, 2015, from http://www.dados.gov.pt/PT/Info/PerguntasFrequentes.aspx

Ambler, L. (2007). The People Decide: The Effect of the Introduction of the Quasi-Jury System (Saiban-In Seido) on the Death Penalty in Japan, The. *Northwestern Journal of International Human Rights*, *6*(1), 1–23.

Amendment to the Constitution of the People's Republic of China. (1999) (中华人民共和国宪法修正案(1999年)), passed and issued on and effective as of March 15, 1999. Retrieved from http://www.npc.gov.cn/wxzl/wxzl/2000-12/10/content_7075.htm

Andersen, K. V., & Henriksen, H. Z. (2006). E-government maturity models: Extension of the Layne and Lee model. *Government Information Quarterly*, *23*(2), 236–248. doi:10.1016/j.giq.2005.11.008

Anderson, P. H. (2011). *Court Information, Privacy, and Technology. Future Trends in State Courts*. Williamsburg, VA: National Center for State Courts.

André, A., & Joia, L. A. (2012). Organizational Structure and ICT Strategies in the Brazilian Judiciary System. *Government Information Quarterly*, *29*(1), S32–S42. doi:10.1016/j.giq.2011.08.003

Angles, R., & Gutierrez, C. (2008). Survey of Graph Database Models. *ACM Computing Surveys*, *40*(1), 1–39. doi:10.1145/1322432.1322433

Anti-Drug Special Provisions Law, 1991, Law no.94 of 1991.

Aragón Reyes, M. (2013, July-December). Dos problemas falsos y uno verdadero: neoconstitucionalismo, garantismo y aplicación judicial de la constitución. *Cuestiones Constitucionales, 2013*(29), 3-25.

Archmann, S., & Kudlacek, I. (2008). Interoperability and the Exchange of Good Practice Cases. *European Journal of ePractice, 2*(February), 3-12.

Arial, D.L. (2001). History of the Federal Judiciary Website: Washington, DC: The Federal Judicial Center. Accessed May 2000. *Journal of Government Information*, *28*(3), 351–353.

Asiimwe, E. N., & Lim, N. (2010). Usability of Government Websites in Uganda. *Electronic. Journal of E-Government*, *8*(1), 1–12.

Asociación por los Derechos Civiles (ADC). (2009). *Acceso a la información y transparencia en el poder judicial. Guía de buenas prácticas en América Latina.* Buenos Aires, Argentina: ADC.

Auld, F. C. (1935). The Comparative Jurisprudence of Criminal Process. *University of Toronto Law Journal*, *1*(1), 82–103. doi:10.2307/823869

Baca, R. L., ... (1971). Automated Court Systems. In *Proceedings of the Fall Joint Computer Conference*. New York, NY: ACM. Available at: http://doi.acm.org/10.1145/1479064.1479120

Baeza-Yates, R., & Ribeiro-Neto, B. (1999). *Modern Information Retrieval* (1st ed.). Addison Wesley.

Barak, A. (2010). Proportionality and principled balancing. *Law & Ethics of Human Rights*, 1-16.

Bargh, M. S., & Choenni, S. (2013). On preserving privacy whilst integrating data in connected information systems. In *Proceedings of the International Conference on Cloud Security Management* (ICCSM'13).

Bargh, M. S., Choenni, S., & Meijer, R., R. (2015). Privacy and information sharing in a judicial setting: A Wicked Problem. In *Proceedings of the 6th Annual International Conference on Digital Government Research* (DG.O'15). doi:10.1145/2757401.2757425

Bargh, M. S., Choenni, S., Meijer, R., & Conradie, P. (2014). Privacy protection in data sharing: towards feedback based solutions. In *Proceedings of the 8th International Conference on Theory and Practice of Electronic Governance* (ICEGOV'14). doi:10.1145/2691195.2691279

Barral-Viñals, I., & Suquet Capdevila, J. (2010). La mediación en el ámbito del consumo. In P. Casanovas, E. Lauroba & J. Magre (Eds.), *Libro Blanco de la mediación en Cataluña* (pp. 301-450). Barcelona: Huygens. Retrieved from www.llibreblancmediacio.com

Barral-Viñals, I. (2011). E-consumers and effective protection: the online dispute resolution system. In M. Kenny & J. Deveney (Eds.), *European Consumer Protection. Theory and Practice* (pp. 82–98). Cambridge, UK: Cambridge University Press.

Barral-Viñals, I. (2014). Reclamaciones de consumo y ODR: Procesos automáticos, small claims y plataformas interactivas. *Revista Aranzadi de Derecho y Nuevas Tecnologías*, *34*, 43–65.

Becker, S. A. (2004). E-government visual accessibility for older adult users. *Social Science Computer Review*, *22*(1), 11–23. doi:10.1177/0894439303259876

Bekkers, V. (2007). The Governance of Back Office Integration. *Public Management Review*, *9*(3), 377–400. doi:10.1080/14719030701425761

Benyekhelf, K., & Gélinas, F. (2005). Online Dispute Resolution. *Lex Electronica*, *10*(2), 1-129. Retrieved from http://www.lex-electronica.org/articles/v10-2/Benyekhlef_Gelinas.pdf

Bényekhlef, K. (2010). La résolution en ligne des différends de consommation: un récit autour (et un exemple) du droit postmoderne. In *L'accés des consommateurs à la justice* (pp. 89–119). Cowansville, Canada: Éditions Yvon Blais.

Bertot, J., McDermott, P., & Smith, T. (2012). Measurement of open government: Metrics and process.*45th Hawaii International Conference on System Sciences* (pp. 2491-2499). IEEE Computer Society. doi:10.1109/HICSS.2012.658

Biber, K. (2014). Inside Jill Meagher's Handbag: Looking at Open Justice. *Alternative Law Journal*, *39*(2), 73–77.

Bickle, A. (1962). *The Least Dangerous Branch: The Supreme Court at the Bar of Politics*. Binghamton, NY: Bobbs-Merrill Company, Inc.

Big Data for Law. (2016). Retrieved February 22, 2016, from http://www.legislation.gov.uk/projects/big-data-for-law

Bobbio, N. (1994). The Future of Democracy. In *The Polity Reader in Social Theory* (pp. 295–303). Cambridge: Polity Press.

BO-ECLI. (2016). Retrieved February 22, 2016, from http://www.ittig.cnr.it/progetti/bo-ecli/

Bollacker, K. (2012). Avoiding a Digital Dark Age. *American Scientist*, *98*.

Bradley, C. M. et al.. (1996). The Convergence of the Continental and the Common Law Model of Criminal Procedure. *Criminal Law Forum*, *7*(2), 471–484. doi:10.1007/BF02197174

Braun, W. (2002). The System Archetypes. *System*, 27.

Burwell, S. M., Roekel, S., Part, T., & Mancini, D. J. (2013). *Open data policy – managing information as an asset* (White House Memorandum on Open Data Policy, May 9). Retrieved June 29, 2015, from https://www.whitehouse.gov/sites/default/files/omb/memoranda/2013/m-13-13.pdf

Büyüközkan, G. (2009). Evaluating Government Websites Using a Multi-Criteria Decision Making Approach. In *9th European Conference on e-Government*. London, UK: Academic Publishing Limited.

Cabral, J. E., Chavan, A., Clarke, T. M., & Greacen, J. (2012). Using Technology to Enhance Access to Justice. *Harvard Journal of Law & Technology*, *26*, 241.

Calderón, C. (2012). Por qué un Gobierno Abierto. In A. Naser & G. Concha (Eds.), El desafío hacia el gobierno abierto en la hora de la igualdad (pp. 27–47). Santiago, Chile: CEPAL. Retrieved from http://www.cepal.org/es/publicaciones/3969-el-desafio-hacia-el-gobierno-abierto-en-la-hora-de-la-igualdad

Canada, National Action Committee on Access to Justice in Civil and Family Matters, Access to Civil and Family Justice: A Roadmap for Change, Ottawa. (n.d.). Retrieved 23, June, 2015, from http://www.cfcj-fcjc.org/sites/default/files/docs/2013/AC_Report_English_Final.pdf

Cano, J., Hernandez, R., & Ros, S. (2014, October). Distributed Framework for Electronic Democracy in Smart Cities. *Computer*, *47*(10), 65–71. doi:10.1109/MC.2014.280

Cano, J., Jimenez, C., Hernandez, R., & Ros, S. (2015). New tools for e-justice: legal research available to any citizen.*Second International Conference on eDemocracy & eGovernment (ICEDEG), 2015* (pp. 108-111). Quito: IEEE. doi:10.1109/ICEDEG.2015.7114455

Cappelleti, M., & Garth, B. (1978). Access to justice: The wordlwide movement to make rights effective- A general report. In Access to justice (pp. 1-30). Alpenn aan den Rhijn: Sijthoff and Noordhoff.

Carothers, T. (2008). Democracy Assistance: Political vs. Developmental? *Journal of Democracy*, *20*(1), 5–19. doi:10.1353/jod.0.0047

Casper, G., & Zeisel, H. (1972). Lay judges in the German criminal courts. *The Journal of Legal Studies*, *1*(1), 135–191. doi:10.1086/467481

Castells, M. (1996). *The rise of the network society*. Cambridge, UK: Blackwell Publishers, Inc.

Castells, M. (Forthcoming). Rethinking development in the global information age. In J. Muller (Ed.), *Higher education and development*. Cape Town, South Africa: African Minds.

Castells, M., Chacón, I., & Himanen, P. (2014). Toward a Welfare State 2.0? The Crisis and Renewal of the European Welfare State. In M. Castells, I. Chacón, & P. Himanen (Eds.), *Reconceptualising development in the global information age* (pp. 89–115). Oxford, UK: Oxford University Press. doi:10.1093/acprof:oso/9780198716082.003.0005

CEPEJ. (2006). European Judicial Systems. Belgium: Council of Europe.

Cerrillo, A., & Fabra, P. (2009). *E-Justice: Using Information Communication Technologies in the Court System*. Hershey, PA: IGI Global.

Cerrilo, A., & Fabra, P. (2009). *E-justice: Using Information Communication Technologies in the Court System*. Hershey, PA: IGI Global.

Chapman, R. A., & Hunt, M. (1987). *Open government. A study of the prospects of open government within the limitations of the British political system*. Londres: Routledge.

Chapman, R. A., & Hunt, M. (2006). *Open Government in a theroretical and practical context*. Surrey: Ashgate.

Chapman, R., & Hunt, M. (2006). *Open Government in a Theoretical and Practical Context*. Surrey: Ashgate.

Chappell, Z. (2011). Justifying deliberative democracy: Are two heads always wiser than one? *Contemporary Political Theory*, *10*(1), 78–101. doi:10.1057/cpt.2010.8

Charalabidis, Y. (2011). *Interoperability in Digital Public Services and Administration. Bridging e-Government and e-Business*. Hershey, PA: IGI Global. doi:10.4018/978-1-61520-887-6

Chatzopoulos, K.-C. & Economides, A.A., (2009). A holistic evaluation of Greek municipalities' websites. *Electronic Government, an International Journal*, *6*(2), 193–212.

Chesbrough, H., Vanhaverbeke, W., Bakici, T., & López, H. (2011). *Open innovation and public policy in Europe*. ESADE Business School & the Science I Business Innovation Board AISBL. Science Business.

Chesbrough, H. (2003). The Era of Open Innovation. *MIT Sloan Management Review*, *44*(3), 35–41.

Chesbrough, H. (2006). *Open Innovation: The New Imperative from Creating and Profiting from Technology*. Boston, MA: Harvard Business School Press.

Choenni, S., Bargh, M. S., Roepan, C., & Meijer, R. (2015). Privacy and security in data collection by citizens. In Smarter as the new urban agenda: a comprehensive view of the 21st century city. Springer.

Choenni, S., van Dijk, J., & Leeuw, F. (2010). Preserving privacy whilst integrating data: Applied to criminal justice. Information Polity, 15(1-2), 125-138.

Choi, J. S. (2014). Korean Citizen Participation in Criminal Trials: The Present Situation and Problems. *International Journal of Law, Crime and Justice*, *42*(2), 83–102. doi:10.1016/j.ijlcj.2013.07.003

Chun, S. A., Shulman, S., Sandoval, R., & Hovy, E. (2010). Government 2.0: Making connections between citizens, data and government. *Information Polity*, *15*(1-2), 1–9.

Cini, M., & Borragan, N. N. P. (2013). *European Union Politics*. Oxford, UK: Oxford University Press.

Civil Procedure Code, 1996, Law no.109 of 1996.

Civil Procedure Law of the People's Republic of China (中华人民共和国民事诉讼法), passed, issued on, and effective as of April 9, 1991, subsequently amended in 2007 and 2012. Retrieved from http://www.npc.gov.cn/wxzl/wxzl/2000-12/05/content_4551.htm

Clarke, T. (2008). *A Unifying Framework for Court Performance Measurement: Final Report*. Williamsburg, VA: National Center for State Courts.

Clarke, T. (2011). *High Performance Courts: Organizational Effectiveness and Enhanced Attorney Advocacy. Unpublished proposal to the Bureau of Justice Assistance*. National Center for State Courts.

CoA Report. (2015). *Trendrapport open data 2015* (in Dutch). Technical Report, Court of Audit of The Netherlands (Algemene Rekenkamer in Dutch, March 31). Retrieved June 29, 2015, from http://www.rekenkamer.nl/Publicaties/Onderzoeksrapporten/Introducties/2015/03/Trendrapport_open_data_2015

Cohendet, P., Creplet, F., & Dupouët, O. (2002). *Communities of oractice and epistemic communities: A renewed approach of organisational learning within the firm*. Strasbourg, France: Universitè Louis Pateur.

Cohen-Tanugi, L. (2016). Case law in a legal system without binding precedent: The French example? *Stanford Law School China Guiding Cases Project: Guiding Cases Commentaries*. Retrieved from http://cgc.law.stanford.edu/commentaries/16-Laurent-Cohen-Tanugi

COM. (2011). *Communication From The Commission To The European Parliament, The Council, The European Economic And Social Committee And The Committee Of The Regions Open data An engine for innovation, growth and transparent governance*. COM/2011/0882 final.

Commission on Trial Court Performance Standards. (1997). Trial Court Performance Standards with Commentary. U.S. Department of Justice, Bureau of Justice Assistance.

Commission's Green Paper, 16 November 1993, on access of consumers to justice and the settlement of consumer disputes in the single market - COM(93) 576 Final.

Conley, A., Datta, A., Nissenbaum, H., & Sharma, D. (2012). Sustaining privacy and open justice in the transition to online court records: A multidisciplinary inquiry. *Maryland Law Review (Baltimore, Md.)*, *71*(3), 772–847.

Conradie, P., & Choenni, S. (2014). On the barriers for local government releasing open data. Government Information Quarterly, 31, 10–17. doi:10.1016/j.giq.2014.01.003

Constitution of the People's Republic of China (中华人民共和国宪法), passed and issued on December 4, 1982, effective as of Dec. 4, 1982, subsequently amended in 1988, 1992, 1999, and 2004. Retrieved from http://www.npc.gov.cn/wxzl/wxzl/2000-12/06/content_4421.htm

Contini, F., & Cordella, A. (2007). Information System and Information Infrastructure Deployment: The Challenge of the Italian e-Justice Approach. *Electronic Journal of E-Government*, *5*(1), 43–52.

Contini, F., & Lanzara, G. F. (Eds.). (2014). *The Circulation of Agency in e-Justice. Interoperability and Infrastructures for European Transborder Judicial Proceedings*. New York: Springer. doi:10.1007/978-94-007-7525-1

Corrêa, A. S., Corrêa, P. L. P., & da Silva, F. S. C. (2014, November 23). Transparency Portals Versus Open Government Data: An Assessment of Openness in Brazilian Municipalities. *Proceedings of the 15th Annual International Conference on Digital Government Research (dg.o 2014)*. http://doi.org/ doi:10.1145/2612733.2612760

Cortés, P. (2011). *Online Dispute Resolution for Consumers in the EU*. Oxon, UK: Routledge.

Cortés, P., & Esteban de la Rosa, F. (2013). Building a global redress system for low value crossborder disputes. *The International and Comparative Law Quarterly*, *62*(2), 407–440. doi:10.1017/S0020589313000109

Council of State Archivists. (2012). *State Electronic Records Initiative, Phase I*. Retrieved July 2, 2015 from http://www.statearchivists.org/seri/SERI%20Phase%20One%20Report%20-%20final%20review%20draft%20-%202012-06.pdf

Council of the European Union. (2013). *Draft Strategy on European E-Justice 2014-2018 (No. 2013/C 376/06)*. Council of the European Union.

Council of the European Union. (2014). *Multiannual European E-Justice Action Plan 2014-2018 (No. 2014/C 182/02)*. Council of the European Union.

Council of the European Union. (2014). *Multiannual European e-Justice Action Plan 2014-2018, 2014/C 182/02*. Author.

Criado, I. (2009). Gobierno Electrónico en Latinoamérica. Aproximación Desde una Perspectiva Intergubernamental. *Estado, Gobierno, Gestión Pública. Revista Chilena de Administración Pública*, *14*(December), 9–35.

Criado, I., Gascó, M., & Jiménez, C. E. (2010). *Marco Iberoamericano de Interoperabilidad*. Caracas: CLAD.

Crime Spotting. (2015). *Website providing crime information for San Francisco*. Retrieved June 29, 2015 from http://sanfrancisco.crimespotting.org

Criminal Procedure Law of the People's Republic of China (中华人民共和国刑事诉讼法), passed on July 1, 1979, issued on July 7, 1979, effective as of January 1, 1980, subsequently amended in 1996 and 2012. Retrieved from http://www.npc.gov.cn/wxzl/wxzl/2000-12/06/content_4373.htm

CSTAF. (2015). *Conselho Superior dos Tribunais Administrativos e Fiscais - Dados Processuais da Jurisdição*. Retrieved May 28, 2015, from http://www.cstaf.pt/Paginas/Estatistica-Processual.aspx

Danish National Archives. (2013). *Strategies for Archiving Digital Records at the Danish National Archives*. Retrieved May 10, 2015 from https://www.sa.dk/en/wp-content/uploads/sites/2/2014/12/Strategy-for-archiving-digital-records-2013.pdf

Darbyshire, P. 1997. An Essay on the Importance and Neglect of the Magistracy. Criminal Law Review, (Sep.), pp.627–643.

Darbyshire, P., Maughan, A., & Stewart, A. 2002. What Can the English Legal System Learn from Jury Research Published up to 2001? *Research Paper in Law*, (1), 1–84. Available at: http://eprints.kingston.ac.uk/23/1/Darbyshire-P-23.pdf

Darbyshire, P. (1991). The Lamp That Shows That Freedom Lives—Is It Worth the Candle? *Criminal Law Review (London, England)*, (11): 740–752.

Data.gov. (2015). *The home of the U.S. government's open data*. Retrieved June 29, 2015 from http://www.data.gov

Data.police.uk. (2015). *Website provisioned by UK police*. Retrieved June 29, 2015 from https://data.police.uk/

Dawes, S. S. (2008). The Evolution and Continuing Challenges of E-Governance. *Public Administration Review*, *68*, S86–S102. doi:10.1111/j.1540-6210.2008.00981.x

Dawes, S. S., Cresswell, A. M., & Pardo, T. A. (2009). From "Need to Know" to "Need to Share: Tangled Problems, Information Boundaries, and the Building of Public Sector Knowledge Networks. *Public Administration Review*, *69*(3), 392–402. doi:10.1111/j.1540-6210.2009.01987_2.x

Dawes, S., & Pardo, T. (2002). Building Collaborative Digital Government Systems. In W. J. McIver & A. K. Elmagarmid (Eds.), *Advances in Digital Government: Technology, Human Factors, and Policy* (pp. 259–273). New York: Springer. doi:10.1007/0-306-47374-7_16

De los Ríos, N. (2010). Los nuevos liderazgos. In C. Calderón & S. Lorenzo (Eds.), *Open government* (pp. 185–197). Granada: Algón Editores.

Dean, M. (1995). Trial by Jury: A Force for Change in Japan. *The International and Comparative Law Quarterly*, *44*(2), 379–404. doi:10.1093/iclqaj/44.2.379

Deb, G. K. (1999). Electronic governance - A vehicle for the new world order. *Electronics Information & Planning*, *27*(1), 29–33.

Decision of the CPC Central Committee on Major Issues Concerning Comprehensively Deepening Reforms. (中共中央关于全面深化改革若干重大问题的决定), passed by the Eighteenth CPC Central Committee on November 12, 2013. Retrieved from http://cpc.people.com.cn/n/2013/1115/c64094-23559163.html

Decision of the CPC Central Committee on Several Major Issues Pertaining to Comprehensively Promoting the Rule of Law. (中共中央关于全面推进依法治国若干重大问题的决定), passed by the Eighteenth CPC Central Committee on October 23, 2014. Retrieved from http://cpc.people.com.cn/n/2014/1029/c64387-25927606.html

Decision of the Supreme People's Court on Further Strengthening the Basic Construction of People's Courts (最高人民法院关于进一步加强人民法院基层建设的决定), issued by the Supreme People's Court October 21, 2014. Retrieved from http://www.pkulaw.com/fulltext_form.aspx?Db=chl&Gid=108953&keyword=关于进一步加强人民法院基层建设的决定&EncodingName=&Search_Mode=accurate.

Defeis, E. F. (2000). Human Rights and the European Union: Who Decides-Possible Conflicts between the European Court of Justice and the European Court of Human Rights. *Dickinson International Law Annual*, *19*, 301–531.

Demeulenaere, B. (1987). La médiation et les droits du consommateur. *Windsor Yearbook of Access to Justice*, *7*, 118–128.

Department of Justice. (2015). *Open Data.* Website of the US Department of Justice. Retrieved June 29, 2015 from http://www.justice.gov/open/open-data

Detailed Implementing Rules on the. "Provisions of the Supreme People's Court Concerning Work on Case Guidance" (〈最高人民法院关于案例指导工作的规定〉实施细则), passed by the Adjudication Committee of the Supreme People's Court on April 27, 2015, issued on and effective as of May 13, 2015. (Stanford Law School China Guiding Cases Project, English Guiding Cases Rules, June 12, 2015 Edition). Retrieved from http://cgc.law.stanford.edu/guiding-cases-rules/20150513-english/

DGPJ. (2015a). *Direção-Geral da Política da Justiça - Projecto Hermes*. Retrieved May 28, 2015, from www.siej.dgpj.mj.pt

DGPJ. (2015b). *Resultados de 2014: Nota técnica*. Retrieved May 28, 2015, from http://www.siej.dgpj.mj.pt/SIEJ/PDFs/Tribunais/Resultados2014notatecnica.pdf

Diez, C., & Prenafeta, J. (2002). E-Government Applied to Judicial Notices and Inter-Registrar Communications in the European Union: The AEQUITAS Project. In *Electronic Government: Proceedings of the 1st International Conference, EGOV 2002*. Retrieved from http://www.springerlink.com/openurl.asp?genre=article&id=N6KCG770FN7795V5

Dinan, D. (2004). *Ever closer union: an introduction to European integration* (3rd ed.). Boulder, CO: Lynn Rienner Publisher.

Dollar, C. M., & Ashley, L. J. (2013). *Assessing Digital Preservation Capability Using a Maturity Model Process Improvement Approach.* Retrieved May 10, 2015 from http://www.nycarchivists.org/Resources/Documents/Dollar-Ashley_2013_DPCMM%20White%20Paper_NAGARA%20Digital%20Judicial%20Records_8Feb2013-1.pdf

Donker-Kuijer, M. W., de Jong, M., & Lentz, L. (2010). Usable guidelines for usable websites? An analysis of five e-government heuristics. *Government Information Quarterly*, *27*(3), 254–263. doi:10.1016/j.giq.2010.02.006

Duggan, A. (2003). Consumer access to justice in common law countries: a survey of the issues from a law and economics perspective. In C. Rickett & T. Telfer (Eds.), *International perspectives on consumers' access to justice* (pp. 66–90). Cambridge, UK: CUP.

Dyson, J. (2013). *Advances in open justice in England and Wales. Hong Kong, China,* Retrieved 14, June 2015, from https://www.judiciary.gov.uk/wp-content/uploads/JCO/Documents/Speeches/mr-speech-hong-kong-lecture-18102013.pdf

Dyson, J. (2013). *Advances in open justice in England and Wales.* Hong Kong: Master of the Rolls.

Dzur, A. W. (2012). Participatory Democracy and Criminal Justice. *Criminal Law and Philosophy*, *6*(2), 115–129. doi:10.1007/s11572-012-9149-x

ECMA International. (2012). ECMA-376, Office Open XML File Formats - Fundamentals and Markup Language Reference (4th ed.). Author.

Economides, A.A. & Terzis, V., (2008). Evaluating tax sites: an evaluation framework and its application. *Electronic Government, an International Journal*, *5*(3), 321–344.

Eisenberg, T., & Wells, T. (2002). Trial Outcomes and Demographics: Is There A Bronx Effect? *Texas Law Review*, *80*(7), 1839–1876.

Elena, S. (2015). *Datos Abiertos para una Justicia Abierta: Un Análisis de caso de los Poderes Judiciales De Brasil, Costa Rica, México y Perú.* Buenos Aires, Argentina: Iniciativa Latinoamericana por los Datos Abiertos (ILDA).

Elena, S., Aquilino, N., & Pichón Riviere, A. (2014). *Case Study: Emerging Impacts in Open Data in the Judiciary Branches in Argentina, Chile and Uruguay*. Buenos Aires, Argentina: CIPPEC.

Elena, S., & Pichón Rivière, A. (2012). *Imparcial, pero no invìsible: justicia, transparencia y gobierno abierto.* Buenos Aires, Argentina: CIPPEC.

Elena, S., & Pichón Rivière, A. (2013). *Acceso a la información y transparencia en la justicia: un recorrido que recién comienza.* Buenos Aires, Argentina: CIPPEC.

Elling, S., Lentz, L., & de Jong, M. (2007). Website Evaluation Questionnaire: Development of a Research-Based Tool for Evaluating Informational Websites. In *6th International Conference, EGOV 2007*. Regensburg, Germany: Springer Berlin/Heidelberg. doi:10.1007/978-3-540-74444-3_25

Ellis, L., & Diamond, S. S. (2003). Race, Diversity, and Jury Composition: Battering and Bolstering Legitimacy. *Chicago-Kent Law Review*, *78*(3), 1033–1060.

Elmasri, R., & Navathe, S. (2004). *Fundamentals of Database Systems* (4th ed.). Addison Wesley.

Esakov, G. (2012). The Russian Criminal Jury: Recent Developments, Practice, and Current Problems. *The American Journal of Comparative Law*, *60*(3), 665–702. doi:10.5131/AJCL.2011.0031

ESPAP. (2015). *GeADAP - Avaliação de Serviços*. Retrieved May 28, 2015, from https://www.siadap.gov.pt/Paginas-Publicas/Servicos.aspx

Espluques Mota, C. (2013). Hacia una nueva noción de "Acceso a la justicia" en la EU a través del fomento del recurso a los mecanismos de ADR: la Directiva 2008/52/CE y su transposición en los diferentes estados miembros. In J. Forner, C. González, & R. Viñas (Eds.), *Estudios sobre la unificación internacional y regional del Derecho internacional privado, Liber Amicorum Alegria Borrás* (pp. 351–376). Barcelona: Marcial Pons Editores.

Estrella, R. (2010). Diplomacia Abierta - Nueva Diplomacia. In C. Calderón & S. Lorenzo (Eds.), *Open government* (pp. 143–163). Granada, Spain: Algón Editores.

EUCases. (2016). Retrieved February 22, 2016, from http://www.eucases.eu/

European Commission for Efficiency of Justice. (2008). *Checklist for promoting the quality of justice and the courts*. Council of Europe. Strasbourg.

European Commission. (1995). *Directive 95/46/EC of the European Parliament and of the Council of 24 October 1995 on the protection of individuals with regard to the processing of personal data and on the free movement of such data, OJ L 281/31*. Author.

European Commission. (2001). *Summary Report: Web-based Survey on Electronic Public Services* (Results of the first measurement: October 2001). Author.

European Commission. (2003). *Directive 2003/98/EC of the European Parliament and of the Council of 17 November 2003 on the re-use of public sector information, OJ L 345/90*. Author.

European Commission. (2007, September). The User Challenge Benchmarking The Supply Of Online Public Services. *Measurement*.

European Commission. (2008). Communication from the Commission to the Council, the European Parliament and the European Economic and Social Committee: Towards a European e-Justice Strategy (No. COM(2008)329 final). Brussels: European Commission.

European Commission. (2008). *Towards a European e-Justice*. Brussels: Communication from the Commission to the Council, the European Parliament and the European Economic and Social Committee.

European Commission. (2009). *Smarter, Faster, Better eGovernment (8th Benchmark Measurement | November 2009)*. Directorate General for Information Society and Media.

European Commission. (2010). *European Interoperability Framework for European Public Services (EIF)*. Brussels: European Commission.

European Commission. (2010a). *Digitizing Public Services in Europe: Putting ambition into action (9th Benchmark Measurement | December 2010)*. Author.

European Commission. (2010b). The European eGovernment Action Plan 2011-2015 : Harnessing ICT to promote smart, sustainable & innovative Government (No. COM(2010) 743). Brussels: European Commission.

European Commission. (2011). eGovernment Benchmark Pilot on Open Government and Transparency: Measuring the potential of eGovernment to foster Open Government and Transparency in Europe. Brussels: European Commission.

European Commission. (2011). *Open data: An engine for innovation, growth and transparent governance*. COM(2011) 882.

European Commission. (2012). *eGovernment Benchmark Framework 2012-2015: Method Paper*. Directorate General for Information Society and Media.

European Commission. (2013). *Directive 2013/37/EU of the European Parliament and of the Council of 26 June 2013 amending Directive 2003/98/EC on the re-use of public sector information, OJ L 175/1*. Author.

European Commission. (2013). *Public Services Online: "Digital by Default or by Detour?". Assessing User Centric eGovernment performance in Europe – eGovernment Benchmark 2012*. European Commission.

European Commission. (2014). *Guidelines on recommended standard licences, datasets and charging for the reuse of documents* (2014/C 240/01). Author.

European Commission. (2014a). Delivering the European Advantage? "How European governments can and should benefit from innovative public services" (eGovernment Benchmark Final Background Report - May 2014). Brussels: Author.

European Commission. (2014b). *Delivering the European Advantage? "How European governments can and should benefit from innovative public services" (Portugal: eGovernment State of Play - May 2014)*. Author.

European Commission. (2015a). *e-Government factsheets. eGovernment in Portugal 2015* (No. January 2015, Edition 17.0). Brussels: European Commission. Retrieved from https://joinup.ec.europa.eu/sites/default/files/egov_in_portugal_-_january_2015_-_v_17_0_final.pdf

European Commission. (2015b). The 2015 EU Justice Scoreboard (No. COM(2015) 116). Brussels: European Commission.

European Economic and Social Committee. Opinion of the European Economic and Social Committee on the "Communication from the Commission to the Council, the European Parliament and the European Economic and Social Committee: Towards a European e-Justice Strategy"COM(2008) 329 final, 32 Organization 1–7 (2009).

Exploring the Emerging Impacts of Open Data in Developing Countries (ODDC). (2013). *Researching the emerging impacts of open data*. Washington, DC: World Wide Web Foundation. Retrieved from http://www.opendataresearch.org/sites/default/files/posts/Researching%20the%20emerging%20impacts%20of%20open%20data.pdf

Eynon, R., & Margetts, H. (2007). Organizational solutions for overcoming barriers to e-government. *European Journal of ePractice, 1*(November), 73-85.

Fabri, M. (2009). The Italian Style of E-Justice in a Comparative Perspective. In A. C. i Martínez & P. F. i Abat (Eds.), E-Justice: Using Information Communication Technologies in the Court System (pp. 1–19). IGI Global.

Fagan, J. (2008). Legitimacy and Criminal Justice. *Ohio State Journal of Criminal Law*, *6*(1), 123–140.

Fallows, J. (1994). *Looking at the Sun: The Rise of the New East Asian Economic and Political System*. New York: Pantheon.

Fashion Times. (2015). *Sony Announces 185TB Tape Storage*. Retrieved June 29, 2015 from http://www.fashiontimes.com/articles/6415/20140506/sony-announces-185tb-cassette-tape-storage.htm

Fernando, P., Gomes, C., & Fernandes, D. (2013). Citius: the Electronic Payment Order Procedure in Portugal. In F. Contini & G. F. Lanzara (Eds.), *Building Interoperability for European Civil Proceedings Online* (pp. 215–272). Bologna: Clueb.

Fernando, P., Gomes, C., & Fernandes, D. (2014). The Piecemeal Development of an e-Justice Platform: The CITIUS Case in Portugal. In *The Circulation of Agency in E-Justice* (pp. 137–159). Springer. doi:10.1007/978-94-007-7525-1_6

Fesler, J. W., & Kettl, D. F. (1996). *The politics of the administrative process*. Chatham, NJ: Chatham House Publishers, Inc.

Fishkin, J. (1997). *The Voice of the People*. New Haven, CT: Yale University Press.

Five-Year Reform Plan of the People's Court (人民法院五年改革纲要), issued by the Supreme People's Court on October 20, 1999. Retrieved from http://www.chinacourt.org/article/detail/2013/04/id/941425.shtml

Foote, D. H. (2007). *Nameless Faceless Justice* [Na mo nai kao mo nai shiho]. Tokyo: Yuhikaku.

Foqué, R. (2008). Criminal Justice in a Democracy: Towards a Relational Conception of Criminal Law and Punishment. *Criminal Law and Philosophy*, *2*(3), 207–227. doi:10.1007/s11572-008-9063-4

Fountain, J. (1995). *Enacting technology. An institutional perspective*. Cambridge, MA: John F. Kennedy School of Government.

Fountain, J. (2001). *Building the virtual state. Information technology and institutional change*. Washington, DC: Brookings Institution Press.

Franklin, M., Halevy, A., & Maier, D. (2005). From databases to data spaces: A new abstraction for information management. *Special Interest Group on Management of Data (SIGMOD) Record, 34*(4).

Fukurai, H., Knudtson, C. R., & Lopez, S. I. (2009). Is Mexico Ready for a Jury Trial?: Comparative Analysis of Lay Justice Systems in Mexico, the United States, Japan, New Zealand, South Korea, and Ireland. *Mexican Law Review*, *11*, 3–44.

Galvão, S. (2009). *Funcionamento dos Tribunais Administrativos e Fiscais*. Lisbon.

Gamero, E. (2012). El objeto de la Ley 18/2011 y su posición entre las normas relativas a las tecnologías de la información. In *Las tecnologías de la información y la comunicación en la Administración de Justicia. Análisis sistemático de la Ley 18/2011, de 5 de julio* (pp. 45–88). Pamplona: Aranzadi.

Gant, J. P., & Gant, D. B. (2002). Web portal functionality and State government E-service. In *Proceedings of the 35th Annual Hawaii International Conference on System Sciences (HICSS'02)*. Waikoloa, Hawaii: IEEE Computer Society. doi:10.1109/HICSS.2002.994073

Garapon, A. (1997). *Bien juger – Essai sur le ritual judiciaire*. Paris: Odyle Jacob.

Garson, D. (2006). *Public information technology and e-governance. Managing the virtual state*. Sudbury, MA: Jones and Bartlett Publishers.

Gascó, M. (2010). Los retos de la colaboración. ¿A qué, si no a eso, pretendemos hacer frente con la interoperabilidad? Paper presented at the XV CLAD Conference. Santo Domingo.

Gascó, M., & Jiménez, C. E. (2011). *Interoperability in the justice field: variables that affect implementation*. Paper presented at the 11th European Conference on e-Government. Ljubljana.

Gascó, M., & Jiménez, C. E. (2011). Interoperability in the Justice Field: Variables that Affect Implementation1. In *Proceedings of the 11th European Conference on EGovernment* (p. 272). Academic Conferences Limited.

Gascó, M., & Sierra, V. (2015). *Technological innovation projects.The role of management and network governance in e-government interoperability*. Paper presented at IRSPM 2015. Birmingham.

Gascó, M., Esteve, M., & Fernández, Ch. (2013). *Managing e-government interoperability.Abandoning projects to develop real management models*. Paper presented at PMRC 2013. Madison, WI.

Gascó, M. (2009). El papel de las instituciones en el desarrollo del gobierno electrónico en América Latina: Algunas reflexiones. *Estado, Gobierno. Gestión Pública*, *14*, 37–59.

Gascó, M. (2014). *Guía de buenas prácticas en gobierno abierto*. Bogota: Observatics.

Gavelin, K., Burall, S., & Wilson, R. (2009). *Open Government: Beyond Static Measures.* Paper produced by Involve for the OECD. Retrieved from http://www.oecd.org/gov/46560184.pdf

Gechlik, M. (2015). *Stanford Law School China Guiding Cases Project:* Guiding Cases *Analytics*™, Issue no. 4. Retrieved from http://cgc.law.stanford.edu/guiding-cases-analytics/

Gechlik, M., Philips, D., & Lee, O. (2014). Survey of judges in China (2013-2014). *Stanford Law School China Guiding Cases Project: Guiding Cases Surveys™, Issue No. 1*. Retrieved from http://cgc.law.stanford.edu/guiding-cases-surveys

Gechlik, M., Zhang, M., & Ye, L. (2016). Cumulative analysis of all subsequent cases referring to Guiding Cases in China (2014 Q1-2015 Q4). *Stanford Law School China Guiding Cases Project: Guiding Cases Surveys™, Issue No. 2*. Retrieved from http://cgc.law.stanford.edu/guiding-cases-surveys

Giard, M., & Proulx, M. (1985). *Pour comprendre l'appareil judiciaire québequois*. PUQ.

Gil-García, J. R. (2012). *Enacting electronic government success: An integrative study of government-wide websites, organizational capabilities, and institutions*. Heidelberg, Germany: Springer. doi:10.1007/978-1-4614-2015-6

Gil-García, J. R., & Helbig, N. (2006). Exploring e-government benefits and success factors. In A.-V. Anttoroiko & M. Mälkiä (Eds.), *Encyclopedia of Digital Government* (pp. 803–811). Hershey, PA: IGI Global. doi:10.4018/978-1-59140-789-8.ch122

Gil-García, J. R., & Pardo, T. (2005). E-government success factors: Mapping practical tools to theoretical foundations. *Government Information Quarterly*, *22*(2), 187–216. doi:10.1016/j.giq.2005.02.001

Glassey, O., & Gordon, T. F. (2005). Feasibility Study for a Legal Knowledge System in the County of Herford. In *Electronic Government: 4th International Conference (EGOV 2005)*. Berlin: Springer.

Gobert, J. 1997. Justice, Democracy and the Jury, Aldershot: Aldershot.

Goff, L. (1997). The Future of the Common Law. *The International and Comparative Law Quarterly*, *46*(4), 745–760. doi:10.1017/S0020589300061194

Gordon, T. F. (2007). Legal Knowledge Systems. In A.-V. Anttiroiko & M. Mälkiä (Eds.), *Encyclopedia of digital government* (pp. 1161–1166). Hershey, PA: Idea Group Reference. doi:10.4018/978-1-59140-789-8.ch175

Gorham, U. (2012). State Courts, e-Filing, and Diffusion of Innovation: A Proposed Framework of Analysis. In *Proceedings of the 13th Annual International Conference on Digital Government Research*. New York, NY: ACM. doi:10.1145/2307729.2307767

Gottschalk, P., & Solli-Sæther, H. (2009). *E-Government interoperability and information resource integration: frameworks for aligned Development*. Hershey, PA: Information Science Reference. doi:10.4018/978-1-60566-648-8

Gramatikov, M. (2012). Measuring costs of ODR. In M. Gramatikov (Ed.), Costs & quality of Online dispute resolution (pp. 125-133). Maklu.

Granickas, K. (2013). Understanding the impact of releasing and re-using open government data. Topic report no. 2013/08. European Public Sector Information Platform. Brussels, Belgium: European Union. Retrieved from http://www.epsiplatform.eu/sites/default/files/2013-08-Open_Data_Impact.pdf

Green, L. (2009). Legal Positivism. In *The Stanford Encyclopedia of Philosophy*. Retrieved 06, June, 2015 from http://plato.stanford.edu/archives/fall2009/entries/legal-positivism/

Groupe de travail sur l'accessibilité à la justice. (1991). *Jalons pour une plus grande accessibilité à la justice*. Sainte Foy, ministère de la Justice.

Guadamuz, A. (2009). Free Open Source Software. In L. Edwards & C. Waelde (Eds.), *Law and the Internet* (3rd ed.; pp. 359–391). Oxford, UK: Hart.

Guiding Opinion of the General Office of the State Council on the Promotion of Coordinated Development of E-Government Affairs. (国务院办公厅关于促进电子政务协调发展的指导意见), issued by the General Office of the State Council on and effective as of November 26, 2014. Retrieved from http://www.yueyang.gov.cn/zcfg2/content_437921.html

Guiding Opinion of the National Informatization Leading Group on the Development of E-Government Affairs in China. (国家信息化领导小组关于我国电子政务建设的指导意见), passed by the National Informatization Leading Group and issued by the General Office of the CPC Central Committee and the General Office of the State Council on August 5, 2002. Retrieved from http://www.nacao.org.cn/publish/main/77/2009/20090114135526965360659/20090114135526965360659_.html

Hammergren, L. (2011). Judicial governance and the use of ICT. In J. A. Caballero, C. G. De Grácia, & L. Hammergren (Eds.), Buenas prácticas para la implementación de soluciones tecnológicas en la Administración de Justicia. Mexico City, Mexico: Instituto de Investigación para la Justicia. Retrieved from http://www.iijusticia.org/docs/Linn.pdf

Harris, B. V. (1995). Equal Access to Justice: A Constitutional Principle in Need of a Higher Profile. *N.Z. L. Rev.*, *282*, 282–309.

Held, D. (1986). *New Forms of Democracy*. London: Sage.

Held, D. (1994). What Should Democracy Mean Today? In *The Polity Reader in Social Theory* (pp. 304–312). Cambridge: Polity Press.

Hengmin, L. I. (2014). Canada's open government policy study. *Technological Development of Enterprise*, *5*, 143–144.

Henriksson, A. T., Yi, Y., Forst, B., & Middleton, M. R. (2007). Evaluation instruments for e-government websites. *Electronic Government: An International Journal*, *4*(2), 204–226. doi:10.1504/EG.2007.013984

Henry, S. (2005). Shaping and Delivering Peace at the Local Level - Learning from the Experience of Peace II. In *Shaping and Deliberative Peace at Local Level?: Learning from the Experience of Peace II. Learning from Peace II* (pp. 8–13). Belfast: Community Relations Council.

Hiller, J. S., & Belanger, F. (2001). *Privacy Strategies for Electronic Government. The PricewaterhouseCoopers Endowment for The Business of Government. E-Government Series*. PricewaterhouseCoopers.

Hoke, G. (2012, May/June). *Future Watch: Strategies for Long-Term Preservation of Electronic Records. Information Management*.

Hongyu, W. C. (2016, February 3). Per-capita GDP of 10 Chinese provinces exceed $10,000 mark. *People's Daily Online*. Retrieved from http://en.people.cn/n3/2016/0203/c98649-9013481.html

Hörnle, J. (2009). Cross-border internet dispute resolution. *Lex electrónica*, *17*(2), 1-14.

Howard, R. (2013). *Smart government key initiative overview*. Report Gartner G00252076. Retrieved June 29, 2015 from https://www.gartner.com/doc/2520516/smart-government-key-initiative-overview

HUANG. Huifang (黄蕙芳). (2014). Taiwan's criminal case system and the development direction of the guiding cases system in the People's Republic of China (台湾刑事案例制度与中华人民共和国指 导性案例制度的发展方向). *Stanford Law School China Guiding Cases Project: Guiding Cases Commentaries*. Retrieved from http://cgc.law.stanford.edu/commentaries/11-huang-huifang

Huang, C. J. (2007). Accessibility of E-Government Web Sites. In *Encyclopedia of digital government* (pp. 11–15). Hershey, PA: Idea Group Reference. doi:10.4018/978-1-59140-789-8.ch002

Huang, K.-C., & Lin, C.-C. (2014). Mock Jury Trial in Taiwan- Paving the Gound for Introducing Lay Participation. *Law and Human Behavior*, *38*(4), 367–377. doi:10.1037/lhb0000080 PMID:24707909

Huntington, S. (1991). *The Third Wave: Democratization in the late twentieth century*. Norman: University of Oklahoma Press.

ICPSR. (2015). *Inter-university Consortium for Political and Social Research (ICPSR) of the University of Michigan.* Retrieved June 29, 2015 from https://www.icpsr.umich.edu/icpsrweb/landing.jsp

Iglesias, C. (2015). *The Benefits and Challenges of Measuring Open Data.* Retrieved from http://opendatacon.org/the-benefits-and-challenges-of-measuring-open-data

Iimura, T., Takabayashi, R., & Rademacher, C. (2015). The binding nature of court decisions in Japan's civil law system. *Stanford Law School China Guiding Cases Project: Guiding Cases Commentaries*. Retrieved from https://cgc.law.stanford.edu/commentaries/14-Iimura-Takabayashi-Rademacher

Inchausti, F. G. (2012). Electronic Service of Documents National and International Aspects. In M. Kengyel & Z. Nemessányi (Eds.), *Electronic Technology and Civil Procedure* (pp. 137–180). Dordrecht: Springer Netherlands; doi:10.1007/978-94-007-4072-3_8

Innovating Justice. (2016). Retrieved February 22, 2016, from https://innovatingjustice.com/en/

Institute of Electrical and Electronics Engineers. (1990). *Standard computer dictionary*. New York: IEEE Press.

Interim Regulation of Wuhan Municipality on Open Government Information (武汉市政府信息公开暂行规定, passed by the Wuhan Municipal Government on May 17, 2004, issued on May 31, 2004, effective as of July 1, 2004. Retrieved from http://www.hangzhou.gov.cn/main/zfxxgk/zfxxgd.shtml

International Association for Public Participation (IAP2). (2014). *IAP2's public participation spectrum.* Retrieved from http://www.iap2.org.au/documents/item/84

International Organization for Standardization. (2001). *Information and documentation – Records management - Part 1: General*. Reference number ISO 15489-1:2001(E).

International Records Management Trust. (2005). *E-records Capacity Tool*. Retrieved June 2, 2015, from http://www.irmt.org/education-and-training/education-and-training-2

International Records Management Trust. (2015). *Module 3: Managing the Creation, Use and Disposal of Electronic Records.* Retrieved June 2, 2015, from http://www.irmt.org/education-and-training/education-and-training-2

International Records Management Trust. (2015). *Module 4: Preserving Electronic Records. Training in Electronic Records.* Retrieved May 1, 2015, from http://www.irmt.org/education-and-training/education-and-training-2

Interpretation of the Supreme People's Court on Several Issues Concerning Judicial Compensation in Civil and Administrative Litigation (最高人民法院关于民事、行政诉讼中司法赔偿若干问题的解释), issued by the Adjudication Committee of the Supreme People's Court on September 16, 2000, effective as of September 21, 2000. Retrieved from http://www.law-lib.com/law/law_view.asp?id=155

Iron Mountain, Inc. (2015). *Data Center for Next-Generation IT: Build v. Buy*. Retrieved June 22, 2015 from http://www.ironmountain.com/Knowledge-Center/Reference-Library/View-by-Document-Type/White-Papers-Briefs/D/Data-Centers-for-Next-Generation-IT-Build-Vs-Buy.aspx#sthash.MYHmjSQn.dpuf

Jackson, J. D., & Kovalev, N. P. (2006). Lay Adjudication and Human Rights in Europe. *Columbia Journal of European Law*, *13*, 83–124.

Jaconelli, J. (2002). *Open Justice: A Critique of the Public Trial.* Oxford: Oxford University Press. doi:10.1093/acprof:oso/9780198252580.001.0001

Janowski, T., Pardo, T., & Davies, J. (2012). Government information networks – Mapping electronic governance cases through public administration concepts. *Government Information Quarterly*, *29*(S1), 1–10. doi:10.1016/j.giq.2011.11.003

Janssen, K. (2011). The influence of the PSI directive on open government data: An overview of recent developments. *Government Information Quarterly*, *28*(4), 446–456. doi:10.1016/j.giq.2011.01.004

Jiménez Campo, J. (1999). *Derechos fundamentales: concepto y garantias*. Trotta.

Jiménez, C. E. (2010). *Interoperabilidad en la administración de justicia: experiencias y buenas prácticas en un ámbito complejo*. Paper presented at the CLAD 15th International Congress. Santo Domingo.

Jiménez, C. E. (2013). Gobierno abierto y back office: Reflexiones para su implementación. Boletín institucional e-Governa, 27, 15-17.

Jiménez, C. E. (2015). *Modernización de la justicia en el siglo XXI: la necesidad de una perspectiva de justicia abierta*. Paper presented at the CLAD 20th International Congress. Lima.

Jiménez, C. E., & Gascó, M. (2012, October/November). *Y ahora... gobierno abierto. Nuevos términos en la constante búsqueda por la transparencia y la rendición de cuentas*. Paper presented at the CLAD 17th International Congress. Cartagena de Indias.

Jiménez, C. E., Criado, J. I., & Gascó, M. (2011). Technological e-Government Interoperability. An Analysis of IberoAmerican Countries. *Latin America Transactions, IEEE (Revista IEEE America Latina), 9*(7), 1112–1117.

Jiménez, C. E. (2012). Implementing interoperability in e-justice's criminal area. *Effectius*, *17*(January/February), 1–7.

Jiménez, C. E. (2014). *Justicia Abierta: Transparencia y proximidad de la justicia dentro del actual contexto de open government*. Barcelona, Spain: Generalirar de Catalunya, Departament de Justícia.

Jiménez, C. E. (2014). *Justicia Abierta: transparencia y proximidad de la justicia en el actual contexto de Open Government*. Barcelona: Centro de Estudios Jurídicos y Formación Especializada del Departamento de Justicia. Generalidad de Cataluña.

Jiménez, C. E. (2014). *Justicia abierta: transparencia y proximidad de la justicia en el actual contexto del open government*. Barcelona: Centre d'Estudis Jurídics i Formació Especialitzada – Autonomous Government of Catalonia.

Jiménez, C. E., Criado, I., & Gascó, M. (2011). Technological e-government interoperability. An analysis of Ibero American countries. *IEEE Latin American Transactions*, *9*(7), 1112–1117. doi:10.1109/TLA.2011.6129711

Jiménez-Gómez, C. E. (2014). *Justicia Abierta: transparencia y proximidad de la justicia en el actual contexto de Open Government.* Barcelona, Barcelona, España: Centro de Estudios Jurídicos y Formación Especializada, Generalidad de Cataluña.

Jiménez-Gómez, C. E. (2014). *Justicia Abierta: transparencia y proximidad de la justicia en el actual contexto de Open Government.* Barcelona, España: Centro de Estudios Jurídicos y Formación Especializada. Generalidad de Cataluña.

Jiménez-Gómez, C. E. (2014). *Justicia Abierta: transparencia y proximidad de la justicia en el actual contexto de Open Government.* Barcelona: Centro de Estudios Jurídicos y Formación Especializada. Generalidad de Cataluña.

Jiménez-Gómez, C. E. (2015). Principios inspiradores de un Estado Abierto en el contexto del Poder Judicial. Análisis y experiencias. *XX Congreso Internacional del CLAD sobre la Reforma del Estado y la Administración Pública.* Lima: CLAD.

Jiménez-Gómez, C. (2014). Desafíos de la modernización de la justicia en tiempos del Gobierno Abierto. *Revista Digital de Derecho Administrativo*, *1*, 225–239.

Jiménez-Gómez, C. E. (2013). *Gobierno abierto y back office: reflexiones para su implementación*. Boletín Institucional e-Governa.

Jiménez-Gómez, C. E. (2013). *Impacto de la Ley Reguladora del Uso de las TIC en la Administración de Justicia*. Barcelona: Centro de Estudios Jurídicos y Formación Especializada.

Jiménez-Gómez, C. E. (2015). Colaboración Público-Privada y apertura de la justicia.*VI Congreso Internacional en Gobierno, Administración y Políticas Públicas GIGAPP.*Madrid: GIGAPP.

Johnes, L. R., & Thompson, F. (1999). *Public management renewal for the twenty-first century*. Stamford, CT: Jai Press, Inc.

Johnson, D. T. (2000). Prosecutor Culture in Japan and the USA. In D. Nelken (Ed.), *Constrasting Criminal Justice: Getting from here to there* (pp. 157–204). Aldershot, UK: Ashgate.

Johnson, D. T. (2012). Capital Punishment and Japan's Lay Judge System. *Aoyama Legal Research Review*, *5*, 269–289.

Jolías, L., & Prince, A. (2013). *Las fuentes conceptuales de Gobierno Abierto y el Open Data*. Madrid, Spain: Telos.

Jones, V. (2012, July-August). *Standards for Establishing records and Information Management Programs. Information Management*.

JRC. (1999). *The Points at Issue in the Justice Reform*. Retrieved from http://www.kantei.go.jp/foreign/policy/sihou/singikai/991221_e.html

Justice Studies Center of the Americas (JSCA). (2010) *Índice De Accesibilidad A La Información Judicial En Internet 2010 (IACC)*. Retrieved from http://www.cejamericas.org/index.php/areas-de-trabajo/tecnologia-de-la-informacion-y-transparencia/transparencia-rendicion-de-cuentas-y-acceso-a-la-informacion-judicial/indice-de-accesibilidad-a-la-informacion-judicial-en-internet.html

Kalidien, S. N., & de Heer-de Lange, N. E. (Ed.). (2014b). Criminaliteit en rechtshandhaving 2013 (in Dutch). Justitie in Statistiek (nr. 4, CBS, WODC, Raad voor de Rechtspraak). Boom Lemma Press.

Kalidien, S. N., Choenni, R., & Meijer, R. (2009). Towards a monitoring tool for crime and law enforcement. In *Proceedings of the 3rd European Conference on Information Management and Evaluation* (ECIME'09). Gothenburg, Sweden: Academic Publishing Limited.

Kalidien, S. N., Choenni, R., & Meijer, R. F. (2010). Crime statistics online: potentials and challenges. In *Proceedings of the 11th Annual International Digital Government Research Conference on Public Administration Online: Challenges and Opportunities* (DG.O'10).

Kalidien, S. N., van Witzenburg, R., & Choenni, S. (2014a). Developing, implementing and evaluating a web interface in the field of e-government. In D. Yannacopoulos, P. Manolitzas, N. Matsatsinis, & E. Grigoroudis (Eds.), *Evaluating websites and web services: Interdisciplinary perspectives on user satisfaction*. IGI Global. doi:10.4018/978-1-4666-5129-6.ch004

Kaneko, A. (2012). Recussation in Criminal Procedure. *Yokohama International Economic Law Review*, *20*(3), 231–243.

Kapczynski, A. (2008). The access to knowledge mobilization and the new politics of intellectual property. *The Yale Law Journal*, *117*(804), 804–885. doi:10.2307/20455812

Katsh, E., & Rifkin, J. (2001). *Online dispute resolution: resolving conflicts in cyberspace*. San Francisco: Jossey-Bass.

Kaufman, E., & Ozlack, O. (2014). *Teoría y práctica del gobierno abierto: Lecciones de la experiencia internacional.* OAS: Red GEALC-IDRC.

Kaufman, E. (2012). *Aportes para el Gobierno Abierto y la Entrega de Servicios: Experiencias canadiencer.* ASAEC y la Embajada de Canadá de Argentina y Paraguay.

Kellner, D. (2000). *Habermas, the Public Sphere, and Democracy: A Critical Intervention.* Perspectives on Habermas.

Kopackova, H., Michalek, K., & Cejna, K. (2010). Accessibility and findability of local e-government websites in the Czech Republic. *Universal Access in the Information Society, 9*(1), 51–61. doi:10.1007/s10209-009-0159-y

Kovalev, N. P. (2014). Selection of Jurors and Lay Assessors in Comparative Perspective: Eurasian Context. *Russian Law Journal, 2*(2), 9–62. doi:10.17589/2309-8678-2014-2-2-9-62

Kramer, L. (2004). *The people themselves: Popular constitutionalism and judicial review.* Oxford University Press.

Kubicek, H., Cimander, R., & Scholl, H. J. (2011). *Organizational interoperability in e-government. Lessons from 77 European good-practice cases.* Heidelberg, Germany: Springer. doi:10.1007/978-3-642-22502-4

Kulk, S., & van Loenen, B. (2012). Brave new open data world? *International Journal of Spatial Data Infrastructures Research*, 7.

Kumm, M. (2005). The Jurisprudence of Constitutional Conflict: Constitutional Supremacy in Europe Before and After the Constitutional Treaty. *European Law Journal, 11*(3), 262–307. doi:10.1111/j.1468-0386.2005.00260.x

Lafond, P. C. (2010). Les modes alternatifs de règlement des différends en droit de la consommation: d'un progrès né du chaos à l'optimalisation. In *L'accés des consommateurs à la justice* (pp. 119–180). Cowansville, Canada: Éditions Yvon Blais.

Lafond, P. C. (2015). *Droit de la protection du consommateur: théorie et pratique.* Comwansville, Canada: Éditions Yvon Blais.

Lakhani, K. R., & Panetta, J. A. (2007). The principles of distributed innovation. *Innovations, 2*(3), 97–112. doi:10.1162/itgg.2007.2.3.97

Lampoltshammer, T. J., Sageder, C., & Heistracher, T. (2015). The Openlaws Platform - An Open Architecture For Big Open Legal Data. In E. Schweighofer, F. Kummer, & W. Hötzendorfer (Eds.), *Proceedings of the 18th International Legal Informatics Symposium IRIS* (*Vol. 309*, pp. 173–179). Vienna: Österreichische Computergesellschaft.

Lanvin, B., & Lewin, A. (2006). *The Next Frontier of E-Government: Local Governments May Hold the Keys to Global Competition.* Global Information Technology Report.

Lauris, É., & Fernando, P. (2010). A dupla face de Janus: as reformas da justiça e a Lei Tutelar Educativa. *Julgar*, (11), 135–146.

Law Commission of Canada. (2003). *Transforming Relationship Throught Participatory Justice.* Ottawa: Law Commission of Canada.

Law Commission of Canada. (2003). *Transforming Relationships through Participatory Justice.* Ottawa, Canada: Law Commission of Canada.

Layne, K., & Lee, J. (2001). Developing fully functional E-government: A four stage model. *Government Information Quarterly, 18*(2), 122–136. doi:10.1016/S0740-624X(01)00066-1

Lee, G., & Kwak, Y. H. (2012). An open government maturity model for social media-based public engagement. *Government Information Quarterly*, *29*(4), 492–503. doi:10.1016/j.giq.2012.06.001

Lee, J. (2010). 10 year retrospect on stage models of e-Government: A qualitative meta-synthesis. *Government Information Quarterly*, *27*(3), 220–230. doi:10.1016/j.giq.2009.12.009

Lee, J. (2010). Korean Jury Trial : Has the New System Brought About Changes? *Asian-Pacific Law & Policy Journal*, *12*(1), 58–71.

Lenaola, I. (2011). Public participation in judical processes. Kenya Annual Jusges Colloquium, Mombasa, 14-19 August. *Kenya Law*. Retrieved from http://www.kenyalaw.org/kl/index.php?id=1934

Lewis, J. A. (2007). *Government open source policies*. Washington, DC: Center for Strategic and International Studies.

Lezcano, J. M., & Olivera, N. (2009). The Electronic Ombudsman. In *Proceedings of the 3rd International Conference on Theory and Practice of Electronic Governance (ICEGOV)*. Bogota, Colombia: ACM. doi:10.1145/1693042.1693086

Li, H. (黎虹). (2013, November 27). Build strong foundations for judicial openness to promote fairness and establish public trust (筑牢司法公开的基石 以公开促公正 以公开树公信). www.ChinaCourt.org*(中国法院网讯)*. Retrieved from http://www.chinacourt.org/article/detail/2013/11/id/1151559.shtml

Li, J. (李健). (2011, September 9). Two dimensions of judicial openness (司法公开的两种维度). *People's Court Daily (人民法院报)*, 1. Retrieved from http://rmfyb.chinacourt.org/paper/html/2011-09/09/content_33174.htm

Linders, D., & Wilson, S. C. (2011). What is Open Government? One Year after the Directive. In *12th Annual International Conference on Digital Government Research (Dg.o'11)* (pp. 262–271). College Park, MD: ACM. doi:10.1145/2037556.2037599

Linhares, G., & Raaen, N. (2013). *To Preserve and Protect: Standards for Maintaining 21st Century Court Records*. COSCA 2013 Working Paper. Retrieved May 1, 2015, from http://cosca.ncsc.org/Policy-Papers.aspx

Liu, X., & Shi, G. (刘晓鹏、石国胜). (2008, June 23). Wang Shengjun suggests during the national meeting of presidents of higher courts: Satisfy the people's judicial needs to the largest extent (王胜俊在全国高级法院院长会议上提出:最大限度地满足人民群众司法需求). *People's Daily (人民)*. Retrieved from http://paper.people.com.cn/rmrb/html/2008-06/23/nw.D110000renmrb_20080623_3-04.htm

Li, Y. (2012). Putting the U.S. National Archives and Records Administration's "Open Government Initiative" into perspective. *China Files*, *11*, 55–56.

Lourenço, R. P., Moura e Sá, P., & Veloso, S. (2015). Avaliação de transparência online: O caso do SIADAP das Direcções Gerais. In CISTI'2015 - 10a Conferência Ibérica de Sistemas e Tecnologias de Informação. Águeda. Academic Press.

Lourenço, R. P. (2013). Data disclosure and transparency for accountability: A strategy and case analysis. *Information Polity*, *18*(3), 243–260. doi:10.3233/IP-130310

Lourenço, R. P. (2015). An analysis of open government portals: A perspective of transparency for accountability. *Government Information Quarterly*. doi:10.1016/j.giq.2015.05.006

Lourenço, R. P., Sá, P. M., Jorge, S., & Pattaro, A. F. (2013). Open Government and online transparency for accountability: One assessing model and two applications. *European Journal of Electronic Government*, *11*(1), 280–292.

Lu. (2016). Review of Taiwan's Precedent System and Brief Discussion of Mainland China's Case Guidance System. *Stanford Law School China Guiding Cases Project: Guiding Cases Commentaries*. Retrieved from http://cgc.law.stanford.edu/commentaries/15-lü-tailang

Luna-Reyes, L. F., & Gil-Garcia, J. R. (2014). Understanding the co-evolution of institutions, technology, and organizations: The enactment of the state government portal of Puebla. *14th Annual International Conference on Digital Government Research*. Quebec, Canada: Digital Government Society.

Luo., (2014). Overseas open government data plan: Progress and implications. *Information Studies: Theory and Application*, *12*, 138–144.

Luzuriaga, J. M., & Cechich, A. (2011). Electronic Notification of Court Documents: A Case Study. New York, NY: ACM. doi:10.1145/2072069.2072077

Macdonald, R. (1990). Access to justice and law reform. *Windsor Yearbook of Access to Justice*, *10*, 287–337.

Macdonald, R. (2010). L'accès à la justice et le consommateur: une "marque maison? In P. C. Lafond (Ed.), *L'accés des consommateurs à la justice* (pp. 4–10). Cowansville, Canada: Éditions Yvon Blais.

Macdonald, R., & Mc Guire, S. (1996). Small Claims Courts Cant. *Osgoode Hall Law Journal*, *34*(3), 509–530.

Machado, H., Silva, S., & Santos, F. (2008). *Justiça Tecnológica: promessas e desafios*. Porto: Edições Ec.

Machura, S. (2003). Fairness, Justice, and Legitimacy: Experiences of People's judges in South Russia. *Law & Policy*, *25*(2), 123–150. doi:10.1046/j.1467-9930.2003.00143.x

Mahrer, H., & Krimmer, R. (2005). Towards the enhancement of e-democracy: Identifying the notion of the 'middleman paradox'. *Information Systems Journal*, *15*(1), 27–42. doi:10.1111/j.1365-2575.2005.00184.x

Malone, P., Cheuk, A., Rowe, S., Kriegman, I., Wong, S., & Fein, D. (2010). *Best Practices in the Use of Technology to Facilitate Access to Justice Initiatives*. Harvard University. Berkman Center for Internet and Society.

Malone, P., Cheuk, A., Rowe, S., Kriegman, I., Wong, S., & Fein, D. (2010). *Practices in the use of technology to facilitate access to justice initiatives*. Boston, MA: Berkman Center for Internet and Society.

Malsch, M. (2009). *Democracy in the Courts: Lay Participation in European Criminal Justice Systems*. Surrey: Ashgate.

Manago, W. (2011, May-June). *Protect, Maintain Information Integrity to Reduce Business Risk. Information Management*.

Márquez, J. M., Vázquez, R., Martínez, M., & Roldán, N. (2013). *Estudio de la demanda y uso de gobierno abierto en España*. Madrid: National Observatory of Teleccommunications and Information Society.

Martínez-Vares García, S., & De la Quadra-Salcedo Janini, T. (2014). *La tutela multinivel de los derechos fundamentales. XVI Reunión trilateral de los Tribunales Constitucionales de Italia, Portugal y España*. Santiago de Compostela: Tribunal Constitucional (Spain).

Maskivker, J. (2010). Participation and Rights in Athenian Democracy: A Habermasian Approach. *The European Legacy, Toward New Paradigms*, *15*(7), 855–870. doi:10.1080/10848770.2010.528902

Matheus, R., & Vaz, J. C. (2012). New perspectives for electronic government in Brazil: The adoption of open government data in national and subnational governments of Brazil. In *Proceedings of the 6th International Conference on Theory and Practice of Electronic Governance*. doi:10.1145/2463728.2463734

McClanahan, J. (2011). Citizen Participation in Japanese Criminal Trials: Reimagining the Right to Trial by Jury in the United States. *North Carolina Journal of International Law and Commercial Regulation*, *37*, 725–792.

McCormick, J. (2014). *Understanding the European Union: A Concise Introduction*. London: Palgrave Macmillan.

McKinnon, C. (2014, January-February). *5 Trends reshaping Records and Information Management. Information Management*.

McLachlin, B. (2014). Openness and the rule of law. *At the Annual International Rule of Law Lecture*. Retrieved June 29, 2015 from http://www.barcouncil.org.uk/media/270848/jan_8__2014_-_12_pt.__rule_of_law_-_annual_international_rule_of_law_lecture.pdf

McLachlin, B. (2014). *Openness and the rule of law.* Remarks of the Right Honourable Beverley McLachlin, P.C. Chief Justice of Canada at the Annual International Rule of Law Lecture. London, United Kingdom. Retrieved 06, June, 2015 from http://www.barcouncil.org.uk/media/270848/jan_8__2014_-_12_pt.__rule_of_law_-_annual_international_rule_of_law_lecture.pdf

McLachlin, B. (2003). Courts, Transparency and Public Confidence-To the Better Administration of Justice. *Deakin Law Review*, *8*, 1.

Meares, T. L., & Harcourt, B. E. (2000). Foreword: Transparent Adjudication and Social Science Research in Constitutional Criminal Procedure. *The Journal of Criminal Law & Criminology*, *90*(3), 733–798. doi:10.2307/1144276

Meijer, R., Conradie, P., & Choenni, S. (2014). Reconciling contradictions of open data regarding transparency, privacy, security and trust. *Journal of Theoretical and Applied Electronic Commerce Research, 9*(3), 45-58.

Meijer, A. J., Curtin, D., & Hillebrandt, M. (2012). Open government: Connecting vision and voice. *International Review of Administrative Sciences*, *78*(1), 10–29. doi:10.1177/0020852311429533

Memorandum on Transparency and Open Government. (2009, January21). 74. *Federal Register*, *4685*. Retrieved from https://www.whitehouse.gov/the_press_office/TransparencyandOpenGovernment

Meng., (2005). On the relationship between government re-engineering in the information age and e-government. *Journal of Chinese Academy of Governance*, *1*, 37–39.

Military Resource Protection Law [*Gunyou Shigen Himitsu Hogo Ho*] 1939, Law no.25 of 1939.

Military Secrets Law [*Gunkihogo Ho*], 1937, Law no.72 of 1937.

Miller, J. J. (2013). Graph database applications and concepts with Neo4j.*Proceedings of the Southern Association for Information Systems Conference.*

Misdaad in kaart. (2015). *Website provisioned by Dutch national police.* Retrieved June 29, 2015 from https://www.politie.nl/mijn-buurt/misdaad-in-kaart

Miyazawa, S. (2014). Citizen Participation in Criminal Trials in Japan: The Saiban-in System and Victim Participation in Japan in International Perspectives. *International Journal of Law, Crime and Justice*, *42*(2), 71–82. doi:10.1016/j.ijlcj.2014.03.002

MJ. (2015). *Ministério da Justiça - Procedimento de Injunção.* Retrieved May 28, 2015, from http://www.citius.mj.pt/Portal/consultas/Injuncoes/Injuncoes.aspx

Moolenaar, D., Choenni, S., & Leeuw, F. 2007. Design and implementation of a forecasting tool for justice chains. In *Proceedings of the 5th International Conference on Law and Technology.*

Morozov, E. (2014). *To Save Everything, Click Here: The Folly of Technological Solutionism.* New York: Public Affairs.

Munoz, H. (2013, July 10). *Lessons from the world's most unequal region.* Retrieved from UNDP: http://www.latinamerica.undp.org/content/rblac/en/home/presscenter/speeches/2013/07/10/lessons-from-the-world-s-most-unequal-region.html

Müßig, U. (2007). *Gesetzlicher Richter ohne Rechtsstaat? Eine historisch-vergleichende Spurensuche.* Paper presented at the Juristische Gesellschaft zu Berlin, February 2006 (No. 182), Berlin, Germany.

NACJD. (2015). *Website of National Archive of Criminal Justice Data.* Retrieved June 29, 2015 from https://www.icpsr.umich.edu/icpsrweb/content/NACJD/mission.html

Nader, L. (1988). The ADR explosion -The implications of rhetoric in legal reform. *Windsor Yearbook of Access to Justice*, *8*, 269–291.

Naser, A. (2012). *Datos abiertos: Un nuevo desafío para los gobiernos de la región.* Santiago, Chile: CEPAL.

National Archives and Records Administration. (2015). *Disposition of Federal Records: A Records Management Handbook.* Retrieved June 2, 2015 at: http://www.archives.gov/records-mgmt/publications/disposition-of-federal-records/chapter-4.html

National Archives of Australia. (2011). *Digital Continuity Plan.* Retrieved May 2, 2015 from http://www.naa.gov.au/records-management/agency/digital/what-is-digital-continuity/plan/index.aspx

National Center for State Courts. (2005). Williamsburg, VA: CourTools.

National Informatization Development Strategy. (2006–2020) (2006–2020 年国家信息化发展战略), prepared by the National Informatization Leading Group and issued by the General Office of the CPC Central Committee and the General Office of the State Council on March 19, 2006. Retrieved from http://www.gov.cn/gongbao/content/2006/content_315999.htm

Nemirovsci, O. (2010). Un cambio cultural. In C. Calderón, S. Lorenzo, C. Calderón, & S. Lorenzo (Eds.), *Open government: Gobierno Abierto* (pp. 87–101). Granada, Spain: Algón Editores.

Netten, N., van den Braak, S. W., Choenni, S., & Leertouwer, E. (2014). Elapsed times in criminal justice systems. In *Proceedings of the 8th International Conference on Theory and Practice of Electronic Governance* (ICEGOV'14).

Neuberger, J. (2009). Volunteering across the criminal justice system. Academic Press.

News 13. (2013). *Judge Belvin Perry testifies about preventing escapes through forgery.* Retrieved June 22, 2015, from http://www.mynews13.com/content/news/cfnews13/news/article.html/content/news/articles/cfn/2013/11/6/judge_belvin_perry_o.html?cid=rss

Niikura, O. (2013). *AGU Insite.* Retrieved from http://www.aoyama.ac.jp/research/insight/column_niikura/page2.html

Northrop, A. (2002). Lessons for managing information technology in the public sector. *Social Science Computer Review*, *20*(2), 194–205. doi:10.1177/089443930202000209

Nosek, B. A., Banks, G. C., Borsboom, D., Bowman, S. D., Breckler, S. J., Buck, S., & Yarkoni, T. et al. (2015). Promoting an open research culture. *Science*, *348*(6242), 1422–1425. doi:10.1126/science.aab2374 PMID:26113702

Notice Concerning Speeding Up the Implementation of Work Related to the Information-for-Citizens Project (关于加快实施信息惠民工程有关工作的通知), issued by the National Development and Reform Commission et al. on and effective as of January 9, 2014. Retrieved from http://www.gov.cn/gzdt/2014-01/15/content_2567048.htm

Notice of the Supreme People's Court and the Ministry of Justice on the Issuance of the Speech by Comrades Xiao Yang, Wu Aiying, and Hao Chiyong during the National People's Mediation Work Conference (最高人民法院、司法部关于印发肖扬同志和吴爱英、郝赤勇同志在全国人民调解工作会议上的讲话的通知), issued by the Supreme People's Court and the Ministry of Justice on July 16, 2007. Retrieved from http://www.pkulaw.cn/fulltext_form.aspx?Db=chl&Gid=110447

Obama, B. (2009). *Transparency and open government. Memorandum for the heads of executive departments and agencies.* Retrieved from http://www.whitehouse.gov/the_press_office/TransparencyandOpenGovernment

Obama, B. (2009, January 26). Transparency and Open Government. (Memorandum for the heads of executive departments and agencies). *Presidential Documents, 74*(15), 4685-4686.

OCDE. (2003). *Open Government: Fostering dialogue with civil society*. Paris: OCDE.

OD101. (2015). *Open data 101*. Retrieved June 29, 2015, from http://open.canada.ca/en/open-data-principles

ODef. (2015). *The open definition*. Retrieved June 29, 2015, from http://opendefinition.org

ODH. (2015). *Open data handbook*. Retrieved June 29, 2015, from http://opendatahandbook.org/guide/en/what-is-open-data/

ODRN. (2015). *Open data research network*. Retrieved June 29, 2015, from http://www.opendataresearch.org/content/2013/566/early-insight-2-definitions-open-data

OECD. (2003). *The e-government imperative: main findings*. Paris: OECD.

OECD. (2010). *OECD guiding principles for open and inclusive policy making. Building an open and innovative goverment for better policies and service delivery*. Paris, France: OECD.

OECD. (2011). *The call for innovative and open government. An overview of country initiatives*. Paris: OECD.

OGD. (2015). *Welcome to open government data*. Retrieved June 29, 2015, from http://opengovernmentdata.org/#sthash.kjB8Ex3v.dpuf

Online dispute resolution for cross-border electronic commerce transactions: draft procedural rules, Working Group III (Online dispute resolution) de la UNCITRAL, Viena, 18-22 November, 2013.

Open Data Portal. (2016). Retrieved February 22, 2016, from https://open-data.europa.eu/en/data/

Open Definition. (2016). Retrieved February 22, 2016, from http://opendefinition.org/

Open Government Directive: Memorandum for the Heads of Executive Departments and Agencies. (2009, December 8). Retrieved from https://www.whitehouse.gov/open/documents/open-government-directive

Open Justice. (2015). *Website Open Justice*. Retrieved June 29, 2015 from http://open.justice.gov.uk

Opinion of the Supreme People's Court on Further Improving the Communication of Public Opinions (最高人民法院关于进一步加强民意沟通工作的意见), issued by the Supreme People's Court on and effective as of April 13, 2009. Retrieved from http://www.chinalaw.gov.cn/article/fgkd/xfg/sfwj/201012/20101200330542.shtml

Organization of American States. (2015a). *Inter-American Program of Judicial Facilitators*. Retrieved from http://www.oas.org/en/sla/judicial_facilitators.asp

Organization of American States. (2015b). *Inter-American Program of Judicial Facilitators. Regulation*. Retrieved from http://www.oas.org/es/sla/docs/facilitadores_judiciales_reglamento.pdf

Orlikowski, W. (2000). Using technology and constituting structures: A practice lens for studying technology in organizations. *Organization Science, 11*(4), 404–428. doi:10.1287/orsc.11.4.404.14600

Orszag, P. (2009). *Open government directive. Memorandum for the Heads of Executive Departments and Agencies*. Retrieved from http://www.whitehouse.gov/open/documents/open-government-directive

Ortiz de Zárate, A. (2010). Por qué esta obsesión con la participación? In C. Calderón & S. Lorenzo (Eds.), *Open government* (pp. 29–49). Granada, Spain: Algón Editores.

Osborne, D., & Plastrik, P. (1998). *Banishing bureaucracy: Strategies for reinventing government*. New York, NY: Plume.

Oskamp, A., Lodder, A. R., & Apistola, M. (2004). *IT Support of the Judiciary*. Asser Press. doi:10.1007/978-90-6704-659-6

OSS Strategy. (2016). Retrieved February 22, 2016, from http://ec.europa.eu/dgs/informatics/oss_tech/opensource/ossinec_en.htm

Ossowski, S., Sierra, C., & Botti, L. (2013). Agreement Technologies: A Computing Perspective. In S. Ossowsky (Ed.), *Agreement Technologies. Law, Governance and Technology* (pp. 1–16). Berlin: Springer. doi:10.1007/978-94-007-5583-3_1

Oszlak, O. (2013). Estado Abierto: Hacia un nuevo paradigma de gestión pública.*XVIII Congreso Internacional del CLAD*.Montevideo: CLAD.

Overall Framework for National E-Government Affairs. (国家电子政务总体框架), adopted by the National Informatization Leading Group on March 19, 2006. Retrieved from http://xxhs.miit.gov.cn/n11293472/n11295327/n11297172/11800751.html

Ozslak, O. (2013). Estado abierto: Hacia un nuevo paradigma de gestión pública. Trabajo presentado en el panel "Gobierno abierto en Iberoamérica: promesas y realizaciones". *XVIII Congreso Internacional del CLAD*, Montevideo, Uruguay.

Packer, H. L. (1964). Two Models of the Criminal Process. *University of Pennsylvania Law Review*, *113*(1), 1–68. doi:10.2307/3310562

Páez Mañá, J. (1994). *Bases de datos jurídicas*. Madrid, Spain: CINDOC, CSIC, Centro de Información y Documentación Científica.

Palvia, S. C. J., & Sharma, S. S. (2007). E-government and e-governance: definitions/domain framework and status around the world. In A. Agarwal, & V. Venkata Ramana (Eds.), *Proceedings of the Fifth International Conference on e-Governance (ICEG)* (pp. 1–12). Sonning Common: Academic Conferences Ltd.

Pardo, T., Nam, T., & Burke, B. (2012). E-government interoperability: Interaction of policy, management, and technology dimensions. *Social Science Computer Review*, *30*(1), 7–23. doi:10.1177/0894439310392184

Pardo, T., & Tayi, G. K. (2007). Interorganizational information integration: A key enabler for digital government. *Government Information Quarterly*, *24*(4), 691–715. doi:10.1016/j.giq.2007.08.004

Park, K., Han, Y. H., & Seong, Y. R. (2010). The Effect of Double Judgments on Public Confidence in Court Decisions for the Trial by Citizen-Participation in Korea. *International Journal of Law, Crime and Justice*, *38*(4), 166–174. doi:10.1016/j.ijlcj.2011.01.003

Park, R. Y. (2010). The Globalizing Jury trial: Lessons and Insights from Korea. *The American Journal of Comparative Law*, *58*(3), 525–582. doi:10.5131/ajcl.2009.0049

Parks, W. (1957). The open government principle: Applying the right to know under the Constitution. *The George Washington Law Review*, *26*(1).

Parycek, P. S. (2003). Electronic democracy: Chances and risks for municipalities. In A. K. Prosser (Ed.), *E-Democracy: Technology, right and politics (paper #174)*. Vienna: OCG.

Pastor, S. (2005). *Cifrar y descifrar volumen 1: Manual para generar, recopilar, difundir y homologar estadísticas e indicadores judiciales*. Santiago, Chile: CEJA.

Pecherzewski, P., & Rodziewicz, P. (2012). ODR and trans-border dispute. In Costs and quality of Online dispute resolution (pp. 39-50). Maklu.

Peng, B. (彭波). (2013, January 8). XI Jinping issues important instructions on properly carrying out political and legal work in a new situation, emphasizing the needs to meet the People's new expectations for public safety, judicial fairness, and rights protection, to promote the development of a safe China with rule of law and excellent team-building, to strive to make people feel fairness and justice in every judicial case (习近平就做好新形势下政法工作作出重要指示强调,顺应人民对公共安全司法公正权益保障的新期待,全力推进平安中国法治中国过硬队伍建设,努力让人民群众在每一个司法案件中都能感受到公平正义). *People's Daily* (人民日报). Retrieved from http://paper.people.com.cn/rmrb/html/2013-01/08/nw.D110000renmrb_20130108_3-01.htm

Petersen, N. (2011). Avoiding the Common Wisdom Fallacy: The Role of Social Sciences in Constitutional Adjudication. *International Journal of Constitutional Law, No, 2011*(22).

Peters, M. A., & Britez, R. G. (2008). *Open education and education for openness*. Sense Publishers.

Phillips, M., Bailey, J., Goethals, A., & Owens, T. (2014). *The NDSA Levels of Digital Preservation: An Explanation and Uses*. Working paper. Library of Congress, NSDA Infrastructure Working Group.

Poblet Balcell, M. (2008). Introduction: Bringing a new vision on online dispute resolution. In M. Poblet (Ed.), *Expanding horizons of ODR, Proceedings of the 5th International Workshop on online dispute resolution*. (pp. 1-8). Firenze: Springer.

Poblet Balcell, M., et al. (2011). Tecnologías para la mediación en línea, estado del arte, usos y propuesta. In Libro Blanco de la mediación en Catalunya (pp. 943-1008). Barcelona: Huygens.

Ponce, A. (2015). *A new way to measure open government*. Retrieved from http://worldjusticeproject.org/blog/new-way-measure-open-government

Posner, R. A. (1993). *The Problems of Jurisprudence*. Cambridge, MA: Harvard University Press.

Powell, L. F. (1965). The Right to a Fair Trial. *American Bar Association Journal. American Bar Association, 51*(5), 534–538.

Pozen, D. (2010). Judicial elections as popular constitutionalism. *Columbia Law Review, 110*, 2047–2134.

Prieto, L. M., & Rodríguez, A. C. (2012). Implementation framework for open data in Colombia. In *Proceedings of the 6th International Conference on Theory and Practice of Electronic Governance*. doi:10.1145/2463728.2463732

Provisions of the Supreme People's Court Concerning Work on Case Guidance (最高人民法院关于案例指导工作的规定), passed by the Adjudication Committee of the Supreme People's Court on November 15, 2010, issued on and effective as of November 26, 2010. (Stanford Law School China Guiding Cases Project, English Guiding Cases Rules, June 12, 2015 Edition). Retrieved from http://cgc.law.stanford.edu/guiding-cases-rules/20101126-english/

Provisions of the Supreme People's Court on the Broadcasting of Live or Recorded Trial Activities by People's Courts (最高人民法院关于人民法院直播录播庭审活动的规定)), passed by the Adjudication Committee of the Supreme People's Court on November 8, 2010, issued on and effective as of November 21, 2010. Retrieved from http://yqcqfy.chinacourt.org/article/detail/2014/01/id/1171568.shtml

Provisions of the Supreme People's Court on the Publication of Adjudication Documents on the Internet (最高人民法院关于人民法院在互联网公布裁判文书的规定), passed by the Adjudication Committee of the Supreme People's Court on November 13, 2013, issued on November 21, 2013, effective as of January 1, 2014. Retrieved from http://www.chinacourt.org/law/detail/2013/11/id/147242.shtml

Raaen, N. (2014, January-February). Order in the Courts: RM Principles for the Judiciary. *Information & Management*.

Raisio, H., Valkama, K., & Peltola, E. (2014). Disability and Deliberative Democracy: Towards Involving the Whole Human Spectrum in Public Deliberation. *Scandinavian Journal of Disability Research*, *16*(1), 77–97. doi:10.1080/15017419.2013.781957

Rajevic, E. (2012). Transparencia: qué están haciendo los gobiernos. In A. Naser & G. Concha (Eds.), *El desafío hacia el gobierno abierto en la hora de la igualdad* (pp. 101–113). Santiago, Chile: CEPA.

Ramírez Alujas, Á., & Dassen, N. (2012). Gobierno Abierto: la ruta hacia una nueva agenda de reforma del Estado y modernización de la administración pública en América Latina y el Caribe. In N. Dassen & J. C. Vieyra (Eds.), *Gobierno abierto y transparencia focalizada. Tendencias y desafíos para América Latina y el Caribe* (pp. 41–71). Banco Internacional de Desarrollo.

Ramírez-Alujas, Á. V. (2011, December15). Gobierno abierto y modernización de la gestión Pública. Tendencias actuales y el (inevitable) camino. *Revista Enfoques: Ciencia Política y Administración Pública*, *9*(15), 99–125.

Ramírez-Alujas, Á., & Dassen, N. (2012). Gobierno abierto: la ruta hacia una nueva agenda de reforma del Estado y la modernización de la administración pública en América Latina y el Caribe. In N. Dassen & J. C. Vieyra (Eds.), *Gobierno abierto y transparencia focalizada: tendencias y desafíos para América Latina y el Caribe* (pp. 41–72). Washington, DC: Inter-American Development Bank.

Ramsay, I. (2003). Consumer redress and access to justice. In C. Rickett & T. Telfer (Eds.), *International perspectives on consumers' access to justice* (pp. 17–45). Cambridge, UK: CUP.

Ran, Liu, & Chen. (2013). Commentary on the progress of implementing the U.S. Open Government Initiative in the Web 2.0 environment (Web2.0环境下美国开放政府计划实践进展评述). *Information and Documentation Services*, *6*, 89–95.

Rawls, J. (1999). *A Theory of Justice*. Cambridge, MA: Belknap Press of Harvard University Press.

Rechtspraak. (2015). *Website of the Dutch judiciary and the supreme court of the Netherlands.* Retrieved June 29, 2015, from http://zoeken.rechtspraak.nl/default.aspx

Regulation of Chengdu Municipality on Open Government Information (成都市政府信息公开规定), passed by the Chengdu Municipal Government on March 4, 2004, issued on March 29, 2004, effective as of May 1, 2004. Retrieved from http://www.chengdu.gov.cn/wenjian/detail.jsp?id=nyaEXXXWnsgW4P2lQdK9

Regulation of Guangzhou Municipality on Open Government Information (广州市政府信息公开规定), passed by the Guangzhou Municipal Government, issued on November 6, 2002, effective as of January 1, 2003. Retrieved from http://www.gz.gov.cn/gzgov/s8263/200211/595736.shtml

Regulation of Hangzhou Municipality on Open Government Information (杭州市政府信息公开规定), passed by the Hangzhou Municipal Government on April 15, 2004, issued on April 27, 2004, effective as of October 1, 2004. Retrieved from http://www.hangzhou.gov.cn/main/zfxxgk/zfxxgd.shtml

Regulation of Shanghai Municipality on Open Government Information (上海市政府信息公开规定), passed by the Shanghai Municipal Government, issued on January 20, 2004, effective as of May 1, 2004, expired on May 1, 2008. Retrieved from http://www.shanghai.gov.cn/shanghai/node2314/node12959/node12967/userobject21ai28762.htm

Regulation of the People's Republic of China on Open Government Information (中华人民共和国政府信息公开条例), passed by the State Council on January 17, 2007, issued on April 5, 2007, effective as of May 1, 2008. Retrieved from http://www.gov.cn/zwgk/2007-04/24/content_592937.htm

Reiling, D. (2011). e-Justice: experiences with court IT in Europe. In J. Caballero, C. De Gracia, & L. Hammergren (Eds.), Buenas prácticas para la implementación de soluciones tecnológicas en la Administración de Justicia. México.

Reiling, D. (2012, June). Technology In Courts In Europe: Opinions, Practices And Innovations. *International Journal For Court Administration*, 1–10.

Reilling, D. (2011). E-justice: experiences with court IT in Europe. In J. A. Caballero, C. G. de Grácia, & L. Hammergren (Eds.), Buenas prácticas para la implementación de soluciones tecnológicas en la Administración de Justicia. Mexico City, Mexico: Instituto de Investigación para la Justicia. Retrieved from http://www.iijusticia.org/docs/REILING.pdf

Reinhardt, S. (1995). Judicial Speech and the Open Judiciary. *Loyola of Los Angeles Law Review*, 805–813.

Republic of Panamá Government. (2015). *Órgano Judicial de la República de Panamá.* Retrieved from Programa de Facilitadores Judiciales Comunitarios de Panamá: http://www.organojudicial.gob.pa/wp-content/uploads/2014/04/PROGRAMA-DE-FACILITADORES-JUDICIALES-2009-2010.pdf

Research Libraries Group (2002). OCLC Working Group on Digital Archive Attributes. *Trusted Digital Repositories: Attributes and Responsibilities*. Rep. Research Libraries Group.

Rhode, D. L. (2000). Access to justice. *Fordham Law Review*, *69*, 1785.

Robertson, A. (2005). Criminal Justice Policy Transfer To Post-Soviet States: Two Case Studies Of Police Reform In Russia And Ukraine. *European Journal on Criminal Policy and Research*, *11*(1), 1–28. doi:10.1007/s10610-005-2290-5

Rocheleau, B. (2005). Interorganizational and interdepartamental information systems: Sharing among governments. In D. Garson (Ed.), *Handbook of public information systems* (pp. 59–82). Boca Raton, FL: Taylor & Francs Group.

Rogers, M. (1998). *5). The definition and measurement of innovation.* Parkville, Australia: Melbourne Institute of Applied Economic and Social Research.

RotM. (2013). *Rotterdam municipality (gemeente Rotterdam in Dutch).* Rotterdam World Port World City. Retrieved July 14, 2015, from http://www.rotterdam.nl/gw

Rottman, D. B., Efkeman, H. S., & Casey, P. (1998). *A guide to court and community collaboration.* National Center for State Courts.

Saha, P., Nath, A. K., & Salehi-Sangari, E. (2012). Evaluation of government e-tax websites: an information quality and system quality approach. *Transforming Government: People, Process and Policy*, *6*(3), 300–321.

Sandoval Almazan, R., & Gil Garcia, J. R. (2015). Understanding Judicial Websites: An Exploration of Portals in the States of Mexico. IEEE Computer Society. doi:10.1109/HICSS.2015.253

Sandoval-Almazan, R., & Gil-Garcia, J. R. (2010). Evaluating Websites in the Judicial Branch: An Exporatory Study. In Electronic Government and Electronic Participation: Joint Proceedings of Ongoing Resarch and Pojects of IFIP eGOV and ePart 2010. Lausanne, Switzerland: Trauner.

Sandoval-Almazan, R., Gil García, J. R., Luna Reyes, L. F., Luna, D. E., & Rojas Romero, Y. (2012). Open government 2.0: citizen empowerment through open data, web and mobile apps. In *Proceedings of the 6th International Conference on Theory and Practice of Electronic Governance*. New York, NY: ACM. doi:10.1145/2463728.2463735

Sandoval-Almazan, R. (2013). *La larga marcha del Gobierno Abierto. Teoría, medición y futuro. In The Long Walk of the Open Government: Theory, Metrics and Future*. Mexico City: INAP.

Sandoval-Almazán, R. (2015). Gobierno abierto y transparencia: Construyendo un marco conceptual. *Convergencia. Revista de Ciencias Sociales*, 68.

Sandoval, R., & Gil-García, J. R. (2008). Limitations of Evolutionary Approaches to E-government. In D. Garson & M. Khosrow-Pour (Eds.), *Handbook of Research on Public Information Technology* (pp. 22–30). IGI. doi:10.4018/978-1-59904-857-4.ch003

Sanford, C., & Rose, J. (2007). Characterizing eparticipation. *International Journal of Information Management*, *27*(6), 406–421. doi:10.1016/j.ijinfomgt.2007.08.002

Santos, B. de S. (1982). A participação popular na administração da justiça no Estado capitalista. In S. dos M. do M. Público (Ed.), A participação Popular na Administração da Justiça (pp. 83–98). Lisbon: Livros Horizonte.

Satola, D. (2007). Legal Aspects of Internet Governance Reform. *Information Polity: The International Journal of Government & Democracy in the Information Age, 12*, 49–62. Retrieved from http://iospress.metapress.com/app/home/contribution.asp?referrer=parent&backto=issue,6,9

Schauffler, R. (2007). Judicial Accountability in the US State Courts: Measuring Accountability. *Utrecht Law Review, 3*(1).

Schmidt, A. (2007). IT and the judiciary in the Netherlands – A state of affairs. *Computer Law & Security Report*, *23*(5), 453–460. doi:10.1016/j.clsr.2007.03.006

Scholl, H. J. (2010). Electronic Government: A study Domain Past Its Infancy. In *E-Government: Information, Technology, and Transformation* (pp. 11–32). Armonk, NY: M.E. Sharpe.

Scholl, H. J., & Klischewski, R. (2007). E-government integration and interoperability: Framing the research agenda. *International Journal of Public Administration*, *30*(8), 889–920. doi:10.1080/01900690701402668

Schrems. (2016). *Judgment in Case C-362/14 Maximillian Schrems v Data Protection Commissioner.* Retrieved February 22, 2016, from http://curia.europa.eu/jcms/upload/docs/application/pdf/2015-10/cp150117en.pdf

Scott, W. R. (2014). *Institutions and organizations: Ideas, interests, and identities* (4th ed.). Thousand Oaks, CA: Sage.

Sebastian, A. (2012). *Harvard Cracks DNA Storage-Crams 700 Terabytes of Data into a Single Gram.* Retrieved June 2, 2015, from http://www.extremetech.com/extreme/134672-harvard-cracks-dna-storage-crams-700-terabytes-of-data-into-a-single-gram

See, H. (1982). The Judiciary and Dispute Resolution in Japan: A Survey. *Florida State University Law Review. Florida State University. College of Law*, *10*(3), 339–368.

Seligson, M. (2001). Lay Participation in South Africa From Apartheid to Majority Rule. *Revue internationale de droit pénal*, *72*(1), 273–284.

Senger, D. (2011). The Japanese Quasi-Jury and the American Jury: A Comparative Assessment of Juror Questioning and Sentencing Procedures and Cultural Elements in Lay Judicial Participation. *University of Illinois Law Review*, *2*, 741–774.

Several Opinions of the Supreme People's Court on Further Strengthening the Construction of the People's Courts'. "Case Registration and Letters-and-Visits Window" (Trial Implementation) (最高人民法院关于进一步加强人民法院"立案信访窗口"建设的若干意见(试行)), issued by the Supreme People's Court on December 25, 2009. Retrieved from http://www.chinalaw.gov.cn/article/fgkd/xfg/sfwj/201012/20101200330536.shtml

Several Opinions of the Supreme People's Court on Making Enforcement Processes of People's Courts Open) (最高人民法院关于人民法院执行流程公开的若干意见), issued by the Supreme People's Court on September 3, 2014. Retrieved from http://www.e-gov.org.cn/ziliaoku/news004/201503/155170.html

Several Opinions of the Supreme People's Court on the Construction of Three Major Platforms to Promote Judicial Openness (最高人民法院关于推进司法公开三大平台建设的若干意见), issued by the Supreme People's Court on November 21, 2013. Retrieved from http://www.chinacourt.org/article/detail/2013/11/id/1152225.shtml

Several Provisions of the Supreme People's Court on Enforcing the Property Portion of A Criminal Judgment or Ruling (最高人民法院关于刑事裁判涉财产部分执行的若干规定), passed by the Adjudication Committee of Supreme People Court on September 1, 2014, issued on October 30, 2014, effective as of November 6, 2014. Retrieved from http://www.chinacourt.org/law/detail/2014/10/id/148014.shtml

Several Provisions of the Supreme People's Court on Open Enforcement [Work] of People's Court (最高人民法院关于人民法院执行公开的若干规定), issued by the Supreme People's Court on December 23, 2006, effective as of January 1, 2007. Retrieved from http://www.court.gov.cn/shenpan-xiangqing-718.html

Several Provisions of the Supreme People's Court on the People's Courts' Acceptance of Public Opinion-based Supervision by the News Media (最高人民法院关于人民法院接受新闻媒体舆论监督的若干规定), issued by the Supreme People's Court on and effective as of December 8, 2009. Retrieved from http://www.chinalaw.gov.cn/article/fgkd/xfg/sfwj/201012/20101200330480.shtml

Share-PSI 2.0. (2016). Retrieved February 22, 2016, from http://www.ercim.eu/activity/projects/390-share-psi-2-0

Siau, K., & Long, Y. (2005). Synthesizing E-government Stage Models - a Meta-synthesis Based on Meta-ethnography Approach. *Industrial Management & Data Systems*, *105*(4), 443–458. doi:10.1108/02635570510592352

Silveira, L., Wazlawick, R. S., & Rover, A. J. (2015). Assessing the Brazilian e-justice interoperability model. *Latin America Transactions*, *13*(5), 1504–1510. doi:10.1109/TLA.2015.7112008

Simon, K. D. (2005). The value of open standards and open-source software in government environments. *IBM Systems Journal*, *44*(2), 227–238. doi:10.1147/sj.442.0227

Six Provisions of the Supreme People's Court on Judicial Openness (最高人民法院关于司法公开的六项规定), issued by the Supreme People's Court on and effective as of December 8, 2009. Retrieved from http://www.chinalaw.gov.cn/article/fgkd/xfg/sfwj/201012/20101200330480.shtml

Smith, A. M., & Heath, M. (2014). Police.uk and Data.police.uk: Developing open crime and justice data for the UK. JeDEM-eJournal of eDemocracy and Open Government, 6(1), 87-96.

Software, C. (2009). *Citius. Relatório de Auditoria ao Citius*. Academic Press.

Soldwedel, A. (2010). Testing Japan's Convictions: The Lay Judge System and the Rights of Criminal Defendants. *Vanderbilt Journal of Transnational Law*, *41*(5), 1417–1474.

Sousa, F. A. de. (2013, May 26). SITAF faz advogados perder dois dias por semana. *Diário de Notícias*, p. 16.

Southgate, P., & Grosvenor, T. (2000). Confidence in the Criminal Justice System - A Qualitative Study. London: Academic Press.

Spigelman, J. (2006). The Principle of Open Justice: A comparative perspective. *The University of New South Wales Law Journal*, *29*(1), 147–166.

Spigelman, J. (2006). The Principle of Open Justice: A Comparative Perspective. *The University of New South Wales Law Journal*, *29*(2), 147–166.

Stanford Law School China Guiding Cases Project. RONG Baoying v. WANG Yang and Alltrust Insurance Co., a motor vehicle traffic accident liability dispute, *English Guiding Case (EGC24)* (Apr. 4, 2014 Edition). Retrieved from http://cgc.law.stanford.edu/guiding-cases/guiding-case-24

Stanford Law School China Guiding Cases Project. Shanghai Cunliang Trading Co., Ltd. v. JIANG Zhidong, WANG Weiming et al., a sale and purchase contract dispute, *English Guiding Case (EGC9)* (Nov. 9, 2012 Edition). Retrieved from http://cgc.law.stanford.edu/guiding-cases/guiding-case-9

Stanford Law School China Guiding Cases Project. XCMG Construction Machinery Co., Ltd. v. Chengdu Chuanjiao Industry and Trade Co., Ltd. et al., a sale and purchase contract dispute, *English Guiding Case (EGC15)* (Apr. 10, 2013 Edition). Retrieved from http://cgc.law.stanford.edu/guiding-cases/guiding-case-15

Stein, P. G. (1992). Roman Law, Common Law, and Civil Law. *Tulane Law Review*, *66*(5), 1591–1604.

Stolz, B. (1985). Congress and Criminal Justice Policy Making: The Impact of Interest Groups and Symbolic Politics. *Journal of Criminal Justice*, *13*(4), 307–319. doi:10.1016/0047-2352(85)90001-7

Subirats, J. (2012). Preámbulo. In A. Hofmann, R. A. Álvaro, & J. A. Bojorquez Pereznieto (Eds.), La Promesa del Gobierno Abierto (pp. 13–17). Academic Press.

Supreme Judicial Court Commonwealth of Massachusetts. (1992). Reinventing Justice 2022. Boston: Author.

Suquet Capdevila, J. (2012). Exploring online consumer mediation in Catalonia: principles and technological uses. *International review of Law and Information Technology*, *20*(2), 124-146.

Susskind, R. E. (1996). *The Future of Law: Facing the Challenges of Information Technology*. Oxford, UK: Clarendon Press.

Sviridoff, M., Rottman, D., Ostrom, B., & Curtis, R. (1997). *Dispensing Justice Locally. The Implementation and Effects of the Midtown Community Court*. Amsterdam: Harwood Academic Publishers.

Syllabus for the National Judicial Examination in 2015 (2015年国家司法考试大纲), formulated by the Ministry of Justice on May 1, 2015.

Takahashi, K. (1990). Contemporary Democracy in a Parliamentary System. *Law and Contemporary Problems*, *53*(1), 105–122. doi:10.2307/1191830

Tang, Z. (2007). An effective dispute resolution system for electronic consumer contracts. *Computer Law & Security Report*, *23*(1), 42–52. doi:10.1016/j.clsr.2006.11.002

Temporary Seditious Documents Law 1936 [*Fuonbunsho Rinji Torishimari Ho*], Law no.45 of 1936.

Temporary Speech Publication Assembly and Association Order [*Genron, Shuppan, Shukai, Kesshanado Rinji Torishimari Ho*], 1941, Law no.97 of 1941.

Thaman, S. C. (2007a). The Good, the Bad, or the Indifferent: "12 Angry Men" in Russia, Part of Symposium: The 50th Anniversary of "12 Angry Men.". *Chicago-Kent Law Review*, *82*(2), 791–808.

Thaman, S. C. (2007b). The Nullification of the Russian Jury : Lessons for Jury-Inspired Reform in Eurasia and Beyond. *Cornell International Law Journal*, *40*(2), 355–428.

The "Twelfth Five-Year" Plan of National E-Government Affairs (国家电子政务"十二五"规划), issued by the Ministry of Industry and Information Technology on December 12, 2011. Retrieved from http://www.miit.gov.cn/n11293472/n11295327/n11297217/14562026.html

The Opinion of the Supreme People's Court Concerning Comprehensively Deepening the Reform of the People's Court—The Fourth Five-Year Reform Plan of the People's Court. (2014-2018) (最高人民法院关于全面深化人民法院改革的意见—人民法院第四个五年改革纲要(2014-2018)), issued by the Supreme People's Court on February 4, 2015. Retrieved from http://www.court.gov.cn/zixun-xiangqing-13520.html

The Second Five-Year People's Court Reform Plan. (2004-2008) (人民法院第二个五年改革纲要(2004-2008)), issued by the Supreme People's Court on and effective as of October 26, 2005. Retrieved from http://www.chinalaw.gov.cn/article/fgkd/xfg/sfwj/200904/20090400132177.shtml

The State Council Information Office. (国务院新闻办公室). (2015, March 10). The SPC Holds Conference to Release the "Judicial Openness of China's Courts" (White Paper) (最高法举行中国法院的司法公开(白皮书)发布会). Retrieved from http://www.scio.gov.cn/xwfbh/qyxwfbh/Document/1396210/1396210.htm

The Supreme Court. (2015a). *Q&A*. Available at: http://www.saibanin.courts.go.jp/qa/c6_6.html

The Supreme Court. (2015b). *Report: The Implications of the Citizen Judge System*, Tokyo.

The Third Five-Year People's Court Reform Plan. (2009-2013) (人民法院第三个五年改革纲要(2009-2013)), issued by the Supreme People's Court on and effective as of March 17, 2009. Retrieved from http://www.chinalaw.gov.cn/article/fgkd/xfg/sfwj/201012/20101200330558.shtml

Thibaut, J., & Walker, L. (1975). *Procedural Justice: A Psychological Analysis*. Hillsdale, NJ: Wiley.

Thompson, E. (2011). Does the Open Justice Principle Require Cameras to be Permitted in the Courtroom and the Broadcasting of Legal Proceedings? *Journal of Medicine and Law / Detroit College of Law at Michigan State University*, *3*(2), 211–236.

Tilbury, J. (2014). *The Active Preservation of Digital Information*. Retrieved May 2, 2015 from http://preservica.com/resources/white-papers/

Tonn, B., Dorian, S., Scheb II, J. M., Glennon, C., & Sharma, H K. (2009). Future of the Courts: Fixed, Flexible, and Improvisational Frameworks. *Futures of Governance, 44*(9), 802–11. doi:10.1016/j.futures.2012.07.005

Transparency International. (2015). *Transparency International Corruption Perception Index*. Berlin: Transparency International.

Tribunal Constitucional. (2015). *The website of Spanish Constitutional Court*. Retrieved June 29, 2015 from http://www.tribunalconstitucional.es/en/Pages/Home.aspx

Trochev, A. (2007). Courts on the Web in Russia. In A.-V. Anttiroiko & M. Mälkiä (Eds.), *Encyclopedia of digital government* (pp. 260–265). Hershey, PA: Idea Group Reference. doi:10.4018/978-1-59140-789-8.ch039

Tyler, T. R. (1990). *Why People Obey the Law*. New Haven, CT: Yale University Press.

U.S. Bureau of Justice Assistance. (1993). *Trial court Performance Standards and Measurement System Implementation Manual*. Washington, DC: U.S. Department of Justice.

UK Government. (2015). *Open Justice. Making Sense of Justice*. Retrieved from http://open.justice.gov.uk/

Ullman, J. (1988). *Principles of Database and Knowledge-Base Systems*. New York: Computer Science Press.

Umble, E., Haft, R., & Umble, M. M. (2003). Enterprise resource planning: Implementation procedures and critical success factors. *European Journal of Operational Research*, *146*(2), 241–257. doi:10.1016/S0377-2217(02)00547-7

UMIC. (2015). *Cronologia da Sociedade da Informação em Portugal*. Retrieved May 6, 2015, from http://www.umic.pt/index.php?option=com_content&task=view&id=3123&Itemid=477

Valenzuela Mendoza, R. (2013). Delimitar Gobierno Abierto para ampliar la colaboración con una sociedad más abierta. In *Revista Estado, Gobierno y Gestión Pública Nº 21* (pp. 127-158). México City, Mexico: ITAP. Retrieved from http://inicio.ifai.org.mx/Publicaciones/La%20promesa%20del%20Gobierno%20Abierto.pdf

Valenzuela-Mendoza, R. (2013). Delimitar gobierno abierto para ampliar la colaboración con una sociedad más abierta. *Revista Estado. Gobierno y Gestión Pública*, *21*, 127–158.

van den Braak, S., Choenni, S., Meijer, R., & Zuiderwijk, A. (2012). Trusted third parties for secure and privacy-preserving data integration and sharing in the public sector. In *Proceedings of the 13th Annual International Conference on Digital Government Research* (DG.O'12). doi:10.1145/2307729.2307752

Van den Haak, M. J., de Jong, M. D. T., & Schellens, P. J. (2009). Evaluating municipal websites: A methodological comparison of three think-aloud variants. *Government Information Quarterly*, *26*(1), 193–202. doi:10.1016/j.giq.2007.11.003

van den Hoogen, H. (2013). Taking care of research data: Outcome of a seminar on managing data integrity in research. Library Connect Newsletter, Issue: Research Data Management, 1(1).

van Dijk, J., Kalidien, S., & Choenni, S. (2013). Development, implementation and use of a judicial data space system. In *Proceedings of the 7th International Conference on Theory and Practice of Electronic Governance*.

Van Schalkwyk, F., Cañares, M., Chattapadhyay, S., & Andrason, A. (2015). *Open data intermediaries in developing countries*. Ottawa, Canada: ODDC. Retrieved from http://figshare.com/articles/Open_Data_Intermediaries_in_Developing_Countries/1449222

Vargas Vianco, J. E. (2006). *Gobierno judicial: La organización y el rol de las Cortes Supremas*. Santiago, Chile: CEJA.

Vasudeva, V. N. (2014). *Open source software and intellectual property rights*. New York, NY: Kluwer.

Velicogna, M. (2010). ICT within the court in the e-justice era. *Effectius*. Retrieved from http://www.effectius.com/yahoo_site_admin/assets/docs/ICT_within_the_court_in_the_e-Justice_Era_by_Marco_Velicogna.207234735.pdf

Velicogna, M. (2007). Justice systems and ICT. What can be learned from Europe? *Utrecht Law Review*, *3*(1), 129–147. doi:10.18352/ulr.41

Velicogna, M., Errera, A., & Derlange, S. (2013). Building e-Justice in Continental Europe: The TéléRecours Experience in France. *Utrecht L. Rev.*, *9*(1), 38. doi:10.18352/ulr.211

Velicogna, M., & Ng, G. Y. (2006). Legitimacy and Internet in the Judiciary: A Lesson From the Italian Courts' Websites Experience. *International Journal of Law and Information Technology*, *14*(3), 370–389. doi:10.1093/ijlit/eal009

Veludo, F. (2014, October 2). Cronologia: um mês caótico na Justiça. *Jornal Público*. Retrieved from http://www.publico.pt/sociedade/noticia/um-mes-caotico-na-justica-1671700?page=-1

Verhulst, S., Noveck Simone, B., Robyn, C., Brown, K., & Paz, C. (2014). *Released: The open data era in health and social care*. Retrieved June 29, 2015, from http://thegovlab.org/nhs/

Vermeys, N. W. (2013). La cyberjustice et l'espace OHADA: Des outils virtuels pour une avancée réelle. Journal Africain de Droit des Affaires, 102- 135.

Vidmar, N. (2000). *World Jury System*. Oxford, UK: Oxford University Press. doi:10.1093/acprof:oso/9780198298564.001.0001

Vidmar, N., & Abramson, J. (1996). We the Jury : The Jury System and the Ideal of Democracy. by Jeffrey Abramson Review by : Neil Vidmar. *Contemporary Sociology*, *25*(1), 97–99. doi:10.2307/2076992

Villeneuve, J.-P. (2014). Transparency of Transparency: The pro-active disclosure of the rules governing Access to Information as a gauge of organisational cultural transformation. The case of the Swiss transparency regime. *Government Information Quarterly*, *31*(4), 556–562. doi:10.1016/j.giq.2013.10.010

Von Lucke, J., & Große, K. (2014). Open government collaboration. In M. Gascó (Ed.), *Open government. Opportunities and challenges for public governance* (pp. 189–204). New York: Springer.

Voorberg, W., Bekkers, V., & Tummers, L. (2015). A systematic review of co-creation and co-production: Embarking on the social innovation journey. *Public Management Review*, *17*(9), 1333–1357. doi:10.1080/14719037.2014.930505

Waller, M., Carey, S., Farley, E., & Rempel, M. (2013). *Testing the Cost Savings of Judicial Diversion*. New York: Academic Press.

Wang,, C. (2006). On opening government. *Henan Social Sciences*, *4*, 5–8.

Wang. (王喜文). (2012, June 21). The United States' "Open Government Initiative" study (美国"开放政府计划"研究). *China Economic Net (中国经济网)*. Retrieved from http://intl.ce.cn/specials/zxgjzh/201206/12/t20120612_23399833.shtml

WangMa. , 2002). Reengineering government in the view of seamless government theory. *Journal of Socialist Theory Guide*, *12*, 27–29.

Wang, Y. (2014). Under rule of law: Open government and public participation. *Scientific Socialism*, *4*, 75–78.

Wang, , Zhou,, , & Li., (2002). An untechnical analysis of reengineering government and e-government. *Reform of Economic System*, *1*, 85–87.

Wass, C., Dini, P., Eiser, T., Heistracher, T., Lampoltshammer, T. J., Marcon, G., . . . Winkels, R. (2013). OpenLaws.eu. In E. Schweighofer, F. Kummer, & W. Hötzendorfer (Eds.), *Proceedings of the 16th International Legal Informatics Symposium IRIS* (*Vol. 292*, pp. 21–23). Vienna: Österreichische Computergesellschaft.

Wass, C., Sageder, C., & Lampoltshammer, T. J. (2015). openlaws.eu - Offene Rechtsinformation. *Proceedings of the 4.OGD D-A-CH-LI Conference Open X*.

Weinstein, J., & Goldstein, J. (2012). The benefits of a big tent: Opening up government in developing countries. *UCLA Law Review Discourse*, *60*, 38–48.

Weiss, P., & Pluijmers, Y. (2004). *Borders in cyberspace: conflicting public sector information policies and their economic impacts*. Cheltenham, UK: Edward Elger Publishing.

Wellington, B. (2015). Measles reporting and the dangers of semi-open data. *I Quant NY*. Retrieved June 29, 2015, from http://iquantny.tumblr.com/post/112113837909/measles-reporting-and-the-dangers-of-semi-open

West, D. M. (2004). E-Government and the Transformation of Service Delivery and Citizen Attitudes. *Public Administration Review*, *64*(1), 15–27. doi:10.1111/j.1540-6210.2004.00343.x

West, J., & Lakhani, K. R. (2008). Getting clear about communities in open innovation. *Industry and Innovation*, *15*(2), 223–231. doi:10.1080/13662710802033734

Wiler, V. (2014, September-October). *Europe and Canada Embrace Right to Be Forgotten. Information Management*.

Willem, A., & Buelens, M. (2007). Knowledge sharing in public sector organizations: The effect of organizational characteristics on interdepartmental knowledge sharing. *Journal of Public Administration: Research and Theory*, *17*(4), 581–606. doi:10.1093/jopart/mul021

Williams, F. V. III. (2007). Reinventing the Courts: The Frontiers of Judicial Activism in the State Courts. *Campbell Law Review*, *29*, 591–735.

Wilson, S. C., & Linders, D. (2011). The open government directive: A preliminary assessment. In *Proceedings of the 12th Annual International Digital Government Research Conference: Digital Government Innovation in Challenging Times* (pp. 262–271). doi:10.1145/1940761.1940814

Wolf, R. (1996). *Access to justice, Final report to the Lord Chancellor on the Civil Justice System in England and Wales*. Lord Chancellor's Department. Retrieved 06, June, 2015 from http://www.dca.gov.uk/civil/final/index.htm

Wolf, R. (2005). *California's Collaborative Justice Courts*. Judicial Council of California. Administrative Office of the Courts. Judicial Council of California, Administrative Office of the Courts.

Wonderlich, J. (2010). Ten principles for opening up government information. *Website of Sunlight Foundation*. Retrieved June 29, 2015, from http://sunlightfoundation.com/policy/documents/ten-open-data-principles/

Woolf, S. H. (1996). *Access to Justice: Final Report*. London: HM Stationery Office.

Work Regulation of the Supreme People's Court on Specially Engaged Supervisors (Trial Implementation) (最高人民法院特约监督员工作条例(试行)), passed by the Supreme People's Court, issued on and effective as of October 12, 2009. Retrieved from http://www.chinalaw.gov.cn/article/fgkd/xfg/sfwj/201012/20101200330479.shtml

Work Regulation of the Supreme People's Court on Specially Invited Counselors (最高人民法院特邀咨询员工作条例)), passed by the Supreme People's Court, issued on and effective as of May 31, 2009. Retrieved from http://www.chinalaw.gov.cn/article/fgkd/xfg/sfwj/201012/20101200330544.shtml

World Bank. (2003). *IRMT/World Bank Evidence-based Governance in the Electronic Age. Summary of Discussion Three: Legal and Judicial Reform and Record Keeping*. Author.

World Bank. (2015). *World Bank*. Retrieved from http://data.worldbank.org/country/

World Justice Project. (2015). Retrieved from http://worldjusticeproject.org/open-government-index

Wu, Zheng, Mei,Ren., (2014). National Science Foundation (NSF) information disclosure and its implications for China – using the "Open Government Data Program" (OGDP) as a research focus (美国国家科学基金会 (NSF)信息公开及对中国的启示——以开放政府指令计划 (OGDP)为研究对象). *Science and Technology Progress and Policy*, *7*, 94–99.

Xiao, J. (肖金明). (2005). Administrative licensing system, as well as open government and government credibility (行政许可法制与开放政府、信用政府). China Public Administration (中国行政管理), 4, 91-95.

Xiao, Y. (肖扬). (2007). Constructing a fair, efficient, and authoritative civil trial system to provide judicial safeguards in the building of a socialist and harmonious society – speech given at the Seventh National Civil Trial Work Conference (建设公正高效权威的民事审判制度为构建社会主义和谐社会提供有力司法保障—在第七次全国民事审判工作会议上的讲话). *China Trial (中国审判)*, 2, 4-8.

Xiaoming, H. U. (2015). From open government information to open government data. *E-Government*, *1*, 67–72.

Yáñez, R. (2008). *L'Oficina judicial a Catalunya. Mitjà d'una Justícia eficaç pel ciutadà del segle XXI*. Barcelona: Centro de Estudios Jurídicos y Formación Especializada.

Yang, Z., & Kankanhalli, A. (2013). Innovation in government services: The case of open data. In *Proceedings of IFIP International Federation for Information Processing*, (pp. 644–651).

Yang, Zhang, & Wang. (杨成、张雨、王泽). (2013, July 4). Zhou Qiang: Promoting impartiality by judicial openness: Openness is the rule, non-openness is the exception (周强:以司法公开促进公正,公开是原则不公开是例外). *People's Daily (人民日报)*. Retrieved from http://legal.people.com.cn/n/2013/0704/c42510-22083161.html

Yang, T. M., & Maxwell, T. (2011). Information-sharing in public organizations: A literature review of interpersonal, intra-organizational and inter-organizational success factors. *Government Information Quarterly*, *28*(2), 164–175. doi:10.1016/j.giq.2010.06.008

Yang, , & Wang., (2015). Opportunities and challenges facing China's E-Government "Thirteenth Five-Year" Period. *E-Government*, *4*, 11–17.

Yarez, C. J. N. (2004). Participatory Democracy and Political Opportunism : Municipal Experience in Italy and Spain. *International Journal of Urban and Regional Research*, *28*(4), 819–838. doi:10.1111/j.0309-1317.2004.00553.x

Yücel, G. & Ozok, A.F., (2010). Quantifying ergonomic quality of governmental websites. *Electronic Government, an International Journal*, *7*(3), 233 – 251.

Zakaria, F. (2003). *The Future of Democracy at Home and Abroad*. New York: Norton.

Zeleznikow, J., & Hunter, D. (1994). *Building Intelligent Legal Information Systems: Representation and Reasoning in Law*. Amsterdam: Kluwer.

Zhang & Wang. (2013). The current situation and outlook of open justice in China. *China Legal Science*, *1*, 131–143.

Zhang, . (2005). Toward alternative delivery systems of public gods and services: A critical review of reinventing government movements. *Journal of Renmin University of China*, *5*, 111–117.

Zhang, . (2014). Open government theory. *Journal of Renmin University of China*, *3*, 79–89.

Zhenming, C. H. E. N. (2002). Reengineering government: Strategies and tactics of public department management reform. *Southeast Academic Research*, *5*, 16–22.

Zhou., (2010). Open government and government data disclosure strategy[Social Science Edition]. *Journal of Guangzhou University*, *10*, 11–16.

ZhuLi., (2014). Government 2.0, open government, and construction of service-oriented government (政府2.0、开放式政府与服务型政府建设). *The Journal of Shanghai Administration Institute*, *3*, 59–66.

Zissis, D., & Lekkas, D. (2011). Securing e-Government and e-Voting with an open cloud computing architecture. *Government Information Quarterly*, *28*(2), 239–251. doi:10.1016/j.giq.2010.05.010

Zuiderwijk, A., Janssen, M., Choenni, S., Meijer, R., & Sheikh Alibaks, R. (2012). Socio-technical impediments of open data. *In Electronic. Journal of E-Government*, *10*(2), 156–172.

Zuniga, R., & Murillo, R. (2014). Draining the judiciary bottleneck: A quasi-experiment in improving a government service. *Journal of Business Research*, *67*(6), 1267–1276. doi:10.1016/j.jbusres.2013.04.003

About the Contributors

Carlos E. Jiménez (@estratic) is a Government-Justice specialist with experience in innovative and strategic projects related IT adoption by public organizations, mainly in Justice field, where he has been working since 1991. Since 2007 he has been working on the functional design and implementation of the several times awarded e-Justice system of the Department of Justice of Catalonia, in Spain. He is a Computer Engineer with a MSc. on Information and Knowledge Society, and Postgraduate degree on Information Systems Management. He also does research in his fields of interest that include e-Justice, Open Judiciary, Interoperability and Smart Government. He collaborates with several Universities, and he belongs to several scientific committees. He is Distinguished Lecturer of the IEEE Society on Social Implications of Technology, and Distinguished Visitor of the IEEE Computer Society.

Mila Gascó holds a MBA and a Ph. D. in public policy evaluation. She is a senior researcher at the ESADE's Institute of Public Governance and Management, where she is in charge of the e-governance, open government and smart cities areas of research. For seven years, she was a senior analyst at the International Institute on Governance of Catalonia. She has also taught at different universities and has done a lot of consulting work with different types of organizations such as the United Nations Development Program, the Mayor's Office in Valencia (Venezuela), the Spanish Agency for International Development Cooperation, the City Council and the Provincial Council of Barcelona, the International Institute for Democracy and Electoral Assistance, the Latin American Centre on Management for Development, the World E-Governments Organization of Cities and Local Governments, the Inter-American Development Bank, or Google.

***

Mortaza S. Bargh is research scientist at the Research and Documentation Centre (WODC), Ministry of Security and Justice, The Netherlands. His research interest areas include collaborative security, secure distributed systems, information fusion algorithms and preserving privacy in big data infrastructures. His work is multidisciplinary by nature, in close collaboration with various disciplines such as administration, sociology, criminology and economy. He has an educational background in information and communication theory.

Inmaculada Barral-Viñals is a professor of Private law, University of Barcelona, Salvador Madariaga fellow at the Ciberjustice laboratory, Centre de Recherche en droit public, University of Montréal, Director of Advanced Research (AQU), Member of IDT-UAB, Director of the Working Group on consumer mediation, White Book of Mediation in Catalonia (2009-2011), member of the IMI task force on ODR.

Jordan Corrente Beck is a corporate associate at Debevoise & Plimpton LLP in New York and an editor of Stanford Law School's China Guiding Cases Project ("CGCP") English-language products and translations. Ms. Corrente Beck previously served as co-managing editor and on-site project manager for the CGCP, where she worked on a number of broader initiatives, including successful proposals for inclusion in the Open Government Partnership Summit in Mexico City and the 2015 Law, Justice and Development Week co-organized by the World Bank Group and the Global Forum on Law, Justice and Development.

Jesus Cano is an IT expert who has been working in public sector for years and currently he is posted at the Constitutional Court of Spain. He has a PhD in engineering, a Ms in Security and Criminology and belongs to some societies such as Education, Communication and Computer of the IEEE, among others.

Sunil Choenni holds a PhD in database technology from the University of Twente and a MSc in theoretical computer science from Delft University of Technology. Currently, he is heading the department of Statistical Information Management and Policy Analysis of the Research and Documentation Centre (WODC) of the Dutch Ministry of Security and Justice. Furthermore, he is a professor of human centered ICT at Rotterdam University of Applied Sciences in Rotterdam. Prior to joining WODC, he held several teaching and research positions at different universities and research centres. His research interests include open and big data management, e-government, cyber security and human centered design.

Di Dai is an associate managing editor for Stanford Law School's China Guiding Cases Project. He received both his Bachelor of Laws and Master of Laws at Peking University and was a China eGovernment Development Index Project attendee hosted by Good Governance International. He has been working at Beijing Haijia Law Firm for the past four years and is now a Doctor of Law candidate at Peking University, focusing on administrative law.

Sandra Elena is a lawyer with a Degree in Political Science and a Master's in Legal Studies (American University, USA). She is a rule of law and open data expert with extensive experience in Latin America and other regions of the world. Since 1990, she has been involved in institutional analysis, civil society coalition-building, and political and legislative reforms in the following areas: the rule of law, transparency, anti-corruption, and open data. Her areas of expertise include qualitative and quantitative research, project management, contract negotiation, and program design, implementation, monitoring and evaluation. Ms. Elena has participated in long-term USAID/WB/IDB-funded projects in Argentina, Mexico, Bolivia, Peru, Haiti, Honduras, Nicaragua, Guyana, Ecuador, Pakistan, India, and Albania, among others. She is currently the Coordinator of the Open Justice Program in the Ministry of Justice, Argentina. Previously, she was the Director of the Justice Program at CIPPEC. As a Rule of Law Senior Advisor at IFES, she was in charge of providing legal assistance and helped implement projects on a diverse set of rule of law issues, including: legal aid, legal rights for women, judicial management and case management, transparency, independence and accountability of the judiciary, open data, and monitoring and evaluation in different regions and environments. Ms. Elena has substantive experience in the monitoring and evaluation of rule of law projects. In 2007, she drafted a report on the state of the evaluation of rule of law reform projects worldwide. This report, commissioned by the International

Institute for Democracy and Electoral Assistance (IDEA), has served as a valuable source of information for evaluation practitioners. She was a team leader of the evaluation of PROJUM (justice sector reform program of Argentina funded by WB). She is currently a member of the monitoring and evaluation team of the Modernization of Justice Program in Guyana.

Paula Fernando is a lawyer and a researcher of the Permanent Observatory on Portuguese Justice of the Centre for Social Studies of the University of Coimbra

Mei Gechlik is Founder and Director of Stanford Law School's China Guiding Cases Project ("CGCP") as well as Founder and President of Good Governance International ("GGI"). Formerly a tenured professor in Hong Kong, she has been a visiting professor at Peking University and has spoken at prestigious law schools in the United States and China. Approximately five years ago, Dr. Gechlik founded the CGCP and GGI. The work carried out by the CGCP and GGI has been presented and commended at the U.S.-China Legal Exchange Conference led by the U.S. Department of Commerce and China's Ministry of Commerce and institutions such as Oxford and Princeton universities. The CGCP is a groundbreaking initiative that aims to advance knowledge and understanding of Chinese law and enable judges and legal experts to contribute to the evolution of Chinese case law through ongoing dialogue on "Guiding Cases" ("GCs") released by the Supreme People's Court of China. GCs are *de facto* binding precedents that help guide the adjudication of subsequent similar cases to ensure the uniform application of law in China. The CGCP has become the premier source of translations, information, and analyses of GCs, with its publications capturing the attention of leading groups such as the Wall Street Journal and the International Monetary Fund, and, most recently, being selected for presentation by the World Bank as part of its Law, Justice and Development Week. The CGCP harnesses not only the resources of Stanford Law School, but also that of an international team of approximately 150 law students, lawyers, and translation professionals, as well as the support of more than 40 distinguished experts, including justices from the U.S. Supreme Court and the Supreme People's Court. GGI, a 501(c)(3) non-profit organization, provides innovative information technology solutions for governments to promote the rule of law, citizen participation, government transparency, and other core principles of good governance. GGI's team has developed an e-government assessment methodology for use in its China eGovernment Development Index, a project to create tools for assessing e-government development in Chinese localities. The project made a big splash in China and was extensively covered by Chinese media, including China's official newspaper, the People's Daily. Prior to teaching and researching at Stanford Law School, Dr. Gechlik worked for the Carnegie Endowment for International Peace, a Washington-based think tank. She has testified before the U.S. Congress on various topics about China and has advised the United Nations and the Chinese government on implementing rule of law programs. Dr. Gechlik is admitted as a barrister in England, Wales, and Hong Kong and is a member of the Bar in New York and the District of Columbia. Dr. Gechlik received her J.S.D. from Stanford Law School and her M.B.A. in Finance from the Wharton School at the University of Pennsylvania.

Conceição Gomes is a Senior Researcher at the Centre for Social Studies of the University of Coimbra and Executive Coordinator of the Permanent Observatory on Portuguese Justice of the Centre for Social Studies and Coordinator of Judicial and Judiciary Training Unit.

Andres Guadamuz is a Senior Lecturer in Intellectual Property Law at the University of Sussex and an Associate Researcher of the CREATe Centre for Copyright and New Business Models in the Creative Economy. He is an international consultant for the World Intellectual Property Organization, and has been involved with Creative Commons in various roles since 2005. His main research areas are open licensing, software protection, digital copyright, and complexity in networks. Andres has published two books, the most recent is "Networks, Complexity and Internet Regulation" with the British publisher Edward Elgar.

Thomas Heistracher is tenure professor at Salzburg University of Applied Sciences, head of research of information technologies and head of dpt of informatics and software technologies at the school of information technology and systems management (ITS).

Roberto Hernández received his M.Sc. degree in Physics, specialized in Electronics, in 1989 at Complutense University, Madrid, Spain. He also received his Ph.D. in Sciences in 1994 at Spanish University for Distance Education, UNED, Madrid, Spain. He is an associate professor at the Control and Communication Systems Department at UNED. He has been Dean at School of Computer Science at UNED for eighth years. His research interests include e-government, quality of service support in distributed systems and development of infrastructures for e-learning, software quality and architecture systems engineering. He has co-authored more than 80 publications in international journals and conferences on these topics.

Yumiko Kita is a PhD student in Legal Studies at the University of Sussex. My doctoral research topic is the evaluation of the new Japanese lay adjudication system which was introduced with the aim of increasing democracy in criminal trial procedures. After completing my LLB in Japan, I undertook an LLM in International Criminal Law at the University of Sussex and an MA in International Criminology at the University of Sheffield. My research interests have developed to include various aspects of a comparative criminal justice system study between different jurisdictions, mainly Japan and European countries.

Thomas J. Lampoltshammer is Senior Scientist (postdoc) at the Department of E-Governance and Administration at the Danube University Krems/Austria. Prior to the current position, he worked as a Researcher and Lecturer in Applied Informatics at the School of Information Technology and Systems Management at the Salzburg University of Applied Sciences Salzburg/Austria. His research interests include - but are not limited to: Semantics, Open Data, Data Visualisation, Geoinformatics, and Software Engineering.

Rui Pedro Lourenço obtained his Bachelor of Computer Science degree from Coimbra University in 1992. Since then, and until 1998, he worked as a systems analyst and programmer at several private companies. In 1998 he joined the Faculty of Economics of the University of Coimbra and, in 2008 he received his PhD in Management Science with the dissertation "Public Participation Support Systems: a Collaborative Writing Model" from Coimbra University where he is currently an Auxiliary Professor at the Faculty of Economics. His current research interest include eGovernment, eDemocracy and Open Government.

Ronald F. Meijer graduated in science of public administration. He worked in universities, doing policy research (Amsterdam, Leiden). He is engaged in research at the Research and Documentation Centre (WODC) of the Ministry of Security and Justice of the Netherlands. His interest is focused on information management, big data, open data, and privacy in the domain of Security and Justice.

Luis Pomed works as a counsellor at the Constitutional Court of Spain and is a lecturer in Administrative Law at the University of Saragosse (Spain).

Nial Raaen is a court administration professional with 40 years experience in court operations, policy, training and consulting for state, local, and international judicial organizations. He has served as a consultant on numerous projects in state and local court systems in the United States and abroad, specializing in operational assessments, delay reduction, enforcement of judgments, and records management. Mr. Raaen is a graduate of Vanderbilt University and received masters degrees in Social Work and Public Administration from the University of Michigan.

Rodrigo Sandoval-Almazán is an Assistant Professor at the Political Sciences and Social Sciences Department in the Autonomous State University of Mexico, in Toluca City. Dr. Sandoval-Almazán is the author or co-author of articles in *Government Information Quarterly, Information Polity, Electronic Journal of Electronic Government; Journal of Information Technology for Development*; American Journal of Business. Also is author of the Book Long Walk of Open Government: Theory, Metrics and Future (2013) (in Spanish), and co-author of the book Challenges and Advances of E-government in Mexico (2016) (in Spanish) His research interests include electronic government, open government and social media in government. Profesor Sandoval-Almazan has a Bachelors Degree in Political Science and Public Administration, a Masters in Management focused on Marketing, and a Ph.D. in Management with Information Systems.

François van Schalkwyk conducts research in the areas of open data, science communication and higher education studies. He has an MEd from the University of the Western Cape, an MPhil in Publishing Studies from the University of Stirling, and a BA(Hons) in English Literature from the University of Cape Town (1995). He is currently reading for his PhD in Science and Technology Studies at the University of Stellenbosch, South Africa. Francois is also the research lead on the Higher Education Research and Advocacy Network in Africa (HERANA) project on university engagement at eight African universities; as well as on the Carnegie Corporation of New York-funded project on the changing revenue models of African universities presses. Completed research projects include the IDRC-funded Scholarly Communication in Africa Project (SCAP), in which he investigated the relationship between collaboration and improved online visibility of academics, as well as three projects as part of the Emerging Impacts of Open Data in Developing Countries project: (1) on the use of open data in university governance, (2) on the institutionalisation of open data practice in government, and (3) on open data intermediaries. Francois is also the research manager for Africa for the World Wide Web Foundation; a trustee of the not-for-profit, open access academic publisher African Minds; and managing director of the publishing services company, Compress.dsl.

Clemens Wass has studied law and economics. After working several years as legal counsel in international companies, he has started his own company with a special focus on legal informatics.

Index

P

R

S

T

U

www.ingramcontent.com/pod-product-compliance
Ingram Content Group UK Ltd.
Pitfield, Milton Keynes, MK11 3LW, UK
UKHW050951290926
15470UKWH00005B/1758

9 781522 507178